● X □ △ ★

Library of Congress Cataloging-in-Publication Data has been applied for.

ISBN-10: 1449575579
ISBN-13: 978-1449575571
First Printing: November 24, 2009
Second Printing: February 2, 2011

Cover Photo: Bob Barry/Jazzography

My Life with

THE CHORD CHEMIST

A Memoir of Ted Greene

Apotheosis of Solo Guitar

by Barbara Franklin

● X □ △ ★

This book is lovingly dedicated to all Ted's students past and future.

● X □ △ ★

Contents

Preface

There are many musicians all over the world that have only experienced Ted Greene through his books. I have been told many times that the impression given through this view alone is of a music scholar, even a genius (always refuted by Ted), given the young age at which he wrote his first and most celebrated book, Chord Chemistry. Since Ted's untimely death from a massive heart attack in 2005, interest in his music studies and his amazing guitar playing abilities has soared. Ted has gained much new exposure through the Internet, through magazine articles and interviews with famous guitar players commending his talent and expertise as a guitarist and musician. Many of these musicians have noted the influence Ted had on their own musical growth. And the interest continues to build.

Besides being an amazing musician, a renowned teacher, and one of the greatest solo guitarists who ever lived, Ted Greene was an extraordinary human being who spent much of his life striving to enhance the quality of life on this earth in many ways.

In the San Fernando Valley, where he lived most of his life, Ted had acquired a mysterious aura. After several years of being featured playing with numerous Los Angeles area rhythm and blues bands where he garnered high acclaim and prominence for his dazzling guitar prowess, Ted took the surprising step of giving up the opportunity of a career in the spotlight. There were several reasons for this decision, one being Ted's penchant for teaching. Due to his choice to teach rather than perform, and his preference for staying at home, many unfounded rumors of a reclusive existence proliferated. Perhaps the extensive book collections; books stacked from floor to ceiling in Ted's apartment fed the rumors. However it happened, he took on the enigmatic aura of a secluded guru. Ted was well aware that many people misinterpreted his way of existence, and refuted these claims but to no avail. Ted's lifestyle and intriguing demeanor were decidedly captivating, yet he did little to enlighten people when questions arose.

However, it is hard to convey what it was like to experience being in the presence of this singular, exceptional person. Therefore, since many people had asked me to write a book about him, this is my attempt at coming as close as I can to depicting who Ted was.

Ted Greene was celebrated worldwide as the author of the book "Chord Chemistry" which is one of the most in-depth studies of chord harmony and theory ever published for the guitar. In addition to Chord Chemistry, he wrote three other books; Modern Chord Progressions Volume I, and Single Note Soloing Volumes 1 & 2, all very much coveted and greatly praised. Ted released only one professional recording under his own name, "Solo Guitar," and this singular album is quite possibly the one that half the guitarists in the world have sought to duplicate.

Less known, other than to Ted's students and those fortunate to hear him when he performed around the Los Angeles area, was Ted's brilliance as an innovative and diverse guitarist. He was capable of playing stunning solos from jazz-style fantasies to neo-Baroque counterpoint improvisation, and sometimes combining two styles. On many occasions he would perform for two hours or more, taking no breaks as he presented a seamless and ever-flowing repertoire blending each piece easily into the next.

Nonetheless, Ted discovered that his most beloved path was as a teacher. With his reputation as a player preceding him and his expertise as a teacher steadily spreading, Ted was highly sought out for his insightful and instinctive gifts in this area. As a testimony to his teaching abilities, for many years there remained a long list of hopeful guitarists waiting for an opening in his schedule.

Everyone fortunate enough to have had the experience of taking a lesson or spending some time in Ted's company found not only a brilliant musician and guitarist, but also a soft spoken man, with a gentle and unassuming nature, (and an almost uncanny natural sagacity). These qualities combined with a kind and generous spirit and his inimitable sense of humor added up to a rare and exceptional person.

Ted's word play alone was incredibly clever. He was a quick-witted punster, using his own idiomatic language he loved to devise. For example, from the interview, *"… so a bunch of Julliard graduates go to Nashville for the summer and take a country gig through a great misunderstanding, and end up sounding like The Vienna Stringbean Orchestra on Nyquil."* Occasionally, to illustrate a point, he would create very comical scenarios, complete with foreign accent. Humor also played an important role in the way Ted communicated and the way he viewed problems. As Ted noted, *"When life has us in a tight corner, one of the first questions to ask is "Can I solve this with some humor?"*

In regard to Ted's teaching ability, he had a unique way of relating to each student on a very particular and individual level. First, and most importantly, he took a genuine interest in each student, musically and personally. This enabled him to establish what type of music the student most desired to learn and to play. With that information, Ted was able to choose the best method of learning suited to each student's personality and work habits. Many of his students not only improved as musicians but in their life goals as well. Consequently, Ted's total focus and caring was woven into every lesson. He truly had a gift for making each student feel very special, so special in fact, many students felt as if Ted was more like a best friend to them, not just a teacher.

Ted was also keen to notice when a student was upset by something going on in his or her life, and if Ted deemed it appropriate, would encourage a discussion, sometimes resulting in a "life counseling session" as opposed to a guitar lesson. On many occasion he would loan out guitars and amplifiers to his students, sometimes for months on end. He truly believed he could trust most people, and this was borne out considering the hundreds of guitars and amplifiers he loaned out over the years, only rarely, were they not returned.

There were many other special characteristics Ted possessed that did not go unnoticed. Ted's compassion for humanity was boundless; he was ultra sensitive to the injustices on the planet, and to the plight of the poor. In fact he was so filled with concern for anyone in trouble or need, friend or stranger, he would go to great lengths to help in any way that he could. Through knowing him, his compassion was so intensely felt, one often became infused with his sense of empathy and kindness. Consequently that aspect of Ted's nature was passed on from person to person.

These were all aspects of Ted's nature and why he was loved so much and held in such high esteem among all who knew him. He literally radiated goodness. Perhaps Ted's insight and uncanny perceptions were why he seemed so "in tune with the universe" on many levels. Ted was a magical being.

About This Book

This book is intended to answer some of the most compelling questions about Ted the musician and Ted the person. It contains some biographical information for a general knowledge of Ted's background and as reference regarding Ted's musical growth, but it was never my intention to write Ted's definitive life story.

The pages herein are divided into sections in order to feature Ted's musical development as it occurred during the course of his life, and how Ted blossomed into the brilliant and innovative musician he was known as.

About Part III

The third section, in the form of a story, details the thirteen years that we spent together, from the very beginning of our relationship and through our various stages of development and personal growth.

My intention is to provide insight into the way Ted perceived life on a daily basis. In this manner I share his thoughts, ideas, sensitivities, fears, joys and sorrows. In addition, I aim to show to how Ted dealt with personal obstacles, and to acquaint you with Ted's many other passions.

In spite of his enthusiastic discussions and interactions with students and friends, Ted took great care to guard his time. He rarely offered any details about his personal life. When I met Ted in early July of 1992, his days were very full, and he had an established routine he rarely deviated from. His teaching schedule included Mondays, Thursdays and every other Wednesday. He began at noon and his last student was booked at 10:00 p.m. Sometimes these last late night lessons would continue into the early hours of the morning. He taught approximately 30 students per week, and occasionally taught on Sunday afternoons as well. At that time, the remaining days of Ted's week were used for practicing, working on student files or new lesson material, personal studies, occasional gigs and the basic and necessary errands that life demanded.

Getting to know Ted proved to be a difficult proposition. All I can say is that I was extremely fortunate and eventually as Ted would state, we were destined to be together. Our relationship was a mutual learning process. We both grew and changed as a result. By the early 1990's most of his major music studies were well formulated, and he continued to refine and rework them. There were always a few new studies in the works and he periodically came up with ideas for new music books. Alas, most of these ideas were never elaborated on, some were merely titles. This was actually Ted's most innovative and creative period in regard to his guitar playing. His contrapuntal improvisational skills were at their height.

The decision to reveal parts of our personal life was something I deliberated over for a long time. I questioned this decision every day as I distilled down 10,000 pages of personal notes. The act of reading through these notes was highly emotional. But I realized I could piece together a chronological sequence of events that depicted Ted's life so clearly in no other way. Because our lives were so inextricably bound, I had no choice but to include personal aspects of my life as well, but not without a considerable amount of natural apprehension.

Revealing our lives in this manner illustrates the many parallels between Ted the musician and Ted the person. I felt it was important to convey how Ted was driven compulsively not just to pursue music, but in pursuing all he loved. He was like that from birth, and as he stated regarding music, *"I didn't choose it (music), it chose me and I had to do it."*

Part IV is an "interview" Ted was working on sporadically during the last couple of years of his life, but was never completed. Eventually Ted intended to write an autobiography, of sorts, and this was to be included. This is the most revealing and forthcoming of all his previous interviews.

Barbara Franklin

● X □ △ ★

The material used to compile this book came from various sources:
My personal journals, Ted's personal notes in his datebooks, my personal observations and experiences, and information directly related to me by Ted.

to understand it? Ted was enormously complex.

There is another book that can be written about Ted. It would be written by *you*. Just as someone could reconstruct almost every moment of Richard Feynman's life, or Albert Einstein, or John Lennon, one could account for almost every moment of Ted's. Is there *anyone* who ever met Ted that doesn't remember everything about that meeting? I've never known anyone who met Ted that didn't have a "Ted story." We never forget.

This book, however, is about what Ted did when *you weren't* around. A love story. At first I thought the title should be: Ted Attempts to Clean His Apartment. It seemed important to them. To me Wow! A young man's dream, all those cool books, magazines, papers, VCR's, guitars, amps, cassettes, vinyl, CD's. Barbara also tells us of their adventures to Guitar Stores, friends homes, family, and seminars. If you didn't already know, you are let in on Ted's intimate feelings about film composers, cars, cats, the Lakers, and the Angels. (I wish I could have shown him my signed photo of Robert Horry's shot that beat the Kings.)

Barbara gives us an exclusive behind the scenes view of Ted completely exposed, i.e., without guitar in hand. What was that like!? We get to know some of his values and lifestyle. We gain a better understanding of Ted. Armed with these insights, one can even extrapolate as to how Ted would face "current" issues. We can speak unequivocally and with confidence as to why, for example, Ted would never trade *his* clunker for cash.

Along, and underscoring, this beautiful and joyous journey, Barbara allows us to see her relationship with Ted unfold. Her deep love for Ted is revealed. As it captures my heart, I feel uncomfortable, like a voyeur. Her love for Ted is so personal, so intimate, so deep. Now, I am fearful for Barbara, as it feels so personal, so revealing. "Are you sure you want to publish this?"

It is her story. A story that she feels passionate about, and needs to tell. So here Ted's history is revealed in the intimate, subtle, and the sublime. A relationship journey told before the guitar story, before the chronology of his achievements, before his character study, and accomplishments. A journey of the heart.

William Perry
September 2009, Oxnard

● X □ △ ★

(grad.) 1963-1964 - with my Silver '63 split window Corvette 360hp Fuelie with American Mags & Goodyear Blue Streaks all around (initially) and the 27 gallon gas tank, road racing suspension. What a time in my life. Of course, I was NOT happy, no, BECAUSE: I yearned so to be able to find all the glorious sounds on the guitar, which I love, and I didn't have a clue. Even though I had been playing for 7 plus years!!!!"

He completed his senior year at University High School and graduated on June 19, 1964 with a Major in Liberal Arts Mathematics.

● X □ △ ★

Meanwhile, Ted's family had returned to Southern California and had moved into a house on Mulholland Drive high above the San Fernando Valley. After graduating high school, Ted moved back in with his family. By now, already considered an accomplished guitarist (by others standards, not by his own admission), a good part of that summer was spent playing with local R&B bands. He also began giving guitar lessons.

In the Autumn of 1964, to appease his parents, Ted enrolled at CSUN (then called Valley State College), as a Business major, but before completing the first year he dropped out, thus incurring the wrath of his parents (who eventually forgave him) and began the permanent pursuit of his true passion, a career in music.

Now, at 19 years old, Ted was able to devote himself full time to the guitar, and the pursuit of knowledge became all encompassing. Ted practiced and studied for hours and hours on end, sometimes remaining in his room for several days. He supplemented the rudimentary education he had gained from his early guitar lessons. In this way Ted gained an extensive knowledge of theory and harmony. For example, if a book suggested doing an exercise in a few keys, such as spelling major triads, Ted would do the exercise in ALL keys, major and minor until he had memorized them cold. Ted learned to instantly recognize everything from interval identification, including being able to sing each interval and distinguish them when listening, to knowing the quality of every chord on each scale degree, the many uses for each chord, the inversions, traditional voice leading, and more. I could go on and on, but essentially Ted absorbed college level music education that was more in-depth than if he had gone the academic route. He utilized many different harmony and theory books and soon began to analyze and refine the way the material was presented in the books. As he acquired this knowledge he was able to determine which methods for learning were most effective. He applied these theoretical studies to the guitar, and slowly began to realize there would be a need to refine these concepts specifically for the guitar. However, since he was just beginning to expand his own learning process, the formulation of his music studies and lesson materials were still a few years away.

He continued to reside at the Mulholland Drive house with his family, and it was during this time, upon hearing guitarist Jay Lacy that his old Telecaster mania began. In April 1965, Ted bought his first Tele, a 1953 for $135.00, and was thrilled to meet and take a few lessons from Jay Lacy.

When in late summer or autumn, Ted and his family moved to Hartsook Street in Encino, he was offered a teaching position at Ernie Ball Guitars in Tarzana and later on his teaching would expand to include the Ernie Ball Canoga Park store as well. Ted's guitar lessons consisted of teaching any musical knowledge he could impart, and sometimes a popular song that was requested. On an old chord chart for "Poor Side of Town," Ted noted in 2001 " *'Poor Side of Town' is a beautiful young pop ballad recorded by Johnny Rivers in what, '66 or 67? Apparently when I wrote this sheet, I did a lot of sheets like this. Very basic changes just so I had a short hand reference page. It was exciting to see my ears getting a little better all the time, and what a self esteem booster to figure out the popular songs of the day. No great feat but felt great and helped me earn a living. I taught songs like these to students when they liked them and gained a reputation for having a good ear. This of course, was all on a fairly meager level - this 'good' ear. But step by step unfoldment it's been."*

For the next few years, along with his teaching, he continued playing in local Rhythm & Blues bands in venues throughout the Los Angeles area. By now, Ted had honed his R&B and Rock n' Roll playing to a sharp edge and was more than well received and recognized locally for his amazing abilities. At 22 years old he was fast becoming legendary, and in demand.

Despite all the positive recognition, and people raving about his playing, Ted was not satisfied with the level of musicianship he had attained. He realized that there was so much more he wanted to be able to express musically, and also realized he lacked the knowledge to do so.

Therefore, around this time he began to apply and experiment with the vast amount of music theory and harmony he had been accumulating and assimilating. In his own words: (c.1968)*"This is likely when I fell in love with J.S. Bach et al and when I started composing those classical pieces and when my ear progressed to the point where I shocked & thrilled myself by figuring out Johnny Smith's chords to "What's New,"*

And, *"This was where I first started tuning down, then especially tuning way higher than pitch and putting harpsichordish filters in the Telecasters. And figuring out my 1st jazz lick: Joe Pass w/Gerald Wilson."* Ted composed many original "Baroque" pieces in this period of his life. His first piece was written in winter/spring 1968 and appropriately titled "My 1st Classical Composition." This was shortly followed by a Processional in B minor. In late October he began a Fantasia in E minor, which he did not complete, but resumed work on it again several years later (June of 1970). Among other pieces written around this time, were an Invention in F, and in January of the next year his Pastoral No.1.

Besides still being *"nuts about & obsessed with composing & playing Bach, tuned up high,"* Ted also began specifically formulating written lesson material, devising his own "diagrams," and song "road maps" for himself and his students. He began translating and refining the many concepts he had studied into a written format for guitar, which he felt was more accessible for the student. Initially the lesson material format was quite rudimentary. The diagrams were tiny red boxes stamped by hand unevenly across the page denoting chords or patterns. The system of dots, x's, triangles and squares, denoting one such as Paramahansa Yogananda, he found much to benefit from.

After exploring many options, he distilled the wisdom from the sources he felt most applicable to help engender the most positive aspects in his own life as well as utilizing his newly discovered philosophies in the area of teaching. The following thoughts and conclusions dated 5/12/74 were written as a result of his search for meaning and his subsequent understanding.

Reasons for Staying with Music as a Profession
1. Latent therapeutic powers for healing and awakening virtues in others, generally improving the quality of life due to the uplifting vibrations radiated out. A person who is striving for things consistent with these concepts can accomplish these things to a much greater degree. The healing forces can have a hard time getting through if the human channel is clogged up with too much ego, self-pride, arrogance, love of flattery & adulation, desire for self-gratification, etc. The wise person is consistently on guard to detect and dissipate these lower vibrations by remembering thoughts that inspire compassion, humility & sacrifice.
2. A person can set an example for others when he is in the position of exposure that the entertainment field creates. Remember the man who reforms himself will reform others.
3. The money earned can be used beneficially in a multitude of ways.
4. My talents lie in this area so it seems that the Creator would have it be this way, although math, puzzles, or COLOR are also possibilities.

Reasons for Self-Control
1. To decrease the focus on self and concentrate on helping others.
2. To build up the positive quality of will-power which coupled with kindness & reason (wisdom) or common sense can produce very great results in the world, positive vibrations are contagious, have repercussions, just as negative ones do. Will-power can transmute a negative emotion such as jealousy into a positive one such as kindness. Imagine that 10 people were kind to you on a certain day - you would be more prone to be kind to someone else (the contagious aspect) a cynic might say, "I would be surprised if 10 people were kind to me." Well, eventually kindness wins out because it reaches that essential spark of goodness in all (I must confess to just a few doubts but I am confident time will hold the answers).
3. To not hurt others through lack of control of self. Remember, the quality of harmlessness; do not "use" others; do not be deceitful to satisfy your own selfish desires; do not radiate thoughts which can harm.
4. To set an example for others: "First become that which you want others to be."
Helpful hints: a) a cosmic viewpoint of life helps in a moment of heated emotion - just relax & think of the universe & how small and insignificant most things

really are: "Is it really worth getting mad at others so much?" Life is too short for most worries.
b) Controlling one aspect can often help in controlling another (be careful here though, not to go so far overboard all at once that you over compensate in another area to make up for the emotional need).

Ted admitted to experimenting with recreational drugs (never 'hard' drugs), for a short time in his very early 20's. He told me he tried psychedelics a few times and did not enjoy the experience. However he did admit to a penchant for marijuana, but stopped using it for the reasons he listed in the following:

Reasons for Giving up Dope
(Quite a few years earlier was the actual occurrence)
1. Self-delusion (illusions, distortions in general)
2. Increased self-gratification sense is more often the case than not. The world needs more unselfish people, more healers, more people devoted to a life of service. This type of life is impossible to one who is too "high to cope" with the physical plane.
3. Dullness of logical thinking - unable to learn quickly and especially to retain information.
4. Unable or unwilling to cope with problems, crises.

Ted gave these reasons for giving up Rock n' Roll, R&B, and ceasing to play in bands:
The Combination of High-Energy, Pounding Beat, Excessive Volume in Music
1. Causes riots.
2. Generally increases frenzy, chaos in the world occasionally if not often.
3. Stimulates the already over-stimulated self-gratification tendencies of mankind.
4. Fosters a high degree of competitiveness: Everybody trying to be the "hottest" or "funkiest" player, trying to "outblow" everybody else. Also it creates more of these feelings in the listeners, they get caught up in who is the "hottest" etc. What is needed instead is more music that inspires kindness, service, unselfishness, compassion and similar virtues to help mankind to live amongst each other in a harmonious way. Alarming sidelight: In some experiments plants died when exposed to loud hard rock music while they flourished on Bach organ music.

Along with Ted's spiritual awakening, he continued to formulate new musical ideas, improve his teaching methods, and find new ways to organize and categorize the material that he wished to expand. Part of this would eventually become incorporated into his second book. Ted often wrote out extensive and detailed "Organization Sheets" to clarify his ideas. This also helped Ted organize the material in his mind and he found making these sheets to be a very satisfying and productive way of thinking.

Shown here is a partial example from 1974

ORGANIZATION SHEET (MAIN AREAS: STUDY, WRITING, TEACHING, PERFORMING, LISTENING) 6-23-74

WHAT TO THINK:

HARMONIC RESOURCES

DIATONIC MINOR

MOODS:

In July 1974 Ted arranged for a guitar lesson with Joe Pass. Ted told me his main reason for this was to find out what Joe was thinking when he improvised lines, but Joe would not admit to thinking anything, such as chords or scales. However, Ted did gain some insights from his singular lesson with this enigmatic man.

Ted's Lesson with Joe Pass

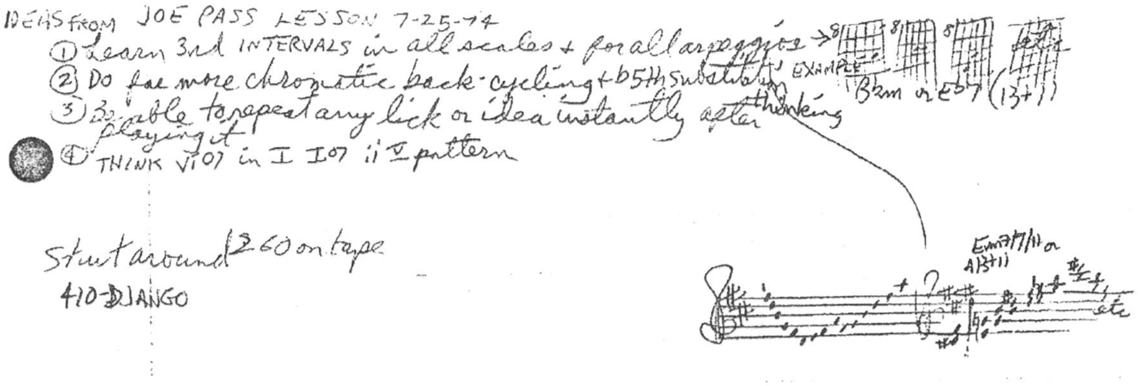

● X □ △ ★

In May of 1976 Ted retired from 11 years of teaching at Dale's (formerly Ernie Ball) and began his home teaching career. He also wrote and published his 2nd book "Modern Chord Progressions Volume 1."

Due in part to the inspiration and education he obtained from J.S. Bach, Debussy, Max Steiner, George Gershwin and others, and due, once again, to the interest and encouragement of students, Modern Chord Progressions Volume I came into being.

His plans for Modern Chord Progressions Volume 2 were in the making, there was much material already written that he wanted to include, however the book was never completed.

Autumn brought Ted's first extended solo guitar gig, Sunday nights at the Smoke House in Toluca Lake. As if that weren't enough to fit into a busy schedule, he also began taking seminars from A. J. Galambos, an astrophysicist, who founded The Free Enterprise Institute. According to Ted's notes regarding the lectures, he was ambivalent about some of these theories, and completely disagreed with others, yet as always, he also garnered much positive and useful information from these lectures.

Many live playing opportunities were forthcoming. In 1977, a new nightclub was established in Studio City and booked Ted and vocalist Cathy Segal-Garcia for the opening night. The club was called The Sound Room and this was the first of frequent appearances there for this very impressive duo. Backing female singers was a particular favorite mode of performing for Ted, as he could relax a bit more because the singer was focal point, enabling him to experiment and come up with some of his most creative accompaniment, including combining some interesting and surprising modulations.

However, the most momentous event to occur at this time was the making and recording of his album "Solo Guitar." Encouraged and produced by his friends, Leon White and William Perry, this project took many painstaking months to perfect and was released in 1977. There were many stories surrounding this tremendous effort, and this was purported to be a very trying albeit ultimately rewarding experience for all those involved. The Album was re-released in 2004 on CD through Art of Life Records, and is still available.

In June 1978, another relocation took place, Ted and his family moved to a house on Penfield St. in Woodland Hills. Despite needing some "down" time after recording his Solo Guitar album, the ensuing year proved productive in the writing of "Single Note Soloing Vols.1 & 2." Once again, he was encouraged by his students to organize his written lesson material, which became the contents for these books.

Not long after completing these last two books, Ted fell into a deep depression regarding his guitar playing. He said he was unhappy and even bored with his sound, his arrangements, and he completely lost his desire to play. He was at an impasse, unable to get through it and move forward. Through musicians Dan Sawyer and Scott Page he met the highly renown jazz guitarist Lenny Breau for the first time. This fortuitous meeting gave the two guitarists a chance to exchange ideas, learn from each other, and form a friendship. Unfortunately, Ted's depression about his own playing continued to plague him on and off for a long time to come.

In 1979, Ted maintained a meager two-day teaching schedule (Mondays and Thursdays), which would continue unchanged for three years. Having become quite renowned from his books, he was now invited to give seminars at various institutes.

In March alone he was booked for three seminars, the first at Musician's Institute (formerly known as GIT), then on the 7th he taught a master class at the University of Southern California, and finally on the 14th another seminar at Musician's Institute. Mid-year Ted noted in his sparsely filled datebook of that time, recording dates with Joseph Byrd. Several years prior Ted had played guitar on Joseph Byrds's now notorious album, *The American Metaphysical Circus,* which was released c. 1969. This album presents a rare opportunity to hear Ted playing psychedelic-rock guitar. Ted did not indicate what these mid-year recording dates were for. Winding up the year were three more seminars, one in October and two in November, all taking place at USC.

Despite having completed 4 books, new ideas continued to pour forth. Throughout the new year, Ted set his mind to evaluating new and old studies and formulated a considerable amount of new teaching material. In March, he gave two more seminars, one at USC and one at Musician's Institute. Then on August 16th, as Ted noted, *"Do the Guitar Video 'Session With the Stars' produced by Ed Sulzer of A&M. The Very 1st Guitar Instructional Video!"* The video was released, but unfortunately, it was not well marketed. However, there are still copies floating around if one is lucky enough to discover such, and it is well worth viewing.

Early in 1981, Ted was offered a very special opportunity, which he graciously accepted, interviewing his friend and mentor, George Van Eps for the cover-story in the

August issue of Guitar Player magazine. The interview was a wonderful experience for Ted, not only was he able to present his beloved mentor to the world, but this article also revealed Ted's talent as a writer.

In May, he attended the fabulous 2-day Norm's Rare Guitar Show, which took place at the Hollywood store. Ted and owner Norman Harris had already formed a long and solid friendship, and this was an especially exciting and rewarding weekend. An elated Ted expressed in his datebook, *"One of my fondest memories these two days."* He bought a 1957 Esquire (near mint) and a 1952 Tele.

Mid-year Ted jotted down this amusing little note to himself, *"6/7 Try No TV for a year,"* well, about that, I can attest to the fact that Ted absolutely loved to watch television, and had it turned on almost all the time whether we were watching or not. He told me the TV was like company for him when he was home alone and working. Knowing that Ted made a note like this implies (to me, at least) that TV was becoming all-consuming, and distracting him from his work. Ted always endeavored to put his time to good use, he loved to be productive and when he found he wasn't being so, it frustrated him.

However, his life would change considerably over the next two years. Ted's datebook at this time contained very few personal comments, it would later become a more detailed account of the days, but for now I quote another one of the precious few, *"Late May: Begin Baseball Card renaissance, (frenzy!). Time off from guitar in large part...(still much pleasure with it, only here & there though. Consistency impossible."*

Due to Ted's sports card collecting frenzy, there is a comparatively scant amount of written material and studies for this two-year period.

In mid summer Lenny Breau was in town, giving the two guitarists a chance to once more spend some time together. Lenny was playing several gigs in the valley, and after attending a show on July 27th Ted jotted this in his date book, *"Lenny at Donte's - great night."*

Despite the sports card craze, perhaps seeing Lenny was influential in Ted coming up with some new conceptions for solo guitar. One area he began to improve on was harmonic structure, which included 2-voice counterpoint with free question and answer using the whole instrument. Other devices were bass solos in up-tempo tunes, walking chords and other chord solos and walking bass with chord punctuations or sustains. A main focal point was improvisation on the melody using ascending or chromatic bass in any one of many tonality types, and parallel movement in any structure.

The summer was equally memorable for another special occurrence; the beginning of what was to become one of Ted's most endearing friendships, that with Valley Baseball Card Store owner Max Himmelstein.

Max didn't know what to make of Ted at first. He told me that early on before they got to know each other that Ted came in one day and spent hours looking through boxes of clear plastic sheets (sheets that housed the cards in notebooks) to determine and discard any sheets that were flawed. Max, astonished and amused by this, said he had never seen anyone do that before. Due to his sports card mania, much of Ted's time was now spent hanging out with Max at the store, frequenting other card shops, attending card shows, (he was compelled to compile complete sets of his favorites) and meticulously arranging the cards in albums.

This was the same year (1981) that Fender Guitar Company decided to design a "reissue" model of their 1952 Telecaster. In August, Ted had his first meeting with the people at Fender and his mint condition 1952 Telecaster was chosen as the prototype for the reissue model. Ted offered suggestions and helped with the new design, which he would showcase at the NAMM show in February of the next year.

The NAMM show took place on the weekend of February 6th and 7th, 1982. Ted performed there playing the "new" reissue 1952 Tele, which he tuned down to Db for the occasion.

Although the Sports Card frenzy continued to dominate Ted's life, 1982 turned out to be quite a memorable year, as this is when he met and became friends with the legendary jazz guitarist Emily Remler. Definitely worthy of mention in Ted's datebook, he wrote, *"Feb. 16 1:00 Get together with John Collins & Emily Remler, A day of musical 1sts: 1.) Reasonably comfortable in role of bass player, 2.) Due to Emily and real low tuning, able to solo in a semi-Wes style & tone with thumb and finger, 3.) Someone who feels the Wes walking bass groove, such as I do."* A few days after their first meeting, Emily went to visit Ted. For the next month, they would spend many hours together jamming and exchanging ideas. Ted noted that he fixed her guitar and transcribed McCoy Tyner for them both. Emily left for Toronto on the 22nd of March, but they continued to stay in touch, and Emily visited him whenever she was in Los Angeles. Their friendship lasted until Emily's premature death in 1990.

Inspired to begin serious practicing again, one area Ted chose to focus on was "textures." He began experimenting with right hand "teams" (team fingering) with interpolation of 1 voice on many qualities, in many voicings and inversions. Then 2-line "chases" on all types of 4-note through 8-note chords or scales. Ted had a multitude of ways to devise texture and he diligently worked through all the possibilities.

May of 1982 earmarked Ted's 1st anniversary of Card Collecting. It is possible that in order to support this passionate habit, in June he added another teaching day - the 2nd Wednesday of every month. But it is also just as likely he wanted to accommodate many new requests for guitar lessons. In September, he was to add another teaching day. He was now teaching on Monday, Thursday, and alternate Wednesdays.

A few music-related ideas came to Ted's mind in between card collecting rampages. He was always considering better ways to disseminate musical information; one idea noted was educational inserts for string packages. In his day planner he jotted down another idea, *"Consider developing your 7- position lever switch and selling the idea to Fender."*

Despite the baseball card collecting, Ted's music studies were never totally disregarded. At this time he also wrote out many Baroque harmony and counterpoint studies and new Chord Voicings Reference Charts.

A partial example of an early attempt to determine options of soprano harmonization in the Baroque style is depicted here.

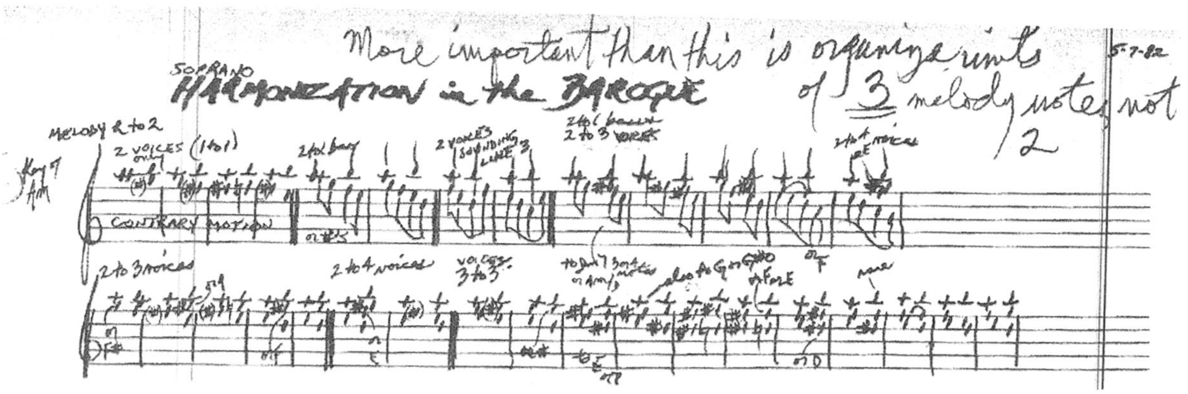

He was also asked by MCA to do an arrangement of the John Williams composition, "Theme From E.T." for guitar, which he did brilliantly. This was Ted's first (and only) published professional arrangement.

● X □ △ ★

Towards the end of 1982 the sports card collecting was beginning to taper off. Ted continued his 3-day teaching schedule, and started to get back to seriously sorting out his musical works. He began a reorganization of all his Baroque material and also writing a plethora of new Cumulative Chord Forms pages. In the upcoming year this led to a complete re-evaluation of his teaching program. The following six months were consumed with working on and improving the latter, but incorporated time for his personal studies as well. This included studying George Van Eps Volume III, organizing all his sheet music and fake book photocopies of the past twenty years, and a musical categorizing of all "loose scraps."

By the summer of 1983 the Sports Card frenzy had abated considerably, and Ted began totally focusing on his playing again. On July 22nd he came to a sort-of revelation and wrote, *"Because I noticed I am loving this naturally (it has evolved little by little, more & more it becomes clear, IT FINALLY COMES TO ME: FRI. NIGHT: In my own fight for and against my playing, it is imperative to first & foremost, PLAY with LOTS of feeling and emotions and a beautiful, lots of reverb, mellow full tone. Fancy fills are nice but not the essence of what I want to say."*

A few days after making that discovery he wrote what was to become his mantra for the next few years, *7/30/83 "It is your responsibility to work hard until you are confident playing music that touches others hearts the way it has yours."*

Over the summer months, his mother had become quite ill, and on the 2nd of August was diagnosed with cancer. Ted told me she had been given little chance to survive, but she confounded all the specialists and lived close to seven more years.

Yet at that time the diagnosis was discouraging. His mother was in and out of the hospital undergoing treatments and Ted did not know that she was to beat some incredible odds. Perhaps this is why Ted dove head long into his music studies with a renewed vigor and a tremendous intensity. As I was to learn later, this complete immersion into working served Ted as a distraction and a comfort during distressing periods in his life.

He finished organizing his personal Baroque notebook of papers from the last 10-12 years and then began studying it, specifically the Baroque key schemes and chords.

Other musical projects on his list would keep him busy through the end of the year. These projects included, "*Study C 7/6 in all 14 spreads, Cumulative Chords showing little inversions on middle 4 strings, top 4 strings & Cumulative Chords, minor 6 voicings with 7 for root, 9 for root, 11 for 5, 6 for 5, 4), modern voice leading progressions, and progressions to learn Systematic Inversions (with or without tune basis).*

This might seem like quite a plateful, but it was not at all daunting for Ted.

An excerpt from Ted's Baroque Organizational Task pages.

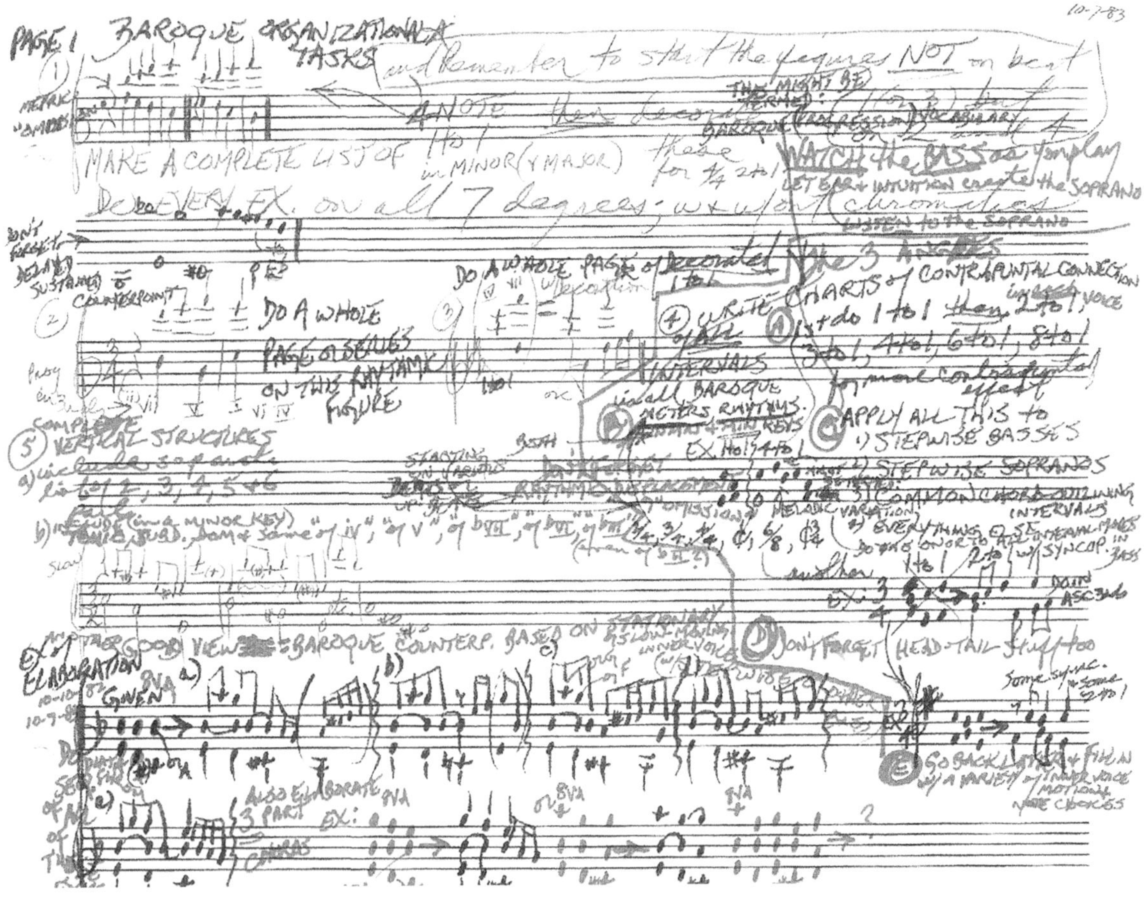

Part II

A Rekindling of Interest and an Explosion of Ideas

(1984-1992)

Upon his mother's completion of the cancer treatments, Ted's parents sold their house in Encino and made a final move to Palm Springs. A new home was found for his grandmother, and after apartment shopping Ted rented unit #9 in the El Dorado Apartment building in Encino. Just prior to signing the lease, he received the somber news that Lenny Breau had died on August 12th.

Then on September 30, just after his 38th birthday Ted moved into his new apartment. Less than a month later his beloved grandmother passed away.

Other than a few short excursions exploring different living situations away from his family, the move into his new apartment found Ted living on his own for the first time in many years. His student roster steadily increased and by the end of the 1980's he was teaching 12 hours a day, three days a week, and even reserved some Sunday afternoons for students with special circumstances, such as those traveling from out of town exclusively for a lesson. It never ceased to amaze him that students would travel from all parts of the United States and occasionally even other countries, just to take even one lesson with him.

In the midst of this productive music frenzy, was Ted's purchase of his first VCR. Thus began his love affair with videotaping. So enamored was he of this marvel, the love affair eventually escalated into his purchasing at least thirty VCR's and taping television shows around the clock. It was not uncommon for him to have several machines going at all times. Those who saw the interior of his apartment were witness to the ramifications, as stacks of videotapes slowly, insidiously began to line the walls.

What did Ted tape, you might ask? Everything! Movies, sports, documentaries, talk shows, situation comedies, essentially whatever was being aired that he thought might be interesting. And there wasn't much that Ted did not find interesting!

Despite his growing student roster and the VCR infatuation, this was the beginning of Ted's most productive years in formulating new music systems and new student lessons. He began seriously developing and elaborating on his Voicing Systems Formulations, a pet project he continued working on and improving throughout the remainder of his life.

Through the rest of the decade Ted concentrated most of his energy on his teaching and personal work. Ted was so incredibly productive during this period.

In light of how productive Ted was during this very fertile decade, I offer a small depiction with a few examples of particular material.

● X □ △ ★

The onset of 1984 found Ted deeply involved with improving old lesson material and formulating new concepts to develop into student lesson material. He worked extensively on clarifying his Cumulative Chord Studies and Harmonic Vocabulary for his students.

In May Ted devised a new plan for himself to finally learn double line textures by *"1. Watching the top note, after you are friendly with the fingerings, which must be tested at a brisk tempo. 2. Play the top voice as a single line occasionally if necessary for visual purposes. 3. Learn one key really well before moving to others. 4.Stay mainly on lower string sets when you have a choice. 5. Do 3 types of studies; arpeggios traversing the whole fingerboard, at least 3 separate positions horizontally, little fragments within these positions, lots of reverb is virtually a prerequisite, 6. Lift the fingers- don't hold the "back two" down unless doing double hammer-ons or pull-offs, 7. Lean back from the guitar so you can see more of what's coming up next, 8.One of the main vehicles: Blues (in Eb) of various types, low strings - upstairs register."*

Ted was inclined toward writing out extensive reference and organizational material. By using this method, he derived the optimal choices, and loved discovering surprising new ones. This type of systematic work also proved to be very relaxing for him to do. Here is a partial example page among the hundreds he worked out.

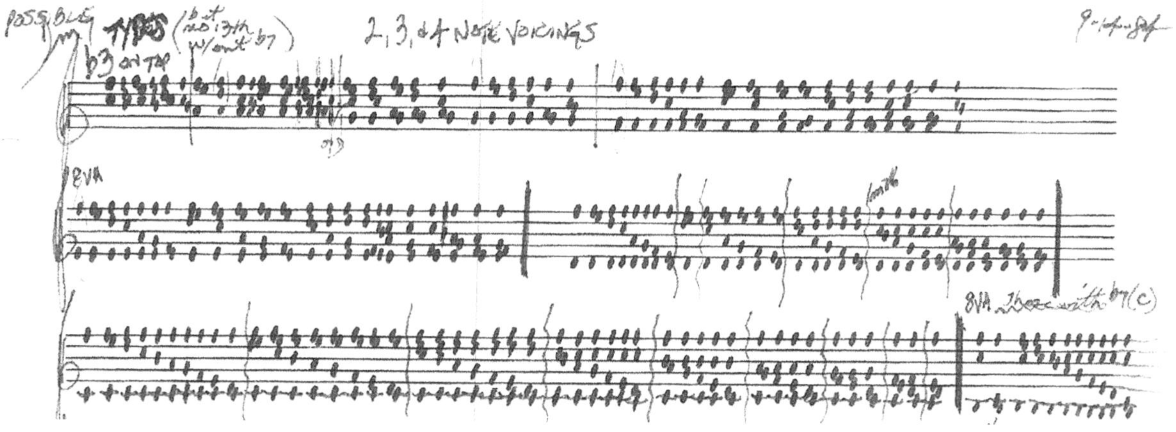

● X □ △ ★

At the beginning of 1985 Ted focused on his Voicing System Studies, first by top note and outer voices to find practical or at least "*reasonable expectations*". This is one example of many that he experimented with as he searched for the best way to organize and present this material.

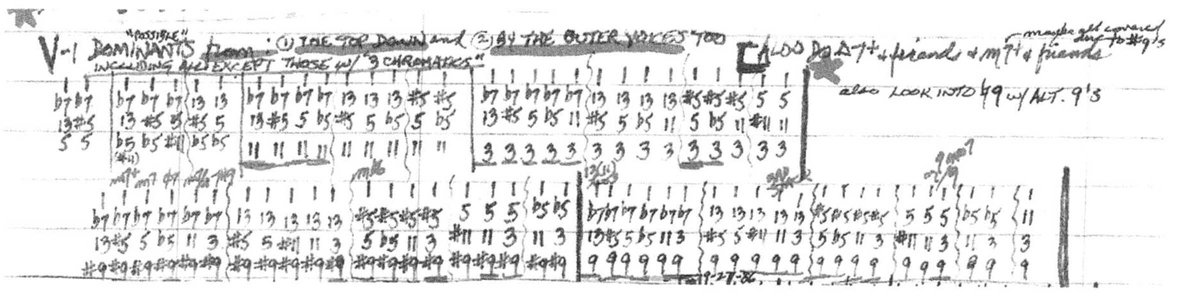

Mid year Ted reflected on the pros and cons of teaching his Voicing System 2. After a year or two of trying the V-2 System, **one set** at a time, and also the V-2 **all sets** at one time; he raised issues to consider and also offered himself a valid argument for each issue. Such as, why teach one set at a time when the crossovers are actually used more? But conversely, the crossovers felt so good that the student may never learn to go up and down each section, one at a time, which he or she will need at the top and bottom of the board. Ted knew he couldn't give most students all the chord forms at once of any one type (say, V-2 Dom. 7) since they couldn't process that much information for quite a long time. The other alternative could be to give them small sections of the neck with crossovers, but many might feel less responsive to the seeming lack of an overall system to this. At least with one set at a time there was a general acceptance and good feeling and results. However, even then it would require lots of review and application for long term absorption.

In late summer, Ted discovered what he termed "a great new method" and began writing out a gradual presentation of minor 7 and dominant 7 type voicings for himself and for teaching. His path was often lead through trying to find ways to show things to the students via different presentations and organizations, which often helped him in self-organizing and retention of the material.

Another idea Ted had been pondering for a while was how to teach Baroque harmony on a fundamental level. He began this method by organizing all bass moves in units of 2, a method he would later revise.

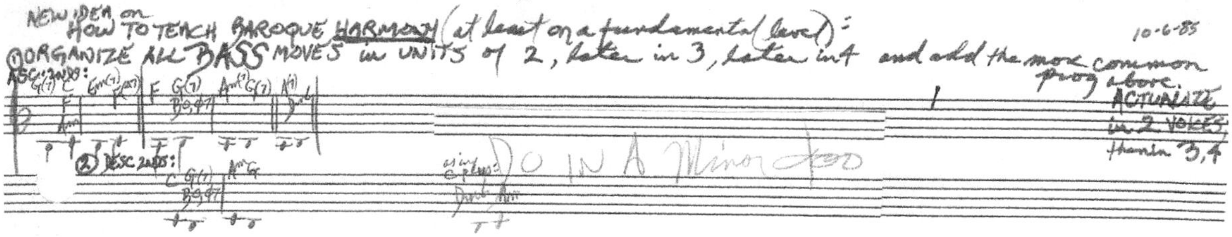

Throughout the rapidly disappearing decade of the 1980's, Ted would periodically drive to Palm Springs to visit his parents. They would share their time enjoyably watching movies and listening to music together. Ted was particularly thrilled when he could bring something new for them he was sure they would love, whether a movie, music or books.

In Ted's never-ending quest for the finest sounds, whether chords, chord progressions, or patterns, he continued experimenting through making organizational charts. This excerpt from an extensive exploration shows part of his "Harp-like Broken Chord Patterns."

In the autumn of 1986 Ted developed a new teaching program comprised of many studies he had refined. He divided the new program into three parts. Part I incorporated a lot of these new studies which he put under the heading of Harmony and Voicings. This included: Cumulative Chords, Harmonic Improvement, Harmonic Tendencies, Favorable Matings, Jazz Turnarounds, Choice Voicings, Blues Progressions, Walking Chord Jazz & Gospel type, Diatonic and non-diatonic 4ths, V-2 top set 1st, V-2 middle & top. V-2 all 3, V-1, master list of large chords. Remember this is **only** Part I!

Then a rare note to himself on Sept. 19, 1986 states, *"From now on when practicing work on a) One harmonic concept or texture, then b) One song & apply above as interlude (TRY)!"*

In January of 1987 he revived and elaborated on some imperatives from May of 1984, titled "The 9 Main Areas of Music" and qualified them for improvisation or extended composition. This now included: "*1. Melody (decoration through ornamentation or embellishment via diatonic or chromatic tones, phrasing) 2. Harmony (chord quality, chord connection, or root movement, voice leading) 3. Register & Spacing 4. Texture 5. Harmonic Rhythm (frequency of change of chords) 6. Rhythm (meter, regular or displaced accents, rhythmic figures, all of this yielding specific rhythm types) 7. Tone Color (instrumentation: density- one instrument? or a group? all playing same notes?, intrinsic variations with each of same) 8. Dynamics (related to volume and to rhythm accents) 9. Form*"

Now Ted was beginning to long to perform live again and on February 27, 1987 he made a rather telling entry in his datebook, *"Plan - get out & play in restaurants (& clubs) where people are noisy so that eventually you (crave?) the quiet concert audience again, this might do the trick."* Four more years would pass before he would make this happen.

In March he began another organizational project, this time to discover all 4-note melodic patterns. A partial example is given here:

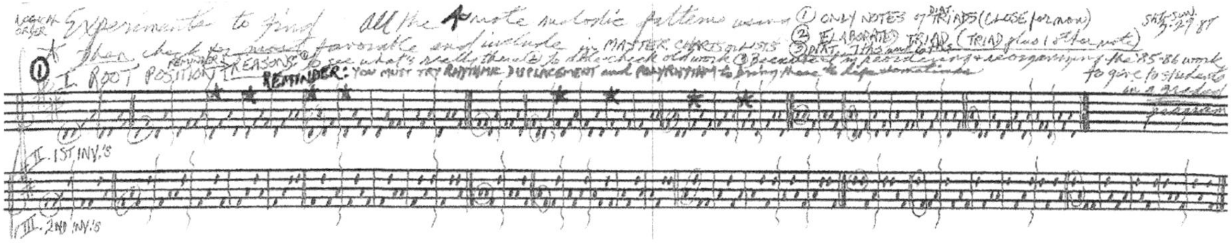

A few other notes of interest were in his datebooks during this time in his life. These suggest that Ted was still going through periods of self-discovery. On March 15th he wrote, *"New Beginning: Try something new or a new way of seeing every day!"*

Then in October an insight regarding his life, *"Observation: The first 25 yrs. of my life were often Sensory Heaven & Emotional Hell."*

● X □ △ ★

With much of his time spent deeply involved with his musical experiments and student lessons he rarely gave pause for reflection on his own life. Now these reflections were happening more frequently. Soon he came to one of his most important realizations, which also became his "mantra" over the next few years. On May 1, 1988 Ted wrote, *"My main purpose in being here: Spread beauty, increase beauty, or increase appreciation for that which already exists here."*

September still found him engrossed in experimentation. Ted would continue this type of procedure for his entire life.

In 1989 he gave much time and thought to his "pet project," his Voicing Systems. Ted had determined three methods of figuring out which voicing group any 4-note (non-doubled type) chord belonged to. Although he had come up with all three methods independently, he realized their amazing similarity at the core. Along with that he more clearly detailed how to devise each Voicing System's style or size.

There is no question that this is a testimony to Ted's commitment to his studies. Throughout the latter part the 1980s the amount of work he accomplished is impressive to the point of being astonishing. A complete list of Ted's student lesson material and his Voicing System material can be found in the appendix. On top of all that, Ted still made time to practice, and find ways to improve his playing.

● X □ △ ★

The start of the new decade brought much grief into Ted's life. On January 2, 1990 his mother succumbed to cancer after her seven-year battle with the disease. The following May he lost his dear friend Emily Remler to a tragic drug overdose; she was only 33 years old. Despite these hardest of blows, he held steadfast to his studies and his teaching, not allowing the grief to overwhelm his senses. Ted had the unusual capacity to grieve silently, accept the pain and continue to move forward.

In the beginning of 1991 he began to rekindle a love for his playing again, as he noted in his datebook, "*More music rejuvenation in the back room with '51 Lemon Nocaster, '63 brown deluxe reverb unit. LOVE my sound again.*" Once more he began giving seminars, in May at the University of Redlands, in July one at Scripps College in Claremont, and also the National Summer Guitar Workshop. He formed a duo with singer Jacie Barry. They spent many months rehearsing and choosing material and performed at private parties and weddings, all the time refining their act to a level of perfection. In January of 1992 they landed their first public performance at Monte Leone's West, followed by a four-month engagement at the Westlake Inn. They were truly incredible! The unique tone quality of Jacie's voice combined with Ted's accompaniment was an inspired blend of harmonic brilliance, phrasing and nuance. And in July of 1992, I tiptoed into Ted's life.

Part III

My Life With The Chord Chemist

● X □ △ ★

Part III

Chapter I

The Extraordinary and the Complex
(1992-1993)

On July 9, 1992 I had my first guitar lesson with Ted. When I arrived, he was finishing up with another student and led me to a back bedroom that he used as a waiting room. I could not help but notice that the whole apartment was filled primarily with books. His massive bookshelves were over burdened and books spilled out and spread everywhere. There were books piled atop and obscuring the few items of furniture, and books stacked floor to ceiling.

Being confined temporarily to the back room, I perused the selections, of which more than half were music books. I also noticed books on movies, cats, history, cars, biographies, and self-help or do-it-yourself type books, but no novels, no literature. It was all factual, informative reading. While I was scrutinizing all the titles Ted opened the door.

The books highly aroused my curiosity about him. I wondered if he'd read many of them, but didn't ask. These thoughts formed the basis for my first impression of Ted. I also sensed he possessed a high degree of intelligence along with a very serene demeanor, and a casual, open attitude.

We spent much of the lesson discussing my musical goals, musical background, and musical interests and desires. He made me feel comfortable and selected some lesson material he thought I might find useful.

After that first lesson, I knew I wanted to get to know this interesting and attractive man a whole lot better.

An excerpt from my first lesson:

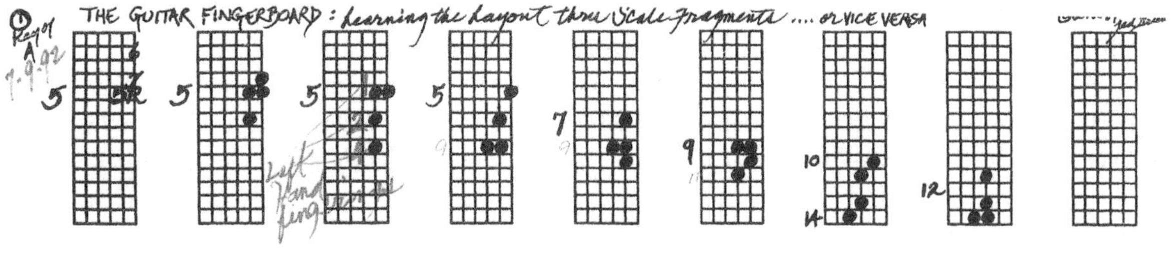

By my third lesson, a month later, our conversation flowed easily; we connected on many levels. I was truly fascinated by him, his many facets, intelligence, and eccentricities. The musical information he imparted that evening served me perfectly. I was not sure how he so keenly perceived what I needed but it was almost uncanny.

A week or so after that third lesson, I called him with a question and hours of conversation ensued. From that initial query, many hours of phone conversation began consuming our late evenings. Eventually I suggested we converse in person, which Ted found agreeable. So, for the first time I ventured over to Ted's apartment not for a lesson. That night he told me some of his childhood stories; about the time he ran away from home to be back in New York; his love for Rhythm and Blues and the intensity of city street life that fed his passion for that gritty sound. His actions brought much dismay to his parents, who believed this entire scene to be unsavory and dangerous.

That story led me to ask why he chose the San Fernando Valley to live since he'd mentioned how much he loved city life. Ted told me that after having moved back to Los Angeles, it just felt like home, and he found the San Fernando Valley and the apartment to be centrally situated and close to the freeway. Location was important to Ted and a prime consideration as he wanted to be as easily accessible as possible, causing the least inconvenience for his students.

We talked about music. He explained his "Theory of Visualization" which entailed visualizing the fingerboard while reciting major scales descending, major chords descending, one key each day, then the minor scales and chords. This exercise could be done anywhere, anytime, such as while driving or waiting in line at the store. Ted never wasted a second of his time; he was always studying, even mentally and encouraged others to try to develop this habit.

Inevitably, as we got to know each other better, the subject of personal relationships came into question. At this stage in his life, Ted had come to the conclusion that he was ill suited for intimate personal relationships. He told me that all his past relationships had failed for various reasons, one of the main factors being that there was never an adequate amount of time he was willing to devote to a relationship that was acceptable to the other person. Another reason was that he found it very painful to be "in love." Given his obsessive nature (he used the term addictive) his tendency was to become consumed by thoughts of the person to the point of distraction and worry which he could not bear.

After that evening, our phone conversations continued, as was Ted's preference. In this manner we gradually began to learn more about each other. He was definitely hesitant to consider becoming involved in a relationship with me, the phone helped to moderate his feelings, gave him time to consider the possibilities, while still maintaining a connection. I found this quite frustrating, but I complied with his preference at that point.

Curiously I had noticed Ted often used third person plural when he left phone messages for me and even occasionally during our phone conversations. When I started to respond in third person plural, he immediately stopped using it for the duration of our conversation. Then he began to use it less frequently and it completely ceased by the end of the year.

On October 1st I had my last formal lesson as Ted and I both realized that we had become more than teacher/student. By then there was a mutual recognition between us of a budding relationship as our conversations had become considerably more intimate. At the end of that last lesson, he bestowed upon me my first gift, a biography "Beethoven the Creator," by Romaine Rolland, because I had mentioned how much I revered this author.

● X □ △ ★

As fate would have it, via the phone, we began to discover many similar interests and surprisingly determined we could easily converse indefinitely on almost any subject. From old cartoons, "*We talk about the old animation, she's receptive (& loves TOP CAT (1962) of all things!,"* to economics, to philosophy.

Eventually when Ted asked me about my family, I told him about the vast expanse of my father's musical career, from New York's Tin Pan Alley to Warner Brothers (movie studio's) Music Department. Through continued inquiry Ted found out that my father not just worked with but had been friendly with Max Steiner, (Ted's all time favorite film composer). Ted was incredulous and eager to meet my father and talk with him.

Soon we made arrangements to visit my parents and I made some wonderful discoveries that day. Not just the magical musical connection Ted had with my father, but I also realized one of Ted's greatest gifts: the ability to bring out the best qualities in others. My parents responded so well to Ted, they were glowing. He took a genuine interest in them, stimulated meaningful conversation and ignited their memories. It was heartwarming to see my parents so responsive and radiant.

Ted had a natural facility for making people feel good about themselves. He told me he had worked hard at it all his life; and that people were of as much interest to him as music. He had always loved to study people. Ted easily captivated both my parents.

After leaving my parent's house, we went to my house for the first time, and he settled in as if he'd been visiting for years. I found him so comfortable to be with. At that point I realized I was becoming quite enamored of this incredible man. However around midnight, as he was leaving, I felt a distinct change, a distance when we said goodbye. Did I do something to anger or upset him? Later I had to call him to allay my uneasiness, and he simply stated it was hard for him to say goodbye. We talked for a while, things I don't remember except this, (and in retrospect this is almost eerie), I asked him what he most feared. He replied it was dying young.

Towards the end of 1992, Ted began to realize he was developing some strong feelings for me. What did it mean when one spent ten hours with someone and the time seemed to go by in the blink of an eye? Maybe that love was in bloom?

Late one evening we took a long walk through my neighborhood then up and down Ventura Boulevard sharing observations, sensations from everything we saw, our faces flushed from the cold night air. It was the most beautiful experience together thus far. Together, time didn't exist; it was just the two of us, and our total involvement in the moment. Further more, we continued discovering things we both loved. Another of those discoveries: Words! We were always coming up with word games, one was making up synonymous song titles for example: instead of 'Ticket to Ride' I offered my rather dull suggestion, 'Entitlement to be Borne Along,' compared with Ted's inimitable humor, 'Passport to Non-ambulatoria.'

That night he also told me about his "pet" Voicing Systems project, a massive study that he began in the '80s. On November 22nd he began another aspect of the project, which entailed organizing the V-1 voicings by Intervals.

Our first actual date-like experience occurred on December 4th, when Ted's friend Norman Harris invited Ted to see Charles Brown at the Cinegrill, and Ted asked me if I'd like to join him. Absolutely elated, I accepted his invitation. Therefore, on a clear, chilly winter night, Ted and I drove to the Cinegrill located in the Roosevelt Hotel, where we joined his friends. In this elegant atmosphere with the architecture painstakingly restored to the glorious splendor reminiscent of Hollywood in the 1930's, we were charmed by the music and warmth of this 70-year-old blues singer. Despite the bedazzlement induced by the surroundings and the entertainment, I was acutely aware of how impassioned I felt being with Ted. When we walked with our arms around each other, or with my hand pressed tightly in his, the fervency of this interaction, the physical connection was overwhelming. More than a complement to the evening, it seemed to eclipse all else. That night I knew I had fallen in love.

Now that I knew how strongly I felt, I was quite hesitant to let on, for although I felt that Ted had strong feelings for me as well, I wasn't sure how comfortable he would be with an intensity of this nature, so I kept it to myself.

A week later, we again spent almost eleven hours together with the cold north wind howling through every crack in my old house. That night, we huddled together on the floor by the little space heater. Besides our usual effusive conversation; he showed me how to use my amplifier effectively and imparted a lot of information helpful to my guitar playing. I noticed too how he enjoyed all the things in my house with the delight of a child having new and wonderful toys; the Les Paul copy, Martin D35, even my VCR! We watched, and afterwards discussed some Tom & Jerry cartoons he brought, which depicted the difference of quality in animation and music in the 1940's as opposed to the 1960's. Together we had discovered even more things that we both found entertaining, stimulating and amusing. He left around 4 a.m. and once in bed thoughts of him lingered leaving me sleepless.

Ted's example of Coloristic Film Chords

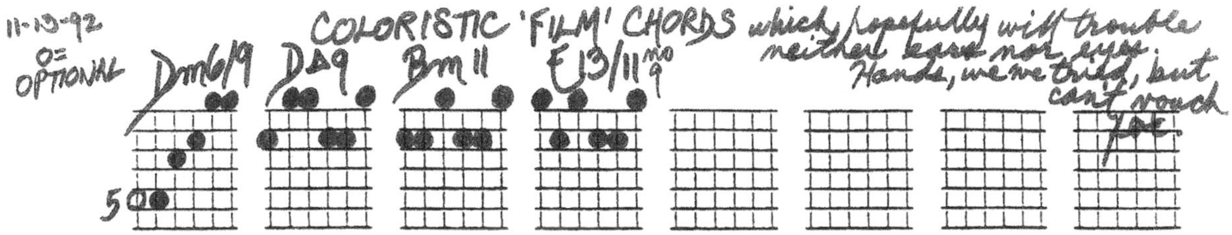

As the end of the year approached, Ted called to offer a rather perplexing proposition; would I possibly be interested in accompanying him to some Christmas gatherings to which he was invited. I was somewhat surprised he had considered going, as neither of us were socially inclined. After much vacillation, we decided to go since Ted wanted me to meet a few of his friends.

The parties were interesting, his friends delightful, but.... we did come to the conclusion that parties were not our cup of tea. What I enjoyed most of all was afterwards, our first time going to the supermarket together. I discovered that shopping with Ted was no ordinary excursion. Supermarkets seemed to energize him. His interest was not solely in buying food, but in many of the other items offered. We actually plopped ourselves down on the floor by the magazine rack and browsed through magazines for an hour. Prior to this I had never laughed so much while shopping, it was wonderfully playful.

During this holiday season we had socialized more than we had done all year. Christmas eve and day we spent with my family. Upon reflection, having Ted along to share the holiday activities certainly embellished the experiences, not just the overwhelming joy of his company, but observing him interacting with everyone, and their open and affirmative responses to him. He was able to draw out so many positive aspects of their natures, and of course, make everyone laugh.

When next I saw him there was no disguising that he was rather despondent and moody, which he admitted was due to the end of the year. I learned the end of the year was often a most difficult time for him, but he didn't want to elaborate on why. It was the first time I witnessed his moody side. We spent a peaceful evening, talked a bit and listened to seasonal music offered on the classical radio station. This was our first New Year's Eve together.

● X □ △ ★

Shortly into 1993, Ted informed me his father would be in town and suggested we pay him a visit. Apparently his father was most anxious to meet me since Ted had been telling him all about the "new woman in his life." Therefore, with some apprehension on my part we went to see him. Ted's father, Irwin, greeted me with a warm, reassuring welcome. He needed no encouragement to talk about his beloved son. A bit to Ted's embarrassment, Irwin spent hours raving about Ted's accomplishments. There was no mistaking that Irwin was one proud father. I found Irwin to be quite charming and we all had a pleasant visit.

Although Ted and I had been spending more time together, getting to know the "real" Ted was not an easy endeavor. There was still so much about him that I found most perplexing and even somewhat mysterious. For example, at this point he did not feel comfortable seeing me more than once a week. Ted explained some of the reasons for his particular behavior in certain instances, one being his need to exercise rigid control over his actions because of his tendency to become obsessive, or as he termed it "addicted." Regarding his reluctance to become intimate, he felt that physical desire wore off too quickly and wanted to be sure there was much more than that to sustain us, to know there was something lasting at that stage in his life. Basically, Ted was still testing us, questioning our relationship, weighing it, unable to trust it yet.

I remember gently explaining to him that underneath the surface of any solid relationship there was an area of understanding that went beyond the common interests people shared. Sometimes what bonded two people was a similar way of viewing life, reaching the same levels of understanding, having the same fundamental values, the same sensibilities. Almost any two people can develop common interests, take up hobbies or sports together, but they cannot develop that unexplainable sense of connection, what is coincidently termed "chemistry." He understood, but needed time to really absorb it all.

Toward the end of January, Ted took a regular gig playing solo guitar at the Seashell restaurant in Encino, Friday and Saturday nights. I began accompanying him to the Seashell every weekend, reveling in his heavenly music, and enjoying the luxury of eating his complimentary dinner.

Ted assumed that because we were together every weekend at the Seashell, that we were spending enough time together. Since he always felt so pressed for time, he figured this situation worked out well for both of us. When I realized he was substituting the Seashell for our visits, I decided to cease joining him there. When he enquired as to why, I brought to his attention that this was unsuitable as a substitute for spending time together. He didn't completely understand but did reluctantly concede somewhat to my wishes and we did resume spending time together, but not with any regularity, not even once a week.

Alas, much to Ted's dismay, these infrequent visits were still not enough to sustain me, and I began to question whether I could maintain a relationship with him. I began to think that maybe Ted was right about the time issue after all.

The next week he told me he was no longer playing at the Seashell Friday nights because the management felt he wasn't drawing enough dinner customers, and that that should enable us to have some more time together. We acknowledged a distance had grown between us and vowed to help each other communicate. We affirmed how much joy we gave to each other, and agreed that together we had something very special. He expressed his desire for the relationship to continue, to learn from each other and asked me not to give up hope. I told him I felt the same way.

Slowly we began learning to communicate as our weekly visits resumed. We spent a lot of our time talking, watching movies, listening to and discussing music and occasionally doing errands together.

During our talks I noticed how easily Ted would go off on tangents. It was difficult for him to stay with the initial subject matter. Was he aware of this? Yes, but he could not converse otherwise. However, sometimes these frequent digressions made it easier for Ted to cleverly circumvent any questions about him that perplexed me. Ted was actually a master at subtly manipulating a conversation.

Another thing Ted explained to me was that all his life he had to be many different people, and had to learn to change and adapt to fit in with whom ever he was with at the time. Who was the real Ted? As I was very curious about him, I would search for little insights into how to better understand him, and also asked him to help me to do so.

● X □ △ ★

Meanwhile, he had been in the process of moving from apartment 9 to apartment 8, and towards the end of February 1993, Ted decided to begin teaching in the front room of the new apartment. Although he had moved some of his belongings, there was still a considerable amount left to move. The amount of work that remained to be accomplished was causing him much anxiety. Upon seeing each other that weekend, I sensed his stress, which seemed to lessen during the course of the visit. We watched one of his favorite movies, "The Young Savages" and had a very enjoyable time together. I remember asking him why we only watched old movies, particularly ones he'd already seen, his response was that he did not want to take the chance of wasting time on the possibility of us not liking something, he would rather go for a sure thing, than take any risk.

Young Savages

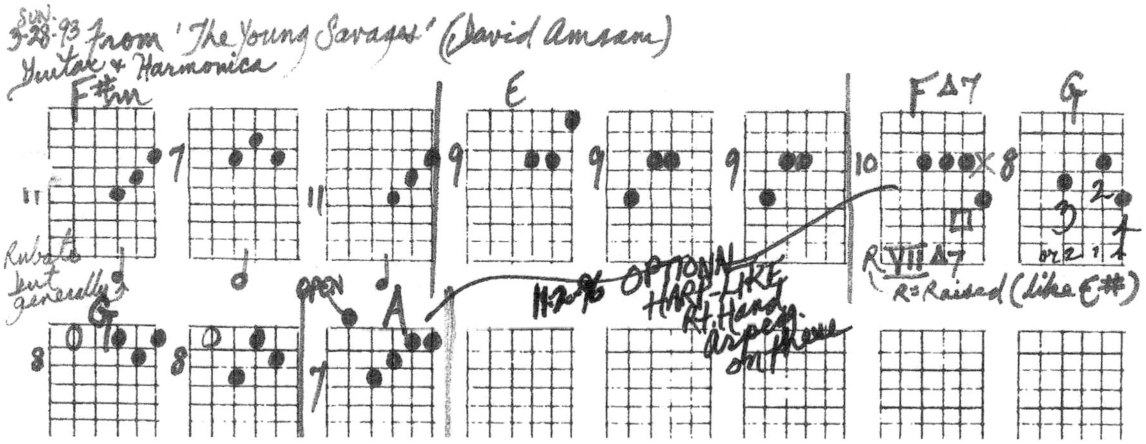

For the most part, his thoughts were now consumed with moving into his new apartment and how he could arrange all his belongings in order to utilize the limited space wisely. At this stage he had only brought what he considered necessities. It was mostly a painstaking thought process, as he needed to plan out how best to achieve an optimal arrangement of his things. He did many experiments by repeatedly rearranging the items he had brought over. I couldn't help but think, at this pace and the way in which he worked, there was no doubt it would take him the rest of the year to complete the move. And besides continuing to move, he was always working on several projects of some sort. As a result, he constantly felt he was behind on everything.

In attempting to use his time efficiently Ted always carried several brown paper supermarket bags, which contained his most current and pressing work. These bags accompanied him everywhere. When at my place, he would work on music studies, student lessons, and any work that was easily transportable. When at his apartment the work was almost exclusively the rearranging and organization of various sections of a room, or the organization of a particular collection of items such as videocassettes or magazines. Regardless, working on organizing his apartment always helped him to feel good, especially when he got a lot accomplished. He loved being productive, which seemed to heighten his enjoyment of our evenings.

In mid April, Ted called to tell me that his Dad had a somewhat serious stroke, but Ted felt assured that his dad would be able to make almost a full recovery. He said also that he was no longer playing at the Seashell Saturday nights, thus entirely ending his gig there. My hope was that now he would have a bit more time to share with me. Unfortunately, this was not to happen for some months.

● X □ △ ★

April 25, 1993. I include this date for it was one of our best days together thus far and eventually lead to a major turning point in our relationship. Having reflected upon this day, I realize it's not what we did, but essentially how we went about experiencing it together. Yet, when I describe the events they will most probably not seem at all extraordinary.

Inadvertently, Ted and I took a rather circuitous route to get to the hospital where his father was recuperating, yet the drive afforded us the pleasure of viewing the diverse sights of that section of the city. When we finally arrived at the rather obscurely marked Cedars Sinai Medical Center, we were taken aback by the strange geometric shape looming up at a bizarre angle. The building was a rather nondescript, olive colored high-rise; nothing at all to indicate it was in fact a hospital. How impressed I was when he parallel parked his beloved Betsy, a huge light blue, 4-door 1972 Plymouth Fury II, perfectly!

We took the elevator to the 8th floor and found his father in the sunny glass enclosed rehabilitation unit. I was encouraged and pleased by Irwin's seemingly rapid recovery. He was spry, lively, walked well, formulated full sentences (with some difficulty) but his spirit and attitude were positive. It was a lovely and encouraging visit.

Then it was off to another world, another slice of life, to the shopping area around Beverly Center to purchase a VCR for me, after which we went down to another level to purchase a portable CD and cassette player. This whole episode in the electronics store lasted at least two hours. Ted scrutinized every minute detail, made comparisons, did trial runs to test response, sound quality, the feel of the buttons, the ergonomics. One could not be more thorough in determining a purchase. What an exercise in patience for me. Yet Ted was great, helped me focus, think about what I wanted and why I wanted it, it wasn't enough to simply like the way it looked.

By the time we left the shopping complex it was growing dark and we walked outside into the brilliance of neon. We drove down Beverly Boulevard marveling at the city silhouetted against the sky, the changing features of each building, the juxtaposing of old and new. Then I happened to glance at a store with a collection of restored old sports cars, and there in the front window - a bright yellow Cobra! Not able to contain my excitement I screamed and pointed at the car. Ted responded immediately with a u-turn and took me back to look in the window. The car was stunning. Ted delighted in the discovery that I loved cars so much. Around nine p.m. we arrived at my house exhausted. We exchanged warm "goodbyes" with a simple kiss I knew I'd never forget. It was our first kiss.

What made this day so extraordinary was that it produced in me a heightened response from all the stimuli, which in turn triggered and heightened Ted's response level to the same degree and intensified Ted's feelings towards me. I was to learn that Ted acquired many of his pleasures in life vicariously.

I thought that the result of having this experience together would be a step forward in our relationship but instead a long interval of regression ensued. Ted's anxiety surfaced. He feared becoming too addicted to our visits and neglecting his work, and he still hadn't finished moving. All this loomed over him. Instead of drawing us closer, phone conversations resumed for almost a month in lieu of seeing each other. A distance seemed to have crept back and formed between us again. I had felt a bond, and that a closeness was firmly established, but I was totally taken aback by his resultant anxiety.

Finally, he somewhat reluctantly conceded to me visiting. Upon seeing each other we just stood there, hesitant, not knowing what to do or say. It had been close to a month since we had spent the day together. What to do? Since he was still concerned about time and had yet to complete moving from apartment 9, to help ease his stress I suggested helping him move, figuring this way we were spending time together and being productive, to which he was very receptive.

Ted had given most of his furniture away, essentially what was left were massive stacks of everything he had collected. That day we moved hundreds, maybe thousands of boxes of baseball cards into apartment 8. After seeing what was still left in the old apartment I was truly amazed at the amount of things he had acquired and accumulated over the years. Every closet and cabinet was full of magazines, baseball cards, amplifiers, there was so much stuff I don't remember it all. Then there were mountains of books, record albums, and video cassettes, phenomenal! We put merely a small dent in what had yet to be moved.

On June 8th, 1993 Ted gave a seminar at Musician's Institute, here I defer to Ted's datebook entry for a summary of what occurred, "*June 8 Seminar at M.I. Playing ranged from not so great to really o.k. - lots of ringing tones. Discussed: keys - Dorian versus Aeolian, learning chords: R5R55R; 5R5R5R also as neutral pads to make the ear hungry and excited for the arrival of some harmony, hungry for the key, hungry for a tonality. Played: Autumn Leaves, jazz, then Baroque florid 20th century expanded diatonic & regular improv. horizontal piece, long free form reprise, Send In the Clowns, Like Someone in Love, Eleanor Rigby (request) God Bless the Chile, slow then double time to this, just had to."* This seminar was videotaped and transferred to DVD.

● X □ △ ★

My requests to spend more time together were still mostly going unheeded, I told him I found it ridiculous that we spent so much time on the phone (conversations spanning 6 hours or more) when we lived so close together. He wasn't exactly happy to hear this since he was perfectly content to spend hours on the phone while leisurely sorting through and organizing his things. I began to suspect he used these telephone conversations as a buffer, so as to not let us get too close but still retain a relationship. He argued this point and agreed to one-hour visits since in his words, "I needed to SEE him." The next Sunday evening we got together, the "one-hour visit" exceeded six hours. Ted had a bad toothache, but I could feel him trying to make the evening pleasurable. Even with his reassurance and renewed enthusiasm, I was anxious and unsure. We spent most of the time looking through music books together. He set aside some classical duets we could play and offered me one to take home. He said he had forgotten how good it was when we were together; maybe he just needed to be prodded (his words, idea). He insisted he had been glad to have me there and wouldn't wait so long again.

That night I told him I detected a change in him in the past month, he said I was very perceptive. What brought this about? He explained he could no longer be carefree, his innocence was gone, his responsibilities loomed and his spirit was drained. He no longer felt he had much time or energy to expend for pleasurable though frivolous activities in lieu of completing his work, and was saddened by that realization.

I reached out to him with my whole heart, and with such sensitivity that I became infused with his pain. I told him I was trying so hard to understand him. He insisted he was not complex, asked me to explain. I told him I felt that he was unnecessarily complicating his life and I needed to think about why.

And I did think about "why" which led me to consider his many idiosyncrasies, and I pondered one possible explanation. Over the past nine months, I had begun to make some interesting observations about certain unusual aspects of Ted's behavior.

I couldn't help but question how much bearing this had on our relationship, and how Ted functioned in the world in general. Some of the most salient actions that aroused my curiosity were: Ted's use of third person plural, his constant rocking back and forth or fidgeting while sitting, the massive accumulation of things, and incessant need to rearrange these things (obsessive/compulsive), unusual diet and eating habits (extreme aversions to most foods and smells), and most especially, his almost constant state of underlying anxiety, and his rigid control over his actions. I knew many of these were traits attributed to Asperger's Syndrome*, (often found among highly gifted, highly intelligent, creative people). Prior to meeting Ted, I had read a considerable number of books in this area. Could Ted have a very mild form of Asperger's? These thoughts I kept to myself for a very long time. What mattered more was that I was now learning to reach out for the first time. He was also learning and trusting me more and more.

* Incidentally, here are a few other famous and gifted people that were thought to have a mild form of Asperger's Syndrome: Eric Satie, Glen Gould, Albert Einstein, and Howard Hughes

Chapter II

Learning: Trust - Compromise - Reciprocation

(1993-1994)

Now, but for the rare occasion, we had begun to spend most of our time at Ted's apartment since he needed to continue organizing his stuff and again, in Ted's words, "I needed to SEE him." Initially, he was apprehensive of my visiting him under these circumstances, but acquiesced to my wishes. He warned me that he would be working the entire time. I assured him I didn't mind. He did appear more unsettled than usual, as he wasn't sure if he could manage to have me visit once a week. To make it a little easier on him, I offered my assistance with anything he chose. I knew he trusted me more now, as he let me sort his mail while he sorted through lessons. We sat on the living room floor with Ted surrounded by papers and books like a symbolic wall built around him. The last hour of this visit, he spent writing me out some music I had wanted for a long time. And I was completely elated when he mentioned that he loved teaching me music.

Next weekend, after a lovely evening, he told me he had to reconsider his decision, that the once a week visits were too much for him. At that point I expressed my utter dismay and told him I was ready to give up on the relationship. A long discussion ensued. Basically, he pleaded with me not to give up what we had, as there was too much good to throw it all away. We wrestled with this the remainder of the evening; questioning, analyzing, trying to understand each other as best we could. We finally got around to talking about "that wonderful Sunday in April," which I suggested was when he began to withdraw from me. He insisted I was totally responsible for his feelings that day, and completely negated his own responsibility. He blamed me for his losing control. I was stunned and exasperated by his explanation. For the remainder of the evening we worked our way through this problem, and Ted, at the thought of losing the relationship, conceded to once a week visits and even a kiss!

When I compared our journals for that day I found them quite amusing; note the discrepancy in each of our entries specifically regarding a kiss goodnight.

From Ted's datebook:

Visit Barbara: "A fine feeling, she comes out in that sleeveless olive green top & the sun illuminating her beautiful green eyes & auburn hair & golden skin....wowza... 'course I told her that she looked beautiful. I make her discuss US again ...to help better vibes. I write her some music, the beginning of a tailored for her key of G solo guitar version of "Here There & Everywhere" First observable chord produced shudder from her (when I show her what the jazz folk would do (II 13 #11 - 2 handed). ***She asks for & receives hugs & before I am to go "Are we ever going to kiss again?" "Sure" & we do & I assure her we can do this each time we see each other....leaving her happy."***

From my journal:

Ted visits: "How genuinely surprised I was to hear Ted say he thinks about me every day. I asked him what, he just stated certain things bring me to mind. I was elated. Truly a wonderful evening together. He wrote me out the first few measures of "Here, There & Everywhere" his choice, albeit a good one, and he played many variations of the song for my amusement, I love when he does this. Then we had a much needed discussion about our relationship. (edited out) ***When I asked him if we were ever going to kiss again, it aroused some anxiety, he responded with something like "But where would that lead to?" And I exclaimed, "Ted, it's just a kiss," he thought for a moment and then said sure, and kissed me!"***

How cleverly Ted was able to manipulate time in order to accommodate my request for once a week visits. Next Sunday we got together at midnight. Ted called to invite me over and answered the door "midnight movies." I found this quite an interesting hour for him to choose. We watched a movie he'd seen many times, "They Made Me A Criminal" from1939, the music score by Max Steiner. Not only did we enjoy it but were truly moved by the story, and of course the music. Sharing this experience helped to reinforce the bond we'd begun to reestablish. Our best emotional connections seemed to be made through a shared "indirect" experience, usually a movie, whether it was poignant or comical.

Perhaps as a benefit of sharing the energy, or maybe it was Max's music, Ted wrote in his datebook, "*Begin studying guitar again in earnest! What inspirations tonight! Culminating in '64 Jazz-Max tuned up a whole step - Baroque near-fugato improvisation. Slowly making my way towards total fugato improv."*

● X □ △ ★

Now it was mid summer and our weekly visits continued with regularity. Next time upon my arrival at the apartment, I found Ted straightening out the cupboard underneath his bathroom sink. I sat on the floor in the hallway amused as he shuffled through his stuff. When he finished he suggested watching a movie and went through boxes of videos trying to decide on one. Then somehow a large stack of music books distracted him, which he began to sort through. We browsed through some during the process, sharing with each other certain passages that interested us. Of course, we never did get to the movie.

The following weekend without even trying we just seemed to connect and laughed a lot. We read lines in books to each other, and especially enjoyed the C.P.E. Bach "Essay" book, laughing as we tried to decipher the convoluted use of language. Then we reviewed the tape of Ted's Musician's Institute seminar from earlier that year. He used my reactions and questions as a gauge of how readily the students at the seminar may have comprehended, as this was not discernible to him during the lecture. He was attempting to figure out what he could have done better and how.

Later, as he reviewed a new study course he was working on titled, Choice Dominant Voices by Soprano, he told me one of the goals he aspired to; which was to change the way music was taught for the better, by formulating a basic method of understanding for everyone who pursues musical knowledge. He was sure he could convey music theory in a way as to make it easily comprehensible and accessible to anyone.

From our discussions, lessons, and the information he imparted to me, I was convinced he would achieve this. It was not just the matter of having researched and refined his theories and ideas, but he also had such a keen insight into human nature as to perceive how differently everyone takes in or receives information and assimilates it. He had an uncanny ability to communicate, although he would disagree. In spite of his inability to regulate certain areas of his own personal life, Ted demonstrated impressive insight in observing the problems of his students and others as well.

Excerpt from the Choice Dominant Voicings study:

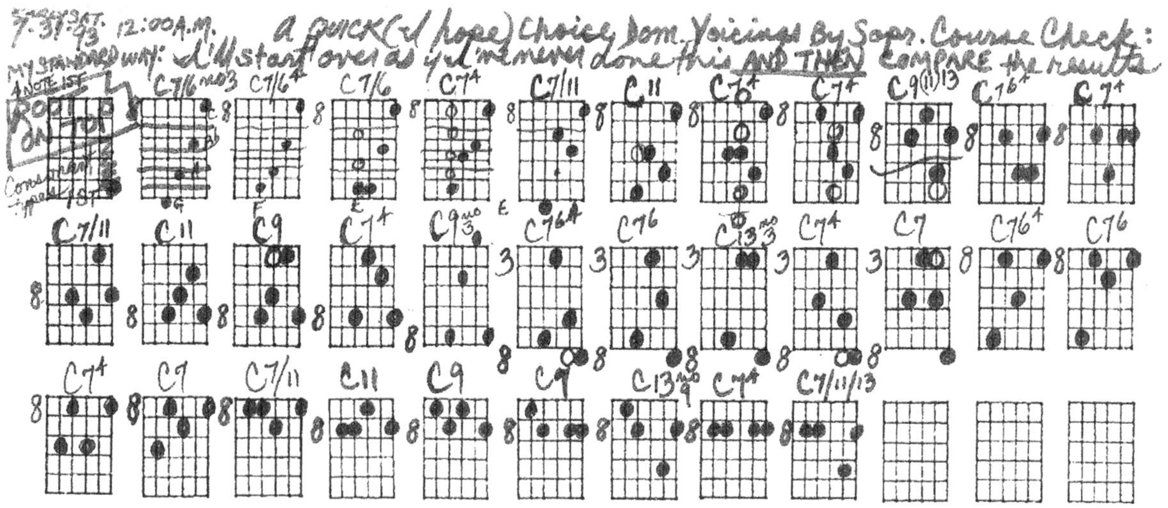

At that time, I was working in the music department at Warner Brothers studios transcribing music for movies and television shows; the schedule could be grueling. Since I'd been working non-stop long days, Ted began picking me up and bringing me back to his apartment because he didn't want to worry about me driving. By then the owner of the apartment building had given Ted a deadline to be out of his old unit. With only three weeks left to complete the move, it was evident how hard he had also been working the past week; as there were piles of books, record albums and video boxes everywhere, creating the massive clutter he sought to avoid. We sat in the back bedroom as he sorted through literally thousands of record albums while deciding where to put them. What took up most of his time was this decision making, this meticulous process of finding the proper places for everything. It mattered little to Ted that it was his 47th birthday, but I did have a very special gift for him, now that I knew how much Ted revered Max Steiner. It just so happened that Max Steiner had given my father a few of his original music manuscripts from the movies they had worked on together. These manuscripts my father had passed on to me. Now I wanted Ted to have one. As he noted, "*Sept. 26 Pick up Barb*

& bring her back here. She fetching in summer dress is loving & supportive. She gives me a) her first ever hand-made card! Beautiful, beautiful....and b) the original hand-written (pencil) Max Steiner autograph "Theme From a Summer Place"!!!! She joins me in the back room as I work on the albums."

For the next month all our time together was dedicated to moving, sorting through all his stuff, and finding an appropriate place for everything in the new apartment. One afternoon we both got distracted by a box of old National Geographics from the 1940's and 1950's and spent the entire afternoon amused by all the old advertisements rather than the articles. This was something that occurred with regularity for Ted and why moving always took much longer than necessary. Even though I felt we had made little progress, he always was appreciative of my help. He said the support and encouragement alone meant a lot. By November the move was just about complete, there wasn't much left in apartment 9.

The next massive task was putting things in order. During the process of accomplishing this Ted reveled in introducing me to old TV shows and movies I'd never seen, which we could enjoy together while he continued to sort through and rearrange all his things. Ted wrote, "*Barbara visits - long & increasingly pleasurable as we watch The Rifleman, The Lone Ranger (love that library music) & Popeye - we turn to the early ones & love."*

● X ☐ △ ★

Late autumn! Warm windy days and cold nights. Thanksgiving we went to my parent's house. The evening was enjoyable, congenial, and interesting. I listened as Ted and my father became engrossed in conversation about the entertainment industry and all the changes that had taken place over the course of my father's career. The food was great and my appetite ravenous. Ted said he had never seen me eat so much, and was quite amused. This particular year Thanksgiving fell on my mother's birthday, and Ted, always thoughtful gave her a movie he knew she wanted, "Written on the Wind," she was ecstatic.

As our first year together drew to a close, I realized how much closer we had become through the many things we were able to share and from Ted trusting me more and more. About a particularly enjoyable December evening, Ted wrote, "*Barb visits. I really clear out lots of space for us & begin reorganizing my videocassettes. We watch & enjoy "Crossing Delancy" & "Rocky & Bullwinkle" - we just think these cartoons are the greatest. We go on a nice walk (it's cold) to the 7-11. We dress her in one of my thick flannel shirts & coat."* During our walk Ted told me that never in his wildest dreams did he think he would care about me this much. He asked me if I knew that Saturday was a sort of anniversary? Yes, the Roosevelt Hotel, he was actually surprised I remembered.

Next weekend being Christmas, I expressed to him how glad I was that he was willing to share that time with me. He mentioned how he was just getting used to sharing enjoyments again after a long period of solo indulgence and had forgotten how wonderful it was to do this. One reason he had stopped is because he found it difficult to be close to someone as the fear of loss still loomed over him. The closer he got to someone the more he feared losing them. These fears recurred periodically, more so it seemed in December.

Christmas Eve and Christmas Day were spent with my family. We were both astonished when my parents generously gave us each $100 gift certificates from Tower Records. Contrary to the previous night, Ted did not bring work along with him on Christmas Day; (no bags at all). He came unshielded and was comfortable, seemed completely at ease with himself and with everyone. Often the work Ted brought along with him acted as sort of a buffer between himself and the surroundings. The work helped him maintain a comfortable distance and quell anxiety especially if a visit became intense.

On New Years Eve we went to Tower Records to spend the gift certificates from my parents. We made ourselves at home in the Classical section and since there were no employees around we began assisting the customers. Finally near closing time an employee came in and was absolutely astounded when he found us behind the counter! We were just changing the CD, but we were booted out of there so fast despite our explanation. We laughed all the way home.

Of all the discoveries we had made about each other thus far, the one that amazed and bewildered Ted the most about me was that I had rarely watched movies or television. Since movies in particular had always been an important source of pleasure and education for Ted, he was thrilled by my willingness to experience any movie he chose, and especially to share in my reaction.

Ted had amassed thousands of videos since the mid 1980's (when he got his first VCR) and began to tape not just movies, but absolutely everything he found interesting, which was, not surprisingly, almost everything. By this time, Ted had at least three or four VCR's simultaneously taping various shows almost twenty-four hours a day. It was wonderful to share the experience of these special movies together, and each time seemed to draw us even closer together. And, as the new year dawned, Ted referred to me as his "girlfriend" for the first time!

● X □ △ ★

On Monday, January 17th, 1994 the Los Angeles area experienced a very powerful magnitude 6.8 earthquake. We were both situated within 10 miles of the epicenter and it was terrifying. Ted was the first person I thought of when I felt the impact (thinking about all the stuff in his apartment) what a relief to hear his voice, just knowing he was okay, and vise versa. That day while straightening up my home, I damaged several of my fingers, one of which took a long time to heal. Little did I then realize, but this trauma triggered in me the onset of what we would later learn to be diagnosed as CREST Syndrome.

A few days later Ted and I went for a walk around my neighborhood, we were amazed by the devastation. Numerous houses and apartment buildings bore gaping holes and massive cracks, some were partially collapsed and many were condemned. Upon returning home, the stress of the past week finally took hold of me and all my emotions came pouring out. Ted held me in his arms for a long time, his soothing voice, optimistic attitude, and inimitable humor, worked magic for me.

Initially due to the move into apartment 8, and now compounded by the earthquake, Ted's apartment was quite a mess. He knew he must begin the dreaded chore of reorganizing all his belongings. Because of his determination to deal with the matter, we spent most of our time together at his apartment. This enabled Ted to continue to sort through and rearrange his various collections and we were still able to share many activities whilst he did such. As Ted put it, *"I continue to work on the back room. We sit in there & listen to records & love Bach Partita (Bb) allemande by Jean Louis Steurman (what a poetic player!), also Jaques Loussier Trio Book, and Lives of the Great Composers - Schoenberg"*

Spending our time together during Ted's reorganization process also afforded us many hours of conversation, and making new discoveries about each other. The more I discovered about him, the more I realized how incredibly unique he truly was. One time he stated that I should not take it personally, but he could go for weeks without wanting to see anyone. I challenged him to see how long he could go without seeing me before he missed me. He wouldn't do it and said he already knew. He even ventured that I would want, and continue wanting more time together. I said yes but it was deeper than that. He said I wanted him to want it. Yes. But I thought about what he had mentioned before; that he was "*wired differently*" and most notably, had the capacity for self-containment that far surpassed the norm. I wondered if Ted would ever be capable of having those deeper feelings.

Sometime in March we began incorporating errands into our visits. On one of the first occasions, he asked if I wanted to accompany him to a bookstore to pick up a book he had ordered. This was still so early in our relationship, I had no clue that buying just one book was impossible for him. Well, we spent the entire evening going from bookstore to bookstore, accumulated a considerable haul of books and ended our excursion at Barnes & Noble, where we stayed for hours. We had lots of laughs; it was pure fun sitting on the floor amid piles of music books reading to each other. Then before we could leave, he decided he needed to organize the books in the music section in alphabetical order, by composer. Of course, to expedite the matter I assisted him with this mission. Afterwards, back in the apartment, he said he felt we made a good couple, and he now knew that we were destined to be together for many reasons.

He told me I was responsible for instigating and proliferating this relationship, that had I not initiated it, it would never have been, and that he'd changed as a result of this, of me. Before, he never would have believed it was possible for him to feel this way, and now he believed it was possible we even had a future. I knew his comments were partly based on my ability to spend countless hours sharing and enjoying the same activities, and that he knew it wasn't a matter of my simply being willing to accommodate his idiosyncrasies. Besides I was genuinely fascinated by the way he did things and my love for him was all encompassing.

Despite the closeness that had developed, many difficulties remained. For example, one evening Ted was a bit tired and fraught with indecision on how to spend our time; I could sense him becoming irritable, really wanting to be alone. Earlier, we had decided to watch a movie, but that entailed hooking up his new VCR, which proved to almost push him to his limit. This was a difficult task because it required incorporating the new VCR into "the chain" of several VCR's already hooked up together. I sat there in silence, knowing it was best just to read and leave him be. By the time he got it working, he did not feel in the mood for a movie, instead he played around with the VCR. Inevitably, we got into a painful discussion regarding our relationship and the discrepancies in our wants and needs. Periodically Ted would experience anxiety about our closeness and would pull away. Also when stress and pressure built up in his life, mostly due to his living situation (not enough space, noisy neighbors), he would reach some limit of exasperation and transferred it to me or "us," blaming the relationship for making demands on his time. By some means, each time this happened we managed to get past it, talked it through and grew from it as a result.

In spite of these problems our relationship did grow, albeit very, very slowly. Now at least the weekly visits weren't questioned, lasted about 8 hours and just fell into a routine, beginning with errands and then spending the remainder of the time at Ted's apartment. Our being "out and about" always included stops at either a bookstore, a magazine stand, a record store, or with growing frequency, all three. Ted's purchases were rarely modest. At least once a month we'd also visit Max at Valley Baseball Cards or Norman, Danny and "the guys" at Norm's Rare Guitars. But, once back at his apartment each visit also involved something new for me, and ran the gamut from Ted writing me special guitar treats, to introducing me to different types of music, composers, movies, TV shows, and eventually his favorite sports. Everything Ted chose was absolutely delightful for me which in turn increased his own enjoyment considerably.

Unfortunately moving into his new apartment didn't solve Ted's problems. He continued to be troubled by the lack of space and the noisy neighbors plagued him constantly. As a result, he needed to completely rearrange the apartment again! He decided to use the books to reinforce the walls as a form of soundproofing. The extraneous noises determined where the book-based sound shield was needed. He would choose the quietest room and use it for teaching and most of his other needs, and that was the room in which he would utilize his makeshift soundproofing. This time he decided to use the living room for storage and utilize the bedrooms for personal use and teaching. I hoped this was a final solution. Alas, there was never to be one.

During this next stage of reorganization, as usual, there was a lot of time for conversation. One time I asked Ted to explain to me how he defined love. I remember his answer very clearly, Ted told me one way to measure love is how you feel when you are with that person, another is how you feel when you are apart, how much you think about that person, long for that person, and above all how you would live if something happened to that person. We agreed that neither of us could bear the loss of the other. Then I asked him that if something happened to one of us, if he truly believed that we would find each other again, somewhere, and he said yes.

Oh, the irony when I think of this now, and how I still want so much to believe it.

On April 13th, 1994, Ted was interviewed on KPFK Radio, on Bill Davila's show at Noon. When I asked Ted how it went, he said he thought it was fine but he had taped it so we could both listen together. We were most amused by how Ted was able to subtly manipulate the conversation to where Ted actually became the interviewer. Later when he brought me home he showed me again, and in more detail, how to use my amplifier, a small Fender Sidekick Switcher. This was when I realized Ted's extraordinary ability to determine the optimal settings for any particular sound he desired. Ted's knowledge of amplifiers was equally as impressive as his knowledge of guitars. His insight was gained through thousands of hours of experimentation.

In mid May, on Mother's Day, after brunch with my family, Ted took me to one of his favorite music store haunts called Musician's Supply. Ted wrote, "*pick up new Bach lute suite music folio & Counterpoint in the Style of J.S. Bach by Thomas Benjamin & old book Bach's Orchestra by Charles Stanford Terry. Then sitting in car in front of her place on a beautiful day, explain my 'magic formula' for Baroque cycle of 4th's: Hold the R & 3, lower the other two tones one diatonic scale step. She loves its ease.*" I was so impressed that Ted had figured this out. Now as I pondered this "magic formula," I began to slowly understand the workings of his incredibly gifted musical mind.

Ted's "Magic Formula" for Baroque Cycle of 4ths

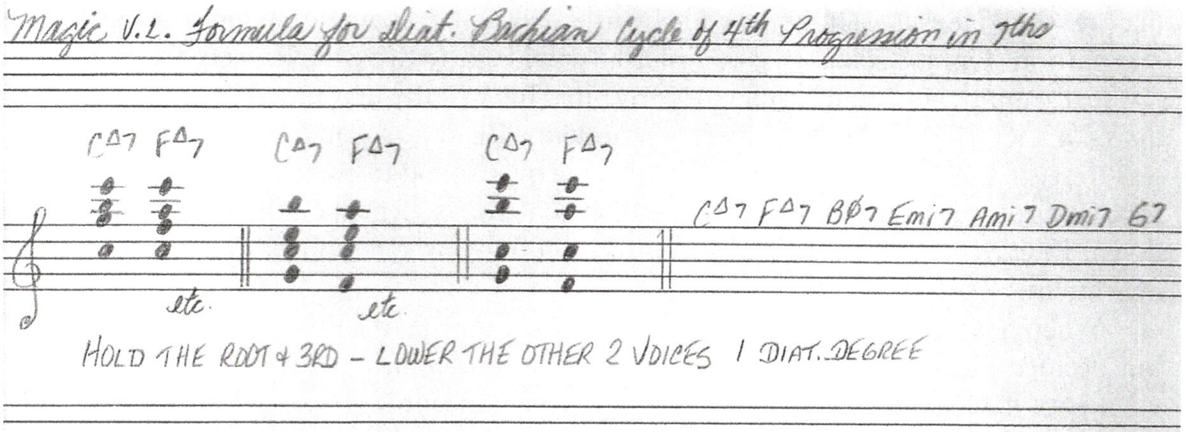

The following weekend I experienced Ted's hypersensitivity to noise. We were in his living room and he was still cleaning out and trying to organize the post-earthquake mess. He became quite agitated by all the surrounding noise, especially the neighbors above him pounding his ceiling with their heavy footsteps. When he could no longer tolerate this, he suggested we go for a walk. As we started up the street he immediately felt better, we walked to White Oak Avenue, sat on the bus bench, went to the 7-11 store then back to his apartment. Calmed by the walk, he resumed shuffling books and magazines from one room to another.

Regarding this reorganization project, I had to be very careful about commenting on what he was doing. There could be not even a hint of futility in my voice. I found this out the hard way, but now to myself I thought, he doesn't have enough space in his apartment to accommodate all his things, and on top of that, he adds a considerable amount of new stuff every week.

As I began to visit more often I also became aware of what he regarded to be his safe boundaries. I learned to avoid issues that produced anxiety or could be perceived as threatening. I wanted him to feel at ease. I remember when I got on the bed for the very first time he fearfully exclaimed, "what are you doing?" and I said simply, "this is the most comfortable place to sit in whole the apartment." Then he was okay about it since he couldn't argue with the logic.

I still had no preference as to where we were or what we did, just that we were with each other. After almost two years, he was still awed by this, and his awe was also laced with a degree of disbelief. He said it was hard for him to get used to because it was new to him, no one else had ever accepted him as he was. He asked me to keep reminding him that I could be happy and content with just being together.

One warm late spring day when Ted pulled up in my driveway, Betsy the Plymouth was visibly overheated; she was steaming and water spurted from a broken radiator hose. Despite the problem, Ted was in good spirits. Deciding to repair it later, we took my Ford Bronco to visit some friends of his that he thought I'd like because they were avid readers like we were. He was right and we all spent a pleasant evening discussing various books and authors. Upon leaving, I asked Ted if he would like to drive the Bronco home. He was not just willing, but totally excited to drive it. This was the first time in ten years he had driven a stick shift and he was thrilled. Actually, I had a reason for letting him drive. It was to see if I felt comfortable with him driving my car and to eventually suggest we use it for our weekends instead of his Plymouth, which always seemed on the verge of breaking down. Besides, Betsy's interior was so utterly cluttered, she resembled the inside of Ted's apartment.

When next we spoke, he said he thought of asking me to help him with the car repair but decided against it, not wanting to cause me discomfort. I expressed to him that I would not have offered my help if I hadn't sincerely meant it. He wasn't sure I was being honest, asked if I would help him understand so he knew that he could always trust what I said. Of course, I would. I thought about how best to define a meaningful reciprocal relationship.

The opportunity to explain presented itself shortly thereafter. The evening went as follows, from Ted's datebook, *"Another beautiful night with Barbara: write her a solo arr. of one of her (& my) favorite songs, "You'll Never Walk Alone" in key of E. Then we go to Ralph's market and she beat me this time, to let her pay for my groceries. I acquiesce. Then back to my place: I file the nut on her Shenendoah, we watch & love the rest of the Rock 'n Roll Special & a great car show I taped for her, Superchargers: very expensive & very fast sports cars."* I thanked him for doing all of these wonderful things for me, he said it was "nothing" and thanked me again for the groceries. I said that's what a good relationship means, being able to and wanting to do things for each other. Then he understood and agreed even though he said it was still hard for him most of the time.

● X □ △ ★

When we were out doing errands, we would usually get food, either at the market or a fast food restaurant. One of my favorite places was Panda Express for the chow mein. One day Ted ventured a tiny taste of mine and loved it. This was a wonderful discovery because it added one more item to the very limited list of food he could eat. Besides his inherent food peculiarities, Ted was a vegetarian. This choice was not for health reasons, but because he objected to the cruelty animals were subjected to during their life and when being slaughtered.

Prior to this time, Ted and I had never eaten a meal together! During family gatherings or other social occasions, Ted never partook of the food. When out on errands which included purchasing food, he would always save his for later. To keep his hunger at bay, he sometimes munched on a carrot or some corn chips. On the other hand, I always ate whether it was take-out or a simple meal Ted prepared for me. However, this time after doing errands, and stopping at Panda Express for chow mein, when we got back to his apartment he was decidedly hungry. We brought the food into the bedroom; I sat on the bed and he a chair. Since this was the first time we were going to eat together, he explained that he was not a "social" eater (which I knew) and suggested I find something to read while I ate, as that was what he was going to do. So as we settled in with our food and books he actually said, *"bye, see you in five minutes"* and we both proceeded to eat and read. We were basically eating simultaneously; not sharing a meal, there was no sharing of the experience. But I was delighted that he finally felt comfortable eating in my presence. To me it meant he knew I totally accepted him.

There were reasons for his food peculiarities, one being his sensitivity to smell. There were many, many smells he simply couldn't abide, mustard or vinegar and numerous others. Once I let him smell the sweet & sour sauce that came with my egg rolls and he was totally repulsed, he wrinkled his nose and backed away, mimicking the reaction of a cat.

● X □ △ ★

All the while, Ted was still teaching me guitar. One day I suggested I'd like to try some blues. My main objective was improvisation and I especially wanted something for us to be able to jam together on. I sat on the bed and read as he wrote out exercises to practice and when he finished we went through them. There were many difficulties to overcome but his patience and understanding pulled me through and gave me encouragement. We went over and over the exercises until I got it, until he was comfortable that I understood and could continue on my own. As all his students knew, he was wonderful in this area. This experience reinforced my thoughts about the fine method of teaching and communicating he had developed. Absolute excellence.

But conversely, out in the world his perceptions, although well intentioned, were not always as keen. The following day, while out on errands and walking back to his car we noticed a man changing a flat tire. Ted stopped to ask if he needed any help. The man replied no and thanked him for asking, but Ted went on to question him about his car, what year, type of engine, question after question. I was a bit taken aback; this man was obviously hot and bothered by the inconvenience and certainly not easily able to converse. Fortunately, he was extremely tolerant of us. I realized that Ted was unable to perceive that this man was in no mood for conversation, and that questioning him was inappropriate at that moment.

In early September of 1994, I met Leon and Judy White for the first time. Our last errand completed we had planned to return to Ted's apartment and watch a movie. Instead, on a whim Ted suggested (intuition he said) that we pay them an impromptu visit. Ted had known them in excess of twenty years. Leon co-produced Ted's 'Solo Guitar' album, and is also an accomplished musician and author. We lucked out as the entire White family, Leon, Judy and their two children Megan and Christopher were home. They were surprised and overjoyed to see Ted and made me feel equally as welcome. Their home was comfortable and they were very gracious and accommodating. What was most evident to me during our visit was how deeply the entire family cared for Ted. We all shared a most enjoyable two hours together. When we were leaving I thanked them for having us in since we had just dropped by unannounced. They gratefully extended the invitation any time. Their friendship became and remains an invaluable treasure for me.

Towards the end of September, we were obligated to attend the semi-formal wedding of Ted's cousin at the Wilshire Ebell Temple of Los Angeles. With supermarket bags in hand, we arrived to a huge crowd. Ted certainly did not enjoy attending weddings, but did his best to appear cheerful. Soon his father found us and was so glad, even relieved to see us. Neither Ted nor his father had any inclination to mingle with the crowd. Prior to the commencement of the ceremony, we three sat on the periphery of the festivities and greeted other family members and guests who came over to say hello. The ceremony seemed to last a long time, Ted and I glanced at each other and rolled our eyes.

During dinner, with the music unbearably loud, Ted visibly uncomfortable, was writing out music studies. Shortly after dinner, we found an acceptable moment to make our exit. We were tired and he was irritable. His mood had grown worse over the course of the evening, as had mine. On the bright side, he was pleased to be able to bring happiness to many people simply by attending, but it was emotionally draining. Driving home his anxiety grew stronger, I could not communicate with him, he just wanted to go home. I was so frustrated; we were both angry and upset when we parted.

He called the next morning. We both were sad, had a difficult time sleeping and knew we needed to make amends. I expressed how unfulfilling the day had been because I felt we did not take advantage of the benefit of our being together. I felt disappointed that we were not able to draw comfort from each other. We both needed soothing, but he was unable to respond to that need last night.

In hindsight, he realized how simple it would have been to assuage my sadness. I suggested that since he had some unpleasant obligations again next weekend, that we share them all. Bearing the burden of the less desirable commitments together would make it easier, and also heighten the more enjoyable ones. This he was willing to try.

At that time, every Friday night there was a car show at a 1950's style diner called Cruiser's. Electric bass player, Danny Duehren, Ted's friend and fellow car fanatic suggested that Ted meet him there. Ted thought we would both enjoy going. We did. It was as if we had walked right into the pages of his car magazines, for displayed all around us were perfectly restored Corvettes (various years from 56 up) Fords, Chevys, even a Cobra. We found Danny, and the three of us walked around and marveled at everything we were taking in. Afterwards, since we just happened to be parked in a Barnes & Noble parking lot, we spent the rest of the evening in the bookstore until closing time.

On Saturday evening we attended a birthday party for Ted's friend Jackie Traynor, an avid animal lover, who Ted had wanted me to meet. Unfortunately Jackie was late in arriving as she hadn't felt very well, so I didn't get a chance to get to know her at that time, but eventually she would become and remain a warm and loving friend. Ted and I both found the rather large party somewhat uncomfortable, but luckily we were able to redeem part of the evening upon our discovery of a pool table! The night gave rise to the question: Why do people have parties?

Sunday, Ted had an appointment to get his taxes done, which wasn't so terrible for us after all. On the way back, a quick stop at Johnny Rocket's for fries then to Ted's apartment to just relax. Later when I was ready to leave, Ted walked me out to my car. He expressed how wonderful our three days together were for him, how each experience was better by sharing it. He was glad and grateful for his willingness to take my suggestion. This was the first time we had spent three days in succession together and I was so relieved he felt no stress as a result. From that experience we slowly segued into spending both Saturday and Sunday together.

Finally a weekend with no obligations, Ted wrote, *"Barb visits. We luxuriate in just staying home and mainly cuddle, talk & then I work on clearing the space in front of the record (45s) cupboard - a big job. We listen to an old R & B tape & enjoy the 'variation city' guitar player on "Soul Twist." Also Barb learns how to find the melody of a song we both love, "Moon River" after hearing Jerry Butler's version & I coach her on the blues and cook her dinner - potato puffs & her beloved little buttered peas. She & I have, as always our great time. We watch the beginning of the PBS Baseball Series. Lovely day & night."*

Yet, despite what he wrote, and even after all this time, he still was having a hard time believing I was happy and content just being there while he worked. He mentioned it again, and again I did my best to impress upon him that just being there with him was entirely gratifying.

● X □ △ ★

Soon I discovered something else very special about Ted: the extent of his humanitarian nature. While out doing errands, we noticed a girl trying to push a large full-size car. We drove on for a few blocks but his intuition told him to go back and see if she needed help. Ted was right, when we drove back we discovered a young couple in trouble, the boy was in a wheelchair, they were lost and out of gas. Somehow, we made room in our car, Betsy, for them and the wheelchair and then took them to a gas station for a can of gas. I offered to let the boy use my cell phone to call his grandmother whose house they were looking for. He was incredulous and exclaimed, "You have a cell phone!" He arranged for his grandmother to meet them at the gas station in fifteen minutes. We took them back to their car, waited until they got it started and followed them to the gas station to make sure they made it there. Afterwards it dawned on me why they were so surprised that we had a cell phone, I surmised it was because they thought we were a homeless couple living in our car. And that is exactly how we appeared; driving around in an old dented-up Plymouth four-door, the interior and the trunk completely filled to the brim with everything you could imagine, besides the fact that we were both dressed in somewhat of a ragged manner. When I mentioned this to Ted, he also thought this to be the case, and we had a great laugh.

Ted's compassion for humanity was boundless. Many times when we were out and about, we would encounter homeless people pleading for assistance and Ted was ever sensitive to their plight. He never passed by someone in need. He always stopped not just to help them a bit financially, but also to chat, to inquire as to how their lives had taken such a difficult turn, and offer encouragement. They always appreciated his caring.

Later, back at the apartment, Ted chose a special treat for me, *"I decide to show Barb the sound (delicious) of the GVE simulated 7-string by tuning E down to A and A down to E - I use my '60 Jazzmaster 'Big Red' We love it. 'Ol Man River by her request. Then back to normal tuning (actually 1/2 step down) and Barb's fav. or 2nd fav. "cathedral guitar" Baroque Improv. and beautiful songs: A Taste of Honey, Tomorrow, (I get a few tears from it's beauty) Georgie Girl. Then all the strings down to B and both our favorite: blue harmony and some blue tunes, Blues in the Night, Willow Weep for Me, Summertine, It Ain't Necessarily So. First was Oh, What a Beautiful Morning, I've Told Every Little Star (Barb remembers it!)"*

The following day at the apartment, Ted wanted to continue sorting through videos so I decided to do something I had been wanting to for a few weeks: clear the bags out of the kitchen. I promised Ted that I would not throw anything away, so with his ever-growing trust in me, he allowed me to do this. In the kitchen, there was a pile of crumpled up supermarket bags, paper and plastic, about four feet high and three feet wide, the floor was barely visible, and there was little room to move about. I began by opening one paper bag, folding the others and neatly placing them inside the open one. The whole pile took me about four hours to complete. When I had almost finished Ted joined me, and together we got rid of six bags of unsalvageable bags and miscellaneous trash. The kitchen now had ample room in which to move about, the floor was now totally visible and this also provided access to the cupboard under the sink.

Afterwards, Ted was ecstatic and stated how he felt so connected to me. He explained that sometimes it didn't matter what we were doing, even cuddling, his mind was elsewhere; he did not feel a connection. I asked if this was a conscious choice or if he couldn't help it - he said both. But that night he felt our minds were totally connected, that we established a bond. Somehow, I had entered "his world." This was an important lesson for me. At times I had lost sight of how to understand him and also to help him understand me. For a while, I had been gently urging him, coaxing him to enter "my world" and had been met with perplexity and resistance. I had remained firmly on my ground and he on his, hindering the ability to communicate, which of course led to frustration. I knew I had to find a way to reconnect. How? By participating with him in "his world." In folding the bags, we worked together towards a common goal. Then I knew I must remain there with him, maintain the bond and through that, we could together venture forward. It was a new insightful beginning.

● X □ △ ★

Thanksgiving, and a celebration for my mother's 75th birthday, she was happy to have all the loving energy. Then back to Ted's place to be alone and relax, as Ted described, *"Barb reads & I work on the back room (magazines). At her request we plug in my '52 Gold Top and I finally correct her wiring which had become more & more apparently in need of hum reduction & change the R pickup tone circuit to the 'bleed' type."*

For the past month or so, Ted had been trying to help me determine what my ideal guitar would be. He kept giving me various guitars to try out, but they all had special qualities and I had been unable to make a decision. I did mention I might prefer a smaller guitar, lighter in weight, and maybe a sunburst.

How uncanny was the circumstance that almost two years ago to the day we came to be in Hollywood again together, neither of us had been there since the magical evening at the Roosevelt Hotel. It was a rather impromptu decision, Ted made a call to Guitars R Us and wouldn't you know the exact guitar Ted was looking for, the one he believed I would find "perfect" was hanging on the wall in that store.

So, off we went to Hollywood where Ted purchased for me what seemed like the cutest, lightest, most beautiful little guitar in the whole world, a sunburst Guild M65 3/4. First he spent close to an hour checking everything about her, then playing her, then letting me play her, Ted was right, she was perfect for me. Afterwards we looked at many other guitars there and in other stores as well. That small area of Hollywood, the corner of Sunset Blvd and Vista had eight guitar stores. It had come to be known as guitar row.

Ted took my new guitar home, set her up and brought her to me the following day. He lovingly noted,*"Bring the new baby to her all set up, shined up & sounding great. She is so happy."* I named my new baby, Daisy. We both took turns playing her, first acoustically then through the amp, she sounded so wonderfully rich.

● X □ △ ★

Twelve Hours. Ten of which were taken up by Ted finishing "fixing up" the second bedroom, what Ted referred to as "the little room." He did not anticipate it would take that long. He asked me not to look in there as it was not quite done and he wanted it to be a surprise. He had fixed up the bedroom for me so I could lie on the bed, read, play guitar, and wait for what he estimated would be two hours. He came in periodically for hugs and kisses then went back to work. He did succeed in his goal and around 2 a.m. brought me in to share in his delight and accomplishment. The room now had ample space for us and the various items he chose to keep in it were pleasingly arranged. He had them stacked in a variety of proportions and it gave me the illusion of being at the edge of a city. He expressed how much he appreciated my enabling him to complete this large project, if with nothing else but my patience and encouragement. He stated he felt we connected spiritually. When he took me back home we sat in the car a moment. After saying good-bye he took my hand, kissed it, then caressed it in silence as he looked downward. I gazed at him and finally asked what he was thinking about; he just said "A lot of things."

The following weekend one of our errands included stopping at Norm's Rare Guitars to pick up a tape of a song Ted needed to learn for the next night. Norm had asked Ted if he would play at his and Marlene's 25th anniversary party. Of course Ted would never have declined this honor from such a good friend. We sat in the living room and I listened and watched as Ted figured out the song in less than an hour, conversing with me at the same time and giggling over many things including Ted telling me he was a licensed hypnotherapist. In Ted's datebook was this, "*Work on '100 Ways' (James Ingram) for tomorrow. And wonderful laughing time for a few hours w/Barb as I plug in Stella (& gradually tune her up higher & higher) and Lola down to Eb. I explain to Barb how I have to hunt for REALLY good ideas & not settle for just anything ok - demonstrate on classical and jazzed up Xmas tunes - she hears it too when it happens now & then.*"

About the night of the party, in Ted's words, *"Norm & Marlene's 25th anniversary party. Pick up Barb at 5:00. An all time supportive vibe night. My dear '52 Tele 'Lola' tuned 1/2 step down & my black face Vibrolux Reverb. Some of the great support: Barbara, Scott Borden (I'd like you to meet the greatest guitarist in the world), Rob Bolger, Danny Duehren, his sister Marianne (she loved the music), Robert Stamps (gave me the "trigger"), his employee Jim (you tore the place up, it was great to hear real music), various musicians who have Chord Chem., Barry Z. and esp. Norm & Marlene both stopped & told me they loved it after their favorite singer Donnie & I did '100 Ways' (in C - B concert) as I was leaving the stage. And the sound the crowd made when he said my name after we did the song, I'll cherish the love sent toward me. It's such a joy to be able to make others happy."*

Soon after that on a rainy Christmas Eve, we spent the evening with my family, and this time my close friend Lori joined us. Ted brought along my white Washburn, (an acoustic/electric single cutaway), whom he named 'Mr. Albinowitz' and serenaded us the entire evening, first with Christmas songs, then medleys from South Pacific and Westside Story. Heavenly!

The rain ceased sometime during the night although the sky remained partly cloudy. By the time we left for my parent's house, it had cleared into a cool windy Christmas afternoon. We had a fine time with my parents; they had come to really love Ted, and now embraced him as a part of our family. By early evening they were exhausted, we said good-bye and returned to my house. Ted had brought with him "Dust Be My Destiny" so we decided to try it. Cuddled together on the couch we shared this delightful and sometimes poignant movie, many moments of which were keenly heightened by Max Steiner's underscore.

We remained on the couch afterwards and talked about a lot of things, one being past relationships, why none were ever "right" and how he knew. He said *"there is only one woman that has ever been right and she's sitting here with me now."* I'm sure I blushed.

Chapter III

Love and Growth

(1995-1998)

The now established weekend routine continued throughout 1995 and would in fact remain the same for several more years. We had also incorporated both days into our agenda much of the time. You could say that was the basic underlying theme to which we would continue to add countless small variations.

At the beginning of 1995, on a rainy January day, Ted noted, "*Pick up Barb go to my place, I begin organizing my CDs, we listen to Brenda Lee, The Skyliner's (Barb really likes & I cry as usual when hearing "This I Swear"), it is so beautiful, so romantic. Then the 4 Seasons (we love the songs, the arrangements and the back up vocals), then we try BLUES: Freddy King, great instrumentals CD (Barb love's it so much, as do I of course). B.B. "Sweet Little Angel" solo, Eric Clapton w/John Mayall, another Wowza, Albert King too.*"

This was some of the music Ted loved and he wanted to expose me to something different, pointing out nuances, harmonic structure, and rhythmic variations, as he knew I was basically unfamiliar with these genres. Ted loved to introduce me to new music that he was quite certain I would love and/or appreciate, so there was almost a constant flow of new experiences we would share. Besides music, Ted's general knowledge was diverse and encompassed many areas. If you asked him a question that he was sure you could solve or learn to solve on your own, he would not give you the easy way out and simply answer the question. I had asked Ted a question regarding "percents," as I needed to calculate something. This turned into a two-hour math lesson. I was quite annoyed but decided I'd better pay attention, or this could go on indefinitely. However, as a "reward" for my sticking with it, (and to this day I can figure out percents, although I rarely use this knowledge), he wrote me out a new Chord Formulas page especially designed for me.

We were now entering into a comfortable place in our relationship. Ted had his own unique and endearing way of encapsulating our days in his datebook, "*a wonderful time for us. We go in her beloved 'Ladybug' (red Porsche) to get me fishing line for my ES345 rewire, then to Fashion Square Mall to Radio Shack for soldering stuff, Walden Books, See's Candy, and Gelson's market. To my place, we watch and truly love and are moved by "Letting Go." Lots of warm cuddling & talk (e.g. what many people we know would think of the movie) for an hour or so. So much love between us, we are so lucky - we share so much.*"

Unfortunately, our bliss was soon to be disrupted considerably by unforeseen, unfortunate troubles. As I recall, Ted had caught a slight cold around the holidays, and consequently I too, ended up with a cold. We thought nothing of it at the time, but two months later I still had a horrible deep cough. I tried to hide it from him as best I could. I didn't want Ted to know how bad the cough really was.

The next weekend he seemed a bit distant, maybe a little troubled but I didn't make mention of anything. We went to Tower Records where he bought me Vivaldi and Chopin CDs, then to get some dinner and after that to his apartment. Once there, he mentioned how much pressure he had been feeling lately. While I sat and played the guitar, he deliberated about the file cabinets and he decided to go get two more. We went to an office supply warehouse and as soon as we got back he began to manically shuffle his files. That's when I knew something was seriously bothering him. I had a suspicion he felt pressure from me, but he finally said he was very worried about my cough, that it was very distressing for him. I had already gone to see the doctor and he found nothing wrong, but he didn't have a cure and told me sometimes a cough will linger for quite a while. The doctor had checked for everything, did a chest X-ray and ruled out all the serious, life-threatening possibilities and thought it was a slow lingering virus. Ted was aware of all this, but it still did not assuage his anxieties or fears.

I was to be plagued with this cough for the next three years, as was Ted by association. Months later we would embark upon a search for a diagnosis and a cure. During the interim, I began to manifest other symptoms such as muscle weakness, but this did not appear to be related.

This was actually harder on Ted than it was on me. Ted was really frightened that I was going to die, and I could not convince him otherwise. Yet I must concede, the cough was awful but I found that Dayquil helped somewhat. A diagnosis was eventually to be found along with a way to suppress the coughing, but no cure. Meanwhile, although the coughing had to be contended with, fortunately there were almost always some wondrous distractions to buffer our fears.

● X □ △ ★

Around this time Ted seriously began to amass his fabulous array of Guild guitars. Early March '95 found him guitar and amp shopping and on the 8th, he found one guitar he had to have but first needed to negotiate a price. The following day the music store called and accepted his offer. Since he was teaching, I volunteered to pick it up for him so he could have it right away. I drove over to the apartment, Ted gave me the cash and I returned with the beautiful Guild 1961 SB X500 we were later to name Gigi. Needless to say, Ted was absolutely jubilant.

Ted's guitar shopping generally took place around this time each year, for this is when he received a residual check for his books. Ted, by design, could not rest until he spent the entire amount. Besides guitars and amps, he went on book buying frenzies, CD and video buying frenzies and indulged in everything he loved until the money was gone. The amount of the check varied from year to year therefore dictating the extent of the purchasing frenzy. Yet, never thinking only of himself, Ted always gave some of the money to charity.

In fact all of Ted's passions were fashioned by design. His interests were not casual. When Ted loved something it was an ardent interest, and the desire to learn and collect everything connected to each passion was fed to the fullest degree. Two more of his passions were baseball and basketball, and it wasn't long before Ted fueled the same excitement in me, at least for basketball. Although I did enjoy baseball, I fell in love with basketball. Ted was overjoyed to find that we could share and even revel together watching his favorite sports. As Ted noted, *"this is when and how it began, Barb visits and we have a fantastic day together watching and loving UCLA basketball, then (she loved this) Michael Jordon and company 3peat championship. She's now loving basketball & Michael Jordon is a revelation to her."*

At this time a very important breakthrough in our relationship occurred. Ted, as everyone who knew him would attest to, was very difficult to get in touch with by phone. He refused to own an answering machine because the obligation of responding added too much pressure to his life. What made this especially difficult is that when Ted was not teaching, he usually unplugged his phone so as not to be interrupted or disturbed. I had been frustrated by not being able to reach him at times. This he knew, and finally conceded to letting me buy him a pager so we could always be in touch. He realized that if I really needed him, he wanted to be available for me. Because of this simple action, I would never doubt how much he loved me ever again.

Despite the underlying anxiety of my illness, and the overt anxiety when it flared up, our relationship continued to grow stronger. For some months now our time together had been wonderful. We were getting along so well, having lots of fun and felt so much in love. Ted commented on this one night as he was dropping me off at home. I told him I felt this too, and it even frightened me a little because it was so good I thought something was bound to go wrong. Ted replied that he knew exactly what I meant.

● X □ △ ★

One of Ted's main musical focal points had always been the study of harmony and counterpoint. Listening to Ted derive beautiful and intricate counterpoint lines, I now expressed a strong desire to learn this art. Ted began giving me lines to experiment with and we delighted in sharing the results together.

Still in guitar buying mode, one day Ted noticed an ad in the local paper for a blonde Ibanez archtop, at a very reasonable price. Ted couldn't resist so we drove over to the residence in Studio City to take a look and a listen. He loved it and also the Ampeg that it was plugged into. He bought both. Afterwards we went to Van Nuys Boulevard to take a walk and browse the pawnshop windows. We walked for several blocks charmed by the atmosphere of what felt like a Mexican bazaar complete with complimentary popcorn.

Looking in the window at Hart Jeweler's a glowing yellow topaz caught my eye and Ted insisted I must have it. I tried to explain that even though I admired its beauty I didn't need to own it, but to no avail. Ted was adamant about buying it for me, particularly since he'd been buying lots of things for himself. We entered the shop and it was priced reasonably, so he bought it. It was the most romantic gift he had given me. And best of all, it gave him much pleasure to be able to give me something I loved.

We got back to the apartment just in time to catch the Dodgers at Colorado, which Ted called "a slug fest." Then at my request, we watched the movie "Forest Gump." He was quite distressed by this movie and it was extremely difficult for him to watch as it depicted too many of the horrors of the times. I felt sad about exposing him to something that caused him pain. Afterwards he told me about the "negative" forces that permeated our society and how difficult it was for him to avoid being affected by them.

By late spring of '95, Ted's major purchasing frenzy had come to an end, since he had completely depleted his residual check. The focus shifted and pressure returned, he felt compelled to finish organizing his apartment and get back to music. All the things he needed to do came flooding through at once. As much as Ted wanted to use every second to be productive, we had planned to get together with my parents for Mother's Day. He knew I had to work that Sunday so we wouldn't be with my family until the late afternoon. Much to his delight, this afforded Ted most of the day to be productive. But when he called me at work, I still didn't know what time I would be finished and suggested paging him when I got home. I did and it worked - he called right back. This was the first time we used the pager and he realized how beneficial it was to be able to always reach each other.

After a pleasant visit with my parents, we went to Ted's to watch an Angel's game. During the game, he showed me some old lanyards he had made and began to try to figure out how he had done it; this compelled him to get into the bottom drawer of the dresser where the rest of the lanyards were kept. He went into to the living room and I followed. When he assessed the situation he said now I would get to see what a "typical" day was like for him. In order to get to the dresser he first had to clean out the corner closet. He explained how doing one thing dictated what else needed to be done "circumstantially" and how that *"led to a process."* The closet was filled with shopping bags, he decided to "take my word for it" and simply get rid of them all. I was silently very proud of the effort. He began tossing the bags into the room and I began condensing them into smaller packages to be removed. Due to our mutual effort this took only about half an hour, which surprised Ted since he thought it would take much longer. We took six bags full of bags out to the trash.

Back in the living room he went through what was left in the closet and found his first classical guitar, which he got out, put a string on and began to play. As he continued, he started improvising, then segued into an exquisite version of "Til There Was You." He picked up and played another classical guitar, very resonant with a deep bass, and finally the blonde Ibanez. After while, he put all the guitars with brown cases into the closet, then began clearing away the stuff in front of the dresser so we could get to the bottom drawer. By the time we did, he had temporarily lost interest in the lanyards after having discovered some old school yearbooks, which we looked through and laughed. When we finally got to the lanyards, two hours had passed. This gave me a first hand glimpse of how each project took on a life of its own due to the many irresistible distractions he encountered along the way.

●X□△★

During our time together, I had the opportunity to experience some very amusing incidents that displayed interesting aspects of Ted's perceptions. A month earlier Ted had purchased a pair of black cotton pants. They immediately became his favorite pants and he had been wearing them almost continuously since he bought them. He asked if I minded him wearing them all the time, I said I didn't, and then with much delight he expressed that the pants did not get dirty! He told me that when he was a kid and wore his favorite pants for weeks, his mom would tell him he had to wash them. He was sure his mother would be amazed that he had finally found a pair that stayed clean! I tried to convince him that the pants did in fact get dirty, but because they were black, the dirt didn't show. I explained that if he wore the exact same pair in white, he would be able to see the dirt, but Ted just said of course the white ones would get dirty! Ted absolutely could not understand my point.

Another time he showed me a small tool set in a plastic box and mentioned that it always had this strange odor. He handed the box to me to smell, it was repugnant, hard to describe, rotten? He, on the other hand found it not the slightest bit offensive, even sort of liked it. His olfactory sense was quite unusual. What was not unpleasant to him was generally unpleasant to most people.

It was the beginning of June, the early morning low clouds and fog moved inland from the ocean to the valley and stayed until late afternoon or sometimes all day. This local phenomenon known as June-gloom hinted my birthday was nearing; Ted wanted to buy me a special gift. I had told him I wanted a small gold heart-shaped locket to put his picture in and wear around my neck. He was very touched by my desire, and had an idea of where we might be able to acquire such a precious item. There was a cluster of antique shops he knew of in Canoga Park, so we headed in that direction. Soon we spied a small antique store and decided to have a look. Inside, nested among many treasures we found the most perfect little gold locket, which Ted graciously bought for me. Then much to our merriment, across the street we found a delicious looking used bookstore. This we couldn't pass up and browsed for about an hour. An old biography of George Sand piqued my curiosity and Ted found a few old music books and a glass ashtray. At last back at Ted's apartment, upon opening the door, we were stunned to see a pigeon sitting on one of the hanging lamps in the dining room! Ted figured it must have gotten in through the fan duct and forced open the cupboard door. What a dilemma, but with a little ingenuity we were able to encourage it to fly out the front door.

We were both very tired and lay down to watch the Angels game. It was the ninth inning and we thought it was almost over but all these amazing things happened. The game went eleven innings with the Angels impressively achieving the win. We were both totally thrilled. At that moment, inspired by these heightened sensations, Ted completely touched my heart; he said that I was the source of his most joyous moments and memories over the past year! My eyes welled up with tears.

●X□△★

After Ted and I had begun eating together, I soon became aware of the effect eating a meal generally had on him. Within a short while after eating he would grow drowsy and fall into a food-induced sleep. Depending on how much he ate, and how sleep deprived he had been, these naps would last anywhere from an hour to four or five hours, much to his dismay. Ted always felt sleeping was a waste of precious time, and constantly cheated the clock. He had no set hours of sleep and would work until utter exhaustion over came him. He could not be convinced that sleep was beneficial. Eventually, sleeping for any extended length of time really began to make him quite irritable and he would become very upset with himself for letting that happen.

On July 4, 1995, Ted gave a seminar at Claremont College, to which I accompanied him. He did not feel it was very successful, was not sure if he really reached them or if he was in fact helpful. I felt that he learned a lot from it. He did agree about that. There were meager notes in his datebook from that day, *"My plan: 1st ask them each what they want me to talk about, and have rough idea of many subjects to at least mention. Kind of a bust, though most had a good time, they're just not prepared enough."*

Rapidly approaching was Ted's father's 80th birthday celebration at his home in Cathedral City, a suburb of Palm Springs. The most interesting and exciting aspect of that day turned out to be the drive there and back. Neither Ted's Plymouth, or my Ford Bronco was reliable enough to chance driving there, and Ted was uncomfortable in my Porsche, which he always claimed was too small. We decided to rent a car and Ted picked out a white Oldsmobile sedan. He was ecstatic about the car, drove maniacally, reaching speeds in excess of 110 m.p.h. according to the speedometer (he thought it inaccurate), when we slowed down to 60, it felt like we were barely moving. To accompany us on the ride he brought lots of cassettes. On the way there we listened to old Rock 'n Roll, a perfect choice for the wild ride. On the way home, we chose classical. Of course we made record time. As Ted noted, *"Bring many cassettes to listen to. Fast (90-110 mph) drive to Cathedral City, arrive by early afternoon, Barb loves it. Drive home at 11:00, rain. We marvel at Walter Gerwig doing that J.S. Bach fugue, what masterful writing and it just goes on & on. I start "speedometer abbreviate's" e.g. WYM (what you mean?) past the 110 mark."*

Shortly thereafter, I became quite ill again and my cough returned with a vengeance. I tried to conceal it from Ted as best I could. One afternoon back at his apartment after a slew of errands, including Barnes & Noble Books, I was feeling awful, had been coughing a lot and Ted was getting very distressed. I sat on the bed wrapped in a tan blanket, looking at my new books, while Ted sat on the floor and ate dinner. I had no appetite but continued to cough so I took some Dayquil, which helped quell it for a while. I promised Ted I'd go back to the doctor next week. He said he would come with me. I crawled over to him and sat next to him on the floor he hugged me, kissed my cheek and tried to explain how worrisome it was to hear me cough so much. Thus began our quest together for a diagnosis and a cure, doctor after doctor, conventional medicine and experimental, every conceivable path.

On November 17th, 1995, Ted gave a seminar at Music Institute, of which he wrote extensively in his datebook, "*Bring V-2 comp: 1. Bluesette (top 4 strings, key of Bb) 2. V-1 Bluesette (middle 4 strings, key of A) 3. Body & Soul (V-2 Top 4) only went over half of it 4. Green Dolphin Street (top 4) did not get to it. In response to their fatigue, I switched gears & talked SUSTAINING notes, while chords move - in style of Lenny Breau, GVE. Told them: they don't NEED a lot of chords if they are willing to be like Wes & know all of the cool names & uses of the ones they do know. In response to questions: 1. Demonstrated (in Dmi) how to use V-1's 7th's, also 4th chords fairly high on ALL degrees over static chord (Dmi7) 2. How to improvise in Baroque style. 3. They wanted to really play in this style so I dug down & played a long thematic improvisation.*"

In next to no time we were again in the midst of the holiday season. On Christmas Eve, Ted did a very special deed for Max and Paula and her family. Ted entertained Paula's father and many of the other residents at the Woodland Retirement Home. His playing and choice of music visibly moved everyone. On this singular evening, the entire experience was wonderfully heart-warming for all of us.

Christmas day we went to my parent's house. We were a bit overwhelmed upon arrival to find a house full when we expected a more intimate gathering. Everyone was fine for a while, but Ted got into a discussion with Sam (a friend of my parents) that became so heated that both of them lost their tempers. Although everyone was civil by the end of the evening Ted remained distressed and quite shaken over the incident. We left around 6:30, stopped at a tiny diner so Ted could get some fries then to his apartment to watch E.T. as neither of us had seen it. He was disturbed by the beginning of it, found it rather eerie and could not watch. With the stress of the day still weighing heavily upon him, he fell fast asleep.

Fortunately, the year ended splendidly, as Ted described, "*Dec.31 Our best New Year's Eve yet! Barbara & I have a wonderful time culminating in me playing Show Tunes from her childhood for her, eventually Angel Eyes and St. Louis Blues. She's fallen in love with the 'one step' minor 6th thing so incredibly exemplified by the verse to Gershwin's "Swanee" also slower bluesy m6 ala Angel Eyes & St. Louis Blues. Write out the 1st part of her new love, Gershwin's piano roll "So Am I," then for many hours the show tunes, e.g. 'Wonderful Guy', 'Around the World,' the 1st music she ever loved, she'd sit at the piano with her beloved dad.*"

On New Year's Day 1996, Ted suggested we visit his friends Tom and Wendy Bocci, both of whom he had wanted me to meet for quite some time. We arrived in the early afternoon to a charming and comfortable home. Tom extended a warm greeting, Wendy was not home yet, so the three of us sat and talked. In a short while, Wendy arrived. As the afternoon unfolded Wendy and I found we could converse easily and laugh endlessly. By the end of the evening we felt as if we'd known each other for years. Ted was elated by our joy, and that we all got along so well. This was to be the beginning of a long endearing friendship for me. What a wonderful way to begin the year.

● X □ △ ★

After observing Ted organizing and reorganizing his apartment for over three years, I had a plan for him, a new idea. He already had a few stacking cubes and I had recently discovered more of the same at a building supply center. I suggested using more cubes to accommodate all the new items that had been accumulating, as there was no more available shelf space and the piles on the floor were growing rapidly towards the ceiling. Ted was most agreeable to this idea, so I began slowly bringing cubes to him every weekend. By the end of the year I must have brought him fifty or more. He used them all.

Occasionally, we took a break from the apartment organization. Circumstances usually dictated errands, and frequently the majority of our purchases were music related. Once home, and eager to listen to new CDs this would lead into having a "music day." An example of such a day as noted in Ted's datebook: *"a beautiful day, and a beautiful time for Barbie and me. She gives me the hard copy of the Guild Guitars book. 1st to Tower for copies of the Feb. 96 Vintage Guitar issue and buy her those Bach Flute & Harpsichord sonatas she loved, Harp CD with Debussy's Danse Sacre et Profane, she wanted to hear an alternate version, & Ravel Introduction & Allegro. Gelson's she sweetly offers to buy the groceries, I let her because she gets the same pleasure from giving that I do. Music Study for Barbara: We study her piano scores from work. Some breakthroughs for her in enjoying studying piano parts. She is so thrilled to be able to see all those augmented chord wonders, e.g. 1) any note in there is the root. 2) there are only 2 whole tone scales. 3) the other 3 bass notes from the scale create 9#11 chords. 4) If 9#11ths bass notes are moved in contrary motion not in their whole tone scale: all are 9#11 (5) +/root up 1/2 step = minormajor7's"* Later that day when we cuddled together on the bed and talked, he told me he found the music activities "romantic" because he felt so connected to me. I laughed and loved this.

In March '96 the Guild guitar fever once again took hold. At the Santa Monica Civic Auditorium Ted attended a guitar show for the first time in fifteen years. Although he spent six hours reveling in the splendor of everything, including running into many friends, he wanted to go again the following day and desired to take me along to share the experience. *"March 10 Pick up Barb and go to the Guitar Show again. She sees the ocean for the 1st time in a long time (she loves that WE see the ocean). Almost paranormal experience: I'm trying to describe to Willie Moseley how great a Jazzmaster or Jaguar can sound on the treble pick up & I mention the scene from "The Patsy" (1964) and he points a few feet away and says "there's the guy who played it!" It was a man named Del Kasher, who tells ME that he's a huge fan of mine & has my album in his car. Who can explain something like this? and what an amazingly good pick stylist (& fingers some) Wow!"*

On the ensuing weekend, still in pursuit of Guilds, Ted followed some leads and took me on a fun-filled escapade, *"March 16 An amazing adventure day for Barbara the sweet and me. We take the Bronco to 1. Monterey Park (Barb is ecstatic about the adventure) to Johnny Thompson's Music to see a 1960 (1st year) Guild Starfire I Serial #13958. It has the earliest style DeArmond pick up, what a sound! She loves the red beauty and feels that it's sad just sitting in a store, it needs a home. I'll fix it up. We get back on the 10 (Barb loves the downtown L.A. silhouette in mist) and realize it will take us right to our next destination, Venice, Guitar Connection: Owner & guitar lover and his favorite amp is the exact same as mine: the Ampeg Gemini II. Check out his early red Starfire early '63, it's actually a II with added Bigsby, opposite of Mona, with whiteface DeArmonds, I love it right away. (Camille, serial #23853) Later ask to see his other Guild a 1987 X170 Blonde (thinner & fancierX175) Barb & I think it's not so great at first but this guitar little by little shows me that it is extraordinarily special: tone & sustain from heaven! I get both. Barb & I are giddy from an extra special day for us."*

Most of the guitars Ted bought needed some adjustments in order to be set up optimally. Ted always found the perfect set up for each guitar. Either with just a tweak, or in some instances a considerable over-haul, he could bring about the best tone quality. He could also determine which guitars were best suited for a specific use. *"Use my old trusty ratchet set breaker bar to fix the stuck truss rod (tighten) in the fantastic 1967 (#EG173) Guild Manhattan. File the nut, adjust pick ups to get rid of extraneous rattle. What an Outstanding feel and superb vehicle for my non-plugged in Baroque improvisations. 1.) Put new (NOS) Mickey Mouse pickup in '70 T100D (tuned ultra high) 2.) Remove wires for IN PHASE sound 3.) loosen rod a tad 4.) add solder to a few strategic places in horribly dented frets. Tune back down to pitch & play her through my loyal lovely Ampeg Gemini II, what a deep jazz guitar tone & as expected with the small pick up, very woody."*

Another Guild, discovered in a Vintage Guitar magazine, Ted took a chance and we waited. This one last purchase, delivered by mail from Tacoma, Washington, a 1970 Cherryburst T100D arrived at my door. The gamble paid off, Ted was thrilled and spent the evening bonding with his newest friend, *"Practice on the new 1970 T100D Cherryburst tuned up to F#. 1.) Giant Steps in Baroqueish 3/4 & Jazzy 3/4 & 4/4. 2.) Just In Time in Baroquish, Baroquish 3/4, Gospel Jazz Waltz 3/4, Medium Swing 3) Ultra Jazz with soulful melodic riff - themes too. Blues upstairs in D"*

The guitar buying frenzy eventually ebbed along with Ted's funds, but left us with the opportunity to take advantage of a long-standing invitation from Ted's beloved Aunt Reva. All afternoon we sat at the kitchen table eating fresh roasted almonds and macaroon cake, as she told us about her life. Ted remembered most everything she told us that day, "*Born in the Ukraine (1910), grew up in Kiev, came to America, she the last of seven kids. We stayed 4 hours, enchanted and entranced by her stories of the early life of the Cottler family and especially her early life in America culminating with her marriage to Harry Gershan (from Cincinnati) in Chicago, 1927 and her prior stenographer job, and how she got it. Ambition fueled by desperation, not hurting at all. Aunt Re was an 86-year-old marvel."* She also told us a little story about Ted when he would come to visit. She recalled that when he was 4 or 5 years old, he would spend hours sitting on her back porch cradling the cat in his arms while rocking back and forth repeating the words "kitty little" over and over. She told me he had always been a bit "eccentric." We all had a wonderful visit and I felt honored to have met her.

Meanwhile, my inscrutable illness continued, flaring up wildly at times. One evening we had decided to watch a movie but after about a half hour into it I began to cough. Although disturbing and upsetting to Ted, this time he had an idea that might help. He suggested if I ate some dinner and did some physical activity the cough might ease up. He put potatoes in the oven then requested that I clear the area in the living room in front of the white file cabinets. At first I just stared at the huge pile of stuff (old mail, junk mail, music sheets, felt-tip pens, remote controls, magazines, etc.), not knowing where to begin, then I just dug in and started sorting out what was there and moving the items to more appropriate places. I felt like I had become Ted. He was working in another area and by the time the food was ready I had completed my assignment. He was most appreciative and said I had accomplished a lot (didn't seem so to me but...). However, Ted was right about my coughing, it had completely cleared up. We retreated back to the bedroom to eat and watch the movie. By midnight we were only half through it because he had stopped the tape so many times for various reasons. Then the doorbell rang. It was Ralph, the apartment building manager, needing assistance with a broken car, and of course, Ted complied.

By mid-year we had added about twenty-five cubes to the apartment and made considerable progress in organizing many of Ted's collectables. In doing this, we had been having wonderful weekends together, accomplishing a lot and all with love. It seemed easy this way. I was even feeling healthier. We both acknowledged how our love enhanced everything we did. For a while now, we had been sharing the entire weekend together, and he did not seem to be distressed or feel any pressure like he used to. In fact it was enjoyable for him. I was so grateful for his love and understanding. I told him how much easier it was to bear any difficulties just knowing he was a part of my life. He said it was like that for him now too. Where as before, he was, as he said, "in his own world - out of sight, out of mind," now his world had expanded to encompass me.

During the summer Ted began working on ideas for a new book on Contrapuntal Approach Chords. He would always begin new books by sketching ideas, and add to them periodically over days, months, or even years.

Here is an example of Ted's initial ideas for his Contrapuntal Approach Chord book:

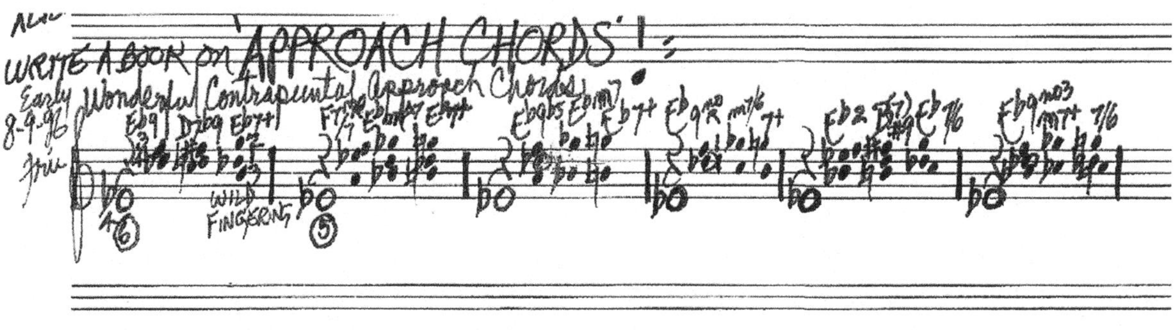

On August 10th we went to CBS Radford Studio to the "Extreme Measures" recording session to say hello to Steve Bartek (a former student and admirer of Ted's) and listen a while. We sat in the booth (in case I coughed). Danny Elfman and Steve Bartek were at the mixing board working. About 20 minutes later they took a break and Steve came over to say hello and visit. He was pleased that Ted had come, as were a few others there who were thrilled to meet a slightly embarrassed Ted. At around 4 p.m. the power failed. We used this as an opportunity to leave. Once out on the street we realized how massive the power outage was. I drove us back to my house and all the traffic signals were out. We loaded three more cubes into Betsy and began to make our way to Encino. At Van Nuys and Ventura, the power was restored, and it was an easy drive back to Ted's.

Hot and tired we plopped down on the bed. Ted put on a tape of various old cartoons. That was when I discovered "Mouse in Manhattan" an old (1945?) Tom & Jerry that was fabulous, one of the best I had ever seen, superior artwork and music! Ted knew I would love this one, as he felt it was one of the best ever made and actually wanted to surprise me with it. He tried to locate others made around that time and found a few, but none measured up, although "Cat Concerto" was also excellent.

Scott Bradley's music in "Mouse in Manhattan" inspired an idea to incorporate into his new book.

● X □ △ ★

On the last day of August, Puddy, my beloved orange tabby cat of fifteen years passed away. He was very ill and my veterinarian suggested I alleviate his suffering. I completely understood, but I was heartbroken and inconsolable. When Ted arrived he offered the utmost solace. Then the two of us, joined by my other cat Willie, sat together in the yard by Puddy's grave, and I wept. After a while Ted felt it best to try to cheer me up. We went to Thrifty's, (a five and dime store) and he bought us toys; puzzles, a miniature pool table, things he thought would be fun. Later we watched some more old Tom & Jerry cartoons. I felt better, but the sadness would take a while to lessen.

Soon Ted's 50th birthday arrived. His preference was to have a memorable celebration for just the two of us. It was a mild September day, partly cloudy and perfect for walking in the city. We were both energetic and our excitement grew stronger as we approached our destination; downtown Los Angeles. Suddenly the buildings loomed up all around us. We found a parking lot on Main St. and began our walk. In one of the first stores we came to we purchased a disposable camera and inside of 10 minutes had taken many photos of fabulous old buildings. We continued up Main St. and within a few blocks came to a store where a guitar and amplifier got Ted's attention. He spent almost 45 minutes there, decided he wanted them and left a deposit. *"A red Squire Strat, just was in need of some love & since she sounded fantastic (on all 5 sounds) especially through that little tan K65 Dean Markley amp (I've wanted one ever since I heard a fellow named Chips in South Pasadena one Friday night in the late 1980's when I bought a wonderful Panasonic 1431 HF VCR from him)."* Then we continued our walk, cutting over to Broadway, which was bustling with people, and lined with all kinds of stores. We explored a huge market; it was like a bazaar, made up of hundreds of individual booths of food. After almost two hours of continual walking, we began to grow a bit weary from all the input. We made our way back to the Bronco and drove to the pawnshop to pick up the guitar then headed for home. Encountering traffic, Ted took a detour, a short cut down Temple, which worked out splendidly. He knew all the streets well, as if he had a detailed map of the entire city etched in his brain.

That summer held some of our best times thus far. We shared many new experiences and we knew the wealth of discoveries for us was inexhaustible. Never had I felt such an overwhelming love from another, nor have I loved another so overwhelmingly.

● X □ △ ★

There were always some unique and humorous experiences while we were out on our errands. One incident in particular gives some insight into Ted's fascination with just about anything. We had planned to make one brief stop at Tower Records then go home. We parked in back where Ted noticed a man servicing fire extinguishers. Ted thought this was a great opportunity to learn something and walked over to talk with him. The serviceman was delighted by Ted's enthusiasm and interest, they conversed at length about fire extinguisher use, function, care and longevity, basically everything there was to learn about fire extinguishers. Ted was very excited about this discussion and pleased to have acquired new and useful information.

Along with Ted's practical side, there existed the impulsive child-like being who was ever full of wonder. Inadvertently, we discovered a store called The Party Shop. We had entered with the intention of purchasing new calendars, but there were too many eye-catching, glittering, and mesmerizing temptations. An hour and a half later we emerged with glowing stickers, confetti, colored paper, felt tip pens and of course the Baseball Stadium calendars. We picked up dinner at Panda Express then headed to the apartment.

That evening, upon my request, Ted allowed me to sleep uninterrupted through the night. Usually when we had fallen asleep, he would wake me up to take me home when he woke up, which was generally around 2:30 in the morning, because it was in these quiet early morning hours that he was at his most productive and when he preferred to be alone. I liked that he was willing to let me sleep, most likely due to my health; at least he learned that my continuing to sleep didn't interfere with his work and we could coexist this way. I awoke around 4:30 or 5 a.m. and he drove me home. He explained that this was a general sleep pattern for him, that he might sleep a bit more later on, then teach from noon 'til

9 p.m., and if needed, catch up on sleep Tuesday. The early morning was cold and crystal clear, still dark at that hour the stars glistened so brightly, we gazed up as if seeing them for the first time.

The cold winter-like weather continued and on Christmas Eve Ted and I met my friends Lori and Sam at the Immanuel Presbyterian Church on Wilshire Boulevard to see and hear Handel's Messiah performed live at Midnight. Absolutely magnificent. Ted noted, *"Pitched fantastically at A = 415 !!!! I love this."*

Then a very social Christmas day, Ted visited with his father then met me at my parents house where he became engrossed in conversation with my father. Ted wrote, *"Dan tells me about going to work for Frankie Laine in 1950, then Warner's & ALL Dimitri Tiomkin scores from "High Noon" on."* From my parents we drove over to Tom and Wendy's where four joyous hours sped by.

New Year's Eve was quiet and rainy. We enjoyed watching a documentary on movies from the silent era to present day. Ted got some work done on his apartment and listened while I watched "An American in Paris" for the second time in one month, and loved it even more, which Ted didn't fail to notice, *"We watch (actually she watches, I listen) An American in Paris (2nd time in weeks) Barbara has fallen madly in love with the music of George Gershwin (as I did years ago)."* At 11:59 p.m. I switched to channel 11 and we watched the detonation of the Hacienda Hotel in Las Vegas at midnight.

As 1997 began, the never-ending apartment reorganization was once again a top priority and consumed the month of January. At the top of Ted's agenda was clearing a path to the main bathroom door so he could get into the bathroom. It was completely inaccessible due to piles of books, magazines, videos and other miscellaneous items having slowly accumulated in that area. Considering that Ted's main objective was to clean out the bathroom, I suggested he let me clear the path knowing that if he attempted to do it, he'd go through each item as he moved it, whereas I would simply pick up whole stacks of items and put them out of the way. Ted agreed with my plan and I went to work as Ted sat on the bed and wrote in his datebook. We both experienced a role reversal and found it amusing. He remarked how strange it was to see me doing his work. The job took me less than half an hour.

We put potatoes in the oven, and then he began rearranging books in the cubes in the living room. In regard to organizing the books, for Ted equally as important as categorization was color arrangement. The books had to be in a visually pleasing rainbow of preference, he shuffled them around until the right combination appeared. After dinner he fell asleep on the floor in the living room. Thus the weekends continued throughout the month and into the next.

In mid February, apartment organization was put aside to celebrate a special day for us, spent quietly and loving at my house which Ted portrayed poignantly, *"Feb. 14 A beautiful memorable Valentine's Day for us. Roses for Barbara. Bring the long awaited "Guys & Dolls" (1955) over for Barb & I to watch & love. Almost a miracle: Barbara flips over this movie as I did & for all the same reasons. We laugh & laugh and a few tears from some of the beautiful music too. How lucky we are."*

Ted's comments about the movie refer to my reaction to the use of language in the dialogue and some lines in particular. He noticed I had reacted exactly the same way to the exact same things as he did when he first saw this movie. The same thing happened with the music too. This was something that occurred frequently with us, but was always a stunning discovery.

The following day, prior to going out on errands, we sat on the couch and talked about our week. Somehow the conversation segued into his eccentricities and through that, he finally got me to acknowledge my suspicion that he might have some mild form of Asperger's Syndrome. It just happened. He was telling me about his strange sleeping habits and I mentioned that I suspected why he had so many peculiarities. He asked me to tell him but I said not until I felt that it would be of any benefit for him to know. He kept pressing and then finally said, "do you think I'm Autistic?" I hesitated, and he knew. I explained to him the broad spectrum encompassed by that heading. He was not disturbed, just curious. I told him about the books I had read and that I would read him some parts directly applicable. He said now he understood my curiosity regarding "physiological anomalies" and why I had read so much in that area. I told him my interest began prior to knowing him but certainly was instrumental in formulating my suspicion about his eccentricities. Most importantly, I reassured him how much I loved him and that all his idiosyncrasies were part of his charm, and very endearing to me. However, I was sure I gave him a lot to ponder.

● X □ △ ★

Towards the end of February, Ted's residual check arrived, and as usual, all his thoughts became focused on new guitar purchases. Naturally, the Guild buying frenzy took over completely. Ted detailed the following weekend, "*To Hollywood: a near miss (just like how I got my 1st gold top) A.) Voltage Guitars: Ready to leave & then happened to look down & say hey, here's a Guild, and bam, there it was, a Duane Eddy 1966, and what an amazingly rich tone through an almost equally astonishing 1968 Silver-Face (but actually black face chasies as these were) Deluxe Reverb. B.) Guitars R Us: I had already walked the floor but just started to do it once more, then bam, "Hey, here's one of those little Guilds we were just talking about" and indeed it was, but after finding a suitable bridge for it, it sounded so quiet and non-dynamic, almost rubbery, but I felt just for knowledge & experience I should plug it in & what a shock, astonishing tone & Supro-like tugboat bass, and when tuned down, forget it. Bought this beautiful little 1968 Bluesbird M75 #DD147. Barb surprises me & Loves it!! In middle of night: Under mounds of stuff, unearth Blackface Twin Reverb & Pro Reverb, wrestle with my conscience about putting those weaker but Blue Oxford Fender speakers in the Twin Reverb. Spray sockets, change some tubes in the twin but she won't stop that horrible intermittent so, Charles my amp tech for emergency visit. Barb & I race up to Sylmar, oh yes, I had decided I couldn't subject a future owner of my wonderful Black Twin Reverb to the possibility of blowing up those lesser rated Pro Reverb speakers (just so I could make say $300. more on the trade in). Charles works hard for quite a long time*

& then finds the broken resistor & when back together: what an immense sound! And then Charles mentions that his favorite amp used to be the Blackface Pro Reverb so I sell it to him for $600. $75 he earned ($525.) he's happy. Barb & I fly down the 2 Fwy then Sunset Blvd. to Lloyd's and they hear how fantastic the Twin sounds, and then somehow Barb & I discover another Guild I somehow overlooked (3 for 3!!!) (how does one explain this ??) It is love at 1st sight for both Barb & I with this ravishingly beautiful late '70s Sunburst X175, and love at first sound too, we giggle & reel. Lloyd graciously allows me $800 on the Twin, what wonderful treatment! Barb is ecstatic. I fix the little M75 and insist Barb take it, she is just wild over it!"

When Ted called to see how I was, he didn't know that Willie my beloved old cat of 18 years had died that day. It was uncanny as he rarely called on Tuesdays. It was as if Ted sensed I was grieving or sad. When I told him about Willie, it saddened him too. He wanted to offer consolation, and also thought a distraction might help and asked if I wanted to accompany him to the market. I did, since I was planning to go anyway. I was just glad of his presence but he seemed to be mustering up all his energy in order to stay light hearted and funny, as if he was fighting his own grieving. Ted allowed himself to cry easily during poignant or sad moments in movies but not over sad incidents in real life. It was too overwhelming for him to directly embrace those sad feelings in relation to himself or his own life. First we went on his errands, in the car we listened to a symphony and drove around until it ended, never knowing the composer because the announcer's voice suddenly became muffled. When we went to the market, he wanted to buy me everything, thinking he could find something to cheer me. He was manic about it even, so overly insistent that I had to fight him in a way. I knew one day I must explain to him how to deal with these emotions, how to accept and understand them. But I was so grateful for his being with me, wanting to try, trying to help. Just that effort alone meant more to me than anything. I told him so.

Now for the first time since I could remember, I was without a cat - for me an unimaginable circumstance. It just so happened that my veterinarian knew of two kittens in need of a home. The following weekend Ted and I drove to Hollywood to look at them and they were beautiful beyond what either of us imagined. Apparently these kittens were semi-feral but seemed calm and comfortable with us, let us pet and hold them. Their names came immediately to Ted - Cocoa and Mocha - which was perfect! Upon arriving home, we brought the carriers into the living room, opened the door and the kittens headed straight for cover, after trying every which way to escape. Oh! Who would have thought getting two eight-month old kittens would cause so much pandemonium? Eventually we got them settled comfortably on the bed, left them there, closed the door and began to "kitten-proof" the house. Ted seemed to have gotten a new burst of energy and used it when he moved the refrigerator closer to the wall. But he attacked it with such force and no regard for his personal safety. I sensed he might regret doing that. When I mentioned it, he agreed but said it was the only way he could have gotten it to budge. His ribs were sore for weeks.

The next day Ted was tired and his muscles ached. We had decided to stay at my place to spend time with the new kittens and help them acclimate. When Ted got hungry he let me fix him dinner for the first time. I loved doing this. He told me that now I completely understood his pleasure in doing this for me. I steamed some green beans with almonds and baked some potatoes. I loved that he let me take care of him; he was more relaxed than I had ever seen him. I gave him the couch all to himself for the movie and sat in the wicker chair. We watched "Pete Kelly's Blues," witty lines and fabulous music. Afterwards, I sat next to him on the floor by the couch and caressed him thinking how much I loved him. This was the first time he actually completely resigned himself to my care, totally relaxed, his mind not distracted by anything else, probably because he was so sore from Saturday. But he smiled and laughed a lot despite the pain he so obviously felt every time he moved.

In March of '97 Ted and I finally got long awaited answers to the nature of my illness. Upon a recommendation I went to see Dr. F, a highly renowned and well-respected rheumatologist. He was the first doctor to diagnose that I had CREST syndrome, and was quite knowledgeable about all my symptoms. Alas, we were informed that it was genetic and also a degenerative disorder with no known cure, but perhaps some of the symptoms could be alleviated. He gave me several options but I needed a while to consider the ramifications of each one. Ted and I were both sad but hopeful, especially since I had been suffering from the symptoms more frequently these past months.

In early April, Ted and I went to Chadney's restaurant to see and hear George Van Eps play with brass player and vocalist, Betty O'Hara and bass player Bob Banes. The place was full beyond capacity. Luckily Joel (my brother), and his wife Stefanie had reserved a table and invited us to join them. For so long Joel had been telling me how great Betty was and now I realized myself. She played trumpet, flugelhorn, and trombone, three instruments among Ted and my least favorite and she had us loving them. She played beautifully, sensitively, and oh when she sang, I fell in love with her. Ted was equally enthralled. Then there was the phenomenal George Van Eps, at 83 living up to all Ted had told me about him, so nimble, agile and effortlessly playing extraordinary changes and fabulous solos. Equally up to the task was Bob Banes, the bass player. We stayed for all three sets and afterwards there was much socializing and revelry. At two in the morning we left with smiles and bags of popcorn.

On the following Saturday, I had a phone message from Ted waiting for me when I got home. Hmmm? unusual for him to call so early. Upon listening I learned that his beloved Plymouth, Betsy had been towed away. When I called Ted back he was understandably upset, but had all the information and was ready to begin the process of retrieval. This turned into a long and tortuous day for Ted. He came to pick me up around noon. First we had to go to the tow service office where it cost $215.00 to gain her release. Next we were instructed to pick her up at a junkyard in Sun Valley but were told she wouldn't be ready until 3:30, as they had to bring her up front. We decided to do errands and went to the newsstand, but then just back to my house to wait. Ted was so upset and he couldn't relax, so he picked up a guitar. Playing helped to ease his anxiety. At 3:00 we headed to the junkyard located in a remote industrial section of Sun Valley. As we pulled in, there was Betsy, looking dusty and forlorn. Upon inspecting her, the front license plate was crinkled and hanging, the driver's side rear view mirror was completely broken and the battery was dead! Shocking! No one at the junkyard would shoulder the blame, they told us to deal with the towing company, but they did help us get her started. We, but especially Ted who was almost in tears, were so relieved. I got in the Bronco and followed him home. We put Betsy in her space in back and locked the gate. Safe! Exhausted, he laid down and fell immediately asleep.

During this very busy month, I'd been coughing incessantly and not feeling too well. I knew I had to make a decision about treatment. Dr. F had also diagnosed me with Myositis, a muscle inflammation and weakness often associated with CREST. Ted and I had discussed the use of medication and side effects since nothing else was helping. After much deliberation and reconsideration, I decided to try Prednisone, which Dr. F had recommended for the Myositis. On May 19th I took my first dose. Within a very short time, we both noticed a remarkable difference. My general health seemed to improve, I had more energy, and I had completely stopped coughing! It seemed like a miracle, and we were both elated.

● X □ △ ★

One day in early summer, Ted got a call from Chris' Guitars about a newly arrived X-500. We brought Gigi, our beloved X-500 along with us to make a comparison. Visually we knew immediately that the one in the store didn't measure up, even though it sounded great. After playing various guitars, Ted discovered a blonde Guild (1954 X375) with three pickups. He was pretty sure he wouldn't like it but I had a feeling otherwise and was right. He loved it. *"I was so shocked. It had the greatest electric jazz guitar tone I've heard in years, maybe ever. Then in measuring, it became clear that it had a long-scale, which always helps & the basic neck pick up vowel sound."* Well that was that, he had to have it. I was able to loan him the money, as I couldn't convince him to let me make it a gift. Back at my house, he plugged her in and was enchanted; re-inspired he played for about an hour. I was so thrilled he was enjoying his playing again, and I loved listening, he could have played for me all evening.

Sometime within the past month I had asked Ted if he would show me his original compositions. He was quite willing but first had to locate them. Ultimately his search turned up the missing envelope. He chose the '63 Gretsch, Hazel, and read through these beautiful pieces he wrote many years ago. At one point we took a break and put two potatoes in the oven then went back to the music. An hour and a half seemed to just disappear. What an absolute joy to experience Ted's Baroque compositions. When he mentioned he had to find a way to pay me back for the X375 I told him he was doing just that simply by playing for me. He loved this idea, but would not accept it. I could have laid there and listened forever, but the potatoes had been in the oven two hours, so we ate then just cuddled on the bed and talked. I asked him if he had mentioned the Asperger's to anyone, he said he had mentioned it to a few people, and they seemed to think it could be an accurate diagnosis. Throughout the weekend he occasionally brought it up "in jest," but when I asked him if he was uncomfortable about it he said no. He now realized his obsessive/compulsive behavior could be a result of the Asperger's syndrome. However, he did not believe that his constant reorganizing was anything but a desire to do just that, get organized.

Ted was exceptionally funny and witty that day and came up with "Twilophobia," fear of twilight, and more funny references to it. Ted's brief reflection on the day warmed my heart, *"My old classical compositions (on Hazel, my '63 high strung Gretsch Tennessean) play through many of them, all Baroque, for Barb. She is so happy. We are so much in love it brings tears to my eyes."*

Now that Ted had re-discovered his compositions he noted, *"My Solo Guitar Pieces: almost finished now with cursory retrospective work and play through. I really did compose a ton of stuff (from '68 through '70-'71) and some of its' beauty holds up really well. Others are strong in spots with flaws that need revising. Given a month or two I think I can do it, if I'm willing to agonize over the 'joins' and or the development- I sure used to. Be honest Ted, you gave 1000's of hours of your life to these pieces, finish them, at least the most worthy, leave some beauty behind for others, if not for you. Not too literally compare but: what if Carl Maria von Weber had said "Aw heck, the world doesn't need another Opus 11 Piano Concerto in C!"*

● X □ △ ★

A musician and teacher of Ted's caliber and reputation could command a much higher fee than Ted was charging for his lessons. Many of his students were shocked when they discovered how low Ted's rates were for one-hour lessons. (At that time Ted was charging $22.00). When Ted needed to increase the amount it would always be by only one or two dollars. Yet, despite the meager request, Ted would always apologize to his students for the increase in fees. But the low amount was simply another aspect of Ted's compassionate nature, he wanted to be accessible to everyone who desired musical knowledge, therefore kept his fees at what he considered a fair but affordable level. If Ted sensed someone absolutely loved music and could not afford his rates, he would charge them less. Ted's association with money and ideas about financial security were quite different than most. Ted lived in the moment and spent most of his money on his beloved possessions. As an example, when Ted was low on cash and came across a guitar he couldn't live without, he would figure out some alternative way to come up with the cash to purchase the guitar. Sometimes he would sell off some of his baseball cards, an amplifier or a guitar he wasn't playing enough. Occasionally he would trade one of his guitars or amps for the desired purchase.

One day, in an attempt to be resourceful, Ted came over with two rings and a bracelet that had belonged to his mother. He wanted to have them appraised in hopes of selling them. This would enable him to have cash in case he loved the Guild we were going to see later in the day. Two different jewelers gave us basically the same information and advice: he would never get the actual value by selling. It wouldn't be worth it. Upon leaving the second jeweler he decided he wanted me to have the bracelet. It was a delicate gold with purple amethysts. He put it on my wrist and I felt so honored. Then we drove to Venice to see a 1958 Sunburst Guild X350, but the guitar although beautiful wasn't right, *"bad binding reaffix, magnet pull (pick-ups too close) and strings hit pick up when lowered to where I like them."*

As we headed back to the valley, stuck in a traffic jam, I sensed correctly Ted was consumed by thoughts of the guitar anyway, he was contemplating if it could be fixed. Ted exited the freeway and took a circuitous route back to his apartment. This cleared out his head somewhat. We ate a light supper and afterwards, he got out the new blonde X-375 and compared the pickups with a Gibson. He was still not sure how he felt but slowly convinced himself he made the right decision. Then he plugged in the new blonde Guild and played and played while I lay on the bed in a reverie. He played all the songs from "My Fair Lady" then "Girl With the Flaxen Hair," then lots of Baroque improvisation. It was after one a.m. by the time he tired.

Next weekend, after playing a wedding gig, Ted came straight to my house upset about his playing. Unbeknownst to him in advance, the gig was outdoors and consequently he couldn't get a good sound from his amp (Lola, his '52 Tele through Peavey Ltd 400), on top of which he claimed to generally be bored with his playing. He was mostly unhappy with the way he played the songs, he felt that they sounded "sappy" and couldn't abide that sound. I adamantly disagreed and told him that when he played for me last weekend it sounded wonderful. He said that was a different situation. This disenchantment with his playing happened periodically and was a real dilemma for him especially because he felt it was his duty to share his music with others. He didn't want to give up, he just needed to reconcile the problems. In this area I felt helpless of course, it upset me to know he was sad and perplexed about this.

On Sept. 23rd, Papashon in Encino featured the first Tuesday Guitar Night Series hosted by Ted's good friend and jazz guitarist extraordinaire, John Pisano. Inaugurating the special event was George Van Eps. Despite our early arrival, when Ted and I walked into the room it was already completely crowded. As we headed to our table people everywhere were calling out "Ted, Ted," clamoring for his attention, which he so graciously acknowledged. It took us ten minutes to get across the room to the table that his friends William and Ahndrea had reserved. Wow! I thought to myself, that is what it must feel like to be with a celebrity, totally overwhelming! I finally got to meet his close friend William Perry, who definitely had Guild fever. GeorgeVan Eps was fabulous and his stories really funny, a truly entertaining and remarkable man. What a special treat.

A few days later, on Ted's request, we let his 51st birthday slip quietly by. I had offered him the day to spend catching up on work, a gift of much coveted time, but he opted for togetherness, although he mostly slept. The following Tuesday, we were back at Papashon, and upon Ted's suggestion we brought my parents along. Frank Potenza and John Pisano got together for the second show, which initially was to be a series of six shows. Their guitar playing was top notch, Frank and John connected so well musically, blending and trading inspired lines. I was glad that my parents were able to enjoy this with us. Afterwards Ted told me he now looked forward to us seeing each other on Tuesdays, said it was nice not waiting so long (all week) to see each other. Interesting to note how his needs in the relationship evolved, Tuesdays too! I was touched by this and quite delighted by this change.

● X ☐ △ ★

During the next week Ted had gone guitar shopping, and he encapsulated the following "surprise" wonderfully, *"Oct. 4, Buy Barb a midget Guild, oh so fetching,'60 M65 #13493. I name her Danielle (Barb approves) I pretend that I didn't buy it, pretend it's a lap steel of my student's that I couldn't sell & seem disgruntled over it for realism) and then I surprise Barb with it. She loves it! I cook her dinner."*

In the past month or so, Ted's compulsion to purchase guitars had all but consumed him, and would continue unabated for another two months. He called early afternoon, after visiting Max to sell some baseball cards to pay for another guitar. He said he was on his way to pick me up and take me with him to Chris' Guitars to buy a Guild that he mentioned was very old, hence the name 'Granny', but also ... *"1959 X-50 Guild - Barb names the guitar "Granny" (much later we find out, I had forgotten, that this model is called the Granada"!!!)* Later that evening we went to Papashon for the third Tuesday Guitar Night. This was one incredible experience. Joe Diorio was absolutely astounding! His playing engulfed you, compelled you along on a journey with his elaborate and unusual musical thought process and together with John Pisano, made a fabulous duo. And what a compliment to a much embarrassed Ted when Joe Diorio announced that Ted was in the audience and mentioned how brilliant a player Ted was and gently tried to coax him into playing one night. Everyone started whistling, yelling and applauding very loudly, and Ted turned red as a beet! After the show so many people (again!) wanted to talk to Ted, we were unable to leave until close to midnight.

The evenings were beginning to get chilly now, only the week before we were barefoot all day and night. The days had turned cool and breezy. A first preview of autumn marked the end of the regular baseball season, and the beginning of the playoffs. Cleveland was in contention and Ted wanted to watch. The games afforded Ted the time to make the much needed and many modifications on all the recent additions to our guitar family, *"The '61 CE100DP Special: Complete transformation into Spectacular sounding 'wood tone' electric archtop by heavy amelioration via a.) wooden bridge b.) lower pick-ups by removing spacers under them (white face DeArmonds) c.) heavy strings: .013, .016, .028 W (half-round) .034, .044, .054 What a tone! Revamp the Sunburst '66 Duane Eddy: find and install a little knob as Master Volume. 2.) file nut slots 3.) heavy strings 4.) find long screws for neck pickup so I can drop it really low for more of an acoustic woody tone."*

Late in the evening on October 21, I got a nightmare of a call from some very kind and thoughtful people. They told me they had found our cat Mocha and that he had been badly injured, hit by a car. In shock, I met them at the veterinarian's but unfortunately Mocha could not be saved. I was totally devastated. When Ted called, I gave him the bad news and broke down crying. He was with me in less than an hour and brought me a fabulous tape he had made of his playing, and said he had been thinking about me while he recorded it. I was very moved, but too sad to appreciate his gesture. He did his best to comfort me and we watched the rest of Game 3 (Cleveland/Marlins), which by chance was the most unusual almost comical 9th inning ever! After the game, Cocoa came in and the three of us cuddled together on the couch and listened to the exquisite chamber music version of Bach's Goldberg Variations. Although still sad, with so much love surrounding us, I felt grateful for that.

Now it was late autumn, darkness fell early, the World Series over and Ted took Cleveland's loss graciously. Meanwhile, my friend Lori had been feeding a pack of feral cats and had told me that amongst them was one little black kitten that was especially tame and very loving. She knew we were considering a companion for Cocoa and pleaded with me to adopt this one and I couldn't resist. Lori brought him to me on November 9th. I named him Quincy. Ted would become particularly fond of this very clever and loving kitten; it would not take long for them to form a special bond.

Heavy rains and Thanksgiving Day ushered in the holiday season. My parents had a houseful for the occasion and shortly afterwards I had begun losing my voice. Ted loved the sound, *"Cute Barb 'whiskey turning gradually to squeaky voice' due to lots of singing practice & a cold (rare for her)."* The rain and my illness confined me inside all week and by the weekend my voice was almost nonexistent.

On Saturday Ted called around noon, wanted to know if I felt like watching football. Sure, did he? It had been so long. Yes. We watched San Diego and Kansas City, a surprisingly "polite" game as Ted observed and commented if that were the new gist maybe he'd watch again. At half time he called a guy in Canada about some Guilds and was on the phone for the entire second half of the game. I made some tea and got a blanket. My cold was getting worse and I was totally stuffed up. When he got off the phone, *"Make soup & garlic bread for my sick darling."* I was genuinely touched by his gesture. Then what to do? A movie was about all I had the energy for so we watched "A Twist of Fate" which was very heartwarming and stirred our emotions.

A month ago Ted had accepted a gig playing at what he thought was a Christmas party. However, the party had turned into a "mini concert" at a student's home. When we arrived, cars lined both sides of the street, we walked up to the house which contained a huge crowd. Ted soon discovered it wasn't really a party and that essentially everyone was there just to hear him play solo guitar. *"Dec. 20 XMAS PARTY Lots of work on Venus, the new archtop, who I'll play for the people tonight. Bring my wonderful 1952 Tele, Lola, Venus, and '54 Esquire "Banana Cream" tuned low, main axe. Attendees gave me so much good energy that I had quite a few stretches where I was able to really play with just the feelings I was trying for and even go beyond and of course I got in a lot of trouble & even bad trouble sometimes too but not for long. Over all my playing ranged from fair to pretty to raunchy. A very supportive & loudly & even cheering crowd, I was a lucky man tonight."*

Shortly after the party Ted caught a cold, possibly from me, since my cold still lingered a bit. Come Christmas Day we were both ill. I went to visit him and brought the card I made for him, which he really enjoyed. He was still not feeling well and certainly not up to going with me to spend time with my parents.

We both remained "under the weather" as the year quietly wound down. During this reflective week, I wondered if Ted would ever appreciate and share with me certain aspects of beauty. Would he ever be moved by the late afternoon sun streaming through the blinds, the smell of the earth after the rain, or the fine white crescent of the moon rising? If I did not point these things out would he even notice? Probably not. The beauty and subtleties of the natural world were not apparent to him and would never stimulate him like the angle of a building, or the graceful lines of certain cars.

● X □ △ ★

The year of 1998 was to usher in some major changes and learning experiences. As the year began we were both feeling better and enjoyed a quiet, pleasant New Year's Day. Ted had really begun to bond with Quincy, our new kitten, and also delighted me with some vastly innovative guitar playing. In his words, *" Her D35 (tuned to Eb) sounds so great as I improvise Baroque counterpoint changing to Romantic harmony to Impressionistic to Jazz harmony to Blues to Gospel."*

A week later, with but few remnants left from our colds, we ventured out on errands. With the Bronco not running and in need of minor repair, we took Ted's Plymouth, Betsy. Long neglected, first we stopped to service her. After filling her tank, adding oil, necessary fluids and air in the tires she was ready to go. We made a brief stop at the newsstand then our very first trip to Target, a discount department store, which proved highly dangerous, especially for Ted with little impulse control. I won't even list all we bought considering we went only for a lampshade and left with two full carts.

Amid seemingly unceasing rain in January, the guitar we sent away for in December finally arrived and I called Ted with the exciting news. The pouring rain was not a deterrent, he came over around 11:30 a.m. and was thrilled with his new purchase. He played her through the Princeton amp, experimenting and trying her various options, all sounded superb. Then he couldn't resist the jigsaw puzzle I'd started, pieced together a tree and played with a much-delighted Quincy. There was always something special about being warm and cozy during a rainstorm, we had a very loving day and kept looking at each other and smiling. Ted noted some changes he made to the new X-350, *"After removing the .05 capacitor wired in parallel with the neck pickup she comes alive! She is a '58 long scale Guild X-350, gorgeous SB with the 3 white pickups. I name her "Desiree" because "one long hoped for is the meaning."*

At the end of the month, George Van Eps was playing again at Papashon. That afternoon we both had felt tired and tried to nap first, as the show usually ended late, but Ted was in a silly mood. He had been revisiting a book on the style of Palestrina and the dissonance. One footnote suggested "the reader" refer to Zacconi's "Prattica di

Musica" c.1622 pages 75 and 230. Ted had written a sarcastic comment about this, which he read to me *"Well sure… it's right here in the front row at Crown Books, and of course at the library (uh…yeah)."* We couldn't stop laughing and after a half hour realized we couldn't sleep. By then we had to get ready for Papashon. We arrived around 8 p.m., it was crowded but not jammed like the first time. Ted went to greet George and have a brief chat with him, then repositioned some of George's guitar switches for a better sound but George put them back. Throughout the evening people continually came over to Ted, to say hello, to meet him, get his autograph, or take his picture. Although humbled, he handled it comfortably and graciously. We decided to leave after the first set even though George's playing was excellent, but before we left Jeanne Pisano, (John's wife), came to get Ted for group photos and Ted was in the next issue of many guitar magazines along with George and the other guitarists there.

This is a study Ted was working on while attending George Van Eps' show.

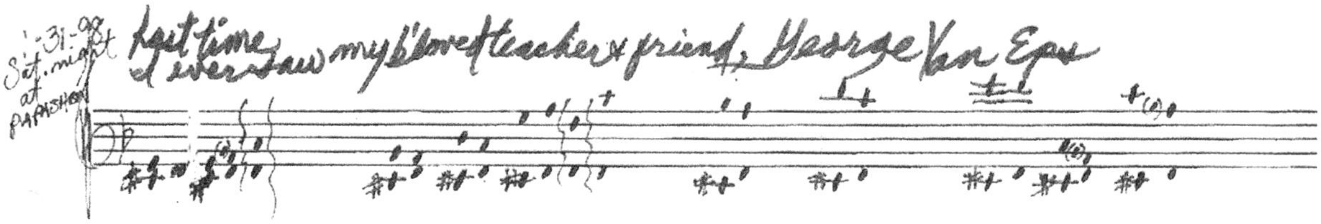

The rain continued relentlessly, loudly pounding the house. Ted practiced many hours for a Valentine's Day party while I read and secretly listened. By early evening the rain abated and had ceased completely by party time. We arrived at John and Margaret's by 8 p.m. as scheduled. He brought Banana Cream, the '54 Esquire, and the sunburst Guild with the Gibson tailpiece and set up in a corner of the living room by the fireplace as per John's request. Ted chose to start with the Guild, and as he began to play the warm woodsy tone slowly grabbed the attention of the guests. In a short while he switched to the Esquire and played for two hours straight. Towards the end of the evening, especially for me, Ted played "Girl with the Flaxen Hair," during which John looked over at me and smiled as tears streamed down both of our cheeks. The next day, we celebrated our Valentine's Day. Ted arrived with flowers and a beautiful card. We leisurely read the newspaper, finished the crossword puzzle then went out on some errands. Later after a sumptuous dinner we settled in together for a short nap. I woke first but remained cuddled up contentedly next to him. When he awoke we just talked and laughed, he was so funny. Later he played me a heart-stopping version of "Our Love is Here to Stay," copious tears flowed from my eyes. A wonderful day filled with so much love.

During the week, an inspired Ted noted and kept track of many hours of productive practicing, *"Feb. 18 The X-50 stimulate hours of practice" main subject: 2 note "skip 1" interpretation. Locked double line on F#7#9, Blue Pentatonic, also Bb7#9, Eb7#9"*

"Feb. 20 Practice 10 hours or so - like the old days, especially lots of locked double line in the blue pentatonic with right hand fingers 2 & 3.'

Late February brought the residual check which resulted in another shopping spree, *"Feb. 21 Barb agrees: one of our finest weekends. Order the 2 ('56 & '57) X-50s from White Plains, New York. To Norm's: Guild M20 serial no. 19447 (1962), Guild X-150 Serial no. 5018 (ergo 1957) and the crown jewel: "Luscious" Serial no. 3155 (1956) The "warehouses" blonde primo Guild X-550 which Barb vacillated back & forth on UNTIL she played it, & then she fell in love with it. Nick freed the frozen pots & then we saw what the pick ups could do. We were sold!"* Walking on a cloud out to the car we were dazed, totally ecstatic. Once home we spent the ensuing five hours reveling in our purchases. We had bought five Guild guitars that weekend.

The following day it rained until mid afternoon. Ted brought the new X-550, who I'd named "Luscious" to compare her to Gigi. Soon we had all the guitars out, taking photos and making comparisons. We both preferred Gigi's looks, but we thought Luscious had the best sound. Brownie, a small mahogany parlor Guild, sounded fabulous, rich and loud for such a tiny one. Later we dropped off the film to be developed at Thrifty's then went to Ted's apartment to pick up an amp plus miscellaneous "stuff" he was going to sell to Norm. *"Decide the early '60 Super (ox blood) & spare old pick ups & tuner & white Tele 7 hold guard."* We gave Norm the money for "Luscious" then Ted discussed what he brought to sell them. Norm and Danny felt badly about Ted having to sell things, especially when they knew the value would increase down the line. Danny offered to actually lend Ted the money but of course Ted refused. Eventually they worked something out. By the time we left it was prime rush hour, lots of traffic. The road through the Sepulveda Basin flooded and was closed, so we wended our way down Ventura Blvd, finally getting to Thrifty's to pick up the film and doted over the photos right there in the store.

Now the Guild shopping spree was in full swing and Ted recorded it all,*"Feb. 27 Trade "Stella" ('66 ES-330TD - wonderful) to the fellows for a '65 X-175 Blonde (#41893) Very clean, no volute, Kolb engraved nickel tuners."*

"Feb. 28 To Norm & Danny: trade in my old wonderful gig amp from '79 (a 70's Silverface Super Reverb) which hadn't been turned on in nearly 20 years, and the JBL'd '62ish brown Deluxe (not working blowing fuses). From yesterday: Jerry's trade in reissue '65 blonde & wheat grill blackface Deluxe Rebverb is the best sounding Deluxe Reverb I've heard in a long time, maybe ever, reverb from heaven, 3 or 4 chords again today to verify- "forget it- that's it" what a Sound! I'm in love with it. Barbara & I stop at my place to drop the amp off, we plug it in & get hung up for hours trying many guitars in it. Barb loves it too & sees why it's so amazing."

Mid-week at my door, I found the two X-50's had arrived from White Plains, New York. With a knife I pried open the cardboard shipping boxes to discover two beauties. Ted was giving lessons that day, but not wanting to wait nor able to contain my excitement I brought them to him. His students, used to some interruptions, didn't mind and we all reveled over these exquisite instruments. I didn't stay long as I was not feeling too well, and also felt I had caused enough disruption of the lessons.

● X ☐ △ ★

A few days later at the apartment, Ted had been trying to straighten up the bathroom and had accidentally caused an avalanche. I went to look and the entire room was a two-foot high pile of books, magazines and papers. The unexpected mess distressed him terribly. At first I thought it best to just leave him alone so I went into the bedroom. A short while later I took a peek and noticed he was so upset that he was just sitting there staring at the avalanche. Somehow I made my way into the bathroom, and began straightening it out, putting everything in neat stacks along the wall where it had been. He was sitting in the hall just outside the door. I began tossing him what I perceived as trash and he gladly threw it away, filling two bags! This made Ted very happy and soon the bathroom was back to its normally organized clutter-filled self.

Towards the end of March, a strong determination took hold of Ted. This time he was resolved to complete the organization of his apartment. He preferred to work during the quiet hours of the night, and would spend the entire night into the next day rearranging his huge collection of things. One late afternoon, after many hours of work, he took a break and came to visit me. It was a beautiful, pristine day after the recent rains so we went into the backyard, played with the cats, and I noticed a very tame squirrel had come to visit. I went into the house and brought out a slice of apple, coaxed the squirrel down the branch and handed it the apple. Ted was amazed, he'd never seen a "tame" squirrel, and thought it absolutely adorable. Later we went to Trader Joe's market for nuts and other goodies. When we returned, Ted went back outside to feed the squirrel. Close to an hour later he came back in the house and remarked how surprised he was that one little squirrel could eat so much. I explained to Ted that the squirrel was probably not eating all the nuts, that squirrels stored them up for the future. Then curiously, I asked Ted if he had noticed all the flowers blooming in my garden, many a brilliant yellow, his favorite color but he said no. So naturally I asked him what he saw when he went outside and he said he saw nothing! He told me he was in his head, as was usual. This time he was thinking the G# melodic minor scale.

Ted worked determinedly on his apartment reorganization, and although he spent more hours toiling away resolved to finish this project, it did not infringe too much on our time together. On a cold, windy April afternoon he came to visit and to fix Lucky, his oldest Tele, because I said that she was buzzing. He found me deliberating over alternative chords for my new arrangement of "Ol' Man River." When I mentioned that it took me a long time to figure out all my options for the guitar, he sat down and wrote me out a chart of chord choices I could easily reference by the soprano voice (top voice - root on top, 3rd on top, etc.), all the possibilities available to me (taking my hands into consideration, that is!) I watched basketball and played Lucky unplugged while he wrote. After he finished the reference chart, he began trying to repair Lucky's switch. This was a long, difficult and tedious process. He had brought the entire drawer full of guitar knobs and switches to my house. Fascinated by all the volume knobs, I took out them out and arranged them on the table. They looked so beautiful we photographed them. The rewiring was a success, he played Lucky and demonstrated the many sounds she was capable of producing. Soon we heard the squirrels arrive, there were now several, and Ted went out with nuts for all. He loved feeding them.

The beginning of "my" chord reference sheet

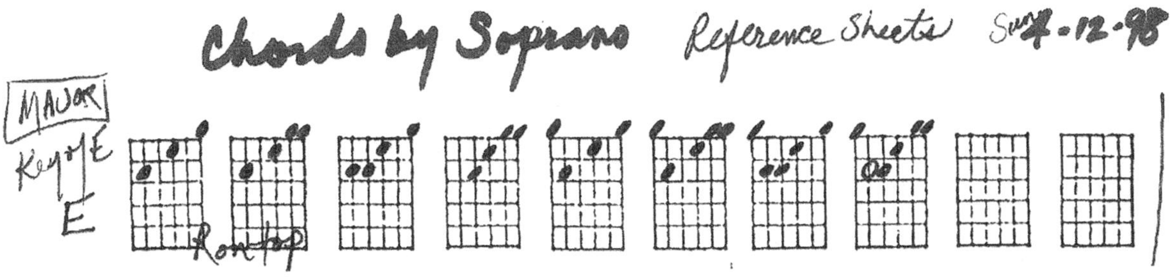

When Ted visited the next weekend, after we'd finished the crossword puzzle and played with the cats a bit, he became very despondent. There was nothing else he wanted to do but work on the apartment. I suggested we do just that, go over there and finally finish it. Nothing else I could have said would have pleased him more. We stopped to pick up spaghetti then went to his place. For eight hours straight we sorted through and made piles of related material and still did not finish! But he was happy we had made a lot of progress. Ted waited until we had finished for the night to surprise me with his new acquisition. During the week he had paid another visit to Norm's and had fallen in love with a '60 Gibson ES-5 Switchmaster, and there she was, so incredibly elegant, I dubbed her "The Lady."

● X □ △ ★

For a long time I had noticed that whenever we did errands, Ted was always in a hurry. This made no sense to me as we rarely had any time constraints, but still we rushed around almost frantically. This day he pulled me along walking at top speed, attempting to race through all our chores. Perhaps because it was such a beautiful day it seemed natural to me to slow down, enjoy being together and do our chores leisurely. Gently I expressed to Ted that rushing was very stressful for me, and asked him if it was necessary. He told me he didn't feel as if we were rushing and that this was his normal pace. However he told me he would try to slow down for me. When we got to Tower Records, I couldn't believe what I was seeing. As he got out of the car, he was moving so incredibly slowly, as if he was in "slow motion." At first I had no idea what he was doing, his movements almost looked like some form of T'ai Chi. He told me he was making a conscious effort to slow down. If it were anyone else I would have sworn they were mocking me, but Ted was completely serious. I mentioned to Ted that we could move at a normal pace and he said he had no conception of what normal was. He asked me to set the pace to show him, which I did. He had trouble keeping it, having a tendency to either slow way, way down again, or when he forgot, went back to rushing. It was very difficult for him to regulate himself. I thanked him for trying and mentioned how this would take time and practice.

Towards the end of April, Guitar Player Magazine invited Ted to participate in an upcoming Wes Montgomery article. Ted spent many hours writing and rewriting the article, refining it to what he considered perfection, attaining a balance of informative reading laced with his unique humor. To do an in-depth study of Wes' playing he brought over a bag full of Wes CDs to listen to and share with me. Four hours passed, as we lay sprawled on the floor, mesmerized, in awe. Wes was truly brilliant!

There was one last Wes CD he needed, so after listening, we were off to Tower Records. The Sherman Oaks store didn't have the one he needed, so we headed to Tower in Woodland Hills, came to Best Buy first, stopped there and found the Wes CD plus a bunch of movies. After that excursion he was tired, and we returned home.

At that time, our cat Cocoa had been missing for three days. I had become very despondent and was beginning to give up hope. Ted tried to remain optimistic, and reassuring. Despite Ted's efforts, and the distraction of our Wes immersion and subsequent excursion, I was still worried and sad.

It wasn't long before the Wes article was finished. Ted and I went to Lori's house so we could fax it to the publisher. At Lori's we visited and talked a while and Ted wrote a cover letter. Lori's fax machine was very slow, it took a long time before the entire hand written article finally went through. Ted was not convinced it worked. As a precaution, he wanted to go to Kinko's to re-fax the article. He was frantic and also totally exhausted, but the craziness wasn't fully manifested until we got to Kinko's and the fax wouldn't go through because Kinko's fax machine was broken, which made him completely nuts. He insisted he would never fax anything again and maintained it was a ridiculous way to transmit information. I tried to explain but gave up. The next morning I got a call from the magazine confirming that they had received the fax (from Lori's machine). I immediately related the message to Ted, who was totally relieved.

By this time our hopes had faded that Cocoa would ever return. In less than a year we'd lost both Cocoa and Mocha. Ted had feared this might happen, as both cats had not been domesticated at an early age. We supposed we should find a companion for Quincy. Neither of us felt emotionally strong enough to utilize the local animal shelters. Eventually, after unsuccessful visits to several large pet adoption agencies, I became quite discouraged and very distraught. Ted suggested some small pet shops. Back at my house, Ted looked in the phone book and called a pet store, and was informed that there were five kittens available, including one orange tabby. We dashed over there; it was love at first sight with the orange tabby. Back home and exhausted, we plopped on the couch as the kitten made itself right at home. Ted came up with the name Pumpkin, which I loved. Soon Quincy came home as well, and we watched as Quincy tentatively followed the kitten everywhere. Thus began the period of adjustment. We also had made the decision to keep our cats inside at night. Our beloved Cocoa was never to return home.

As the end of May 1998 neared, I was down to 1 mg. of Prednisone and full of trepidation about completely withdrawing from this drug for fear that my respiratory problems would recur. Dr. F had prescribed it for the rheumatic problems, but inadvertently it worked for my respiratory problems as well. He felt that the Prednisone had helped in the area he had prescribed it for but was reluctant to keep me on such a powerful drug. He suggested I see a pulmonary specialist if I wanted to continue taking this medication for my respiratory problems.

At the beginning of June, Ted received the galleys for the Guitar Player Wes article. Sadly they had cut out more than half of what he wrote and almost all the warmth and humor was gone. The magazine was to be issued on the 24th of June. On top of that bad news, I started getting very sick.

The next day, when Ted arrived I was still in bed, so we just read and watched some TV; I was coughing a lot despite taking some medicine. Ted dealt with it pretty well, I was glad for his calming influence. Before he left to go home he went to the market, brought me back soup and yogurt but I couldn't eat.

When Ted returned the following day I was still coughing a lot, and was barely able to talk. After watching the Chicago Bulls win their 6th championship, *"Game 3: Astonishing Chicago Bulls 40 points over Utah Jazz. Barb better just watching this,"* we watched and loved the movie "As Good as it Gets." Despite his enjoyment, the movie brought Ted much concern over his own obsessive behavior. He had so many questions and I had to reassure him more than once he was not as extreme as the movie. He knew this but he needed to know just how "weird" he was. I knew we still had much to discuss.

Now that the Wes article was completed, Ted became all consumed by his apartment organization project again. He stressed the issue of needing even more time to finish the apartment and of course didn't have a clue as to how much longer this would take. He told me he wouldn't be coming here as often until the project was completed, and pleaded with me to lend him my support. I was very distressed about having less time with him under these circumstances, but it was futile to discuss this rationally. It was virtually impossible for me to get him to realize it was in fact obsessive/compulsive to be constantly stacking and restacking, moving things from one room to another. He was in complete denial, he justified his reorganizing as productive, truly believed there was an end. But after five years, I now had my doubts. However since he implored me for more time now, convinced that this time he would indeed finish if I accommodated him, I conceded to his wishes. Although Ted knew I was upset, he so graciously worded in his datebook, "*Barb tries so hard to make me comfortable & happy during this apartment renovation period. No one could ask for a better life partner. She's almost all well now after that bronchitis, and so much happier now that the weather is sunny and warm again."*

● X □ △ ★

Bought from a student on July 3rd, Ted termed his purchase as a *"Rescue mission: Buy 1958 #6782 X-350 (Chubbie)"* Ted came here in the mid-afternoon with "Chubbie" who was beautiful. First he played her for me then proceeded to work on filing the nut, got it right and put her aside. Then he worked on the original "uncut" version of the Wes article, which he planned to hand out to his students. There were just a few notes to add before making copies. Our plan was to drop off the article at Kinko's, do marketing, pick up the article then go home for dinner and a movie. However when we got to Kinko's, Ted's fastidious nature prevented him from trusting them to do the work. Due to the close margins, placement was precarious, I realized this was going to take a long time, and I was a little irritable. Finally I took the Bronco and went home. He would call me when he was done. I ate some dinner, got the cats in and tried to read, but couldn't concentrate for thinking about Ted and our day together so far. Of course we hadn't planned any of this. I began to feel sad, he had been there forty-five minutes already; I missed him and decided not to wait. So I drove back to Kinko's to lend him my support, for which he was very grateful. Amazingly he was almost done.

My health had never completely returned after the Prednisone withdrawal. I had been seeing a pulmonary specialist and trying other alternatives to no avail. Fortunately Dr. P finally conceded and prescribed a low dose of Prednisone, which I was to remain on indefinitely. Ted and I were understandably relieved, as this drug had worked wonders for me. That night we watched a TV special on allergies I had taped. Afterwards Ted fooled around with the tape, dubbed the segment onto another tape and in the process showed me all the "tricks" he'd learned about dubbing. He loved to juxtapose shows, small pieces of shows, fragments and especially voices. He was really interested in voice modulation and pitch and spent a lot of time trying to determine what key people spoke in, and now he could do this quite accurately.

One warm summer day, after a slew of errands we went back to my place intending to watch a movie but ended up talking for a long while about many things. I questioned him about how he felt neglecting his special talents for so long while he focused on putting his apartment in order. I stressed that his distinctive gifts were such an important part of his being and should be the focal point. He realized this, but said he needed "order" first before he could focus on anything else. We talked a long time and the discussion led to other obsessions he had dealt with and how eventually they were resolved, which was mostly by being replaced by another obsession. Fortunately, many times his deep passion for music would eventually consume him completely again. He told me if he thought he'd be putting his apartment in order the rest of his life he'd not want to live (and was serious about this). Feeling my dismay, and even some doubt creeping in, Ted suggested I not return to the apartment until it was finished, totally organized. It was now early August 1998. He told me the project would be done by his September birthday. I speculated it would take until the end of the year, if not longer. This was a very difficult situation to deal with, and we were both sad. From that day on, we rarely spent any time together at his apartment. A new chapter in our relationship was about to begin.

New Arrangements and Adjustments

(1998-1999)

How could I have comprehended at that time the consequences of spending all our time together at my house? On the other hand, Ted must have deliberated over the situation during the ensuing week since he thought about all the things at his apartment that I loved and would most likely miss having available to enjoy. There were also many things at his apartment that he had put aside especially intended for us to share, and with only good intentions, decided all of those things should be kept at my house. These were charming and heart felt gestures on Ted's part, and for a long while I did not consider it could be a problem.

The next Saturday Ted appeared extremely cheerful as he came in with a huge rectangular case. He said he had brought a Fender Jazzmaster. Since I had rarely heard him play one, I was curious to hear the differences in tone quality. He laid the case on the floor, flipped open the latches, lifted the lid and instead of a Jazzmaster, there was the beautiful thin Gibson, a 1960's ES125TCD, cherry sunburst, "Cherrima!" He had decided to surprise me and leave her with me to be loved. She had always been one of my absolute favorites; the joy brought tears. When he plugged her in and showed me all the possible sounds she could get, I was simply blissful. Then he handed her to me and brought in the real Jazzmaster. When he began to play I noticed the deep rich tone it had and he played so beautifully. I'd missed hearing him play, as it had been such a long time and I didn't want to go on errands because I wanted him to continue playing. He promised to continue when we returned. Wonderfully, all our errands turned into fun and delightful excursions. This was a fabulous day; we shared so much happiness in mutual enjoyment of all we did. Just the kind of day we needed after so much anxiety over the apartment situation.

The following weekend Ted arrived with four shopping bags full of videos. He told me he had worked twelve hours straight sorting videos yesterday. He sat on the couch and emptied the bags, and told me about the great shows in store for us. Afterwards he brought the videos into my extra bedroom, which I used as a studio. He sat down on the floor and began putting them in the three large built-in drawers I told him he could use. The whole process involved much deliberation about the best order in which to store them and he sorted and filed them by drawer. I sat and observed for a while and was fascinated by his determination to arrange them in the most logical and optimal manner. During the process he said he was starved so I put potatoes in the oven and he finished the drawers by the time his food was ready. We ate dinner and read the newspaper. Was he even aware that he had spent more than four hours sorting videos?

That he spent almost the entire weekend, first at his apartment, then at my house sorting through videos was astonishing to me. He tried to reassure me he was more than half way through them and again mentioned it was taking longer than he had anticipated. I offered no comment. He liked that answer. He said although he had sorted through his videos many times in the past he had never done it right, so this would be the final process. Also he assured me he wouldn't be bringing over this many again. The space I allotted him was almost full anyway and now we had enough here to last at least a year or two. But he was so excited about all the wonderful tapes we had to watch it touched my heart.

Ted called the following evening to tell me he finally had sorted through every single one of his videos, thousands, and had put them in related piles. Now he thought the hardest part was finished and just needed to figure out where to put them. He wanted to store some here that he may never watch. I thought maybe we could put them in the file boxes he had stored in the garage. I had begun to fear I would suffer from a sense of clutter if I continued to allow him to fill up every inch of space in my house.

In spite of working resolutely on his apartment, Ted still found time for his music studies. Here is an example he began in April and continued again in September. This particular procedure or more aptly "process of elimination" had the same calming influence as doing a puzzle, plus the added benefit of organizing the thoughts in his mind.

The beginning of Ted's Diatonic 7-Note Scales Chords organizational sheet:

Later in the month, I learned how Ted's apartment organization frenzy had manifested again with such fury. We lay on the couch and talked for over an hour about his anxieties, about his compulsion to put his apartment in order, the books he wanted to write, and how he could cope with performing in the future. Then Ted reminded me about a comment I made earlier in the year. It was this: I said since I'd known him he had never completed anything he started. I remembered saying it in frustration and perhaps to give him impetus to finish one of his books. However, that one comment had disturbed him so much more than I ever anticipated. Now he was impelled to finish all he started, and the apartment was first on the list. All because of that one statement I made. He said it kept floating over and over through his mind. Oh why did I say that? Perhaps out of exasperation, but the repercussions were disastrous! He stressed he couldn't be happy until he finished organizing his apartment.

Of course it was impossible for him to realize it might never be done, because each week he acquired more "stuff" compounding the ever-growing problem. He knew it added up but couldn't see it making that much of a difference. How could he not see that with countless new guitars and amplifiers, videotapes, books, and fifty new magazines added each month? I was exasperated. What, if anything, could I do to help him? I was at a total loss for fear of completely alienating him. I was depressed about the whole situation. This compulsion had been consuming him now for months and was beginning to wear him down physically and mentally. It seemed to be getting worse and worse. He truly saw an eventual end but I saw a cycle, and I gently tried to point this out. I reminded him that at one time or another each room had been completed, and then compromised. He finished one room, but when he began another the completed room would get messed up again. I did not think he had enough space for everything; conversely he thought he did, if only he could arrange it right.

These discussions regarding his continuous accumulation of goods and the ramifications seemed endless and futile. In my effort to try to get him to understand his actions I kept groping for examples. One day I explained it was not just the apartment. I mentioned that if we considered all the cars on the road, not one would look like Betsy or the Bronco inside. He agreed it had gotten out of hand but that he couldn't help it. He said he had been this way since he was a child. Then he expressed his incessant lament that it was taking longer than he thought. I used that as my case in point, initially he thought he'd be finished by his September 26th birthday, which was yesterday. Now he realized he wouldn't, but still thought just a few more months. I told him I would remind him in a few months so he could assess the situation again. Perhaps this way he would come to the realization it was a never-ending process, and modify his behavior to some degree. We would not talk about it again until the end of the year.

● X □ △ ★

Mid-fall baseball play-off time, Ted here and straight to the TV! " *Barb & I watch and highly enjoy the San Diego Padres (underdogs) in their home park before 50-60,000 rabid fans! over the Braves - Padres lead series 3-0"* Ted was ecstatic. Then we watched an episode of Guiding Light from Friday. (Yes, he had gotten hooked on a soap opera!) He said he'd already seen it but could watch it again. In fact he told me he watched some scenes over and over sometimes because he wanted to understand how certain emotions were conveyed through subtleties. He realized the character had conveyed an emotion but he couldn't always determine exactly what the character did, either through gesture or expression. I found this extremely fascinating, and it made total sense, as it emphasized his perpetual interest in studying people. I had wanted to discuss it but by then the second baseball game had already started and Ted's beloved Cleveland Indians were losing.

Towards the end of the evening Ted became a little pensive about his upcoming interview the next day for the Lenny Breau documentary. Providentially it went very well, as Ted noted, *"Oct. 11 Lenny Breau interview for the documentary on his life. Emily Hughes (his daughter) interviews me on film & I explain certain things about Lenny's style & demonstrate (on Luscious & Lulu) & reminisce. Good vibe with the whole experience."*

The documentary on Lenny Breau's life was completed in 1999 and made available for a short time.

Well in advance, many plans were already being made for Ted's participation during the NAMM show weekend (a major musical instrument trade show) in January 1999. Ted had gotten a call from John Pisano offering Ted the opportunity to give a workshop for Guild Guitars at Papashon one evening during the long event-filled weekend. The idea was well received by Ted and he eagerly agreed to do this.

Although the NAMM show was months away, Ted's yearly gig at the Reagan Library was forthcoming and both seemed to inspire a considerable amount of practicing and new discoveries. Ted wrote, *"More wonderful colors of film music through (rhythm pattern) in Lydian and much else, Overtone dominant counterpoint: 2 & 3 voice, and 4 voice: oblique motion with 2 primary moving ones & 2 stationary. A first for me too on some of these."*

Ted's gig at the Reagan Library proved to be a very enlightening experience, which he also noted in his datebook, *"Reagan Library gig 6-9pm. (Ruby & creme deluxe) Some break throughs: This is the first time I was successfully able to play SOLO guitar versions of open hand & maybe pick & fingers too (did I?) a) Drifter's tunes b) Shirelles c) From This Moment On with a spontaneous groovy churning bass underneath with almost a "When You Dance" (1955) feel."*

Then shortly after, on a beautiful October afternoon, with the sun streaming through the windows, together we cuddled on the bed and settled in for Game 1 of the World Series (Yankees/Padres). We remained there for the entire game, except when he briefly got up to make popcorn. When he returned both cats had curled up on the bed with me. He handed me the popcorn and joined us. That was a blissful moment, and I told him, just the combination of him, the cats, the popcorn, and the game, blended into a perfect serenity. I felt so much love and affection for him and from him. How I wish I could have stopped time then and there, on that rare trouble-free and ideal day.

Usually after being away from his apartment for any excessive length of time (about15 hours), Ted would begin to get irritable. When this anxiety happened he had an overwhelming need to be alone. One evening I noticed this anxiety beginning to manifest. He sat at the table for a moment to write a note to my dad in a special magazine he'd gotten for him. As he was writing I pointed out that I was aware of the change in him and said as I hugged him, "Poor baby needs to be alone, he's had enough for the day." This caused him to smile and even relax. The fact that I had recognized and pointed out the mood change, even pin-pointed when it happened seemed to have alleviated it, (Wow! I considered this a major breakthrough). The barrier that always went up after a certain amount of hours finally began to collapse this time. He noticed the crossword puzzle and pulled it over to glance at the few remaining unsolved clues and between the two of us we solved all but one! Very satisfying. Then a more relaxed, less anxious Ted expressed his gratitude with an abundance of hugs before he left.

In mid-November a major dilemma developed. The new tenants in the apartment above him were driving him to distraction with loud and constant noise. Ted was totally distressed and almost at his wits end. By Thanksgiving it was still going on, and he arrived here very early to escape the constant clamor. With his oldest Telecaster, the 1951 'Lucky' in tow and in need of minor repair, he completed the procedure while we watched the touching "Thanksgiving" episode of Guiding Light. Pleased with Lucky's sound now he noted, *"What a sound, like a stand up bass with a throaty ES-5 on top."* Then we had to rouse ourselves to join my parents in a combination Thanksgiving Day and birthday celebration. Ted gave my mom the multi-CD box set, "Ella Sings Gershwin Songbook" with arrangements by Nelson Riddle and she was overjoyed by this gift. Then I encouraged my dad to entertain us by playing his wonderful original songs on the piano. He was glad to comply with my request, and really enjoyed that we all loved his songs.

Later that evening back at my house, I cherished the fact that I could offer Ted a sanctuary from the turmoil his life had become and that he could relax here so comfortably. But being driven from his apartment meant that he could not continue his organization project, and it was sad to see him almost resigned at times, and occasionally totally despondent. The organization project was far from completion as the end of the year rapidly approached.

At the beginning of December, Ted called early one evening with the sad news that George Van Eps had died a few days ago. (Ted's beloved mentor had died on Nov. 29, 1998). Ted was decidedly sad but accepted it. Then he called back to ask if it was okay to come over after teaching. Of course it was! He canceled his last student and was here by 9 p.m., visibly tired. Due to the new upstairs neighbors waking him at all hours, it was now almost impossible for him to sleep at his apartment. He absolutely couldn't continue to live that way and was waiting until after his gig at Papashon to concentrate on finding a solution. Yes, his gig with Cathy Segal-Garcia on December 10th loomed soon and they had hardly rehearsed. However, he was calmer about it than I'd expected, maybe too tired to feel much anxiety. I figured the coming weekend I'd just feed him, let him sleep and practice if he wanted. I loved him so, so much and wished I could do more to help him, to make his life easier, less stressful.

The day before his gig at Papashon Ted came here in the early afternoon to try different amps and guitars so he could determine what to bring. He brought out the Peavey Ltd. 400 (his old favorite), and began to experiment with various guitars: Granny(X50), Amber (late '80s X170) tuned to Eb, Duane Eddy, Mambo (Jazzmaster) & Deedee (M75). Mambo didn't work at all in that amp - buzzing. Amber and the Duane Eddy both sounded great but DeeDee got the most exceptional sound. He continued to play her, his playing was exquisite, all the right ingredients, hands supple and coordinated from practice with beautiful tone quality. He played for many hours and the music became increasingly more moving, his emotion poured into it culminating with "You'll Never Walk Alone" which brought tears to ***his*** eyes, a most desirable and satisfying goal for him. He said when that happened he had reached the place he was striving for musically. It was absolutely incredible! At that point he said he must tear himself away or he would never stop.

Lori and I got to Papashon early to have dinner and by the time the show began the restaurant was filled to capacity. I thought Ted and Cathy blended beautifully together and Ted played brilliantly. Everyone there was riveted to his every nuance. He generally held back but on occasion threw in some fine jewels. Ted's accompaniment accentuated the deep sensual qualities of Cathy's voice. The show lasted until 11 p.m. About that night Ted somewhat humorously penned, *"Dec. 10 AN INTENSE EXPERIENCE TONIGHT. My old dear friend Banana Creme tuned to Eb with the creme blonde Deluxe Reverb. (I'm shocked, this is still my best set up Tele with 3 pick ups, tuned down) Cathy charms the crowd, we have some really gorgeous moments & also some really deep bluesy ones. Sadly many just O.K. or whoa, how'd we get thru that in spots too. But the people overall applauded & cheered and due to their fervent wish to be enraptured, were. And I did catch some magic shimmering moments that just hung in the air & thrilled the crowd it seemed, so gratitude is in order. So much love in the room, this out weighs my reservations."*

After a busy and stress-filled week, as soon as Ted arrived he went into the bedroom to take a much needed nap. Later when I heard him stirring, I got on the bed and snuggled up next to him. It was then after thinking and verbalizing his distress over performing he came to the conclusion *"I tell Barb that I think I'm most comfortable here with her in her house, and she is touched."* I *was* so very touched, and asked him "more than anyplace in the whole world?" and he said yes. I told him I felt the same way. I wasn't sure if he would ever be able to experience this feeling and it was such an incredibly wonderful moment. To me this marked a major milestone in our relationship. His ability to "just completely be himself" with me and be completely comfortable in doing so even astonished him. He commented, *"We are so lucky."*

A lovely couple of holiday weeks intervened, but on New Year's Eve when Ted arrived he told me the noise from upstairs had been intolerable that day. We relaxed for a little while and then before it got too late Ted went out to get cigs and stop at the newsstand. In the interim I read, and then realized he had been gone a rather long time, just then the phone rang, it was Ted. The Bronco had broken down; he was stuck at the newsstand. I rushed to pick him up and we left the Bronco there. Once home we figured we would deal with everything tomorrow if possible. We just laid around watched a little TV but we were tired, decided to nap and ended up sleeping 'til 11:55 pm just in time to see the ball drop in Times Square.

When I awoke around 6 a.m. on that first day of 1999, Ted was sitting on the couch with the TV on. I made myself coffee; Ted opted for hot water and an orange. Around 9 a.m. we called the Auto Club, met the tow truck at the newsstand and had the Bronco towed back here. As it was New Year's Day there was nothing else to be done, which was just as well. My parents came by for a short visit, surprised us with spaghetti from Barone's restaurant and played with the cats. But mostly we just lazed around, watched TV and had a lovely and relaxing day. I was overjoyed about Ted being comfortable here in excess of 24 hours!

Most of the month, other than teaching, Ted worked on organizing his apartment. He was still very distressed by the incessant clatter from the neighbors above him, many nights it was agonizing for him to remain at his place. Therefore, after his last student, he would come spend the evenings with me. He would stay until the quiet hours of early morning offered him the opportunity to return to his apartment and work there in peace prior to beginning his teaching day.

Ted began a "Catalogue of Bach's Melodic Moves" for both of us.

● X □ △ ★

The NAMM show was a week away. Ted began making preparations for his seminar and the George Van Eps Tribute, which he detailed in his datebook, "*Back to Barb. Begin going over & compiling a prospective list of tunes for the George Van Eps tribute concert at Papashon on Sat. night.*" For seminar: "*Solo guitar pick-style driving rhythm guitar plus tune melody, include at least 1selection 'double Green'.*" Ted described his "double Green" style in the Jan. 29 seminar notes.

Other than the NAMM show preparations, we enjoyed many amusements that weekend as well. I defer to Ted's notes; *"Sat. Jan. 23 Barb & I try to finish (1953) "The Jazz Singer" but alas, the music is too good! & we end up trying to figure it out. Some cues are definitely Max Steiner. Play Savannah, the '57 X-150 Savoy whom we most certainly adore. Barb makes potato pancakes for us. Sun. Jan. 24 we just about finish a very tough Sunday N.Y. Times crossword puzzle, 2 squares vacant. Finish The Jazz Singer. I am so thrilled that Barbara loves all this same music, same songs, same cues, independently!"*

That we shared identical reactions to the same exact moments in movies, and music cues never failed to absolutely stun Ted.

Ted's Transcriptions from "The Jazz Singer"

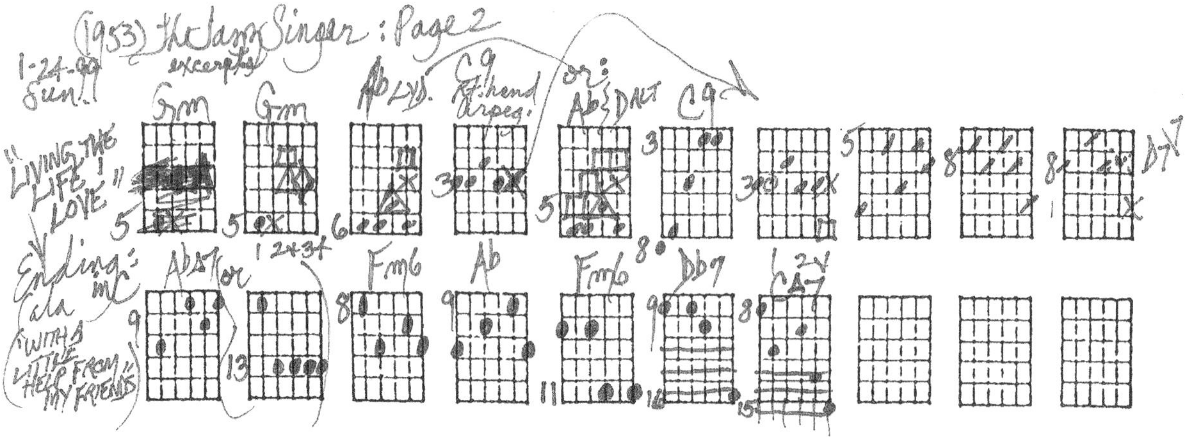

The days sailed by and the event-filled weekend was soon upon us. Ted had a very full schedule. Friday night he would be giving a seminar at Papashon. Saturday day he would be playing for Fender/Guild at the NAMM show, and Saturday night at Papashon he was participating in the George Van Eps Tribute.

Ted wrote rather comprehensive notes about his Friday night seminar, *"Jan. 29 NAMM Show Weekend (hired by Guild/Fender) Friday Night Seminar: Topics covered by request & my own initiation:* ***1.)*** *The near foolproof method for learning all scales in all positions: descending from the pinky. 2.) How to memorize chords, a) hook the new to the old friends, b) Visual roots: mandatory, 3) My Voicing System up to V-10, 4) My double "G" style: simultaneous pick style 'Freddie Green & me, Ted' Greene me on melody, the rhythmic diverseness, suggestions & demonstrations for solo guitar using "Here's That Rainy Day" 5) 'Andrews Sisters' chime chords. 4 Guilds though the supplied Fender amps, I bring Brandy (who feeds back), Savannah (likewise), Deedee (who sounds cool except in the weak 1st string) & the Duane Eddy. Analysis: My playing was just average or worse except for my 'double G' stuff on 'Foggy Day' & 'Stompin at the Savoy' Public debut: Savannah"*

That night I brought my journal with me and wrote my own notes about the evening, later Ted slightly embellished and amended them. Ted's notes are shown here in bold italics. From my Journal, Ted's seminar:

> "We are now at Papashon's and the lighting for writing is miserable. Ted's attention is immediately taken by setting up his equipment (he brought Deedee, Savannah, the Duane Eddy and one more, who? ***(Brandy)*** and by numerous people vying for his attention. He was surprised ***extremely dismayed*** to find upon arrival here, that the room set aside for the seminar was "now" too small to accommodate the rather large crowd assembling for this event. So he is on a stage in a larger dining area and soon hundreds of people will be

descending upon us. It's a quarter to seven, hardly anyone is in the room but just now there's an announcement that everyone is welcome to enter and be seated. He seems slightly anxious but is hiding it well. The seminar is about to start. No one at first seems to be comfortable asking questions, Ted is comfortable, ***uncomfortable*** or so it seems and ***therefore*** tries humor, finally someone asks "how do you break down the fret board" which he explains through scale steps and easily digresses into other areas; pentatonic scales and where the same note exists. 2nd question - how do "you" remember all the chords, the massive amounts in his books for example - visual root - voicing systems - spacing's, another digression, "Teddy Greene" rhythms - segues into the quality of sound contingent on where one*'s **right hand is placed.*** He started on Deedee but for rhythmic examples went to Savannah. Someone wants him to play, just play a song so he switches to the Duane Eddy and renders a beautiful version of "Let it be Me." Then rhythmic variations on "Rainy Day" ***The normal & in essence here dismissed grooves being: a) ballad b) swing c) bossa 1. Gospel 3/4 2. jazz waltz 3. 12/8 gospel & doo-wop which is just south of jazz swing*** jazz waltz vs. gospel through phrasing. Question on harp harmonics - back to Deedee, which sounds fine. ***adequate.*** Then it's over.

Ted comes to sit with us. Earlier I had invited Ted's good friend William Perry, and his friend Ahndrea, to join us at the table reserved for us by the management. I'm also thinking about the seminar now that it's over and realizing that the atmosphere is not really appropriate for learning. He carried it a lot on his own, elaborating on the questions, and only having an hour to disseminate information is not long enough, even though Ted had planned and prepared material. Mundell Lowe sounds great, mellow and gets the "right" sound, I can't explain, hollow and deep woodsy like Gigi. ***Easy it's a 1965 aged Gigi (Bl. X 500 with mini-hums)"***

That night when we came home Ted was still energized, sat on the living room floor and played the X150 Savannah Savoy and sounded great! Generally after a performance, he was rarely pleased by the way he played. He would ruminate over the details, or other aspects that troubled him, for example the sound, amps, all the many areas for potential problems.

On Saturday Ted played at the NAMM show most of the day (Ted said I would "hate" being there, the crowd, the noise level) then in the evening played at Papashon for the George Van Eps tribute. I sure missed him, it was so rare not to be together on a Saturday and lately we had been spending a lot more time together. When Ted arrived, he said he missed me this week. He said it seemed a long interval between visits but in actuality it was only 3 1/2 days. About his day of playing at the NAMM show, Ted wrote, *"Saturday, JAN. 30 NAMM SHOW Play for Guild, Fender & DeArmond. The Duane Eddy & my prayer to make others happy really came through today! Drive Betsy, I bring the Duane Eddy (tuned down to Db) and Savannah ('57 X-150, stay in trunk). I begin like an hour & a half early and play for most of the next 4 to 5 hours!!! Great to be able to play soulfully for all these people. The Duane Eddy through a '65 Twin Reverb reissue really turned me on & I may never have played with more feeling & daring."*

Ted mentioned to me that he would understand if I didn't feel like going to the George Van Eps Tribute as it would be very crowded and would begin at a late hour. But Saturday evening there was no question about going to support Ted, I loved him and wanted to be there for him. It was that simple. When I arrived it was so crowded! William and Andrea spotted me, I waited with them and fortuitously they'd reserved a table. The tribute didn't even get started until close to 11 pm. All the performers were situated in a small waiting room near the stage. I sensed Ted was uncomfortable just glancing at him through the glass in the waiting room. It was a while before he even noticed I'd come. When it was time for him to play he stunned the crowd with exquisite renditions of 1) Embraceable You, 2) One For My Baby, 3) Girl with the Flaxen Hair. The crowd went crazy. Afterwards he went back into the glass "waiting room" for a while before he joined us. He greeted me with a warm, loving kiss and I think a sense of relief. We sat and listened, everyone who played that night was great. The show lasted until 1 a.m. Ted had gone back into the waiting room and was surrounded by admirers. I felt so proud of him, so moved by everyone's reverence for him. Here are his thoughts from the tribute, *"Saturday night, Papashon - George Van Eps Tribute Night and Concert, Surprise: Barbara attending! Also attending: George's daughter Kay, George's grandson, Scott (Scott's Lullaby) who tells me that I was likely his grandfather's favorite pupil, such a heart warming thing. Howard Alden (he sounded JUST like George up there!). I chat with audience, reminisce about George & play 'Embraceable You' "One for my Baby' (on the Duane Eddy) Kay tells me later that "Embraceable You" was her mom & dad's song!!! 'Girl with the Flaxen Hair' on my '54 Banana Creme Esquire".*

What a weekend for Ted! He told me the NAMM show was a major highlight in his life. He admitted to playing brilliantly there (a rare admission from him) and it thrilled me that hundreds of people experienced the epitome of that brilliance. The atmosphere (his booth), the amp (twin reverb) was conducive to his achieving the sound he wanted and loved, and he felt comfortable. Now, of course I wish I'd been there to share that, but mainly I was so incredibly happy that it happened for him.

Although the NAMM show weekend was for the most part a joyous experience for Ted, events of that nature always brought a high degree of stress. Compounded by the stress from his upstairs neighbors, Ted subsequently caught a bad cold. The following Monday I called him when I thought he would be finished teaching, he was in a bad mood and answered the phone "I can't say another word." I said okay just listen, and I briefly explained about how he could use soundproofing. He insisted it must completely block noise, not just muffle it. Then he mentioned that the noise was so intolerable, there was a ninety percent chance he would have to move. I did not comment about that during our conversation. What he didn't realize was the nature of his situation. If he did move to a new apartment, any new manager that saw the inside of his apartment would not allow it to remain in that condition. He was very lucky that Ralph, the manager of the El Dorado, was so tolerant and understanding. Really lucky.

For the next few days he tried earplugs, slept a little but finally couldn't take it anymore. The disturbance from above was interminable. When he got here he was extremely stressed and his cold had worsened. Feeling chilled he was drawn to the warmth of the bedroom, where alone in the quiet he could think. I heard him speaking on the phone and later he told me he had called Ralph and implored him to take some action. Ralph promised to deal with the problem at the earliest opportunity. Ted was somewhat placated by the conversation, but remained skeptical. At least he had been able to vent some frustrati[illegible] We stayed in bed until two in the morning reading, sleeping, or watching TV. He a[illegible] worked on the George Van Eps tribute article for Just Jazz Guitar magazine. We enjo[illegible] ourselves, laughed a lot and he got some much-needed rest.

In mid February, Ted received his yearly check, and new guitars consumed most [illegible] the weekend. *"To VOLTAGE: Lloyd shows me his '63 blonde DE 500. Mid '70s M[illegible] Aristocrat, 'Francesca' "Franny" dark Italian looking sunburst, not unlike Danette X-[illegible] from '58. Home & tell her, then at her pleading: bring Franny over to show her. Work [illegible] setting up the little baby, rubber grommets to help isolate & boost of the neck pick up. T[illegible] switch around correctly, file nut slots. We watch Thurs. & Fri. Guiding Light: Dramatic!*[illegible]

"To Voltage: for the amazing 1976 X-500 Blonde #144 & 1971 T-100D SB #51, and bring them to Barb, show her the X-500 1st in the SUN. She reacts as I did: complete ecstasy over its stunning beauty, gorgeous tone and wonderful feel! Wow! 6:00 Surprise 25th Anniversary Party at Leon & Judy's, a beautiful gathering of their friends & their 2 beautiful now seemingly grown up kids." During the day we took photos of the new guitars and played a bit, but soon it was time to leave. We had to be at Leon and Judy's by six for the surprise party. We parked around the corner and down the block but to *our* surprise, ran into them as we were walking up the driveway. They had a knowing look but were really glad to see us. They continued walking, as their kids, Christopher and Megan needed to get them out of the house. We went inside to help out a bit before the other guests arrived. The party turned out to be a small, intimate gathering of friends. The house was filled with warmth, sentimental reminiscence and laughter. Leon and Judy were so pleased and grateful to be surrounded by their closest friends to celebrate their 25th anniversary.

Then during the week Ted had a wonderful visit with Norman Harris and made another new irresistible purchase, *"go to Norm's: he asks for a little written piece for his new book about to appear, we b.s. I come up with something, which we're both pleased with. The 1977 blonde Guild Artist Award (#149723) has a beautiful warm voice, especially breath taking when played with thumb far away from the bridge. I've tried to resist this guitar on 4 or 5 prior occasions but she calls me too strongly and I take her home. (also the 1958 ES-225 TD SB is a total knockout)."*

● X □ △ ★

On March 24th, all my plans for the day came to an abrupt halt when I received a phone call from my closest friend Lori. She had been in a very bad car accident in Ventura County, was in the emergency hospital and wasn't sure of the extent of her injuries. Her family and I drove up there. After an interminable wait, tests revealed a fractured neck and emergency surgery was scheduled. During the operation I called Ted with the shocking news. After another seemingly interminable wait we finally saw her wheeled out of the operating room and the news was encouraging. The operation was thought to be successful. I got back to L.A. around midnight. A day later Ted and I drove to Ventura to visit her in the hospital. She looked much better and although the recovery would take a long time, she was expected to be fine.

And Ted caught yet another cold. But on the bright side we had new guitars to cherish and J.S. Bach's Musical Offering re-entered our life, this time it inspired a passionate desire to explore and analyze all the components. Ted's cold lingered for a month, and he was finally prescribed some antibiotics.

A short time later by Parcel Post special delivery, *"SANDY" arrives '72 T-100D blonde #71486 from Arpeggio Music in Pennsylvania. She's beautiful, but will need quite a bit of set up work in order to work with heavy strings, although she sounds very good even with lights."* She came all the way from Pennsylvania in a day by plane to my door. I loved unwrapping those packages. So here she sat, loose strings, bridge out of place and unplayable. Pretty blonde maple, almost flawless and around twenty years old, Ted had told me. No sooner did I choose what to use the remaining evening hours for, Ted arrived with yet another guitar; Smoky. His upstairs neighbors had come home so he made a hasty exit to avoid confrontation. He was hot, stressed but settled down. He'd brought Smoky to try the pick guard on the new guitar. He opened the case, approved, tightened the strings, placed the bridge properly and was able to attain pleasant and desirable sounds. Then began a long process of working on her, a process initially deemed easy.

Chapter IV

Sharing a Home
(1999-2000)

It was May 1999, and at this juncture in our lives, besides our weekends, Ted was coming here every evening after teaching. He would generally arrived around seven, as if he were just "coming home" after work. Almost every evening I would fix us dinner. Eating was always accompanied by reading, usually a music book. Later, with the TV always on, at times just in the background, there might be the Lakers or baseball and he would quietly practice, continue reading or do other work. Some nights when I grew weary, I would get in bed, read and listen to him play until I fell asleep. This was basically our new routine, with some variations. Due to the new neighbors above him, all his plans for organizing the apartment had once again come to an abrupt halt.

Despite the apartment problem, which Ted viewed as only a temporary setback, he utilized the time to work on ideas for new books he intended to write. Some nights, much to my delight I'd find Ted excited about writing again. *"Breakthrough in Baroque classification for my book: 2 voice counterpoint, 2 intervals (2 units) at a time, 2 to 1 motion (oblique motion) in one voice only at a time, 3rds & 2nds (and of course 2nds & 3rds) 8 + 8 = 16 motifs available. Bring Barb a new 'Bach of the week' a collection of Bach's greatest organ preludes, fugues & fantasias (The Great...). More work on Sandy."*

Other nights, Ted would bring bags of music to sort through and get distracted by some forgotten project he rediscovered. One time he was experimenting with different types of harmonization on the Musical Offering theme, another time it was Bach's 48 Preludes and Fugues, always coming up with some outstanding possibilities. I found this note on the table one morning: *"Barbara darling, Thought you might like to follow along w/those great Bischoff editions on certain fav. pieces that capture your fancy. Try the C#mi fugue it's slow... be patient you'll be amazed at the writing. Love, Theo"*

Bach's Musical Offering ala Ted 5/18/99

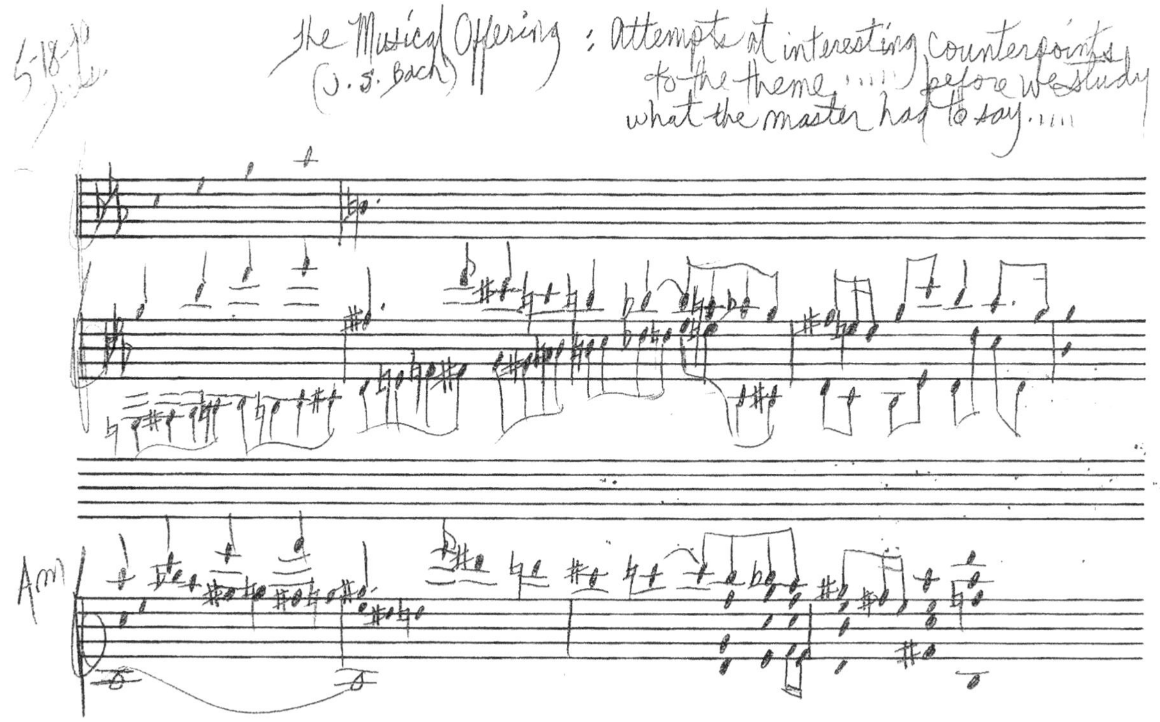

One evening I was in a very bad mood and I wanted to watch the Lakers but Ted's priority was a show he needed to tape, which he said he must monitor. While he was doing that, we listened to a John Williams CD, then Salsa Caliente. Both were great but after the show he was taping had ended, he became further distracted by going through stuff he bought at Tower. By then my mood had gotten worse and had begun to affect him. To stop this cycle, I fixed us each a whisky & 7up (Ted's favorite and a very rare indulgence), and somehow we ended up learning how to read a marked deck of cards and marveling at how we could amaze our friends. Feeling better, we ordered dinner from Ameci's, ate and watched some fabulous old Tom & Jerry cartoons until Ted fell asleep. This is what I had to remember: Not only did Ted derive his pleasure vicariously but also his sadness and other negative emotions. He was literally a sponge of my moods so I had to be extra careful. I knew this! I knew this! It was so just hard sometimes.

By the end of May it was basketball playoffs, other amusements, and little change in our routine. One afternoon we watched the Knicks at Pacers during which Ted made adjustments to a guitar, *"Work on Stella II's bridge pick up, surprises abound, but no true rectification of its weakness - the shock is it measures out at somewhat the same as Deedee's strong pick ups."*

After the game, I asked Ted if we could watch a movie with Ronald Reagan in it, as I wanted to see him as an actor, Ted put on "Knute Rockne," but the music and those arrangements were much more captivating than the movie, we got through less than half of it. Even I knew we wouldn't finish this one, it was close to midnight and this time I was the one falling asleep.

Then the following evening we tried to watch the rest of the "Knute Rockne" movie but Ted kept stopping the tape for various reasons other than music. I mentioned that he was stopping the tape too many times, which ruined the continuity. At first he seemed annoyed then realized how many of the moments he wanted to point out were of little consequence. He got very upset with himself because of his "quirkiness" and not understanding why he was that way. He wrote, *"my crazed idiosyncratic ways of stopping the tape to re-watch too many little things gets in the way. I make a decision to not inflict this on Barb anymore - enough is enough."*

This need to stop the tape wasn't new, but he used to do it almost exclusively to hear a musical phrase or chords. Now it had escalated to include his obsession with vocal mannerisms, nuance and anything unusual to him. I think his intrigue over vocal inflection began about a year ago, but it had increased considerably over the recent months. Many times his focus was not on what was being said, he was not paying attention to the actual words, he was intently listening to tone quality and vocal modulations. Whether on television, or otherwise, anytime he heard an unusual sound it absorbed his attention. Unless he brought the sounds to my attention, I wouldn't have noticed or given it a second thought. Now it was difficult for him to listen "normally." Even certain "meows" from the cats fascinated him! What possibly began as a challenge to him to further refine his ears had really gotten out of hand. The next time we watched TV, he gave me the remote control after he realized he couldn't have it near him, as the act of stopping the tape was so habitual he couldn't resist. He didn't even realize he was doing it! This was an exercise in restraint for Ted, but without any interruptions, we took much pleasure in the entertainment, *"We watch & enjoy the amazing 'twin towers' San Antonio Spurs sweep of Portland Trailblazers. She cooks us potato pancakes and a beautiful vegetable plate. Much to Barb's delight we watch & love "A Bug's Life" especially because I am blown away & find it a near miraculous artistic achievement - so much to marvel at."*

● X □ △ ★

By June of '99, merely six months after Ted decided to spend our time exclusively at my house, I could easily see how Ted's apartment got out of hand. In addition to almost daily accumulation of stuff, he tended to leave projects conspicuously lying around to remind him to get to them. All the projects he intended to get to were piled up in various areas. Meanwhile, as he continued to come up with or discover new projects, the piles grew higher and higher. The newest project always superseded the rest. The piles consisted of music, magazines and books, videos, mail, broken electronic items, and other things. Eventually I had to find shelves for these items because if I did not put things away after he left, the living room would become totally cluttered by these piles. His leaving things out as a reminder did no good, what was at one time important, eventually got buried, defeating the purpose.

On June 27th, Ted gave his first seminar at Boulevard Music in Culver City. All Ted wrote regarding this seminar was, *"Play the early '62 X-175 thru a) B's Princeton and b) the Gibson L-5. Success!"* However I sat in the very back and with pen in hand followed the best that I could. Here is what I wrote:

> "Ted's first topic of discussion is neck layout via Ray Charles moving to Seattle, showing where the same pitch is achieved in various places via "lap guitar" then through using "Figaro." Then on to movable chords and positions and how to use them, and the advantage of using 7 positions: You need the high strings more than the bass for soloing. Now for practicing scales, the neck layout, starting on various strings, descending scales and different fingers - pros and cons. Next he discusses chord substitution, harmonic improvement and chord enrichment. They want to know how he goes about choosing each chord. He's giving examples of various altered chords and progressions - then an explanation of diatonic, Dorian and scales in general. One thing so instantly leads to another. Tonality types. Then takes a simple melody and shows how we can go from minimal harmony to maybe excessive harmony. He's using "Can't Buy Me Love" as example to show harmonic motion, to show various ways the song can be altered using different chords, intervals. It's almost 2:00 p.m. already, I probably won't keep trying to take notes, it's too difficult to keep up and I can't write fast enough. He's still discussing harmonizing "CBML" he interjects how important a function "key" plays. Then the overtone series and he gives examples, he's also very funny. Ted can go on for hours when he has gathered momentum and the energy in the room is good. He's playing "When You Wish Upon a Star" sounding marvelous, they are transfixed and they loved it."

On the last day of June, John Pisano called: Just Jazz Guitar Magazine wanted to put Ted on the cover and do a story! Initially Ted was a bit apprehensive, but I was so excited it didn't take much to encourage an eventual yes. One concern was the two-week deadline for submission to make the August 1999 issue, but Ted planned to submit a revised version of an old interview. The next day Ted began to review the old interview and make decisions.

During the July 4th holiday Ted got involved in what I thought a most comical project, *"Take apart & salvage what I can (part-wise) from my old 1st portable boom-box Digitech Sound Lab: lots of great screws, fabulous wire & some groovy switches."* The project came about as such: Late in the afternoon we decided to rent a movie, but as we were getting into my car which was parked in the garage, he noticed the "bag o' junk," the way I fondly referred to the old boom-box he couldn't throw away. He said he would work on it during the movie. After several attempts to get it to work he realized it was a lost cause, so he began dismantling it to salvage the parts. Ted proved to be much more amusing than the movie. He was really very funny to watch and expressed utter fascination as he slowly discovered many tiny components. He kept showing me various things, like minute screws and telling me how valuable they were and could come in very handy for something. The same with the thousand threads of colored wires, incredibly useful he said. As he sat amongst the odds and ends now strewn about the room, the boombox looked as if it had exploded around him. The project continued for many hours, but soon after midnight I finally grew weary of watching, kissed him good night and got in bed to read. I heard him tinkering until I fell asleep.

The cool summer weather pattern finally broke as a fogless morning ushered in a hot summer day. Ted sat on the couch in the stream of the air conditioner. He was drenched from driving to my house in Betsy with the broken heater unable to be switched off. Cooled down, and ready to get to work on his interview, he happened to notice I had put the two little speakers he had taken out of the broken boombox, in a bag with things going back to his apartment. He said he thought I might want to keep them because they were so tiny and cute and had magnets, but I said no. Then he began looking around the house for a place to put them and placed them atop the refrigerator, and again I said no. I told him that I didn't want them lying around the house and suggested he put them in one of the cupboards with his other stuff. But he wanted to leave them out in order to remind himself to "do something" with them, to which I responded if he left everything out in that manner, my house would look like his, to which he had to agree. Then.... miraculously he decided to just throw them away! That was a big step in his realizing how junk accumulated *and* a bigger step in exercising his ability to dispose of something!

Writing the Cover Story for JJG Magazine
Perfectionism, Patience and Exasperation

For the entire month of July, other than teaching, Ted worked exclusively on the cover-story. He began by trying to use some of the original interview that was never submitted, and soon discovered there were many aspects he needed to completely change. After much deliberation, he decided not to use any part of the original interview and began afresh with a new format. Although he utilized the idea of an interview, it was more in the form of a dialogue, which he felt was a more personalized way to express his views. He became the interviewer and the person interviewed. Yes, Alexandra Adler was Ted after all. He worked hard on trying to imbue the article with a certain sensation to give the reader the feeling of being in the same room and participating in the discussion with him.

There was so much information Ted wanted to include; it eventually became necessary to separate the article into two parts, to run in two consecutive issues. Furthermore, Ted wrote this out entirely by hand.

Unfortunately, Ted could not meet the deadline for the August 1999 issue. The magazine was a quarterly publication so the following issue would come out in November.

Luckily the publisher was not at all averse to running Ted's cover-story in the November issue. By August 11th, the article, now titled 'My Life in Music', was finished and faxed to the JJG offices. There was still one more feat to accomplish, to choose and submit the accompanying lesson material.

Although relieved that the majority of the article was completed, weighing on Ted heavily was my upcoming trip to Europe. A journey to France was planned for September. Lori, now recovered from her car accident and grateful to be alive, had found and rented the two of us a 15th century farmhouse in the Loire Valley for three weeks. Although we welcomed Ted to join us, he was very disinclined toward traveling of any kind at this time in his life. But my heart broke when he told me that if he thought about me going to Europe, he cried. So banishing the trip from his thoughts he worked almost continuously throughout the remainder of August on the lesson material to be submitted with his cover-story.

As the month drew towards its end, Ted was still, "*re-writing & submitting Blue Bossa Comping & Ain't Misbehavin' Walking Chords to JJG for the 'lesson' requested to go with my cover-story for the Nov. issue.*" Then Ted received some rather startling news, *"Aug. 28 Inadvertently : Watershed Day: Call JJG, 3 talks - we agree, we'll wait to put my cover-story on the NAMM Show issue."* That night Ted came bearing the change of plans for the magazine cover-story. Now it would grace the February 2000 issue instead. Unbeknownst to the publisher, the assistant editor made many changes in Ted's original. It would take too long for Ted to change it back in time to meet the deadline for the November issue. Ted was very distressed, as the publisher had promised no changes would be made to Ted's text. Other than us having to wait so much longer, Ted felt that the February issue would give him much better exposure due to the NAMM show.

The following day both of us were feeling a little down, partially due to my imminent departure, and also the delay of the article. In the evening Ted became moody and irritable and apologetically said he wouldn't be okay until I returned. After dinner, he took out Luscious (X-550) and played long into the early hours of the morning. He poured out some of his most beautiful and profoundly heartfelt expressions and went into a very deep trance-like state. I knew this because I'd accidentally jolted him for a moment and startled us both. I knew he was escaping into the music and that it helped to soothe him. Oh! His playing was breathtaking! I felt truly blessed for having him in my life and sad about leaving on my trip.

All too soon for Ted, September 1st dawned upon us. This was our last night together before my journey to France. All evening we pretended as if everything was "normal" as to avoid the pain of our thoughts. Not until we hugged and kissed goodbye did my eyes well up with tears as did his, but he fought it so.

During the time I was away, Ted made no entries in his datebook. The only thing written was his student schedule and that he'd come to my house every night to comfort the cats. The night I returned, he told me he had completely "shut down" since I'd left. He said he was so utterly depressed it was the only way he could deal with my absence. Now, he needed time to "readjust" as did I, so he went about his work as if I'd not come home, while I continued to slowly unpack, occasionally stopping what I was doing to caress him reassuringly. After several hours I got in bed exhausted. He said the time I had been gone seemed an eternity.

It wasn't long before we settled back into our comfortable little life together. Ted continued to bring over more things that he wanted to keep here. Besides the stuff he brought from the apartment, many times he purchased new items on his way over and brought these in as well. As a result my house was beginning to look like his apartment. I had tried to make more room on shelves, in cupboards, anywhere I could, to accommodate the excess but now I was running out of space and piles of things were springing up in various areas of each room. Of course, he didn't even notice.

At this stage in Ted's life, his birthday was met with some trepidation (due to his premonition). On his 53rd, he began listing *"certain salient Rock n' Roll, R&B and Pop tunes by their HARMONY,"* with the intention of writing a new book titled "The Harmony of American Music." He explained to me how this would initially show a *"chronology of harmonic evolution,"* and shared some examples of early rock from the 1950's based on the I IV and V chords. Afterwards I gave him his birthday gifts beginning with the six rolls of paper towels. He was thrilled with these because he used them for "everything" and went through them so quickly. I told him the paper towels were an impromptu gift I found at Ralph's market at an amazingly low price. Then his favorite chocolate chip cookies, followed by the composer postage stamps I knew he wanted, (he loved these), and finally, the card by which he was visibly moved. Then a quick decision to accomplish a few errands, we didn't dawdle at all, left upon making the decision, (a rarity), got gas, the Ray Charles book at Crown Books - just walked in, got it, paid and left (wow)! Then, he couldn't resist the great deal on the paper towels, so to Ralph's, but here we ended up shopping idly. Later at home we found a retrospective of "Saturday Night Live 25 Years on TV," interesting and very funny. For me it was the introduction to pop culture I'd asked for. We watched together as he continued working on his new book, but still able to enjoy the show and tell me who everyone was. When I ask him if this had been a good birthday, he admitted that it was, in part due to his being productive, in part due to my love.

Mid October he decided to revise the cover-story, **"***Work on recasting page 1 of my article for JJG February 2000 cover-story."* He worked assiduously, interrupted only by the World Series. *"Yankee's win three straight. Wow."* Now he had a new deadline to meet, November 15th, and it was rapidly drawing near. As he worked, we discussed the different styles of language he incorporated, from "street slang" to formal English. I asked which one he considered the "true" Ted and he said all of them. He explained how he adapted his language to each situation as was appropriate, and actually became the person he felt best suited to a particular interaction. He said he was all of these people. He had absorbed language idioms and mannerisms over many years. This was the way he learned how best to relate and be accepted by different groups of people. He explained that it was like he had tapes and just put the proper tape in his head.

Halloween Night and a major steppingstone for Ted, *"Oct. 31 roses for Barb. Learn computer tonight: begin typing my JJG cover-story for issue #22 - 1st of year 2000 issue."*

Fortunately it was a quiet Halloween night for us. Ted had done errands before coming here, one being our marketing, which I'd already done earlier. We discovered we were both thinking about sparing each other the trouble of shopping. Consequently we had a ton of groceries, but he brought me roses! Prior to tonight Ted had resisted learning to use the computer. His main reason was he feared addiction to the Internet. When I assured him he could use the computer without any fear of even accidently logging onto the Internet, he conceded to try learning because he felt that maybe it was about time he caught up with the rest of the world.

Obviously using the computer had many advantages for Ted, who wrote everything out by hand. I thought the computer would more easily facilitate his ability to complete the cover-story and meet his new deadline. However, teaching Ted how to use it proved to be an agonizing and frustrating process, pushing us both to the limit. He had no clue as to how involved it was; in fact, he had no realistic idea of how a computer actually functioned. It was completely exasperating for him. After showing him some of the basics, he slowly began entering the article, occasionally asking my help but not before he had pressed keys randomly which only added to his frustration and mine. I implored him to ask when he needed help, but he insisted he didn't want to bother me. I stressed emphatically that it would bother me much more if he didn't ask and something went wrong. I knew this was going to be a long night. I had never seen him get so angry at anything before, but now he understood why I used to yell at it. Ironically, Ted's main complaint was how illogical the damn thing was!

In a few days I sent some files to the JJG office to make sure they were compatible. There was no problem, but there was bad news: JJG went ahead and put together the NAMM Show Issue without Ted's cover-story! Ted was understandably saddened and distressed, even mildly angry. Apparently the publisher was worried that Ted would not make the deadline for the February 2000 issue. Considering that Ted had missed one deadline, was now running late on the second deadline, and had asked for a little more time, it wasn't surprising the publisher didn't want to take any chances with that all-important NAMM show issue. Well, the cover-story wouldn't be in the February issue but at least JJG was still willing to publish it in the next issue or the next. Whenever it was done.

The past month had weighed heavily. The stress of missing deadlines and the countless amount of hours Ted spent on revisions was exasperating for both of us. The magazine article had consumed every minute of our time together.

● X □ △ ★

That night I wrote in my journal, but it was mostly sort of a plea to Ted:

> "I don't want this to come between us anymore it's been the biggest source of frustration, estrangement for us both in a long time. Please, please don't let it continue to be. If I had foreseen all the problems that would be incurred as a result of this article, I would never have encouraged it. Sometimes I think it was almost selfish on my part because I wanted you to be honored

by having your picture grace the cover of a magazine. Not that that was all, I knew it would be a boost for your career and an opportunity to express your ideas to a large audience but if I only could have realized how much trouble and pain it would cause us both and oh Ted, it shouldn't have. You and the publisher definitely had some communication problems, and you stated to me that every business deal you were involved in with your career had been extremely difficult just as this is, why is that so? Yes, some things will not turn out to your liking but some will and it will continue to be so and you keep moving forward and at least that which is to your liking is out there. Do you see? Does this make sense to you? How can I make it make sense? Because I think that I can see from another vantage point and the problems are more apparent to me. How can I help you see? I do believe in you, I love you, but all my faith, love, patience and understanding won't help you see. I see you struggling so hard and I lend you support but it doesn't lessen the struggle! How can you lessen it? It is possible."

The next week Ted reviewed what he had "completed" and revised it again. I had now lost track of how many times he'd revised it, but it must have been at least 30 times. And while working on the computer one night he had accidentally kicked the restart button, consequently losing a portion of it. He was seething. At least he remembered what he'd written, calmed down, fixed it and deemed it wise to press "save" after each sentence. When I woke the next morning I noticed the lights were on, and realized Ted was still here working. I got up, made some coffee and brought the newspaper in. He took a break, had a cucumber and a Pepsi and together we watched some early news and did the crossword puzzle. Soon he fell asleep on the couch. He had asked me to wake him in a mere half hour, I tried but it was impossible. He slept four hours before he awoke on his own. After having a small, unique meal of lettuce, cucumber and Fritos corn chips, he went back to work. I was amazed, astonished and impressed by his fortitude! On Monday morning, this is the note I found from Ted: "*Sun. 11-14-99 Thanks for your loving support honey, the last 2 -3 days & nights. If we're lucky Pt. 1 will be done pretty soon, rest easy, Love T.*"

During the following weeks, Ted continued to work incessantly on the article every day, pouring out thousands of words, revising, and getting very little sleep. Soon the holiday season was upon us. On Thanksgiving we had a particularly nice time at my brother's house where we also celebrated my mother's birthday. My cousin Jerry and Ted made a fine musical connection. Ted depicted our entire day in his datebook, ***"Nov. 25*** *Thanksgiving Day. Celebrate Anita's 80th birthday (actually yesterday) she's happy, at Joel & Stephanie's. Anita's cousin Jerry LeShay and I play music together, what a fine singer & composer. Pretty fine time had by all. Barb & I listen to (for 5 hours!) & revel in Handel's Concerti Grossi a) Opus 3 - which are new for her, b) the last 4 of Opus 6 (which I'd never heard). We are blown away!!!! Bring out the T-100D figure out 3 or 4 of his incomparable extended cadences. I was tired & she says "Handel will wake you up, and she was right!"* Prior to leaving for Thanksgiving dinner Ted had disputed my idea that we would displease everyone by not arriving on time. He was convinced that people never really meant what they said. But everyone had indeed been waiting for us. Ted had difficulty discerning when to take someone's word seriously. Many times he found that people would just "say things." Also he had spent so many years during his childhood "literally" believing everything someone had said and consequently had frequently been let down. All that led him to be skeptical of anyone's word because of his inability to read between the lines, or make a distinction in each particular case.

Ted's transcription's of Handel

For almost the entire month of December Ted worked on the article every night until dawn, his persistence was unbelievable. How did he do it? And how could he be so impervious to the weather? Any weather, no matter excessive heat or bitter cold, he wore the same clothes: plaid flannel shirt and jeans. He said he didn't think about it. The weather never affected how he dressed.

The second week in December I became quite ill again. One morning I felt so nauseous, I couldn't even get out of bed, which is where Ted found me. He tried to encourage me to have some tea, which I could barely get down and within minutes got sick. Miraculously the nausea was gone. Still tired and achy I remained in bed, slept and read, Ted periodically bringing me soup or tea. He worked on the cover-story the entire time. By early evening my cough had escalated, and Ted tried to suffuse me with any and all hot liquids he could get me to drink. We were driving each other crazy. Finally I took some Codeine, which helped, but Ted came in every time he heard even the slightest little cough, insisting I had to have more tea. This went on all night. I just wanted to sleep and he was trying to get me to have soup at four in the morning. He couldn't let me be, he was fixated on the idea I must continue to drink hot fluids. I didn't have the energy to fight him (except the soup) or to explain that if he just would have left me alone for a minute, and given the Codeine a chance to work, I would have been able to sleep without coughing!

The illness lingered for five days before I felt almost back to normal. Dr. P had prescribed some antibiotics, which must have done the trick. One more good night's sleep would seal it. I availed myself of the CDs Ted brought, and I found the Concerto for Two Keyboards, the one we had heard on the radio. During the weekend, Ted did our food shopping, but otherwise he spent the entire time on the computer.

When he returned the next evening I felt much improved, and was actually sitting up watching the Lakers and playing Lala, (the '53 Tele that matched my wall paint). Ted said I had unknowingly painted the living room "Telecaster Yellow." He went straight to the computer and stayed long after I'd gone to sleep. I was not sure how much progress he had made toward completion, except the note I found in the morning sounded encouraging. *"Early Mon.12-20-99 Truly sorry for all the delays honey. It's just that I have a vision - Pt. 1 will get done soon. This was a chance to turn on the readers to a bunch of players I wanted to let people know about. I do believe that's finished now. (yea!) The teaching part of Part 1 needs cleaning up. Then it's done. Thanks for your non-sulking and the food. It's nice to see you (& the Quince) feeling better again. Rest easy. Love, Ted"*

We did share Christmas Eve and part of Christmas day with my family. Still not totally recovered from my illness, my energy was readily spent. Everyone understood, as they knew I'd been ill. The following day was a delightfully lazy Sunday. Ted and I lingered long over the newspaper and ate leisurely throughout the day. Later he sent his very first email (to Tom Bocci). We watched Friday's Guiding Light and a special on cats, both poignant. A pleasantly unfettered day spent together, no article work, no obligations, just rest, relaxation, mutual enjoyment and love. A most welcome respite and desperately needed for us both.

On New Year's Eve, it seemed that the entire world enjoyed one 24-hour period of pure harmony. From around the world each celebration ushered in the new century with hope. There was so much positive energy happening, it was truly overwhelming and offered much encouragement. Ted even ceased his work for one minute to count down to midnight with me, and we shared our first kiss in the new century.

● X □ △ ★

New Year's Day 2000 dawned on Ted at the computer slaving away on what he now termed, "*Part One of the extremely revised article.*" He thought it to be near completion. The deadline to submit the article in time for the May issue was January 5th, he had three days to finish and submit it and insisted he could do it. I hoped so. It was wearing thin on my patience.

"Jan. 4 The last day to work on Pt. 1 Cover Story for JJG May 2000 Issue, the last changes, additions & deletions to be made. Take to Barb all my pictures to her house so I can choose maybe 5 to submit, she helps enormously. Finished by 4:45 a.m. (!)" While he worked I went through the three shopping bags full of photos he had brought over, narrowing down the choices through process of elimination. I left out about fifty pictures for him to pick from to accompany the article; it took three hours, the length of the Lakers game.

The following morning I found a note attached to the cover-story, Ted said part one was done and I could send it to the publisher. I was truly stunned, called Federal Express and sent it without delay. Then...... *"Jan. 9 make cut & paste new 1st section. The printer goes nuts again, B fixes, I in a snit, up till near 5 before home."* Four days later, hypersensitive and stressed, Ted was still deliberating over the photos. When he stopped to once again proofread through the cover-story, I held my breath. It seemed that the segue between parts one and two did not meet with his approval and he had to look for an alternate cut off point. I was beside myself, and couldn't speak. I put on Bach's Orchestral Suites, made soup, which I wasn't in the mood for but Ted liked it. Much to my dismay, he was now back on the computer reworking the cover-story and all I could think about was how the publisher was going to take this for which Ted had many explanations.

He woke me at four in the morning, exasperated because the printer was not operating again. Somehow I fixed it, but he was over tired and in a frenzy when he left. Federal Express came around eleven, and then I took a deep breath and did what Ted had requested; called the publisher. The conversation actually went well after the initial shock and amazement, and the publisher assured me he'd call when he received the "new improved" cover-story. His main curiosity was Ted, he was absolutely baffled by Ted's actions and wondered what made Ted function in such an unusual manner. I did my best to explain Ted's work habits and gave him a basic idea of Ted's fastidious nature. The publisher was still amazed, which was understandable. However, my goal had been accomplished for now. He was willing to read the "new improved version" and consider using it instead of the first one we'd already sent. I knew that this could not continue and I was a wreck as a result. If the publisher was willing to concede, at least Ted would have some of his work published, even if he never got to the balance, which was now in total disarray.

Much to my relief JJG was willing to publish the "new improved" version. They would send us complimentary issues in April. I couldn't believe it was actually going to happen, finally utter elation and relief. Ted too was comforted that this leg of the journey was complete. However, now due to his latest revision, we had no Part Two.

That night Ted intended to sort photos but ended up on the computer instead. I hesitated to think about Part Two but if he wanted it in the next issue it had to be on the publisher's desk by May 1st, and held to seven pages. Ted thought he could do it easily but I knew from experience what that really meant. Besides his health was really the priority, he desperately needed to rest and take care of himself. And I needed a break too since it had been no less stressful for me.

● X □ △ ★

Mid-month, after a short break, and under less pressure, Ted noted in his datebook, *"Jan. 15 Begin formatting Pt. 2 of JJG article." Play Duena for Barb: her request: "How About You" plus my surprise "Somebody Loves Me' She loves these, while she watches her beloved Lakers with sound off. Barb cooks me up a dinner."*

The "office," as Ted had begun calling the extra bedroom, was beginning to look like a room in his apartment, bags of stuff piling up one upon the other. I brought it to his attention, and we laughed about it, but we both knew how easily it could get way out of hand. He was spending almost all his time in that room so I supposed it was hopelessly natural for the clutter to pile up. Funny how to him it didn't appear unsightly even in the context of my house, but it didn't. The Ford Bronco was full of stuff again too; I had cleaned it out twice, so I just gave up on it. Now each morning I would awaken to find the prior nights efforts waiting for me, always with a note stating it was close to completion. What astonished me most was how he functioned on such minimal sleep.

A week later Ted regretfully said Part Two was proving to be much more involved than he had originally intended. A typical notation from his datebook,*"Jan. 23 at B's. Many, many hours on Pt. 2. 5:00 a.m. Finish the Pt. 2 essentially (so I thought)"* Ted had been working every night until five in the morning, with very little to eat, although he appeared alert and triumphant when he thought that he had finished. He told me he needed a day's break from it and then would review it again. Why, why, why did I think he was almost done last weekend? Having been through this for many months now, shouldn't I have known better? It was wishful thinking, I wanted our life back to "normal" and this was driving me crazy. I was concerned for his health and I missed him, missed our time together.

One afternoon, Ted arrived in a huff as if one magazine story wasn't enough, a call this week from another magazine wanting to publish an old phone interview he gave in '97? That explained the somewhat cryptic message left for him on my answering machine. He was not at all pleased, this cresting upon a week in which his patience was strained to its maximum. He couldn't bear any more stress and when he received only half my attention, causing me to ask an unnecessary question, he was momentarily pushed right to the edge. Angry and frustrated he sat at the table for three hours, sorted through all his material, all the while saying he would be done in a minute. Our relationship had become painfully strained through his writing of this article. Not helping was Ted waking me at three in the morning to inform me the printer's ink cartridge had run out. I was incredulous and as irritable as he was and for the next half hour we argued. I complained about the stress this article had inflicted on me, he countered by exclaiming he was doubly stressed and on it went.

A Finished Product

Then came the long awaited moment that assured me Part Two was indeed completed. On February 3rd I found the finished article and a note with instructions for me on what to say to the publisher. Later that day on the phone with JJG, the publisher was agreeable to all of Ted's requests except for sending the blue lines back to Ted to be proofread. Why was I not surprised?

The publisher stressed that once we sent Part Two, Ted could not make any changes in the text so it was imperative that Ted was absolutely sure he was happy with it. Ted was quite surprised when I related this information, as if he didn't understand why this was mentioned. It was so difficult being the liaison between those two but I had no choice, otherwise nothing would have gotten published.

I read the "final" version of Part Two and really liked it, felt it was wonderfully written and very informative and I didn't want to risk it getting back into Ted's hands. When I called Ted and told him I had mailed it, he actually alleviated any last gasp of apprehension I had from dealing with this entire project. Ted was calm and reasonable about how the editor dealt with his requests, realized and somewhat accepted the fact that he would not be granted the opportunity to do a final proofing. Perhaps Ted was just grateful to have gotten this far, that the entire article was actually going to be published and would have an audience and that brought some satisfaction and relief? Regardless, he promised that our weekend would be for relaxation, a marathon of sleeping, eating and movies. Would he be amenable to that still by Saturday? I hoped so.

We did have a leisurely weekend. Ted needed it to rejuvenate, being so depleted and on the verge of illness. But after a nap on Saturday he needed a project, he said, to stave off his ailment and he began reorganizing the videos. That took three to four hours, it being 1 a.m. when he was finished and uttered his well worn lament, "It took longer than I thought." And Sunday afternoon late, awake before dinner after a long nap, miraculously revived by that and a large plate of spaghetti, he felt much better than he had in weeks. We watched some of the Great Composer series, Wagner and Tchaikovsky. I had bought Ted some photo albums so he sorted though half a bag of photos, absolutely enraptured by this project and only half attentive to the show. We laughed a lot. I was relieved to see the improvement after only two days of rest; he kept his promise for the most part and benefited from it. For me, even the nap I had earlier couldn't pause a yawn when approaching one in the morning. My energy spent, I went to bed, his energy steady, intent, reawakened he stayed late arranging pages of photos in the albums. About the weekend Ted noted, *"She requested due to recent readings: B & I watch ch. 28 Great Composers - Wagner. Wagner: Tannhauser Overture, B loves as much as I do. B7b9/5 - B7b5/b5 E - wonderfully clever 2 voices move - 2 don't."*

As if making up for months all at once, the next weekend yielded us a feast of three movies and we took the opportunity to amuse ourselves, with little else a distraction except his Aunt Reva's 90th birthday party on that rainy Sunday. We had to attend for a few hours. Ted's playing sounded fabulous, the room lent itself splendidly to his choice of guitar and amp. He played the entire time; I stayed half with him, half obligingly socializing. In his datebook he voiced his pleasure with his playing and his trepidation about new upstairs neighbors. *"Feb. 13 Rain. I'll play. 12:00 Reva's 90th birthday, W.H. Country Club. Smokey & the cream Deluxe Reverb dazzles me with tone. Wonderful party. Humongous baked potato & fabulous green peas. New neighbors moving in."*

With the new neighbor situation an impending threat, an already distressed Ted arrived here to even more unsettling news which I had received: his dad had been hospitalized. Upon calling the hospital, Ted was somewhat relieved to be told his dad was basically okay; his condition appeared to be nothing serious. However Ted's financial situation was a disaster, he had run out of money and was totally perplexed as to why or what had happened. My guess was lack of sleep had fogged his thinking. Fortunately his residual check was due to arrive very soon. His life was again unsettled due to the rental of the unit above him, again he existed in dreaded anticipation of a new intrusion. I coaxed him into eating some dinner and relaxing. We watched several episodes of Beakman's World. Close to midnight he was overcome with exhaustion.

Much to Ted's benefit, he was to have one more joyful week, a reprieve before a storm unleashed its fury and consumed his life. *"Feb. 24- 2 new guitars: buy the mid '70s gorgeous blonde X-175 (#155233), also Cesar P's '63 Sunburst T-100 DP #21634"*

Facing the Inevitable

Although Ted received his check, he only had time to make two new purchases. A difficult new episode in his life was about to unfold. Within a day or two after his father's hospitalization, Ted learned that his father was indeed quite ill due to complications arising from his scleroderma; the doctors recommended his father be transferred to a nursing care facility. That was not an easy mission to accomplish. The harsh reality began to set in.

Scanning back over the last few days, the past weekend laid in disarray. I tried to function among a multitude of intrusions and inconveniences such as the kitchen sink being clogged, that all faded shortly after Ted arrived. It was a frightening sight to witness him writhe in pain on the couch, constantly shifting position, finding no ease. His arms were aching unexplainably, and he could find no way to stop the pain. At a certain point he even considered seeking medical attention, then reconsidered. Not wanting to feel helpless, I offered my only other suggestion, a bowl of hot soup and channeling his thoughts into the engaging text of his favorite reading. This was the familiar diversion he had utilized his entire life to fend off anxiety, and to both our relief proved successful.

In hindsight and in sorrow, this may have been the onset of a series of heart attacks, but at that time neither of us had an inkling of a suspicion that it could be heart-related. We reasoned that too much strife and personal neglect caused that devastating effect. It wasn't solely the new neighbors above, enough in itself, but the urgent matter of taking care of his father who had so suddenly become incapable of caring for himself. This dilemma not only entailed researching alternatives, but also there was the possibly devastating financial ramifications for which Ted was ill equipped to manage. He was at a loss as to how he would be able to uphold his part of the burden. Fortunately I was able to calm him and he was willing to put aside all troubling thoughts. I convinced him to focus solely on himself, healing and resting. This he unresistingly did all weekend with only one minor set back caused early Sunday evening by a phone call. He answered the phone without knowing, against my warning, and was forced back into the throes of the unsettled dilemma regarding his father. After that call the spasms in his arms came back. I helped him to the bed and he tossed restlessly until sleep overcame him. He slept three hours and upon waking was much revitalized, and the pain had faded. Then he was able to get up and enjoy a TV feature on one of his favorites, The Beach Boys, and sort through more bags of photographs, both activities were very beneficial. That weekend he realized the importance of his needs being met without thinking himself selfish.

Many days would be taken up making inquiries, *"Feb. 29 Call retirement hotels and assisted living places. Call social workers for list of appropriate skilled nursing facilities & assisted living facilities. Constant oxygen tank. For Dad: Dept. of Social Services: they recommend "Connections" Go to Tarzana Hospital get the brochure "Lifestyles" Visit Board & Care, especially Valley Village - very impressive place and highly recommended (the dough is frightful 'tho)."* I chipped in my assistance, sympathetic to Ted's crisis and applied my time to finding the right information, slightly easing Ted's share of the burden. There was much to discuss regarding his following up on recommendations. Although he toured but one, he was impressed with the set up, cleanliness and all of the aspects we were to note were more than adequate. Yet we both agreed a comparison was needed, and this would be made by soon viewing other places. His energy depleted, I treated him to a hearty meal, recreational reading, TV, sleep. A glorious thunder and lightening storm underscored the evening.

"March 4 visit more Board & Cares, Encino Elderly Care, Sterling Home Care, long visit with each. March 5 Still more: Fine Gold Manor, Northridge Regency, Tarzana Hills." Ted arrived, a tornado in the midst of a pit stop, gathered his wits and was gone again, narrowing the list, figuring to return by seven. Shortly after the Lakers gained their 15th straight win, a most elated Ted returned with roses, food and encouraging news. Ted had found a place rating his approval, a home had been chosen, and at least that dilemma was settled. Best of all it had many amenities he believed his father would deem pleasing.

Ted made the arrangements, *"March 7 Call Rita (Valley Village) we agree to meet at the Board & Care again. Terms are agreed upon (she even comes down $400. on the single) the fantastic room for Dad at her place for $1800 a month - no hidden charges. To Barb. Bank : get print out. Call Dad's hospital, call Rita, back to her board & care with my initial $300. check. Back to Barb, try to watch Mon.'s GL with B. Sleep. Barb & I love Schumann's 1st Symphony."*

"In my thoughts, Impatiens, tiny pink and red petals spreading everywhere, spreading red. Popping up dotting the garden. Oh! What a mess! Ted insists on driving Betsy to Cathedral City tomorrow. Betsy the Plymouth residing here and rusting for months, soon to be readied for her last hurrah. I'm totally distressed, can't even write about it now."

Within minutes came the muffled chugging of the Bronco, uh-oh. Late but no mistake Ted arrived determined to drive Betsy against any defense I could render. He had the faith of a saint in her. We embraced and said our good byes as if it could be the final time. After an endlessly aching wait he called to say he safely made it but complications regarding the task at hand had his return uncertain. He would continue to issue me updates and placate my frayed nerves. Yet the fact was that I couldn't relax until he was back despite a sip or two of cognac. Betsy at best should have been used as a statue, a light blue tribute to the automotive audacities of the 1970's.

"March 10 Cathedral City, load Dad's stuff, pick up Dad. Move Dad into Valley Village Board & Care." When Ted called to inform me of his successful trek back to our neck of the woods back to our niche, my apprehension was finally quelled. I silently rejoiced in the sound of Ted's voice and I was amused by the news that his dad, tuckered out from the trip had readily accepted that strange place and was sleeping peacefully.

● X □ △ ★

That first night's peaceful bubble burst as Ted spent much of Sunday administering to his father's wishes, needs and comforts. He arrived here at 11 a.m., dropped off what he bought for us and left to do errands, gather odds & ends for his father. He made a brief stop back here around 1 p.m., intending to return in a reasonable amount of time, but it wasn't until early evening that I would see him again. Tired, overwrought, the demands of his life slamming him sideways, he fumed over other's attitudes and was totally taken aback by well intentioned but misguided actions.

My first concern was to comfort him, but he needed to vent his welling resentment. I reminded him that nothing insured love, but luckily we were able to seek those that please us, and create our own meaningful family, which he and I had become together. Slowly he was able to settle down, a plate of his favorite spaghetti and many incidental amenities helped. The remainder of the evening was pawned off to TV and conversation, casual and relaxing leading to sleep.

All the while on another front, Ted continued to be tortured by noise from the apartment above him, now housing four new tenants. Living in his apartment had become absolutely intolerable for him. Despite that and all else, he conceded to performing with Cathy Segal-Garcia at Rocco's in June. Perhaps because the date of the performance was two months in the future, and he was so consumed with his other troubles, his usual anxiety over playing live did not manifest at that time.

"Gelson's for Pop: bananas, to Dad: more eye level squinting eye contact - has favorites. Tell him funny vignette stories: more laughing (great to hear him laugh again) & act out with body language & voices, more discussions about his incentive to get well. More negotiation with him about food. To Barb." After teaching all day, then visiting his dad, Ted was quite weary when I welcomed him home. He told me that he had more luck eliciting a positive response from his father. Ted sensed at least a trace of motivation in Irwin, who seemed to have risen from the grips of his despair consuming him that afternoon. Ted's mind was eased but as usual lacking sleep he was sagging, the area around his eyes a dark beige like badly painted vampire make up. He slept, almost comatose, for five hours. Tuesday too it was the same scenario.

The daily visits to his father were slowly taking their toll on Ted, who was doing his utmost to cheer and amuse this now recalcitrant man,*"To Dad: bring special books for him. To Dad - 3 shakes. Shop for music cassettes for Dad, Jazz: swing combo big band & vocal music. Misery with Dad and his living arrangements. So many problems & issues keep surfacing. We listen to Swing music. I tell him stories."*

Ted arrived in a mild rage sometime during the Lakers game. More problems. He had again run into difficulties regarding his father's care, which he continued to deal with here by phone. He finally worked it all out with everyone but I'd had enough. We needed a break for the sake of our sanity. My patience was wasting away, a slow erosion of composure. He understood and agreed. We watched the Lakers win a close game. Then he wanted to watch the Academy Awards, which had already started. We actually had a relaxing evening, for which he was most grateful and desperately needed. He fell asleep easily after the show.

The situation at the Board and Care, and consequently Ted's life, alternated between moments of calm, "*Barb brings Dad her spare gloves. He loves them. To Dad: bring lamp bulb, 3 shakes & Kleenex. He loves the new light or what is now a new look of warmth & keeps commenting on it. To Barb: We are happy together & the 'boys' (Quincy & Pumpkin) love being with us too.*" And moments of craziness, as Ted sweltering, half frantic, disposed of his groceries in the 'fridge and was off in a mad dash to attended to his dad's demands. I remained in the wake of that fuss waiting for the dust to settle, it did in seconds, the storm moved through to Valley Village.

Then on April 10th, 2000 upon returning home after late lunch with my parents, I found a message from Ted. Last night his dad had been taken to the emergency room and was now at St. Joseph's Hospital. Apparently Irwin's kidneys were failing and he was having difficulty breathing. He had refused dialysis.

Ted came directly from the hospital too upset to discuss any of it, more stressed from the process than the idea of his dad's impending death. The weight of the resulting problems was impossible to bear. His arms ached again, the same unexplainable ghostly pain. Ted needed a meal and some rest and was soon soundly asleep in bed. Never before had a more formidable ordeal stifled his life, and consequently mine.

The morning was consumed sifting through rumors of Irwin's release and plans for transfer to a nursing care center in Northridge, for three hours we waited for word. Then we picked up basic necessities for him from Valley Village, minimal needs until we assessed the situation. Once notified by the nurse Ted headed for the new care facility. "*To Valley Village. To Dad at new nursing care facility, nice nurses (very accommodating to Dad's impertinence with the food). Bad arm attack, very bad, 4 Ibuprofen, bread, water… make it to Barb's - soup & sandwich & relaxation.*"

Although I knew nothing of the "arm attack" he had that day, I now am aware (through Ted's datebook), of the frequency with which they occurred. Ted never mentioned any others and I was only aware of the ones I had witnessed. Unfortunately, it was Ted's nature to shield me from as many of his physical troubles as possible.

● X □ △ ★

On April 21st a box containing six issues of the Just Jazz Guitar cover-story arrived at my house. For the most part Ted was pleased with the way his interview was presented but was extremely sad and upset that all his italics were lost. The title of the cover-story had been altered from 'My Life in Music' to 'Music is My Life', to which Ted exclaimed to me, *"Music isn't my life, **you're** my life."* Consequently, he reviewed the entire text and in each advance copy underlined the words he had wanted italicized. I watched the Lakers in Game 1 of the Playoffs, elated by the win over Kings. Ted worked on filling his photo album the entire time, ignored most of the game, but caught the final seconds, grinning at my ridiculous grin. After which we both napped on the bed, I was too restless to sleep, but stayed to be caressed. The best aspect of the day was no interference or any dilemmas; Ted didn't even visit his dad since he'd been there the prior two days. It suited him; he was relaxed and subsequently productive the entire night.

By the end of April we knew that his father would not be returning to Valley Village Board and Care. Therefore his father's possessions had to be collected and removed. I was surprised to find Ted had arrived there before me. We both had in mind an early start in packing up his father's belongings. An excessive amount, taken in haste during the initial displacement and we found the packing-up a daunting ordeal lasting several hours. Filled our cars, stored it all in my garage temporarily, for where else?

Now, with both parts of the Just Jazz Guitar interviews finished, I felt Ted needed another "project" so to speak, which I decided to facilitate. Ted had begun working on a new interview for another guitar magazine that had offered him a cover-story. The initial interview had been done by phone months ago. Inevitably he needed to rewrite it and make corrections. The article had been long neglected, so I entered it in the computer for him because I thought it would offer a much-needed diversion from the turmoil, plus give him incentive to finish. The article could be worked on at his leisure, as no deadlines were set. A good move on my part for it fit its function for him on both fronts. The article was never completed, but that wasn't the main objective at that time.

We now found that we could both freely go about life here unimpeded by each other. I could even practice the piano for hours, which was in the same room with the computer without feeling I was disturbing him, or do anything and it was fine. We lived as we would have if alone, but with a bonus. Because when we wanted to converse, or just wanted a hug, we simply expanded our individual worlds outward and there we were, easily reachable. It had taken many years to attain this plane of co-existence, which was highly desirable.

On May 3, 2000 the Just Jazz Guitar issue began to arrive in subscriber's homes. Ted hoped for a lot of feedback about his interview. The day was almost one long and welcome yawn except for watching the Lakers win Game 1 of round 2 in the play-offs. Ted insisted on watching with me. Well, he attempted to anyway, as he glanced occasionally at the plays while he tampered with several broken amps with which he sat encamped amongst on the floor. It was afterwards though that our attention really connected when he plugged in Deedee (M75 Bluesbird) and chanced on a new tuning. We both swooned as he cruised through songs with the wonderful chords this uniqueness afforded. Except for the low E, he tuned the guitar up a whole step then tuned the low E down a whole step (D B E A C# F#).

Soon he began preparations for his performance at Rocco's with Cathy Segal-Garcia in June. *"Rehearsal with Cathy Segal-Garcia. I use Desiree (X350), tune her to Eb & the*

Silver Face Deluxe." Ted continued to practice amidst our days, during Lakers games and also worked on his new guitar magazine article. *"Watch Lakers at Phoenix, game 3 - they pull it out. She's so pleased that I enjoyed the game with her - a creature of sharing she is. Computer: cover-story till 3:00 a.m."*

One evening when I was home alone, the Lakers were too exciting for the mere radio, (we didn't have cable, so could only watch "away" games). During the half I scampered to watch with my dad. Wow, blow out, Lakers nailed it in five. When I arrived home it took a long moment to notice I wasn't here alone. A light glowing from the "office" led me to Ted using the computer. As I did not expect Ted to be here, I was overjoyed and relieved to see him but it threw me a fine surprise. Why didn't I surmise something amiss, since I'd left only the stove light shining, when upon entering again two lamps were lit? Ted said my mind was just on something else. But I loved what he wrote, *"To Barb: Computer. She returns from her folks and is delighted to see me - such a loving woman she is. Computer till 3:00 a.m. again."*

The days of May dwindled away along with Ted's father's health and mental state. Irwin was on dialysis daily, had very little appetite and had lost what little energy and strength left to him. But somehow his will to live persisted. When we went to visit, we found the situation very depressing. Ted was frustrated by what appeared to be a lack of reasonable and responsible care given by the new facility. Ted noted, *" Dad (now in #35) Dad has fallen again & has a terrible rash. He loves seeing Barbara & fumes over medication."*

Fortunately the following day was wonderful for us and helped to offset Ted's slight depression. We enjoyed the Lakers victory over Portland in Game 1 of the Semi-finals. After the game and dinner we shared hours of music listening pleasure. It was so special when we did this together because we experienced the same sensations, unique between us, we were deeply and truly moved. Later, Ted awake from his nap, we lay on the bed, talked and laughed before he arose to use the computer and continue work on interview number two.

The next day went equally well, as Ted expressed in his datebook, *"May 26 1:00 Cathy Segal Garcia a fine rehearsal. Bring Blonde X-500 & Peavey Special. Excited by our new rhythms & chords applied to the wonderful Beatle tunes we rehearsed today. 7:00 To Barb: A fine evening. Game 3 semi finals, Lakers pull out dazzling come back on the road with great defense against the hugely formidable Portland Blazers (who killed them in Game 2) Barb & I so happy."*

The days continued to alternate that way, Ted's distress about Irwin's diminishing condition was counteracted by loving evenings; movies, Lakers, music. I devoted my time to providing comfort and love during this very difficult period in Ted's life. Again I defer to Ted's datebook for some of his touching words, *"Barb & I watch most of "Bugsy" and are impressed, great music & singing by Ennio Morricone. She read a book on him years ago. Barb beautiful & happy and both boys, Quincy & Pumpkin (so affectionate & responsive) so happy with 'Mommy & Daddy' Computer till 4:00 a.m. for guitar magazine cover-story."*

The two of us now became hopelessly consumed by the Lakers in the playoffs. One night, we thought it may be the end for them, my hopes grew cold with the notion of defeat, the Lakers trailing by 15 in the 4th quarter when a dramatic rally began that afterwards was claimed as "the greatest comeback in sports history" culminating in a 5 point victory over Portland, advancing the Lakers to the final round! Even Ted, somewhat complacent all season was ignited with excitement as the Lakers sprang to life, and shared in my exhilaration, *"June 4 Lakers at home down by 15 in 4th quarter, find their heart and pull out one of the most satisfying comeback wins ever! (Portland had won the last 2 games) Deep in 3rd or 4th quarter I run to the garage to get a boombox to tape Chick's radio call (& the fans). Barb & I go crazy in last 15 minutes, SO GREAT - she's overjoyed (the win & me getting into it with her again). Computer till 4:00 a.m. Restructure the article by relocating huge sections all over the place. Much better now (I hope) A re-read tomorrow will tell."*

Mid June Ted readied himself for his upcoming performance with Cathy at Rocco's, practicing into the small hours of the morning. The day of the gig soon arrived, this was Ted's assessment of the evening, *"June 13 Cathy & I play at Rocco's. Packed house. '54 Esquire 'Banana' tuned down a half step & '64 Vibroverb. 1st set: trouble from me, gradually better playing, she sounds incredible tonight! and the people are I think thrilled with her. I took many, many chances up there tonight in my desire to be oh so vocal & bluesy like expressive. Was hanging by a fingertip more than a little but stayed out of the abyss 'cept for 1st set, Skylark, never had memorized the road map to that song - have it now. Feeling & daring - good, accuracy - fair. Barb proud & happy to feel people's love for me. Exodus (non jazz) quite good - even the tone - the tone: never what I hoped for in this big room."*

Ted and I had made it through another difficult and demanding week relatively unscathed, just tired and grateful for its cessation. But on Sunday, Father's Day I was shocked upon witnessing the condition of Ted's father. It was a most distressingly sad and frightful sight, he was in almost unbearable pain from his recent operation and emaciated from his inability to eat. In his agony and frustration he wanted only to hold my hand and cry which I encouraged him to do, and I cried too. Communication had been reduced mostly to yes and no, so we silently stayed, Ted played guitar for him, and I think Irwin really listened.

From this visit it was on to my father and mother, the latter's attitude deteriorating rapidly as impatience with her recovery (fractured pelvis, more eye surgery) increased to an intolerable degree. Ted intervened on everyone's behalf, gave her a realistic view, which seemed to at least appease her. My dad, always glad to have us, had donned his usual easy-going demeanor. Ted was mentally and physically drained so it was a brief stay for us. Immediately upon arriving home, Ted readily fell asleep on the floor, so relieved that our obligations were over. A big bright spot in the day: The Lakers became the NBA Champions!

● X □ △ ★

The following datebook entries by Ted encapsulate the final three days he spent with his father prior to his father losing consciousness. *"June 23 To Dad: In such terrible shape & the tragic news on likely amputation. To Barb."*

"June 24 To Dad: After Dad is safely in the dialysis transportation truck, I explain to him that if this condition of extreme pain, suffering & no life persists even after the likely amputation (according to Dr. R. who did Dad's leg surgery) that it's ok to know that one can say good bye with dignity - it's ok to die. To Barb"

"June 25 To Dad: set his TV close to him. Temperature in his room gone berserk. We watch & enjoy Dodgers & Vin Scully. To Pic 'n Save: "toys" for Barbie & Ted. We play pitch & hit in the yard, we do the 'Teddy Bear's Picnic' rectangle jigsaw puzzle. What a contrast/bridge from yesterday."

After the last visit that Ted noted, I know his mental state was very troubled. He did not mention in his datebook entry his immediate actions upon leaving the care facility, although he did relate them to me. That weekend the toll on him almost taken, he needed an escape from the chaos churning inside; a means to accept and assimilate in his own way, what he knew was his father's imminent demise.

With the thermometer still poised at ninety degrees, Ted arrived here late afternoon. He explained that he had visited his father, and then wanting to surprise me, had stopped in a vacant parking lot where he could polish the Bronco. Although he only managed to do one side of the car, he used an unusual method, tissues and spit. At least it seemed cleaner, albeit unevenly streaked. My guess, that was the first step in an attempt to help him become calm, collected and come to some acceptance. It did not occur to him to wash the Bronco here in the shady driveway with hose and rags, the way in which one would usually tackle such a project. And that wasn't the end; he also had stopped at Pic & Save, a discount five & dime throwback, and bought bundles of toys, a hard plastic bat and ball, jigsaw puzzles, candy, and dozens of colored pens. He totally succumbed to impulse and like a child, treated himself to all that enthralled him. Not without me in mind however, for it was all bought with the thought of sharing the various treasures. Our first indulgence was the bat and ball, my suggestion to relieve tension, we alternated being batter and pitcher until we lost the ball over the backyard wall. Then it was a jigsaw puzzle to the accompaniment of a movie. He insisted on both at once, wanted to drag the big table over to the TV. I was reluctant, but this he explained, was his ability to adapt to and enjoy change. His idea of change was moving the table to a different location. So I acquiesced. All of these activities were especially effective in lessening his stress. He knew what he needed. It all worked perfectly, the movie a light romantic comedy charmed us, and he continued to work on the puzzle long after I went to bed.

The next time Ted went to see his father, mercifully it was to be his last visit, *"June 27 To Dad: unconscious in dialysis, nurses say he may have to be hospitalized afterwards, his arm has turned blue & he refuses to eat."*

That same evening Ted and I went to see jazz guitarist Russell Malone at the Jazz Bakery. Ted needed a night out and a distraction. In his datebook he noted, "*Go with Barb to see Russell Malone at the Jazz Bakery. He blows us all away!!!! prediction: super stardom. Also in attendance, John Collins - such a warm & wonderful man and he introduces me to Bob Barry, stupendous photographer & warmest fellow. John Collins and I just have a wonderful talk- reminiscing about Emily & more - what a vital guy at 87!"*

Irwin was hospitalized either that night or the next day. On June 29th, 2000 Irwin David Greene died around 4:30 in the morning.

Aftermath

It was one long spate of days we wallowed in throughout the long 4th of July holiday, ill placed for the timing in our lives. Ted's depression crept into every crevice, the loss of his father weighed heavier than he thought it would. He hadn't expected it to affect him so, but how could he have known, and how could it not?

When I awoke the next morning Ted was still here, just waking also. He said he had decided I'd like it if he stayed a while to share a portion of the morning. I was relieved that he was able to sleep through the night considering the dark circles ringing his eyes. He eventually left, only to return a few hours later, spurning his apartment due to the obstreperous tenants above him, but made the most of his outing. At KB Toys he stopped for another ball to replace the one we'd lost and also bought half a dozen jigsaw puzzles. We then indulged in a movie during which he was overcome by sleep. But the following day watching old NBA tapes put us back on track for a while at least. Then he slept here again, but as it was Monday morning he soon left to teach. When he returned that afternoon, still sad and lost, I thought a jigsaw puzzle might help him sort his thoughts. It worked wonders along with the classical radio station playing an array of engaging music, so much so we stayed up did the puzzle and listened until 2:00 a.m.

July 9th was our chosen anniversary. This one marked the 8th year from the day we met. There was no celebration other than fond acknowledgement. Our love for each other remained solid. The time passed quietly each to our own device, living side by side. His lingering mood had no room for me as a multitude of troubles surrounded him; he blocked the world out or locked himself in, self-contained in his own way, alleviating the pain. Ted had agreed to another performance at Rocco's, this time playing solo and it was a week away. Ted dreaded that obligation; as for his father's death, he said he just felt numb. But his biggest difficulty was still his living situation, the same strain on and off since I'd known him, the only reprieve was when the apartment above was unoccupied. Yet despite his despair, he sweetly acknowledged the day in his datebook, *"July 9 B & my 8th anniversary. So much love between us."*

Another week swept by, not under a rug luckily. Yet, Ted slept a large part of it, saying he was depressed mostly from the barrage of noise at his apartment, his endless lament, an unsolvable problem. We attempted a movie Saturday night, an old rendering of "The Razor's Edge" and actually lasted through to the end, he only due to the lavish cues of Newman's music, me out of curiosity for how carefully the novel was dramatized.

When I suggested we rent the more contemporary version he exclaimed emphatically, "*oh no we won't*" so spontaneously it was very funny, well we found it so.

Suddenly, almost abruptly it was the 17th, Ted's solo performance for the one-year anniversary of Guitar Night at Rocco's. Ted dreaded playing the sold-out show and to my dismay did not want me to go with him or even attend the show. He gently said that he just wanted to get it over with and get out of there. Although he was never comfortable being the sole focus in the collective intensity of a dense crowd, his anxiety was heightened, worse than ever I'd witnessed. He swore he'd never do a performance like this again. Practicing last night I thought he sounded great and I stayed awake late to listen. As for his show, reluctantly I conceded to his wishes and here defer to his datebook notes as an account of the evening, *"July 17 To Barb: bring Banana tuned one whole step low & the Gibson LAB 5. John Pisano's 1 Year Anniversary of Guitar Night at ROCCO'S. John, Mundell Lowe & Herb Ellis. HUNDREDS of guitar players there, staggering,... close to overwhelming, and stunning reaction to my not-so-great playing, just roaring approval. They were primed to love music this night and certainly wanted to love me & the music I tried to offer which was: A Dream is a Wish, April Showers, Lover Man, When Sunny Gets Blue. Back to Barb."*

● X □ △ ★

Soon the time arrived for Ted's dreaded mission to Cathedral City, his father's house. There was no choice in the matter; he knew he must do this. Late in the evening prior to his departure, after mentally readying himself for his loathsome journey as best he could, he settled in to eat, rest, and await the pre-dawn hours of the next morning. He had planned to fortify himself with a nap, which to his chagrin, lasted throughout the entire night. His hand slammed the alarm, needing more sleep though not meaning to. So when I awoke at 5 a.m., I was surprised to find him here. He still was able to make an early getaway, imperative to avoid the heat of the day and called me at 10 a.m. alerting me he'd arrived safely at his destination to reluctantly begin rummaging through his father's things. Now I knew how he felt when I went to France. These mere two days I missed him so and worried about his safe return, as the Bronco's reliability was questionable. I wouldn't be relieved until he was back home with me tomorrow evening as he planned.

"*Aug. 6 10:00 a.m. departure, 12:00 noon: safe arrival at Barb's - she's so happy.*" With a Bronco full of stuff, Ted steaming from the heat came home laden with boxes. Items deemed useful, some of which were brought in and soon strewn about the room to sort through. A brown paper bag containing his dad's ashes sat atop the washer until together we would distribute its contents amongst the flowers in my garden.

He chose mostly books, CDs, videotapes and a few old photographs. But with an utterly cluttered apartment and no room for anything more, he only sought more of what he tended to collect most. And selected for me, one item especially, a book on James Joyce, so thoughtfully chosen with hopes of how much I would love it, and chanced I didn't have it. I didn't and was most grateful. We listened to music while we spent the remainder of the day going through the contents of the boxes and trying to decide what to do with it all.

Not intending to, Ted slept through the night. We awoke together and lingered over the early shows and the newspaper. In the dull sunlight of late morning we sprinkled his father's ashes amongst the flowers, which caused his arms to ache. Association? Finality? Two Advil, a bowl of soup and bread with peanut butter helped him to feel better. We mused over how many years it took him to feel so at home here, where now he could be completely at ease, with little inclination to leave but.... he had to teach at 1:00.

Upon his return he brought me flowers, then practiced for hours for his upcoming seminar on Sunday. In his datebook, a mere mention, *"Aug. 13, 4:30 Seminar at Sam Ash Music To Barb, bring our wonderful 1956 X-550 Luscious - give seminar - back to B's she's happy that it went well."*

As Ted was leaving to give his seminar, I walked out with him to the car. I happened to notice hundreds of Irwin's neckties piled high on the back seat. I carried armfuls into the house. As I headed up the walkway, he exclaimed gleefully "I must have five hundred neckties!" My guess - he loved the colors.

When he returned, his face bore traces of elation. He told me the seminar went extremely well, better than expected. He related some of the experience to me, beginning with the large turn out. A crowd exceeding a hundred was crammed in, listened attentively and asked questions. He was amazed to see so many Asians. Many brought his most popular book "Chord Chemistry" for him to autograph. He was truly flattered. And best of all he played well, was pleased with the tone.

The seminar medium served him well, it was his most comfortable and effective way of communicating in public. We did regret he hadn't taped it, he said he covered many topics, and infused humor into the mix as well, but didn't recall much else. He told me he "goes into a zone" focusing and concentrating so he can read the needs of the crowd. The energy it takes is intense, and equally intense is the energy he receives. Afterwards he is totally depleted.

For the remaining weekends of that scorching August, we'd awake around midday and spend a few hours reading together in bed. He had begun writing out a new chart of voicing systems (alto voice down 2 octaves becomes the bass). The days segued pleasantly, late lunches, supplemented with fabulous classical radio selections, or sampling the new CDs he'd bought, especially the fine rendering of The Musical Offering, and Andre Previn playing Gershwin. We reveled together over the superlative genius of it all, mutual adulation exclusive between the two of us. A late dinner and Woody Allen's "Manhattan," with an all Gershwin soundtrack, during which he completed his voicing study and then analyzed some of the arrangements of the soundtrack, topped off one evening. That was an especially loving time for us; he comfortably knowing this was his home.

Excerpt from the V-12 study

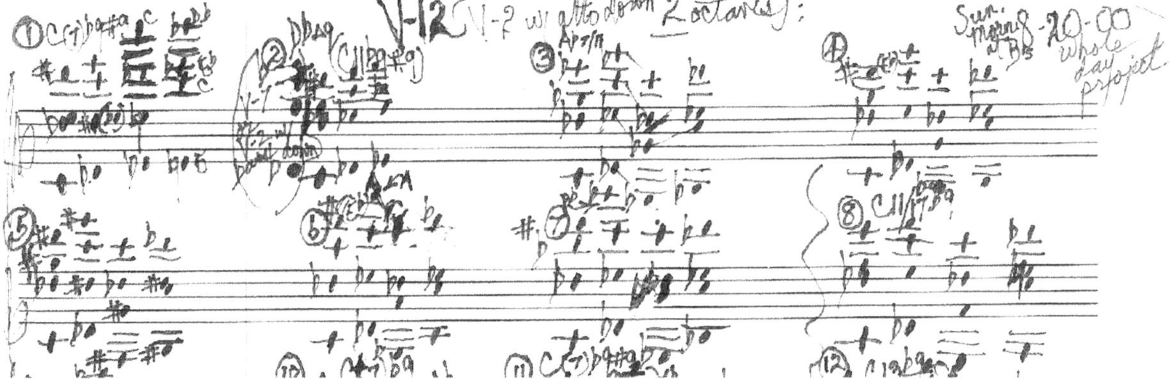

But soon there were underlying subtleties of unrest. Ted was distressed about my upcoming venture to Paris, that inkling of risk, though small could cost him my loss. He couldn't lose the thought, so it ignited anxiety about the ten-day separation and temporary parting of ways. All those days alone in this house, he would count the hours until I returned, tears were already beginning, flowing from both of us. We wended our way through the days with the usual soothers: food, music, a movie, sleep.

Sunday ushered in a radical change in the weather, a cool preview of autumn. Though a relief from weeks of heat, the breeze and scattered leaves only added to my sadness, that it hurt him so when I traveled, and I couldn't do anything to alleviate the feeling or his pain. He simply wished I didn't have to go. But I had to, maybe just this one final trip. Oh, I thought if only he would chance to travel too, I'd love to have him with me, maybe some day.

In the early evening on August 31, 2000 my parents celebrated their 50th wedding anniversary at Cafe Cordiale. They were glowing. Afterwards, at home *"We listen to Beautiful music, e.g. Schumann's 1st Symphony (Ormandy), David Diamond's Romeo & Juliet Music, Fabulous version of the Grand Canyon Suite (BPO James Levine) Finally rewire Toby, the lovely '62 T-100 D SB (#21634) a) phase: in b) Reverse wires on neck pick-ups & volume control."*

A week later, tears in our eyes, a tear streaming his cheek, we kissed. It was more than just a kiss good night, but he tried to pretend that was all it was. For we knew that ten days would pass until the 15th, when at last I would be back. For him I hoped time passed as rapidly as it usually did, I felt my heart heavy with his hurting. On September 6th Lori and I left for Paris. And again during my absence Ted's only datebook entries were his student lesson schedule. Then upon my return, *"Sept. 15 Roses for her, TWA 4:15 p.m. Barb returns. Begin working on my new guitar magazine cover-story."*

● X □ △ ★

Now that the path ahead seemed free from "obstacles," Ted once again began putting many hours into his article for the new cover-story. His goal was the NAMM Show 2001 issue. For Ted's 54th birthday I requested hearing his original classical compositions, and Ted happily obliged. After playing through each one, he began reworking them from his now more sophisticated vantage point. I did ask Ted about his premonition regarding his 54th birthday, as he was very much alive and obviously grateful to remain so. He said couldn't explain it, but needed to think about why he had fixated on the number 54.

When I woke the next morning I found him asleep on the couch. I woke him around 6:30 knowing he had to teach at noon and it always took him a while to orient himself upon waking. He stayed until 11:15, we watched the morning news and ate our respective breakfasts. Ted left just in time, but tired. I knew he didn't get enough sleep as usual. When I called him a little after 12:00 noon, he said his first student was stuck in downtown L.A. What a break, he had another hour to sleep.

October was a tranquil uneventful month. Each day brought more of the same. Fine for us, considering how stressful the first half of the year was - no complaints. The time was spent reclusively, peacefully in this little nook quietly finding and enjoying mutual amusements while baseball playoffs framed the background of the days. Ted worked on the magazine article. And one day after a fun four hours at Tower spending his gift certificate on us both, he filled our home with music until midnight when he decided to write out a Bach aria for me, which I analyzed until I was too tired to see. On another night I cooked us homemade spaghetti for the first time, and totally delighted him. After supper he improvised glorious counterpoint on J.S. Bach's Musical Offering theme. Late October brought an all New York World Series. And one afternoon at lunch with my parents, my dad reminiscing about Italy quipped, "I'm gonna Rome all over Venice with Florence." Later at home when I related this to Ted, he added, "Genoa?" Punsters both.

From October gracefully into November, and on the 3rd, Ted recorded at Will Ray's studio in Burbank for Will's new CD. Ted came here directly from his session surprisingly pleased with his playing; only one cut on what would be a compilation of various artists. Four hours spent refining that one cut, Ted was weary from the effort, ate then slept.

Then on a very fine November night, from Ted's perspective, "*Barbara very happy because: I play at B's request, The Chaconne, sight reading - not too bad. Sounds unbelievably good on The Lady unplugged. Then plugged in, then Gershwin, then on Ruby: April Love, A Certain Smile, I Got Rhythm (verses & all), Someone to Watch Over Me, Topsy & such. Computer: hours on the article.*" Ted treated me to a 4-hour concert beginning with the Bach Chaconne followed by an entire display of his versatility. His playing was exceptional, I felt so privileged to be the sole recipient of the splendor of his musical expression.

Soon it was Thanksgiving Day. A lesson learned earlier this year: never knowing when the last supper might come. Considering our aging parents, Lori and I decided to make Thanksgiving dinner for them here. Ted stayed on the couch the entire time engaged in conversation with all. I knew it was not easy for him but he survived better than I. When finally it was over, a big sigh of relief, at last Ted could eat. By 7 p.m. I was in bed reading, Ted on the computer. The house almost back to normal, the cats glad after being confined to the bedroom for most of the afternoon because Quincy was unusually social, or it was a ruse, all the while eyeing a way to escape?

Then on December 1st, the magic spell of autumn days was abruptly disrupted by bad news for Ted regarding his apartment. It seemed his massive piles of stuff; the forever growing mess might be in jeopardy. Ralph, the manager, informed Ted that the owner of the apartment building intended to have the building inspected by the fire marshal on Monday. Ralph offered to try his best to divert them from Ted's apartment but couldn't guarantee anything. Consequently Ted spent the weekend frantically trying to rearrange things in order to make his apartment appear "normal." I couldn't believe this was not a futile endeavor, but he had the illusion he could do it. All I could hope was that his guardian angel was watching over him and would somehow keep the marshal out. That was the only way he could be saved from being issued a warning, or worse yet, an eviction. He had three days to accomplish an impossible job. He didn't make it, but the potential calamity was averted. Fortuitously, an inspection of the interior was deemed unnecessary.

Along a similar line, Ted had asked me to save all my newspapers for him, which I did, but at some point realized he had been storing them all in the garage. He had planned to sort through them some day. I knew they were a fire hazard and told him he would have to sort through them by the end of the year or they would have to go. An enormous job, but he understood. The next weekend, I watched Ted diligently digging through the bags of old newspapers as the year's end drew near. He had ransacked half, and had two weeks to complete the task. Some were so old they secreted a moldy aroma and emitted a faintly visible cloud of decaying dust. We both were seized by frequent fits of sneezing. But like a blind eye blaming its surroundings he resisted many little insights I tried supplying.

We avoided festivities on Christmas Eve and chanced an untried movie, which delighted us, "*We watch an incredible movie: (1993) "The Sandlot" We're both so surprised, even shocked at how great this movie is.*" And Christmas Day, mid-morning Ted and I at my brother's, joined my parents and others, too many others, too boisterous, so soon back home. We watched the remainder of the game here, Lakers lost, fueling my already escalating sour mood, and Ted's mood was not much better. I got in bed and read until the radio airing of Bach's Christmas Oratorio, which we listened to in its entirety, close to 3 hours. Neither realized it was so long but it was inspired brilliance. We felt much better. Bach: a definite mood improver, which lasted into the next day. *"Dec. 26 Save-On, Tower: Buy Christmas Oratorio & St. John's Passion CDs for B, likewise "We're Off to see the Wizard" Barb's: Play the DeArmond X-155 and Bettina (our best all-around Guild) for her: including metamorphosis of Malaguena via different textures & tonality, and Bach, Gershwin, Tchaikowsky, also Blues tone ala my old days (& with dime for pick), the Princeton reverb cranked all the way!!! Quincy peeks out, indignant "what the h is going on?" B loves it."*

Second to the last day of the year, Tom and Wendy came bearing pinecones and home made cookies, Ted had gone for a can of gasoline. So it was the three of us that greeted him as he poured two gallons into Betsy's empty tank. As a thoughtful precaution, Tom followed Ted to a service station, as Wendy and I remained inside, brewed a pot of coffee, talked and crossed our fingers in order to ward off misfortune, relieved when they returned without incident. The four of us spent the next three hours in coffee-powered animated conversation until the Lakers game began and they had to leave to feed their dog, Daisy. I watched as the Lakers beat the Clippers by the skin of their teeth in overtime, all the while Ted pored over his studies, occasionally glancing at the game and later fell asleep on the floor.

New Year's Eve and Ted in an end of the year sullen mood, tried to be cheerful. He was outside tending to poor Betsy, dust covered, rusting in the street as I breathed fetid exhaust that wafted through the cracks. Now we'd invested so many years, which yielded a solid bond of love, sewn tightly over time, although the edges had begun to fray a bit, our lives interwoven, would remain so forever.

● X □ △ ★

January 2001 and the nights were growing really cold. Ted even turned the little heater up despite his tremendously high tolerance for cold. Now our life had settled into a commonplace sameness, a pattern that sometimes happens after so many years when left untended. We had begun to learn that nothing was perfect, although it seemed so for many years. Yet we were content to coexist, sharing whatever joys we found, but we could not deny the tension slowly growing between us. So when approximately had the change begun to occur? When did I slowly begin to notice? A few months ago? His piles of stuff had accumulated, steadily spreading into many rooms throughout my house. The storage space I had offered could no longer accommodate all he wanted to store. All his projects lay in disarray. In a way, he had simply created a new base of operations, living here and continuing the same sometimes-manic activities. All those years ago I used to wonder what he did with his time, now it was clear. Such was how we integrated our lives, one spilling into the other, yet separate, and each focusing on our own goals.

But luckily the love survived. The love was the fundamental underpinning, ever-present. Were we too used to each other; just comfortable enough that we took for granted this way of being? Because we had trouble even discussing things, it was frustrating. Oh, I didn't know, maybe we both wanted our way but the hardest part was that he had become so discouraged about most everything, always found a problem even with simple things. Was this truly new or had I just recently opened my eyes? He made his life so much harder than it had to be but he couldn't see it. He complicated it with self-created obstacles, but that was not new. I really thought for a long time I could help and I tried. I think I got tired from trying so hard, so I let the course spin itself and now it seemed he was close to drowning, still bound in fears of dying. Although his premonition had been wrong, he clung to the thought, and I had no idea how those notions rose inside him.

And I thought about how many books he had begun, tossed aside, lost, ideas written and strewn about both house and apartment. How many thousands of hours had he spent instead, shuffling his stuff from room to room, sorting it out, piling it up and insisting he must finish before he could work on his books? He still couldn't see he'd never finish and if I dared to suggest, he went into a rage so I let it rest. So why now had this become more frustrating for me? I still loved him so much; I knew I would always love him. Maybe it was sad for me to continue to witness it all now. The sad fact was that we'd been stuck in a rut for months. I should never have let it get to this.

The days remained tainted by our strained relationship both taking notice of the growing distance, wringing out the words, hurting inside and trying to repair the rift. But one night, after an explosive moment, (by that saving grace), we made some headway. A mutual recognition hit us and as the dust cleared we saw each other with a new sense of wonder, with an intense desire to rejuvenate all that had been lacking. We were reawakened to the fact that a relationship stagnated if left untended. We not only needed to put in a concerted effort, but also must continue to nurture each other. We agreed that it was certainly worth the effort; we had too much to just give up. The first step was to renew our communication and rediscover the joys that best connected us.

Slowly the holes in our relationship would begin to mend. With a renewed fervor, Ted had resumed work on the cover-story. However he would not meet his self-imposed deadline for the NAMM show issue. In fact this interview was never to be completed. However, Ted optimistically noted the nature of his phone conversation with the publisher, *"Nice call, the cover-story on me ON whenever I get it done: the 4 things: a) the story, b) the recording I submit & they have to transcribe, c) and I have proof read."*

One afternoon I took a break from playing piano and chanced to glance at Ted's new self constructed interview. I read less for content, as it was similar to the initial work, but what was impressive was his clever use of words. It was a much-improved version of the original. Later when I related my admiration of the writing, he was delighted that I took the time to read it and pleased that I found it to my liking. That evening we had planned to begin watching the Ken Burns multi-part series on Jazz. Ted had mounded up a bunch of pillows and was sprawled comfortably on the floor. A most inviting sight, I decided to join him there. A better decision I couldn't have made, something just clicked and unexpectedly we connected. It was like a picnic, Ted made popcorn, and we ended up watching NFC Championship Football, Baltimore at Oakland. We rediscovered having fun.

At the end of January 2001, Ted gave a half-day seminar at USC, what he referred to as a master class. After a quiet lunch with my parents I came home to find Ted lying on the couch waiting for his dinner, which he was warming in the oven. Tired but satisfied by the success of his seminar, at my request, he ventured to tell me the details. I defer to his datebook for his actual account, *"Give a seminar at USC. Subjects I discussed: How I decide what to do in arranging a piece for solo guitar (mood, rhythmic types 1st) Intros, 4th chords, a) see from top down 2,3,4 & 5 voice, counterpoint, b) that beautiful Debussy Pat K. requested "Girl w/t Flaxen Hair." Lulu (my beloved all time probably greatest stock '52 Tele performed magnificently (her 3rd straight time 3 for 3) as did Smokey, the breathtaking mid '70s X-175 huge Guild archtop."*

After he'd eaten and napped for about an hour, still in the mood to play guitar, he spent the evening gloriously pouring out songs, the evidence of his "genius" apparent to me. Yet he refuted the use of genius applied to him, contended it was just a million hours of patience and practicing. So, in deference to Ted, however one would term his abilities, no amount of hours one could put in would render the results that Ted achieved through his instinctive ability, his innate sense of understanding and feel for the music.

On Valentines Day Ted braved the pouring rain and brought me an adorable stuffed bear holding a basket of candy. We watched the Lakers but he grew dismayed by their playing, so instead, he penned two luscious arrangements for a student, a small fortune in gorgeous chords. The next day, Ted waited for the mailman with the aching anticipation of receiving his residual check, which alas did not arrive. This was the beginning of an agitation that was to escalate as the day progressed bringing mishap upon mishap all resulting from the delay of that much needed payment to compensate for a financially barren month. Drained from the incessant tension, he slept, and the check appeared like a miracle in next day's mail. His financial woes disappeared in an instant, forgotten during the long hours browsing at Tower, even some treats for me, *"To Barb's: give her the CDs I got for her: a) Schumann (double CD) Piano Trios b) D'Indy Tone Poems (late works), c) Jacques Loussier (double CD) of jazz Bach - el delicio."* Nor could he resist the blonde '77 ES 175D, bought from a student, without a thought of remorse.

'Twas a rainy hell of a week, at least for me. When Friday finally came I unplugged the phone, preferring to sulk alone. I was letting the day unfold, and hoping to get some work done, when Ted showed up. He was worried at not having been able to reach me. The rain continued relentlessly, but impervious to weather, Ted did errands for us, enabling me to remain warm and dry the entire weekend, as he graciously gathered our immediate needs along with some delicacies. Mentally he worked for hours, his mind fixated on finding the right title for his new book about bass enhanced triads, and an acronym for what he termed the *"hideously named slash chord."*

Days later and still raining, I spent half the day in bed reading. When Ted called asking what I wanted him to bring, he wouldn't hang up until I chose something for lunch, so I conceded. He arrived soaked to the bone, no raincoat, no umbrella, a bother both, and again piled goodies high on the table, having made several stops in order to procure various items decided upon a whim. How I appreciated the luxury he indulged me with by bringing the fried zucchini with apricot sauce, a request he pried from me during our conversation. He treated himself to gigantic French fries so we ate together, then he slept while I watched the Lakers, waking later during the 4th quarter and watching the rest with me. Afterwards he treated me to his playing. For almost two hours I languished in the sound, he chose old ballads from the 1930's, most of which were show tunes with beautiful melodic lines he elegantly embellished.

The rain continued unremittingly. Ted on the computer, where I predicted he'd be throughout the weekend, said he was close to finishing. Actually he did go out to do errands. I stayed home consumed by weather related petulance, pouted and played the piano. When he returned much, much later, my wonder over why he took so long was directly dispelled as he held a Macy's bag in his hand and slowly removed a gray canister and handed it to me. I knew the nature of the gift though not the choice, but I readily discovered a beautiful crystal Toucan. As I was admiring it, he handed me another gray canister, which contained a crystal Cobra (snake, not car) fabulous and as I thanked him, exclaiming of course I loved them but he shouldn't have, he handed me yet another, the smallest, and oh! my favorite of the three, two tiny crystal turtles, absolutely adorable. Considerably cheered by this sparkling array gracing the room, that afternoon we both worked somewhat productively, Ted on the computer, I playing piano and listening to the Lakers game on the radio. All this in the same room at the same time and Ted insisted he didn't mind. I couldn't imagine why, it probably made quite a racket of dissimilar sounds, his powers of concentration - amazing.

One bit of important news we had chosen purposely to ignore: Ted's apartment building had been sold and we had no idea of the intentions of the new owners. Ted was obviously concerned, and the concern turned to worry. Soon and yet again he would need to work like crazy to try and make his apartment presentable. We knew if he had to move it would be a nightmare.

● X □ △ ★

From where I left off last when trying to write in my journal, tending towards the muddle of something and vying for time, at that moment there was none. Ted wanted to leave at that instant, lest I changed my mind. Although we needed to go sometime, so we went again, back to the mall. We had to exchange a shirt I had bought him because the color was too light and he thought it would show stains of perspiration. As he searched for an alternative, he wet each shirt with a lick at the tip of his finger applied to the fabric and just when ready to give up he found a bright multi-colored one, Hawaiian style, his very first Hawaiian shirt. That discovery led to a new trend in his preference of shirts till the end of his days. Prior to this find, Ted almost exclusively wore plaid flannel. One chore completed, now I had to convince Ted that I had more than enough crystal ornaments and I finally succeeded by allowing him to buy me a purse instead. That at least I needed.

A most tiring experience barely survived by both. But it was that time of year when he got "that check" and intended to spend it, insisted on something for me too, in reciprocation for all I did for him. With his desire to buy things sufficiently sated for a while, I implored him to save an ample portion as a precaution due to the unstable state of his living arrangements. That evening we easily relaxed, watched "Bullets Over Broadway," he fussing with something for the first hour, emptied and organized the clutter clogging his pockets I think. After the movie, I had to comment regarding his choice of priorities since he had contended he may not have much time on this earth. I suggested, even though I didn't put much credibility into his vision, that perhaps his time would be better spent finishing his books. He said he knew I'd say that, then stated he was taking a risk in case he lived, hoped it would improve his chances of not having to move. Given that, I asked him if he realized how much his stuff was controlling him, his life, constantly impeding him from doing more important and valuable work but he said he couldn't stop, any more than I could not go to Paris or do my Sunday crossword puzzle. I countered by explaining that those activities didn't hinder my existence and he had to concede. Nonetheless, his obsession took precedence.

One Sunday afternoon he called from Super Crown Books. I had mentioned they were going out of business so it wasn't entirely surprising to hear him tell me he'd been there a while, had a pile of books to look through and then would come home. I drove over there figuring I might find something and to see the mountain of books he'd amassed. I found him sitting next to a pile of quite a considerable height, swooning in ecstasy over the selection, which he was in the midst of perusing. I meandered through the isles for an hour, scanned the shelves and found several books I'd wanted. Then I left him there to continue pondering, all the while knowing the irony of his actions.

Back home and just when I was getting settled to practice piano, Ted arrived. He allowed me the time to play after all and worked on his music, "*Begin serious work on finding all 4 note (non-doubled tone) chords in the Overtone Dominant Scale (key of Bb),*" so both busy for about two hours until the Lakers game.

The game was exciting, extremely well played and completely engaged Ted's attention, causing him to miss the first fifteen minutes of the Oscars, to which we switched after the win and continued to watch together. There was one funny sort of revelation brought about during the Oscars. Ted pointed out Tom Hanks and reminded me we had seen him in "Big," which led me to comment on my favorite scene where Hanks discovered a plate of baby corn at a buffet table and unsure of how one went about eating it, picked it up and began gnawing at it as one would a normal size ear of corn. Then Ted asked me innocently, how else would one eat it?

On the last day of March 2001, the verdict was in. The El Dorado apartment building in which Ted was living had officially been sold. Word had it the new owner would most likely inspect his new premises, unit by unit. In light of this inevitable event Ted began working single handedly, frantically, almost non-stop, determined to deliver to the eyes of the new procurer a presentable, orderly view of his living quarters. By doing that, Ted hoped to quell any misgivings on the new owner's part, if upon seeing Ted's unit, the owner had reservations about allowing Ted to remain. Yet the work could have been in vain if the building was slated for renovation or a sizable rent increase. Ted was still in the dark regarding any intentions but needed to remain optimistic. The alternative was worse and I could only pray that his guardian angel (for surely he had one) would once again intercede on his behalf.

After taking into account all the information provided regarding the new owner's actions, I came to the conclusion that in the interim between now and when Ted's lease expired in September, he was probably not in imminent danger of major changes. I explained to Ted that I perceived no need for the new owners to check the interior of his living space. It was an opportune moment for he was prepared to listen to my reasoning and I suppose what struck him most was my question of what possible reason would the new owners have for wanting to see it, for which he had no answer. That seemed to ease his mind considerably and after a month of labor he was in need of a break.

Earlier in the day he had retrieved his old Standel amp and now here it was, sitting in the living room. As a result we indulged in what had been a rarity of late, jamming together on anything, but today it was the blues. From Ted's datebook, *"Flat wound strings (3rd string singles) at Stein on Vine. Pick up my old Standel Amp from Albert, (Guitars R Us). Nice visit with Albert & Dave. I try out his old Guild amp with reverb, a boss amp & he shows me what may be the 1st lefty '54 or '55 sunburst Tele style (with contour's body) P- bass! To Barbara: Put flat wound .022 3rd on Goldie, show her the wild reverb sound on the Standel amp CRANK IT with Goldie at B's request. Plug in Daisy (& later Lala) & play Jimmy Reed & Gospel style AND… B, at her request learns the Db minor pentatonic, we jam on bluesy 'twist' feels or triplets."*

Now each day seemed to gently flow into the next with little variation from one to another, except for special occasions such as Mother's Day Sunday. The early afternoon was spent at my parents. Our family was newly reunited following my father's hospital stay and all seemingly back to normal for now, which made the occasion all the more meaningful. My mother was particularly thrilled by Ted's gift of a beautiful crystal butterfly.

That our life seemed to revolve around routine was nothing new and routine suited us best. Each routine formed circumstantially, oftentimes around the Lakers or baseball games. But luckily, there had been little to keep us from the productive pursuits to which we'd grown accustomed. Since I had become comfortable practicing piano while Ted was using the computer, that also turned into a routine, and now I found it quite satisfying to be working side by side, all the more motivated by Ted's encouragement and praise despite my not feeling deserving of half of it.

Meanwhile, the outside of the El Dorado was getting renovated; roofers and painters had descended upon the premises. The Lakers were in the play-offs. Ted alternated between his apartment reorganization, the new article and music studies.

● X □ △ ★

We watched the Lakers sweep the semi-finals. Two sweeps in a row, first Portland, then Sacramento. We watched the Lakers take the first two games of the finals, in San Antonio no less! During the games, Ted got in a lot of fabulous practicing, and came up with some great new book ideas, *"A Book I must write: something like "The 3 (or 4) Great Methods for Learning Scales" 1). My 7 position scales, descending, top 2 strings only. 2). "Drenching Yourself in One Color, One Key at a time. Top strings, descending from a root in lots of tonalities. Top strings at first in (Lydian, Major, Mixolydian, Dorian, etc, later Melodic Minor, Gypsy Major, Gypsy Dominant, Gypsy Minor (b3,#4,b6) and more. 3). One Fingering, One Key: on lots of frets, i.e. in many positions to produce lots of tonalities, all in one key. All over taped chord progression couplets."*

Shortly after that, on a particularly inspired night due to, "*My new awareness of reading, study "Studio de Contrapuntly."* I shared the benefits of Ted's new insights. *"Some of the best Bachian improvising I've ever done. On the 1977(?) ES-175 D blonde with today's new strings: acoustic bronze bottom 3 .032 .042 .054, Flatwound 3rd .026, top 2: .013 & .017 The acoustic sound & wide neck are PERFECT & inspiring for this style. Hours of practice."* Heavenly!

Towards the end of May 2001, Ted was scheduled to give a seminar at Sam Ash Music in Hollywood. As the date neared, Ted began his preparation, and the night prior to the seminar he was playing exceptionally well. I lay in bed and couldn't even read, so compelled was I to listen, what a pleasurable segue to a peaceful sleep. Regarding his playing, even he agreed, *"Prepare for Seminar tomorrow, improvise on Savannah & Lucia both of whom are sounding SO delicious in the Princeton Reverb. Play deep minor modern jazz, lots of vamp echo near slap bass low end answer lines. Some of my very finest playing ever."*

Much to our dismay, Ted's seminar was scheduled on the afternoon of what would later be remembered as Historic Game 4. The Lakers swept the Western Conference Finals, bulldozing San Antonio. What a phenomenal winning streak, 19 straight, 12 in the playoffs! But I had it on tape and would watch it again with him afterwards. Although he said the seminar went well, the notes he wrote were meager, *"May 27 4:00 SAM ASH SEMINAR Bring the 2 Guild archtops. Diatonic 4th chords in 6 tonalities, one key. Pick style rhythm jazz guitar (a little), Misty in B."*

On Sunday, other than the usual crossword puzzle and such, we watched Game 7 of the Eastern Conference Finals, to learn that Philly would face the Lakers for the Championship. Following the post game show Ted got sidetracked by other programs, including some shows he had taped. I'd had my fill of TV, not he, rarely he, but eventually it would get to me, the eerie glow, the incessant talk, but as with all the things he loved, he indulged excessively.

The first week in June, the Championship match began. How much faster could my heart possibly beat, or longer yet could my breath be held? Who knew that a mere game could produce such extreme reaction bordering on insanity? Ted knew, went through it years ago as an avid fan and now he had learned to be calm. I could finally unclench my fists and sink back into the pillows as the Lakers prevailed in Game 3. So what does it mean when you get everything you've asked for? Maybe nothing. Luck. Ted and the beautiful weather would have been enough but for the Lakers to win Game 4 and their 2nd straight championship on my birthday? Perfection.

Spring flowed unnoticed into the months of summer. The days framed in haze. Ted had begun watching baseball, Angels' games, and was trying to rekindle my interest. The long drawn out days seemed well suited for the slow going nature of baseball. It also afforded the illusion of more time. Ted had received a request to record some music cues for a documentary produced by one of his students. In the quiet hours of the night, Ted plugged his guitar into a recording device and achieved 74 minutes of inimitable miscellaneous improvisation. A spicy variety suited to enhance any number of scenes. Many of Ted's cues were used as part of the underscore for two documentary films, "Art City" and "Richard Tuttle, Never Not an Artist" both produced by Chris Maybach, and the DVDs are still available.

Ted, pleased with the subsequent results and the success of the recording method was inspired to tackle a project I'd wanted him to do for a long while: make a CD for me. What

I initially requested was a CD of our favorite songs. Alas, this he never really did. The Pod was a new toy, he was enthralled and wanted to experiment with the endless selection of effects. So instead he recorded not only one, but two CDs of wonderful, interesting and uniquely devised improvisation. *"July 20 Record 1st CD for Barb: 1) 4 1/2 m. of (5b on the Pod, I think) with Delay, jazz blues single line with chord things too. 2) 70 m. or so of Baroque (mainly) Improvisation with tempo medium-fast straight 8ths, delay used as echo. Wow! (some blues, jazz blues & other) Hand went numb in a few spots either played thru or when this became fruitless shook it off while right hand continued. Also, as usual, lots of pain in spots requiring great strength & agility at the same time."*

In the oppressive heat of mid summer Ted gave another seminar at Sam Ash Music, his notes reflected the initial lack of energy transformed into what inevitably went very well, *"July 29 4:00 SAM ASH SEMINAR (#3 in last few months) I bring Bettina (her debut gig for us) & Lulu - play into Line 6 Spider. Starts very stiff, no participation from the 20 or so attending. Then room energy combined with me really digging in hard to GROOVE HARD and cracking off some spontaneous funny lines, the seminar takes off & ends up for the whole last hour as a kind of roaring resonance."*

As a result of many requests, Ted had depleted the supply of business cards I had made for him. A project Ted hadn't initially intended, presented itself. As I was getting ready to print a new slew of cards for him, he decided he wanted to redesign them. A difficult proposition since he was totally unfamiliar with the program, which caused some frustration and this combined with his ultra fussy nature consumed quite a few hours. He was especially humorous. At first when redoing them Ted chose a most incongruous background for a musician, opted for one with a paintbrush simply because he preferred the colors, but changed it to one more suited to music lessons. When he was finally satisfied with his new improved business card he began a song list, his initial intention. After a short while, I couldn't stand it, I was lost in uncontrollable laughter as I watched while he perused the font selection, eliminated many because he hated the shape of one single letter! This A is too rounded on top, or this C is too fat! I found this hysterically funny and he was glad to at least have been able to amuse me. At midnight I withdrew to the bedroom with a book, by then he had found an acceptable font, and was in the midst of organizing his song list.

In the scorching month of August my father came home from a rather prolonged hospital stay. A simple pacemaker replacement resulted in pneumonia; an overnight stay became two weeks. Ted and I went to welcome him home and see if he needed anything. Fortunately both of my parents were coping very well but grateful for our concern and caring. Ted spent most of that weekend on the computer working on compiling a master song list. An innocuous project, but considering the fact that he'd been compiling lists for years by hand, he already had hundreds. There would be hundreds more to come, another compulsion although not a new one, just new doing the lists on the computer. Ted actually loved making lists, it was another way he organized things in his mind.

Alas, if only those simple and basically untroubled times could have lasted. But in less than a month everyone's life was destined to change forever.

Chapter V

Facing New Obstacles - Life Lessons
(2001-2004)

"SEPT. 11 Disaster: N.Y.C Attacked!!!! Twin Towers destroyed! Go to comfort Barb. TV: the news is riveting if horrifying." That was all Ted was able to state in his datebook. A day of horror and disbelief reflected world wide, as the collective consciousness of much of the human race sustained a state of shock at the vile, senseless act of terrorism upon the World Trade Center and the Pentagon. I didn't know what else to write, I felt sick and I was trembling inside. Ted and I reeled from that nightmare for days, grateful only to have each other's comfort. And although I would sometimes complain about the ubiquitous city noise, the ensuing silence was eerie. No airplanes. No helicopters. Just a faint trace of traffic.

That horrendous event was to foreshadow a seemingly relentless torrent of extremely sad events scattered amongst the next 36 months.

A week later the Ford Bronco took what we thought would prove to be its last blow. Ted was heading east on Ventura Boulevard, went through a yellow and collided with a Lexus turning left. No one was hurt but apparently the Bronco took the brunt of it. Ted was able to make it to my house *only* because he didn't need to make a right turn. A friend came to help and armed with a crow bar and a two by four he pried at the fender for over an hour as Ted periodically turned the wheel to check for clearance. Eventually they were successful. However, the radiator was leaking and then we noticed the fan blades were pushed into the housing not allowing the fan to turn. Ted and his friend were able to cut the housing out enabling the blades to rotate but still the radiator would not hold water.

Ted was quite shaken by the experience; he just sat on the curb and stared at the Bronco for a long while. When he came in we attempted to discuss the ramifications and options but soon both of us were frustrated as our opinions differed. Ted insisted he wouldn't file a claim against the other party, he reasoned it was both of their faults and felt it wouldn't be right. No matter how I tried to explain how the "insurance system" worked he held his ground.

This was Ted's point of view: The other driver was a very nice man, had a young son, and Ted didn't want to further inflict difficulties on this person. Ted gave the man his word that he wouldn't file a claim and must uphold it. He felt since they were both at fault the other man should not have to compensate him (Ted) for the damage to the Bronco. He said this is what was right in his heart and must follow that feeling. There was nothing I could say to change his mind. Although admirable, close to saintly, close to martyrdom, I had to question his rationale. However, I just dropped the subject. I needed a day to catch my breath, I felt emotionally drained. That night while Ted and I were watching something on TV, I passed out sound asleep on the couch, very rare for me. Somehow I mustered up just enough energy to get in bed.

All too soon we woke to news that the U.S. had started bombing Afghanistan. The news was unsettling and we thought it might set the stage for more terrorist activity here. Consequently, Ted spent most of October and half of November organizing his most treasured belongings, packing them in specially designated shopping bags, in case, as he put it, we had to evacuate the city. Regarding the reality of being able to evacuate, we argued our respective points into oblivion. Preposterous.

But despite frayed nerves, the days brought some wonderful diversions. We began collecting the newly minted state quarters, and were delighted when either of us happened upon one we were still missing. We watched the World Series of course, that year the New York Yankees and Arizona Diamondbacks. Ted rooted for New York with all his heart.

Then so seemingly, suddenly soon, our lives were sent reeling again by an unexpected and anguishing loss. On Saturday she seemed so vibrant, then around 10 pm that night my brother called to tell me she had been taken by ambulance to the hospital. She had collapsed. The paramedics were not able to revive her. Upon arriving at the hospital we were told her heart had failed. The shock was the most overwhelming I had ever felt, a complete state of disbelief. There was nothing left but to go home. It was a Saturday night, the17th of November 2001, my mother died.

Now time had become so distorted. Each moment stretched endlessly in unbroken hours while the prior days had receded to such a distance it was impossible to believe any time had passed at all. The remainder of the month was a blur. A sad holiday season, and in the midst of that grief, on December 29th, Ted lost his beloved Aunt Reva.

On another front in our life a different grief, more aptly a sad realization took place. On the 3rd of January 2002, Ted's 1972 Plymouth Fury, Betsy, which had been sitting in front of my house for over a year, got a 72 hour parking violation. Ted finally made the decision to send her to car heaven, which might have seemed a simple process except that she was filled to brimming with his things. It took him at least 7 hours to empty her out, the front of the house and street was a sea of newspapers, paper bags, books, and magazines, everything he was inclined to collect that reflected the years she served him. The next day I watched through the window as Betsy was being towed away. Ted was standing in the street forlorn, the sun setting, that sad picture told the tale. I got it with my camera but would it capture the anguish of what I saw? I know he shed a tear or more. And all the stuff now crammed into the Bronco and the Ford Escort, (Ted's new and much needed little car, a gift, which resulted from our recent grief laden days). Ted was to fondly dub her, Miranda.

During the next week Ted slowly began to resume his usual obligations. Ted was never one to be afflicted by grief; he had developed an acceptance of death, which enabled him to let go. His own belief system, which encompassed the idea that there is a reason for everything, combined with a natural resiliency and an ever-present optimism in the life process or forces, impelled him forward.

Over the telephone Ted gave his first installment of an interview with Jim Carlton. Ted's coin collecting fever escalated from state quarters to an avid interest and love of all coins. He bought a coin book for us to study. Many evenings we immersed ourselves in beautiful music and he often brought me flowers.

Then only seven weeks after the death of my mother, life sent me reeling backwards with another heart-shattering and powerful blow. On January 14th, 2002 only two weeks into the New Year, I lost my most dearly beloved father. I lapsed back into a state of grief so deep even Ted couldn't reach me.

Ted remained strong, leant me all his support, brought me dinners, and spent entire nights going through my parent's belongings when I could no longer bear up. He cheered me for brief moments with special little treasures of theirs he found. I couldn't even write in my journal, but he kept a record of the days for us, *"Jan. 20 Go with Barb to Dan & Anita's condo: sort through the music books, manuscripts & odds & ends. B holding up a little better. Music as healer: B plays the Elgar Elegy for Strings for us. Then the 3 fabulous gospel numbers from "Corrina, Corrina" Next: The ULTRA-great HUGE reverb el perfecto N.Y. pit orchestra sound of Gershwin arranged & played at a very top level by Tom Pierson: the soundtrack from "Manhattan." We always LOVE this. Then the Helene Grimaud version of Gershwin's Concerto in F And we repeat the slow & last movements a couple more times so B can really start to absorb it & notice that it's really as if GG was laughing inside & saying "I'll just kind of rewrite the Rhapsody or write the extension of it and/or just switch the order around of certain notes..." also in the equation: The 3 Preludes (esp. the 2nd maybe) They sound like a rewrite of The Concerto."*

While I remained bound within my sorrow, Ted continued to do everything to soothe my wounds and still maintained a remarkable stability to deal with the demands of his own life. A fortunate break came when his noisy upstairs neighbors vacated their apartment, which gave Ted a temporary respite, allowing him some peace and quiet to work there undisturbed. Last June he had accumulated many of his father's belongings, and combined with a considerable portion of my parents' possessions, along with his own substantial mass of things, the interior of his apartment bordered on chaos. While Ted sifted through, sorted and tried to put things in order, he also continued with his phone interview, worked on some music studies, gave lessons and took care of me.

He was relentless in his attempts to pull me out of my sadness. Alas, it was too soon for me to cease grieving, and as a result, Ted suffered the pain of my pain well past the second month of the New Year.

In late February, when his check came, he was able to curb his fervor at first, and only purchased one guitar, *" Guild rescue - CE 100D - buy a rejected mid '60s from a student for what he paid Norm. Even tho her strings are light What a responsive tone machine!!!! And with my favorite pick ups - the Guild small humbuckers."*

It was difficult for Ted not being able to help me, to pull me out of my sadness. He would spend most of March trying to put his apartment in order. For me it was just one endless string of days. I would not accept the irrevocable change, my thinking, my own being, was strangely foreign to me. As spring neared, the hours seemed already too long because of my state of mind, and I wondered if ever again I'd welcome the long warm summer evenings. At that juncture nightfall was already long in coming and I couldn't seem to easily make the adjustment. Soon we would change the clocks ahead, in two weeks? Yet I wasn't ready. The darkness suited me better.

Until one April morning, the sky was crystal clear and the wind visiting, a strong presence, it dried out the ground completely and rendered the short soaking of rain little use to the garden. In fact if I hadn't heard it the night before I'd not have known the rain had fallen at all. I knew I was beginning to make a distinction again, separate dream from reality and wanted to embrace Ted's theories about life. He said I was definitely coming around. We began to plan for my 50th birthday party, which I had now decided to celebrate in a special way. We listened to and loved The Musical Offering by our hero, J.S. Bach, it was my favorite all time music now. The warmth was back and flowing between us. We shared our first nice REAL kiss in a long time. I was surprised by his initiative.

We had begun to enjoy our time together again. How long had it been ...? One evening after a sumptuous supper, we watched the Lakers' nerve wracking, double overtime loss to Portland. Then to restore calm, Ted played guitar and it was such a pleasure to once again hear him, had it been months? I became so emotionally moved by his playing, and he graciously accepted my requests of special songs I loved, along with many others on a multitude of different instruments, the room strewn with guitars. I reveled in this ecstasy until the early hours of the morning.

● X □ △ ★

However, once again at Ted's apartment building, new neighbors were moving into the unit above him. The long hours there, sifting through our parents' things were cut back considerably since there was no buffer against the noise. What wasn't yet sorted got lost in the shuffle, as he spent more time here again. Besides it was time for the NBA playoffs and the Lakers were once again in contention. That night he played Savannah, our beloved 1957 X-150, improvising contrapuntal accompaniments and variations on The Musical Offering, I was so impressed, and he commented, *"very satisfying that I can!"*

Some days the loss of my parents still weighed heavily. Sometimes it was just a short lapse, luckily, such as one evening when I sipped the last of the wine Ted so thoughtfully brought me. Then, a rarity, he played guitar and we sang together. I harmonized "This Little Light of Mine" and Ted thought we sounded pretty good, *"bring her favorite Sterling Merlot wine and pull out Bettina & Barb sings after I get the ball rolling. She sings great harmony to my "This Little Light of Mine."* I was never sure of that, but of this: he pulled me up out of my depression so wonderfully well, just what I needed. Many days I teetered on the borderline, not knowing which way I'd fall.

After all, it was only May and my emotional state still vacillated daily. The Lakers' win moderated my moodiness, but Ted decided we should remedy the cause of a particular irritation. Hence, we went to replace my old, faulty coffee maker. After two days of watery coffee - not fit to drink- and two days in a rage over it, my temper flared. I came close to throwing the useless brewing unit across the room. Upon returning home with the new brewer, I made a good strong cup to make sure it was functional. Then we gathered our strength and drove to the cemetery. Now that the bronze plaques were placed on my parents' graves I wanted to see them. Standing there it was still so hard to believe, and I was crying again. The new polished bronze stood out stark amongst the old weathered ones, a reminder that so little time had passed. As we left the cemetery, I wondered if by the time the years had tarnished the bronze to a gray green patina, would the pain have lessened? I suspected no, it would simply stab less frequently.

A half hour was enough shuffling through old music books, used and water damaged, on the back shelf at Baxter Northup Music store. I developed hoarseness in my throat plus a slight stuffiness from the dust, or so I assumed, until later that evening when a cold began to bloom. It woke me at some predawn hour, my throat so sore I couldn't swallow. I got up for a teaspoon or two of honey which helped but I couldn't get back to sleep, so just lay in bed grew sleepy towards morning, then the cats got up. Ted heard it in my voice when he called and stopped off for a large container of soup for me on his way. My throat soothed, we watched the Lakers take Game 3 in San Antonio while Ted worked on some music studies. For three days in succession Ted administered to my illness. He plied me with strawberries, apple juice and more soup. Although much improved by Mother's Day, I feared a relapse caused by sadness; I was congested again from tears. But the feeling slowly faded when Ted and I watched the game, a sure cure as the Lakers took Game 4 in a fist clenching, pillow gripping, nick of time win at the last minute. Spectacular finish.

As Ted arrived for Game 5, I witnessed a comical vision through the window. Blocking the path to my front door a giant cloud of gnats had stopped Ted in his tracks. Stuck he stayed, his expression perplexed until bravely waving his arms he dispersed the amorphous swarm. Such was Ted's first tangle with a travesty of gnats. I had to laugh. Ted and I listened to Game 5 on the radio as we sat at the table, he working on his Pentatonic System, I analyzing Bach Chorales until the intense ending completely drew my concentration to each play. Lakers won the Semi-Finals, another gripping finish. Whew!

Days later and still chilled I made tea and stayed in. Would I ever get over this cold? On Saturday, Ted and I were stunned by a superb Game 1. Lakers played exceptionally well winning in Sacramento, quelling any inkling of a tinkle from even one cowbell.

For a while now our lives continued to basically revolve around the NBA Finals. Ted's datebook, a testimony to his enjoyment of the game, *"Wow! What a thrill!!!! Game 4 Western Finals Lakers down 2-1 against the deeply talented Sacramento Kings. Lakers thrill us: One of the great 4th quarter come-backs (actually 2nd, 3rd AND 4th - down by 24 at home in 1st quarter) culminating in Robert Horry's last .8 of a second 3 pointer for a 1 point win, when all seemed lost.... Barb & I scream & scream. Euphoric bedlam at Staples Center."*

Ted taught here on Memorial Day, more I think for peace and quiet, which he'd been craving much of lately. The organization of his apartment once again put on hold due to the new neighbors, his two-month respite ended. In the mood for Italian food, we ordered in pizza for me, and spaghetti for Ted. The game had started, but Ted had put on a Mozart CD while we ate, so we came in a little late, Lakers lost anyway. The following day there was no game, Ted practiced on Amber, his beloved X-170 orange-blonde stream of sustain, entertaining us both until late in the evening. Then the next night he sat calmly amused, staying contained while still sharing my elation as the Lakers thrilled us with an overtime win against Sacramento, on the road!

June ushered in an early heat wave, days in excess of 100 degrees and we needed several fans blowing from every direction. A week of NBA Finals, Lakers versus New Jersey and on the 12th the Lakers accomplished their goal, a four game sweep! That win maintained the Lakers championship for the third consecutive year, and was being cleverly coined as a "three-peat." We were thrilled!

My Crest disease kept taking its toll, worse each year through its natural course, now compounded by stress as well. And soon I would be fifty. Fifty! Oh!

For my fiftieth birthday, I had hired a string sextet to play live at my home for Ted and me, and a scant handful of friends. The ensemble consisted of 2 violins, 2 violas, and 2 celli, chosen specifically to play the 6 Voice Ricercare from J.S. Bach's Musical Offering. With that piece, the performance began, followed by the Trio Sonata from the same work. Next was what Ted and I considered "our" fugue, (the way many couples have "their song"), Bach's "Little" fugue in G minor, and then other favorite Bach pieces, an encore of the Ricercare, (even better the second time), and probably the most beautiful version of Happy Birthday I'd ever heard, (except Ted's version). After the concert, as we ate and drank champagne, Ted played beautiful Baroque counterpoint on the guitar in accordance with the already established musical agenda. But the gathering soon "degenerated" after we drained several more bottles of champagne, into a ridiculous sing-along as Ted accompanied us on such numbers as Row, Row, Row Your Boat, and all the other frivolous but fun silly ditties we could think of to sing; a bit too much champagne.

The spring and summer seasons overlapped as did the sports venues, from indoors to outdoors, basketball to baseball. Ted and I watched the Angels for the first time this season. Again I'd forgotten how relaxing it was only having to pay half attention, so I diverted the other half to playing guitar quietly, softly but not quite so, since apparently Ted could hear enough to make helpful suggestions. Afterwards Ted went on errands, and returned with a dozen multi-colored roses, we ate a simple dinner. Then with the TV on in the background Ted amused himself on the guitar and detailed later, *"Wow: Amazing blues in B improv on the perfect guitar for this key, Sadie, a) Jimmy Reed style intro, b) more 3 note IV7, more approaches into open triads on high strings, on V, IV, even bII & c) other low locked double line tough edge, d) back to Gospel bottom 4 strings (High register 1st, then...) a) expanded diatonics, e.g. bII, bVII, IV 7, no bVI at 1st, b) straight diatonic sweet choir, gradually, e) more jazz a) many shades of blue, b) sweet major colors, c) occasional raunchy riff focus & generator d) extensions on expanded diatonic roots. B is very pleased & we watch the 'Freeway Series' Baseball, Dodgers at Angels - nice change of pace for us."*

In the beginning of July, the little carnival that occasionally came to the Hazeltine Park set up for the holiday weekend enticing Ted and me on a Saturday afternoon. Not at all fancy, but reminiscent of an old-time good time that as children we would have been dazzled. So in a way we became spellbound for a few hours. Although we didn't try the rides, we let the game booths tempt us. It was as hard to win as ever, yet we came away with an armful of stuffed toys: two fish, a ladybug and a parrot, because as the carnival man said, there no one ever loses. Then we walked through the house of mirrors, infinite us negotiating the maze. This was fascinating for me, however I realized while inside, Ted was very uncomfortable. He would not look in the mirrors, but kept his eyes on the floor saying "don't stop, just figure out how to get to the end." He was in such a hurry to exit. Afterwards he explained that he only went in because he didn't want me to go in alone! Oh Ted! So we bought three bags of fresh popped popcorn, and headed home.

With a renewed outlook on life, Ted and I celebrated our 10-year anniversary. The house was filled with flowers, mostly roses, which he added to again and again and there were roses everywhere. For him, I finally had the six rolls of film developed that had been sitting in the desk drawer for months. Three of the rolls were from his camera, photos of his students and, astonishingly, guitars! For Ted, there were never enough photos of these precious treasures. The other three rolls of photos were from my camera and equally unique, the cats, more guitars, but one was of my 50th birthday celebration. I was so grateful Ted took the time to record that afternoon on film for me. Anyway it gave us both much pleasure to finally know what was on those six rolls. We also watched the All Star Baseball Game, the first hour being tributes and retrospectives and by far the most engaging aspect of the show. The game only got our attention occasionally, except for the way it ended - in a tie! He was shocked, in all of baseball history that had never happened.

When I woke next morning I realized he was just leaving and found him outside the front door in the midst of carrying bags to his car. No wonder I was able to sleep so late undisturbed by the cats, he'd considerately kept them from waking me. It was a lovely commemoration of our special day and most especially the loving card he gave me.

● X □ △ ★

On July 14th, 2002 Ted gave the first of what was to be several seminars at California Vintage Guitar. We arrived early to a warm welcome by Danny and Rob at their new huge store where a hundred seats were set up to accommodate the attendees. I made myself comfortable on a couch in the back, waited and read. Ted had begun setting up; soon people began to wander in, and in no time at all the place filled. When it was time to start there was standing room only, the store was full, my guess, in excess of 150 people! I felt his seminar was a complete success. As always, he was funny, highly informative and played exceptionally well, although this he refuted, but was most grateful for the love and support of so many people. Alas, neither of us took notes.

Within a mere six months Ted's new car, Miranda the Ford Escort, had accumulated an abundance of stuff. In other words it was stuffed with "stuff" and now resembled the inside of his bygone Betsy and the Bronco. Naturally there was no place for me to sit. Since Wendy's 50th birthday was coming up, he suggested we go to a nursery so he could pick out a birthday gift. He promised he could clear enough room in Miranda so I could sit comfortably, and that he could even do it in seven minutes. Needless to say I was skeptical, but much to my surprise he accomplished the chore. The passenger seat and the floor beneath were completely rid of things so I easily could fit, however when I glanced behind me the pile was so high the entire back seat was not visible, nor was the rear window. Yet we drove to the nursery, looked around, and when he was about to give up, as nothing seemed appropriate within his price range, at last I found a terra cotta thermometer I was sure she'd love. I had a hard time prying him away from shelves and bins of knickknacks magnetically attracting him. He was only slightly annoyed at my insistence he didn't need anything there and only slightly added an additional handful of odds and ends.

A sad note to add at this time, meaningless for some, but very pertinent and distressing for both of us: on August 5th, 2002 Chick Hearn, the Lakers long-time inimitable announcer passed away. We were very saddened by the news. The Lakers without Chick's consummate play-by-play commentary - unimaginable!

On Saturday night, August 17th, our now "mutual" best friend Lori, a fine oil painter, had an exhibit of her work at the Constellation Gallery in North Hollywood. Ted and I had offered our assistance, he would provide the music and I would host the bar. We went in separate cars, due to lack of room (as in a flash, Miranda was stuffed again), and besides, Ted had to fit in all his equipment. The event rendered a considerably large crowd; a fantastic turn out. Lori sold three pieces and many people truly admired and appreciated her work and recognized her talent. Ted's playing was of course, exceptional. Six hours we were there. By the time we left, the late night air was laden with dampness and the moon dipped in between the thin layers of drifting fog. Ted followed me back home and was still wound up from all the attention and energy. To dissipate it he sat in the living room and played again as I got ready for bed and fell asleep once again to his beautiful music.

That experience gave Ted a profound insight into his playing, which he detailed the day after his account of the artshow,*"7:00 Constellation Art Gallery, I play at Lori Markman's Art Show. Bernice 1st, then finally settle on Brandie for 2 hours or so, then switch to Lulu. Brandie not surprisingly is great for the jazz things even, and especially occasionally, with no reverb & large wide mid notch. Lulu & The Peavey - nothing else had worked, I turned up the mid-range a little, (the subtle, hollow mid semi-acoustic tone was lost amidst the conversations), and went for the "On Broadway" fantasy, also the Tequila fantasy. Then suddenly after rejecting it due to boredom I suddenly found myself going into a soulful "Georgia on my Mind" in Db, Ab, (F?), E with Lulu just soaring, singing to a hushed crowd. This was magic, even able to thrill myself, Barb & everyone. This was not unlike some of my experiences 30 years ago at the very beginning of my Solo Guitar Career. Lulu suddenly springs to life, sounding & becoming the soulful purveyor of great beauty that she is. Lulu, born in 1952 celebrating turning 50 this year, the finest stock Tele I've ever been allowed to be the custodian of, WAS THE STAR."*

"Aug. 18 Wow! It's been building inside me for years and now I do sense that: 1.) LAST NIGHT WAS A TURNING POINT in my life or at least in my SOLO GUITAR CAREER: I'm going to make straight 8th grooves & tunes to play this feel (regular & New Orleans bass & near boogie & R&B Latin, nasty blues, faux Latin) MY GUITAR PRIORITY until I've got a whole bunch of them 2.) close behind: rock-a-boog (which is really a form of jazz) tunes ala "See Ya Later Alligator"

Throughout the next month the days were punctuated by Angels baseball. Ted was back on the computer working on his song list, which he revised to emphasize the straight 8th tunes. He wrote me bass lines to harmonize. Made his best popcorn yet. There were jigsaw puzzles for blue afternoons. And Ted began organizing the big categories of his "How Bach Generated Chords & Chord Progressions" book. All was relatively well.

Then in September I pulled down my dusty luggage from the top of the closet. Two years it sat stashed there, I think. Yes. My last trip was in 2000. More tears shed again, and on September 16th, Lori and I left for France. Ted never easily accepted my need to travel, but always kept Quincy and Pumpkin company while I was gone. I called him from Paris on his 56th birthday, reminding him I would be home in four days. Four days after that phone call, I had returned from my journey and our reunion underscored the love we felt so strongly. In less than a week, everything had fallen back into place as if this two-week gap, a mere skip of a beat, hadn't even happened. But soon the dream of a lifetime was about to come true for Ted.

During the summer Ted's favorite baseball team, had risen through the ranks, made it to the play-offs and had won their first play-off series ever, inching them one step closer towards the World Series. Ted's beloved Angels had taken him to the heights of baseball ecstasy. When the Angels prevailed over the Minnesota Twins, he was absolutely euphoric. The Angels were actually going to the World Series. Ted had felt the Angels were on a destiny course that year; his datebook filled with detailed descriptions of each game that could make a book in itself. This was Ted's delightful depiction of the evening and the game that sent the Angels to the World Series, *"Oct. 13 Game 5 Twins send their nasty sinker ball pitcher who shut us down in Game 1 Joe Mays, I knew that the Angels could move 3 inches - 2 inches -on the plate. Twins go up 1-0 in 1st, we get good wood but no runs. Twinkies up 2-0 in 2nd, B worried. Adam Kennedy hits solo homerun - 2-1 - hits Scott Spezio next inning likewise - 2-2. Adam Kennedy hits a 2nd homerun - Angels lead 3-2. Excitement short lived, Twins fight back with 3 hitters, lead 5-3. B asks, "Are you panicked?" "No," I say, "our fans are too strong and our boys have too much heart and desire, I see Tim Salmon squirting champagne with huge shocking headlines as the Angels stun the baseball community." And then up comes the 7th inning our 1/2, 2 men get on and a script of the gods, who's coming up- A.K. I say "Barb, just think, if he can hit a homerun here what a story he'll have for the grandkids someday, and he is locked on today if they give him another high pitch, he really well may do it." And a supreme thrill seen by so many, he did do it. His 3rd homerun of the game, the Angels lead again 6-5 with no one out AND the top of the order coming up. And they get 7 more runs, 10 in all, and there's delicious pandemonium of ecstasy. They lead 13-5. And they are going to the World Series. We've had few bigger sports thrills. After finishing 41 games out last year & a 41 or 42 year wait, the curse is gone, the monkey's off their back & was a wonderful part of why they've won their 1st pennant EVER. Rejoice, Gene Autry."*

Those past two weeks I had watched Ted's hope slowly grow game after game, the Angels beating the Yankees, then the Twins, and I'd never seen him more ecstatic. I couldn't have wished for him anything better. I marveled at his keen appreciation of the subtlety and nuance of each play and I shared his excitement during the most explosive moments of the innings in which the hits, homers, seemingly endless in succession propelled the inevitable success in each game. In less than a week the World Series began. Ted faithfully detailed each day, each game, the culmination and his reflections, *"Oct. 19 Game 1 World Series Angels and Giants Oct. 20 Beautiful purple Irises for Barb. Game 2, fan support like I've never seen in Angel baseball, a roaring, stomping, clapping throng and Angels 11-10. One of the great post season battles ever... and Tim Salmon a BIG hero, to tie the series against Dusty Baker's Giants. Oct. 22 Game 3 - Angels thrill us yet again, up in S.F. (up 8-1 at one point!), win 10-4. Pumpkin bonds with daddy. Oct. 23 Giants fight back and tie series 2-2. Play Gigi for B to a) cheer her, b) later decided the opposite tho' unintentionally funny for both of us, to help her cry more & get the tears out. B loved all this. Oct. 24 Giants clobber the Angels, we're down 3-2 BUT going home to those amazing fans on Saturday & Sunday. We have a fine chance, for they seem to often inspire our boys to their very best. Oct. 26 2002 World Series Game 6: Wow! Angels greatest comeback a) in their history, b) in 98 years of World Series history! Down 5-0 in bottom of 7th & their bats dead, rally in 7th & 8th & win 6-5! fans at a new level of support & enthusiasm & love & appreciation.*

Oct. 27 Culminating in a Series (both meanings) - actually 3 of miracles & guts & glory DREAM COME TRUE: Game 7: The astonishing Anaheim Angels 50th comeback win this year, win the WORLD SERIES! "Pinch me I must be dreaming" Just a little more than a month ago, I said, "Gosh, they could make the play-offs, honey." Then when I found out they faced the Yankees, my thought was the curse... but what if they BEAT the Yankees??? Wow! What a dream...but they lose the 1st game. Well. Game 2- They come out and stun the crowd (at N.Y. stadium of course) then at home (series tied 1-1) for Game 3 & down 6-1 they electrify their rally monkied crowd with comeback of massive proportions and win, what 9-6! Wow. Then Game 4: Angels win and defeat mighty Yankees & make believers of them, esp. Derek Jeter "I don't see anybody (except themselves) stopping them, the way they're playing."

Upon waking next morning, I saw the now familiar light through the crack of the bedroom door indicating Ted was still here. Last night he stayed awake for the duration of the revelry, glued to the TV, euphoric. His 42-year wait, his patience and faith finally rewarded in utmost grandeur with the culmination of the World Series. Through 7 games, the Angels had emerged as the victors. As I lay in bed I could faintly make out the TV, when shortly I heard a car engine slow then the plop of the newspaper on the walkway. Anxious to see the headlines, the deification of the Angels and more so to show Ted, yet somewhat reluctant to leave the warm bed, but I really had to get up, so squinting in the bright lamp light in the living room, I found him fixated by the continuing celebratory coverage. The living room redolent with the perfume from the stargazer lilies in the mixed bouquet Ted brought me days ago, I dashed outside in the cold dampness, grabbed the newspaper, handed him the main section and the sports section, then headed to the kitchen to put on a pot of coffee. He was still in a state of delirious ecstasy, even having slept he thought, about four hours. For a month I'd been on this roller coaster ride with him, the entire post season. We never gave up hope and just as I was about to, a rally happened, and happened again and again. I was so happy for Ted, the elation he felt for this team, and I felt it through him, his joy.

● X □ △ ★

Ted's joy soon turned into apprehension as once again another alarming apartment incident portended a potential problem. On the second to the last day of October, an ominous notice at Ted's apartment building, some kind of housing inspection. He didn't know what it meant but he was in trouble if the interior of every apartment was to be inspected. There was no indication when this might take place but there was never enough time for Ted to make his apartment presentable. He had been lucky for so long I prayed it held up. Again the possibility of eviction loomed, and I shared in his anxiety. The following day we found out that the inspection was scheduled for December 4th. Ted had about one month to pass the test, to get from mess to immaculate.

Ted worked extensively, long days until late, as I waited while the lengthy hours of the day faded and solitude was punctuated with a hot pot of tea, sipped from my mother's floral cup of fine china. Upon closing the blinds, I would sink into reading or writing time. Then Ted came, bringing different rhythms and changing the hours around but as midnight passed and the candles burned down he would be asleep on the floor, me in the midst of a thought. I would glance at him serenely sleeping, so deeply after expending a tremendous amount of energy, more than a day's worth in less time, such were the demands he needed to meet for another deadline. The dreaded apartment saga again, and sometimes it saddened me, when I thought about how he was bound to that strange quirk of fate.

The end of November, a late date for Thanksgiving Day; we filled the house with the warmth of close friends to quell the emptiness of missing my parents. That was my idea, and Ted didn't mind, but afterwards I realized what Ted already knew; that just having each other was always enough and we much preferred it just being the two of us. Alone together, slightly weary from company, we listened to Handel's Opus 6, closed our eyes, grateful to be so lucky to have each other.

The building inspection on December 4th had come and gone, fortunately bearing only minor consequences. The only thing the inspector objected to were the piles of newspaper, which Ted had a month to remove. The fact that Ted had an abundance of belongings was of no importance. Apparently the most visible and predominant of all were his books, which were deemed not objectionable, possibly impressive. Anyway Ted seemed to have dodged another bullet. He almost had me believing in angels.

December sent us splendid days of winter rain, and the year diminished without incident. Regular television offered its special holiday fare and despite the commercials, we took advantage anyway. We watched "It's a Wonderful Life," for the millionth time and it never failed to bring tears to our eyes. Another evening we viewed the "Sound of Music," he'd never seen it in its entirety and was overwhelmed. On Christmas Eve a fulfilling visit from Tom, Wendy and Tom's childhood friend of 50 years, Brennan. After which Ted and I had a rare nice long conversation. For hours we just chatted about all sorts of things including our first date, all our tender warm memories, gently eased us into sleep.

Then a lazy Christmas day, Lakers, a mid-afternoon dinner here, the two of us with Lori, her sister, Andi and their mom. A quiet, rainy week intervened; seven insubstantial days vanished into a quiet, restful New Year's Eve together. Lori visited for a short while, left for home at 10 and by 10:30 Ted was sound asleep. I watched and listened to a fabulous performance of Beethoven's 9th, totally unaware midnight had come to pass.

● X □ △ ★

The sky blushed as summer's company came for a visit this New Year and I savored these warm days hoping to hold them in long after all changed back. I was okay at first but, as happened frequently now, a sadness slowly descended upon me, penetrated my being, and depression set in by the evening hours. Ted had another deadline, and had been working feverishly. The building inspector was returning on January 24th to be sure Ted had removed all the newspapers, and to check on other minor violations of the code. When Ted finally arrived, I was so grateful for his presence, we watched "Fly Away Home," very poignant, enabling my tears to come, and felt better for the moment.

Nearing our eleventh year together, some of our most trying times were still ahead. 2003 had just begun and in the eighteen months to come, we were to face many difficulties that tested and strained our relationship to the utmost. Fortunately our love remained the underpinning.

With my emotional state still so unstable, Ted even risked not finishing his apartment cleanup, and returned next day full of surprises for me. A Shaquille O'Neal bobble head doll! Oh so incredibly ridiculously adorable. Also that night, a movie on TV I'd wanted to see for years (he knew I'd be surprised as I rarely checked the listings), "101 Dalmatians," the original version. I was ecstatic, my mood changed instantaneously. Of course he taped it, we reveled in the animation and fabulous music. One of the things about Ted I loved most was that he knew these ostensibly simple offerings would bring me utmost joy, and his joy was in being able to do that. Although he said he was simply reciprocating all I did for him and that these were little things, his gestures took thought and application as opposed to my rather perfunctory acts. My thinking about him happened so naturally, while on errands if I noticed something he'd love, I'd revel too being able to surprise him with something delectable. But I was basically just taking care of his general needs. He didn't see it that way, and was always most grateful for having all his favorite foods and comforts.

●X□△★

One eye-drop from the bottle was more than the eye could hold; the excess welled up dripped down streaking my cheek, a simulated tear. The miscalculation in the size of the tiny hole structured to release the precise amount needed, only succeeded in displaying another example of waste. Even the most seemingly insignificant thing loomed large in its inefficiency when my moods magnified every mishap. Blown out of proportion any leeway for forgiveness was lost. Affronted on all sides, tiny pinpricks while inside all was churning. Who was this person? Who was this person now with no perspective so tangled in knots with frayed loose ends, none to pull free, pulled it only got worse.

I had thought my mood swings were caused by the grief, now I realized my hormones were totally out of control. The grief masked it at first. I couldn't bear to continue living that way, nor putting Ted through such torment, so I went for treatment. I was given Estrogen pills, the doctor called it hormone replacement therapy, a low dose to be taken once a day. I thought it would be low risk for me. In eighteen months I was to suffer the consequences.

Soon the day for the apartment building re-inspection dawned. Talk about the gods smiling upon you! Ted happened to be walking out to the front gate of the apartment building when in walked the inspector whom Ted greeted and pleaded to for more time, in fact to be the last unit viewed. The inspector informed Ted that most of the units including Ted's were not going to be checked. Ralph, the manager had retired, his daughter Patty now managed the building. She would be overseeing everything and was bound to carry out and complete the instructions given during the prior visit. Just a month ago what was all so troubling and worrisome, was now nothing more than a gigantic sigh of relief, an indefinite reprieve. But Patty still insisted that Ted continue straightening up to thwart off any possible problems in the future. Patty was a blessing and went to extraordinary lengths to "protect" Ted from as many apartment problems as possible for the remainder of his days. Although, the reality was, if he didn't continue diligently, in five more years there would be no more room for him to even move about inside. However, life seemed to have a way of working things out in his favor oh so fortunately, of which Ted was well aware and spared no expression of gratitude to the powers that be.

Gale force winds and pouring rain pelted many days in February. My sleep was broken several times by gusts strong enough to rattle the windows. When out and about I felt tossed like a brittle twig. All month Ted catered to my every wish and whim, I could not dissuade him as he wanted so much for me to feel better. The month also encompassed the usual, Lakers or movies, an occasional serenade but now he brought me flowers every day, and for Valentine's, three dazzling bouquets and a loving card.

Mid-month, Ted spent one evening far and away doing what he claimed he was born to do through obligation and gratitude of his talent. At the very end of Lindero Canyon Road he played solo guitar at Leila's, a small restaurant and bar, for an amount far less than he was worth especially considering the length of time it took to drive there and back.

Those thoughts arose in me at times when I would spend the evening alone, but I knew he wasn't considering the meager pay. He knew he'd probably just break even on this gig. Yet, if only one person responded well to the beauty of his playing, he felt successful, and this was enough to confirm the worth of all his efforts.

In Ted's quest to brighten my spirits, he sought the origins of the songs I loved from my childhood. Consequently, we both developed a craving for old musicals. The first weekend in March he found "Annie Get Your Gun" which we watched and loved that Saturday night. Betty Hutton totally captivated us, wonderful, perfectly cast and oh those songs brought back many childhood memories, and tempered my mourning of the loss of my father. What did we watch Friday? Oh yes, the Lakers broke their winning streak in a miserable game against Seattle. Then Sunday night we watched "State Fair," charming but the best part; the two songs, "It's A Grand Night for Singing" and "It Might as Well Be Spring," which we had always loved. And he made us fresh popped popcorn, one of our favorites, and fast becoming a staple in our diet.

● X □ △ ★

First I must hearken back a day when a simple impulsive purchase caused a chain-reaction the following day. It began with a desire for Chinese food, the usual Panda Express. The best one was in the mall. Then also a thought, or more a craving for chocolate caused us a detour to the lower level where Ted ever so mindful of his needs begged my indulgence for a moment to go into Radio Shack for wires and things. I deferred and wandered about the store but became bored within minutes. Ted noticed and suggested I look at the DVD players since I'd been threatening to buy one for months. Whether due to circumstance or boredom, I did indeed purchase a DVD player. Ted lugged the heavy package to the candy store, a box of my favorite butterscotch, then upstairs to Panda Express, just putting out fresh chow mein. It looked so good we bought mountains to go. Home to unload our goods. We deferred our dinner, had just a taste to satisfy, before we ventured back out for a movie on DVD, as we owned none, and were curious to try the new toy. We came back with "Roman Holiday," Ted figured out how to hook the thing up which didn't take long. We watched "Roman Holiday," it was okay, but that paved the way into the next day, when at some point during the Lakers game I found "My Fair Lady" had miraculously appeared on the dining table. Where did that come from? What a joy to discover, and how clever Ted was. That was only the beginning, for throughout the evening at varying intervals he performed his magical acts as more and more DVDs appeared all around the house, in places I'd least expected to find one. Ted loved doing this; half the fun for him was seeing my reaction upon discovering so many of our favorite musicals in such unusual places.

The following evening we suffered another Lakers' loss, two in a row. After the game Ted tantalized me with what he termed his *"theory du jour,"* a lesson on some of my favorite chord sounds, some surprising facts about them, and how to use them most effectively.

Chord Types for Piano March 3/5/03

When I woke next morning, magically more DVDs had appeared, cleverly nestled in various places around the house. Oh Ted! Mid day it rained buckets, dark like night and four leaks in the kitchen roof. Ted came late, waited for a break so the gutter water could run off. Lakers again, and won this one. The next morning was gorgeous after all that storming, a sparkling world, with clouds occasionally floating by. But soon the winds came again, brutal bellowing, worse as the day progressed, an element that tortured and tormented everything. A portent, as oh so unfortunately it seemed by the end of the week the U.S. would be at war with Iraq.

Suddenly, the unpredictable winds died down, a reprieve was I dreaming? But on the evening news in March 2003: United States began bombing on Baghdad, if only this were a bad dream on an ominous night. It was not. For what was to follow? Our night brought their dawn, our dawn their night. We might know by morning tomorrow, for surely events unfolded as we slept. What then? Everyone seemed on edge, and Ted was especially pensive, as we all waited for retaliation, when, with what or where?

And winds were howling again, why so many windstorms these past months? Everything seemed in tatters and scattered about; we longed for a pause from these storms, and sought solace. The only store that had a crowd sold candy. In this age of anxiety, chocolate was most highly desired to cheer the spirit and calm the nerves. Who said you couldn't buy a smile? Not Ted. And in lieu of the Lakers, for we really needed calm, he played guitar for many hours. I reveled in the sweet sounds with him and when I grew sleepy, got in bed left the door open so the music could still reach me.

At the end of March I surprised Ted with his very own Xerox machine. He was thrilled with it, stayed up the entire night photo-copying and sorting through all his hand written guitar papers. At that rate, it wasn't long before he would use up the ink cartridge. The next day we went to Staples Office Supply to buy another cartridge and that was when Ted discovered luggage. Suitcases, valises, any and all small portable storage cases. He bought several pieces of luggage on sale at Staples that day. Due to all the tension he felt about the war in Iraq, he was more convinced than ever that we might need to evacuate the city. What could more easily transport his most precious papers and books? Nothing but luggage.

● X □ △ ★

The forecasted rain held off until last night late so the day before the sun peeked in and out as the clouds gathered. Nature graced us all with perfect weather for Tom Bocci's first actual birthday party. Tom and Wendy had prepared for two days, made food and decorated their house. Ted was last to arrive after a rare day of teaching on a Sunday. The party was a great success. The rain began as we all left the Bocci's, just a drizzle at first but during the night it grew quite heavy and woke me. I knew Ted was still awake in the living room, but I didn't call to him not wanting to fully awaken. The rain continued steadily all afternoon into early evening. Ted bought more DVDs of old TV shows. We spent one night watching episodes of the Beverly Hillbillies, innocuous inane fun and again he magically made his perfect popcorn. Then the Lakers off to a roaring start in the playoffs slaughtered Minnesota. We knew if they continued to play at that level no one could beat them. We were both so uplifted and energized we actually decided to battle the market during the Sunday afternoon rush, but it wasn't so crowded as we forgot it was Easter. Later Ted picked up the guitar to show me something and the song he began to play, "Can't Get a Man With a Gun" was the song going through my mind at that very moment! This uncanny almost eerie perception happened quite often with us but I was always startled by it.

Ted preserved two other examples of this mysterious perception in his datebook; both happened one week after my mother's death, on what would have been her 82nd birthday. Ted began singing a song my mother used to sing to me and that I'd never heard Ted sing before, I didn't even realize he knew that song. From Ted's datebook on11/24/01, *"We discuss (somehow) "A Bushel and a Peck" after I start singing it to her, she is quite amazed as this is a song her Mom sang to her. And LATER when she comes in to the computer room to ask me, do we have a 'Guys & Dolls' Songbook, it is exactly when I'm entering the song "Guys & Dolls"!!!!!"*

In early May, we had cable TV installed after reading in the newspaper that otherwise we would miss the first three play-off games. Thus we only missed the first one, a disappointing loss anyway. Ted and I were gleeful at the prospect of watching all of the games and sat poised for game 2, in which the Lakers were again beaten to pieces. That season the Lakers were eliminated in game 6, crushed by the San Antonio Spurs.

Nonetheless, the cable was a total fascination for Ted. For a long time we had hesitated to have it installed, Ted being acutely aware of his addictive tendencies, promised he would try to be judicious in regard to videotaping everything. The first show he so delighted in finding was the Tom and Jerry cartoons. Ted had been slowly collecting each episode of Tom and Jerry and only a few were missing, he was sure to find the remaining ones. With an interest and curiosity that spanned the spectrum, soon he was to become completely enraptured at having so many channels to choose from. For that reason, we compromised at a limit of 3 VCRs to keep here at my house.

On Sunday, May 18th Ted gave his 2nd seminar at California Vintage Guitars, a successful effort on Ted's part for the benefit of about sixty attendees. Instead of the usual open discussion, as most students were reluctant to ask questions, Ted used a new tactic, he handed out lesson sheets with specific topics he planned to cover, and concentrated solely on those areas. His playing of course was brilliant. The seminar was video taped by Ted's friend and student, master electric bassist, Phil Chen and transferred to DVD.

The following months, reasonably uneventful, were spent watching all the musicals Ted could find on DVD, interspersed with viewing various things Ted discovered on the cable. When not engrossed in a TV show, there were always harmony and counterpoint studies, or books to share, we were so lucky to never expend our wealth of amusements. In addition, Ted kept adding to his ever-growing luggage collection. In his excitement after returning home from a particularly nice find, he would exclaim, something like "This 3-piece set will be perfect to put all my writings into." With each purchase Ted always had something specific in mind, designated for some special treasure.

My fingers were now manifesting worse problems due to the CREST disease, and it became very painful for me to play the guitar. Many days my fingertips were so sensitive to the slightest indentation, I could not press down even the lightest strings, so I had begun to play piano more and more. An ever-encouraging Ted wrote me out special piano arrangements for some songs I loved, plus fun exercises, with the intent to challenge and inspire me.

● X □ △ ★

Summer was dealing her worst days; the air was thick and still, laden with moisture turning the heat into steam. It was impossible to sleep at night as barely a breeze entered though the window. One day, trudging around on errands in the heat, Ted brought home a 5 piece dark blue luggage set, commenting merrily, *"a steal at half-price."* By now I'd lost count of how much luggage he'd acquired. More than would fit in both cars I thought. Now, in the cool living room, ready to settle in, Ted discovered that the DVD player was broken which sent him into a fit. He configured every possible fix to no avail. Fortunately there was time to run to the store and purchase a new one, and we purchased two. That calmed him, but of course he insisted on keeping the broken one. "More clutter" I said, but he was resolute in case one day it could be repaired. "Not worth it" I maintained.

To change the mood, we watched "Rocky and Bullwinkle" cartoons. Afterwards we got involved in studying counterpoint from a fascinating chapter in a Bach book in which Johann Philipp Kernberger, a student of Bach's, wrote out a canon that modulated through all twelve major keys. The initial work was depicted on 5 staves, which I began converting to 2 staves, for ease of playing. While I was writing this out, Ted on the computer discovered the color palette and multiple options for using color. He spent many joyful hours experimenting with every possible combination. Eventually he came up with 100 new colorful business cards, ten sheets of card stock, ten cards on each sheet, and each sheet a different blending, fading and shading of colors. Ted's love for color sometimes rivaled his love for music.

While exploring the numerous cable options, Ted and I came across and started watching a very charming show called "Monk," about the adventures of a detective who had Obsessive/Compulsive disorder. I was curious about Ted's reaction to Monk's idiosyncrasies and had to laugh when Ted commented on how quirky Monk was and then asked me if I thought he (Ted) was that quirky. I told him no, not that quirky, but certainly very unique, and that he definitely had his quirks. He asked me for an example, and I offered his preference for sleeping on the floor, which in itself was not too unusual. However, that was not Ted's sole criteria for a serene sleep. Ted also preferred to remain fully clothed, and needed two lights on (two, in case one burned out), as he was uncomfortable with total darkness. That habit developed after the 1971 Sylmar earthquake. I reminded him that many people experienced that earthquake, and the 1994 earthquake as well, but did not manifest that behavior as a result. He conceded and understood my point. But that first earthquake had a strong impact on Ted and he never again wanted to find himself unprepared in any emergency, hence the new luggage frenzy.

● X □ △ ★

"Aug. 26 Teach at Musician's Institute - Open Counseling from 1 to 5, at least 5 teachers there, all ex or current students." When Ted came home from Musician's Institute he was pleased at how successful the day had gone, but as usual after an experience as such, he was still wound up. And that night the planet Mars was to pass closest to Earth it would ever be in our lifetime, and was purported to appear in the sky quite a bit larger than usual. I stayed up as late as I could, he sat on the bed playing examples of jazz styles ("Baroqueish" 3/4 vs. Jazzy 3/4 vs. Gospel Jazz Waltz) until I was close to drifting off then remained awake to rouse me at 3 a.m., which he did. When we went outside, Mars looked to be the same as the night before though, or maybe a little brighter perhaps because of the late hour. We didn't know what to expect to see. Mars the size of a ping-pong ball at least? Really knew it wouldn't be. But I was pleased we both took the opportunity to view this phenomenon. Although Ted rarely if ever looked up at the nighttime sky, I knew he really thought about what he was seeing when he made a plea to the Red Planet to bestow benevolence upon the universe. I thought to myself, what a splendidly heartfelt request.

For some time now Ted had begun teaching at my house on holiday weekends, and Labor Day weekend was no exception. His students were always welcome, and we made them feel quite comfortable here. Over the holiday weekend, other than his teaching, he cleaned out Miranda's trunk and was surprised to notice how much higher off the ground she sat as a result. Afterwards he did errands, went to the mall for chow mein, and surprised me with a box of See's Bordeaux chocolate. Then another trip to Office Depot yielded four or five more pieces of luggage, and now having accumulated so much, all of it needed to be organized and labeled.

It was late summer and the Santa Ana winds were fierce. From the east the sun cast an eerie orange glow through the smoke and I knew that fires were still raging many miles away over thousands of acres. A blast of October heat lasted all week. The fires were inevitable almost every year, the air thick with particles of ash, irritated our eyes. We stayed indoors; I worked on writing 2-part canons while Ted studied and watched the baseball playoffs. When the games ended, I hoped he wasn't disappointed, but he was pleased even though the teams he had rooted for lost, he just loved the game so much.

Soon Ted made what for him could have been a dangerous discovery, the cable Shop At Home channel. Initially, he held himself to a gold-clad State Quarter set and a coin vault. At Border's Book Store he purchased more books on coin collecting to study. The end of October brought the Lakers season opener, a new starting lineup, with unbelievable superstars of the game. Ted and I thought no other team in the entire NBA would have a chance.

One late November evening, Ted told me that a few months ago he had befriended some homeless women. I don't think he had intended to tell me anything until his plan had come to fruition but he couldn't contain his enthusiasm any longer. He clearly had a vision of resurrecting these sad lives, rescuing them from poverty and the indignity of living on the street. Something had instilled hope in him that this was possible. There were three women; a mother, her daughter, and a friend of the mother. Ted said that the mother spent the day begging for money on the steps in front of Borders Books and that was how he met her. He had been giving her money for months and now they had sort-of become friends.

A kind gesture. His heart always ached for others and I felt his compassion, and that his intentions were commendable. Encouraged by my initial reaction he began to elaborate and by doing so, gave me cause for concern and aroused my suspicions. Apparently these women were not exactly "homeless," they actually lived in a hotel room and even had pets. Then he confessed that he was now giving them half of all he earned! At that point, I thought to myself, the cost of a hotel for one month was almost as much as his rent and my mortgage combined, and considering he was just squeaking by financially himself, this upset me quite a bit.

After he had explained, I was quite disturbed, which was not the reaction Ted had expected from me. In fact, he was utterly disappointed with my response, as he thought I'd be so proud of his actions. What troubled me most, (and this was a major point of contention between us), was that these people might be taking advantage of him. He contended I was questioning his judgment. I told him that I thought most of the time his judgment was quite accurate but anyone could misjudge a situation. But he wouldn't listen and insisted I was questioning his entire ability to make judgments as a whole. I didn't want to argue. I knew time would reveal the truth, and hoped he was right. We didn't discuss it much from then on, but I knew he intended on following through with his initial convictions. I just didn't want to see him get hurt and disillusioned but there was nothing I could do. Unfortunately this incident became a wedge between us that would take many months to dislodge, and would eventually turn out to be a hard and costly lesson for Ted. However, it would not discourage nor deter Ted in his efforts to help others.

A few days before Thanksgiving, Ted gave another phone "interview" to Guitar One magazine. For the most part he simply detailed information about his music lesson appearing in an upcoming issue, and again the entire article had to be rewritten. Totally stressed, he would be at the computer all night since there was a Wednesday deadline. This happened every time and he kept saying he would never do another article this way and always relented. When he reviewed the final drafts sent to him for approval, they inevitably failed to meet his extremely finicky and particular standards.

Thanksgiving Day started out to be the worst ever for both of us. I spent much of the day engulfed in sadness, tried to fight it, baked us an apple pie only to have it slip from my fingers as I removed it from the oven. Half of the pie dripped down the side of the stove and onto the floor. When Ted arrived late in the day he was in a worse state of mind than I. What a sorry pair we made. So we made use of the TV for what it was intended, the ultimate diversion. Ted had saved special little treats he'd taped just for such an occasion. Fortunately it worked, *"We watch Shaq on J. Leno from a recent rerun that I taped for B & it sure changes my foul mood & thrills Barbie!"*

● X □ △ ★

As the year 2003 drew near its conclusion, Ted accepted an extraordinary gift from a good friend and student, guitarist and music producer John McClain. Ted generally did not accept gifts, but made a one-time only exception because he knew it was guaranteed to thrill me. I closed my eyes and held out my hands as Ted had requested, and in them he placed 2 courtside tickets to a Lakers game! I thought I was dreaming, a gift to top all gifts, a most incredible moment, almost immeasurable, barely believable. I was stunned.

On Sunday December 14th, Ted gave another seminar at California Vintage Guitar. How I regretted that illness prevented me from attending that afternoon. He comforted me by the promise of other seminars, yet I knew afterwards this had been a special and highly successful one. At least the night prior I had the opportunity to enjoy all the Christmas songs while he was practicing. His arrangements of these seasonal pieces were some of his most tender and heartfelt. Ted made no notes in his datebook regarding what was discussed during the seminar, however it was videotaped by one of his students and transferred to DVD. A day or so after giving the seminar Ted came down with a horrible cold or flu.

When the day for our first live Lakers game finally arrived, Ted still had a bad cold, but we risked the possibility of my catching it, as we wanted to share this once-in-a-lifetime experience together. When we arrived at Staples Center that night, Ted was carrying his usual old grocery bags full of music, books, papers and pens. This triggered the alarm as we walked in and Ted had to empty everything out. The management at that time (post 9/11) didn't allow anything to be brought in but Ted argued so effectively they made an exception. We found our seats and as we waited for the game to begin Ted took out the Bach Chorale book and began analyzing Chorale #17; he did not stop when the game began. Somehow he was able to work and enjoy the game including catching an out of bounds ball!

The experience was dreamlike from the moment we entered the stadium. We stopped to gaze all around and then walked down to our seats which were right there on the court; unbelievable! That dazzling arena, after only seeing it on TV, became true to life. Merely inches in front of us the two teams thundered back and forth on the court, and every scream of excitement, every sigh of dismay was echoed 18,000 fold - a simultaneous collective emotion. And it all culminated in a thrilling victory by the Lakers over the Phoenix Suns. Unequivocally, one of the most incredible experiences of my entire life!

Two drizzly and grey days later, I with a sore throat and stuffy nose, had definitely caught Ted's cold. I knew it was probable, but certainly worth it to have shared that special night together.

Come Christmas Eve, I was very sad when Ted told me he would not be joining me, and then he totally surprised me when he appeared here after all. Sometimes he did that intentionally, especially when I was blue, for it cheered me all the more. We were both still quite ill and spent the evening listening to the beautiful holiday music offered on the classical radio station. Then a quiet, nondescript Christmas Day, the Lakers lost to Houston, but at least we were together.

The last week, the slow closing of another year, both still sick with our colds, the days crept by, turned over like the final pages of some huge tome.

● X □ △ ★

From the window the sun shot one straight ray and I focused my gaze on the sparkling particles of dust floating freely but appearing confined inside that one singular shape. Had I glanced a minute later, the light angle changed, the dust, ever present, would have floated unnoticed.

Complicated days followed. In January 2004, Ted began contemplating which guitars he could part with, he loved them all, but he had amassed so many and some rarely were played. That was his main justification and he did feel sad that some guitars were languishing in their cases. Also, he knew how much happiness he would bestow by fulfilling a student's fervent yearning for a special guitar. That in turn brought Ted much pleasure. *"1/12/04 Bill P. absolutely falls madly in love with Mona and his arms, hands, shoulders don't hurt when he plays her. So I will have to sell her to Bill. 1/13/04 Maybe the finest Jazzmaster I've ever heard. Sell J.C. the '63/64 big neck, dark rosewood L series Jazzmaster to fulfill his dream."*

But he also sold them partly to have extra money for himself, or oftentimes he had succumbed to another guitar's irresistible charms, and sometimes to help others in need. I had never questioned his reasons, but due to the recent disparities on that one particular subject, I remained silently concerned.

Causing further consternation our cat, Quincy, had been getting into a lot of fights. In one week alone, three altercations. We had to do something, and resolved to keep him indoors. I bore the fallout of that pronouncement, since Ted spent the days teaching at his apartment. The decision to transform Quincy into an indoor pet displayed its many flaws and drawbacks. After about a week I weighed the pros and cons, and was leaning towards going back to the original arrangement. When Quincy wasn't complaining vociferously he was holed up under the bed in such a state of despondency as to break my heart. Quincy's nature thrived outside, that would never change, so Ted and I relented, Ouincy was once more allowed to go outdoors.

● X □ △ ★

Each day passed like a bead of rainwater slowly forming on an eave, filling and swelling until heavy its weight caused it to fall. A slow unbroken pattern, and into that pattern swelling the drop fatter, though not more rapidly, was an endless stream of complexities. I was finding every-day life more and more difficult to deal with, and after relentless battles with Ted, friends and with myself, I reluctantly conceded to getting a prescription for anti-depressants and began taking them on the 21st of January.

Apparently, only a week later, even though I couldn't tell, Ted noticed the difference. He said I was much calmer, and he thanked me graciously for making the effort. The love was reflected and reciprocated and we shared an especially loving Valentine's Day. That same week we received the March '04 issue of Guitar One in which Ted's lesson was published, and both of us were quite pleased with the presentation.

The rain came again on a Saturday lasting long into the night. No fancy dress, no high heels, especially not the velvet coat, a rare chance at elegance lost but for my Grandmother's diamond ring that fit so perfectly. Ted and I attended a dinner party for eighteen to celebrate Leon and Judy White's 40th wedding anniversary at the Bistro Gardens Restaurant in Sherman Oaks. In a dimly lit corner at a table too long for connections from end to end, Leon and Judy smiled the entire night, thrilled with the gift of giving thanks for what life gave to them. I ordered for Ted a plate of mashed potatoes, he said it was the best he'd ever eaten, a wonderful and well-spent evening for everyone.

Due to the continually worsening condition of my fingers, I had begun using the piano as my main instrument. The small Baldwin console I had was adequate, but the action was tight and could be frustrating and painful, so Ted suggested we look for a more suitable piano. Our search took us to Keyboard Concepts, where I found a 1923 Knabe 5.8 Grand with the perfect action among other fine features except the price, and possibly the size for the room. A week later the store called me about another piano I might be interested in looking at. Ted and I drove over there and although not quite as nice as the 1923, it did have many of the same features, including light action and lovely tone. Ted refused to give me any opinion until after I made a decision, so I thought about it on my own, and bought the 1961 5' Knabe baby grand, to be delivered in one week. Afterwards, Ted said he felt I had made the right choice. The piano arrived and was gently maneuvered into the back room at an angle. The wood floor increased the naturally embedded resonance in the instrument itself. I played all afternoon, learning its touch and the precise pressure and resistance to modulate the tone.

Meanwhile Ted maintained his quest to help the homeless women, and despite my suspicions he would periodically update me on the situation. I knew he was hoping to allay my doubts, and engender my support. I remained silent when he would offer the latest information, such as helping them to buy a cell phone, a new bicycle (allegedly the old one was stolen), and pay their hotel rent. He accepted my silence; I think he viewed it as neutral, which he felt was better than negative. Those brief exchanges were infrequent and we would go on to enjoy our time together, such as one night analyzing a piece I was learning on the piano, J.S. Bach's invention Number 13 in A minor. In an attempt to help me understand the piece, he described the use of the cycle of 4th's and diatonic 7th's via Musica ficta, (feigned music) as the sharpening or flattening of particular notes to avoid awkward intervals. We began to spend even more time dissecting music together, Ted always loved helping me learn, which also seemed to inspire his personal studies, and of course his knowledge was easily transferable to any instrument.

Not unusual for spring, the city was in the midst of a late April heat wave and Santa Ana winds abounded. Perhaps the valley climate was cycling back to its semi-desert state, the way I recalled it when I was growing up here. The regular basketball season had ended and we were now enjoying the Lakers in the play offs. Also, after studying many books on coins, Ted's passion for coin collecting really ignited and he made his first purchase after two years; beautiful Peace dollars, and Franklin half-dollars. He delighted in sharing his passion with me, showed me how to use the magnifying glass, and would point out the unique and beautiful nuances of each coin. He even began photographing the coins in various lighting, as certain angles of light enhanced a distinct aspect of beauty.

● X □ △ ★

Soon a most wonderful and fateful opportunity appeared on the horizon. John Pisano had gotten Ted a gig playing for the Sunday brunch crowd at Spazio's restaurant. For Ted, it seemed an almost perfect circumstance, the optimal conditions he preferred for publically playing solo guitar; a comfortable place where he could remain in the background, and unobtrusively infuse the room with his beautiful music. This would turn out to be the beginning of semi-regular performances he would give throughout the remainder of his life. His first gig was on Sunday, May 2nd, 2004. In his datebook he noted the preparations he made the night before, *"May 1 The night before 1st Spazio's Brunch, Unearth my dear black face Vibrolux Reverb, variac and clean that driver socket! ah! much better. Then reverb goes on the fritz, terrible distortion (pot 3), lift and bang pan and jostle reverb tubes VOILA! she's back. Play: me - nothin' happening. Duena, through both black face amps not quite right for me this time. Try Banana my old faithful friend. Nothin' for me and her at first, but after a couple hours of trying WOW suddenly did she ever step up to the plate. What a transformation. Stunning that now I went from crap to playing as well or better than I ever have! Magic!"*

On May 2nd at Spazio's Ted played during the brunch from 11 a.m. 'til 2 p.m. He told very few people about it, although the details were posted on many Internet guitar sites and there was a wonderful write-up in the Los Angeles Daily News full of praise and encouraging music lovers to take advantage of this rare opportunity to hear a true virtuoso. Consequently, quite a large crowd showed up and he dazzled everyone. Ted's playing was unbelievably beautiful that day. However he was rather uncomfortable because of the set up in the restaurant as he felt it was more like concertizing as opposed to just being in the background providing music. It might have been the background for someone else, but when a crowd came specifically to listen to Ted play, he became the sole focus. Ted wrote about that afternoon, *"Banana (down a whole step) with black face amps. I went into a creative zone in response to the (surprise!) near concert quiet and 'the creator' was very kind as I played many things I've never played before. I was barely present."*

● X □ △ ★

Now almost half way through the year, my moodiness continued, although somewhat mitigated. The anti-depressants were not a panacea, so to quell potential depression I had Mother's Day brunch with Lori and her family. When I came home Ted was already here, the Lakers were on TV and it was about 3 minutes before the half. Ted informed me they were playing exceptionally well. We watched the second half together as the Lakers routed San Antonio. The game over, Ted and I both napped about an hour, and afterwards a groggy Ted went to get us dinner. I watered the yard to awaken myself, and wondered what was taking him so long. An hour later he returned home with our dinner and a surprise CD, the soundtrack from Mary Poppins!

Later, upon my analyzing some music, perhaps one of the chorales, and finding myself confused as to naming some of the chords, Ted explained the "root unplayed" Bachian 7b9's (Ted said Bach used thousands of them). For instance here is Ted's example of *one group*: E7b9: G# B D F, G7b9: Ab B D F, Bb7b9: Ab B(Cb) D F, Db7b9: Ab Cb D F (or the enharmonic of this one). When I continued my study I was amazed at how often "root unplayed" occurred. Ted had a way of opening one's eyes to grasp a clearer understanding of a concept. And by using just one example, he opened up a world for one to discover. Ted found it equally thrilling and rewarding when I grasped a concept and in turn got so excited by all the possibilities.

On Tuesday May 11th, Ted gave his third "open counseling" at Musician's Institute. All he mentioned in his datebook was, *"Bring Lulu & Chubbie - both sounding simply spectacular in the school's Fender 'Blues Jr.' amplifier. To B's Wow everything moving on Highland & the freeways like back in the '60s!!!!"*

As always, stimulated from the energy at the seminar, once home Ted played for about three hours straight; everything I loved, the songs that he transformed with his mystical gift into the most magnificent renditions imaginable. Later that night his playing had inspired me to play and I channeled my Ted-infused energy into the piano while Ted worked in the same room on the computer. As he worked, he listened and offered me suggestions on how to practice. I did as he asked, dissected the troublesome bars beat by beat. One bar that had been a stumbling block was finally realized. He was very pleased, and explained that was how one overcame the difficult spots, by breaking them down to the minutest increments. He was right of course, and yes, it was a tremendous amount of effort, very intense, totally effective.

During the week I had noticed the little carnival had returned to Hazeltine Park. Sunday afternoon was mild and we decided to go take a look. On a fluke I tossed a dart at a board of balloons and popped one on the first try! The booth vendor said I won, so I let Ted pick out the prize, he chose a small framed print of Betty Boop.

We went on to other booths of skill, we each won Tom & Jerry drinking glasses by tossing quarters into disarrayed piles of dinner plates, glassware and vases of various shapes, sizes and colors. At the same booth were a mother with two children, a little boy and his younger sister. Ted and I watched as the children tossed quarters, the little girl so proud when she won a saucer. However the little boy, quite dejected, had not won anything and now they were out of quarters. That is when Ted so generously began handing the little boy quarters and soon the boy's spirits soared when he won a coffee cup.

But what Ted really wanted was a stuffed smiling-faced sunflower, which we tried to win by tossing rings around floating ducks moving about in a small pool, no luck. Ted finally won the flower at another booth, more easily achieved, scooping up rubber turtles bobbing in a tub, using a net attached to the end of a stick. Six tries, six turtles won him the flower. Satisfied, at last we headed to the food stand for two huge bags of popcorn and a caramel apple. Home and tuckered out, we ate all we bought, watched the Angels and napped. A loving and lazy evening complemented our playful day.

Towards the end of the month, Ted was put in touch with someone who wanted to reissue Ted's 1977 record album on CD. The man was Paul Kohler. He had a small company called "Art of Life Records" and Ted felt very comfortable with Paul as a person and the idea of the re-release. Ted just had to get a clean sound source ready to send to the company.

Soon, Ted's friend Dan Sawyer (masterful jazz guitarist and composer), found a studio and the original tape was re-mastered. That same day the order of the songs was changed. This came about because Ted said he wanted the new CD to start with "Watch What Happens" because it was in a solid 4/4 rhythm. He felt that hearing the record start with a ballad would put off modern listeners, as it had on the original vinyl record. Dan Sawyer made up a list of the song titles in the new order. Ted thought about it for a while and then agreed. The final results met with Ted's approval and the CD is still available today.

● X □ △ ★

The 3rd of June. Discovery inadvertent. Ominous lump. Left breast. My first inclination was to ignore it, pretend it didn't exist. How? When it kept creeping into each thought. Is that what fear is? It was late afternoon on a Friday, and nothing could be done until Monday so I kept the news from Ted until then. What an actress I tried to be, but Ted knowing me so well, sensed there was something wrong. I think I told him I just didn't feel well. Later I told Lori, and then wished I hadn't, but I knew she would make me face it. Monday was a nightmare Lori and I shared, from initial exam to mammogram to ultrasound to surgeon. Turning numb to his words, all I heard, "looks suspicious" then I went blank.

In the interim, on June 10th Ted had his 4th open counseling, 3rd month in a row and 3rd this year at Musician's Institute. *"In the small room, bring Bettina my beloved '54 X375 Stratford Guild."* No notes. We watched the Lakers lose to Detroit - twice. Ted bought us the Camelot DVD, we grasped and held fast to any distraction.

Monday, the day before my 52nd birthday, a biopsy, the lump was excised and although malignant hadn't spread. Sore, but fine. *"Lori calls: B went through the surgery fine, they removed the growth, it was not benign but the meds are confident they got it all and after removing one lymph node also that it had not spread. To B she looks...... good!"*

Tuesday came and my birthday perfect and relaxed, Ted, Lori and I watched the Lakers lose. The loss meant less considering the circumstances. I was so grateful to be okay that everything was placed in perspective. Time had elongated, from the initial discovery of the lump, through the process to the conclusion. It seemed more than a week. Finally all those mind-numbing daunting thoughts and the fears that were strangling me had vanished.

Relieved and healing, over the next few days we watched "Carousel" and "Around the World in 80 Days." Ted lavished us with Panda Express and See's candy. While I rested, Ted practiced many hours on Chubbie and got into a long fantasy improvisation on 'America' from "West Side Story." I listened, in awe and fixated, it was his most brilliant improvisation to date.

Then we found out the nightmare was not over with! After I had been told everything was okay, they had been mistaken. My calm was shattered by a call from the surgeon; the secondary pathology report detected a small cluster of cells in a lymph node. I would have to relive that awful experience again, another surgery.

A week of quiet well-spent days of distraction. As Ted gave lessons, my afternoons were whiled away in the garden under the trees with the cats. I gazed up into the green canopy of leaves as sparks of sun shot through and thought how the sun is a star and here I am, this tiny life form just here now and pondered again those age-old questions to gain some perspective which somehow I found comfort in. And the hot flashes returned. No estrogen - ever again. Definitely thought to be the cause of the cancer. Eighteen months ago, "low risk" I was told and now Estrogen was the prime suspect.

On June 30th I went through the second surgery. Ted and I would bide our time awaiting the findings, not knowing anything until after the long July 4th holiday weekend. He was doing his utmost to hide his fears from me, but still I could sense his trepidation. One night we watched "My Cousin Vinny" for the second time because we needed so badly to laugh a lot. The next day Ted went crazy at Tower Records, came home with a million gems of entertainment to help mitigate another endless waiting period. During this time Ted entered in his datebook a very revealing insight about himself, *"July 2 We watch and enjoy my FAVORITE movie I think 1939 "They Made Me A Criminal" This movie embodies so much of what I feel, who I am, what I've lived, how I've lived. The Max Steiner wonderful triple theme score also seems to this humbled soul to portray in tone my very essence, as he's done countless times with me. His notes in certain places ARE me. I weep with joy at some non-understood inner recognition."*

Right after the holiday weekend we received the best news, the pathology reports came back negative! O the absolute elation, the weight lifted, the tension released, after having been burdened for a month with the unknown, the fear. I became so light-headed and grateful for the reprieve, to live. Now it was merely the process of healing from the second surgery, perhaps a month of mending for the arm to be fully functional.

With summer in full bloom and the temperature well into the 90's, on July 9th we celebrated our 12th anniversary. Even the heat spell couldn't cast a pall on our joy. Ted brought over The Wizard of Oz DVD, but we never got to watch it, so filled with exhilaration we couldn't stay focused on any one subject. Even our conversation zig-zagged like a jagged path all over the planet, we laughed and were just grateful for everything.

● X □ △ ★

Soon Ted granted the most ardent wish of one student, *"7/15/04 Chris N. is absolutely overjoyed with his new purchase of my '70s natural finish, ash bodied Tele, Egg, or "The Egg Man" with the '50s lead pick up and the Gibson humbucker in the neck pick up.*

Ted had asked me about selling Egg and expressed to me how much his student loved it, I told him I thought that was wonderful. Egg was a bit too heavy in weight for me so I never played it much, nor had Ted for a long while. Actually Egg had been out "on loan" on and off to several students for quite some time. So we were both grateful it would have a good loving home.

With some money in his pockets Ted couldn't resist an excursion to the coin shop and came home with a variety of old dimes, quarters, Peace dollars and Morgan silver dollars. I always enjoyed him showing me all the coins, his excitement and enthusiasm was contagious. But the enthusiasm was ruined like a pin in a balloon, when he decided to update me on the changes in the "homeless" situation. Perhaps he thought at last I would feel some compassion? He told me that mother and daughter had checked out of the hotel and had disappeared. But he ran into their friend at Borders Books who told him the mother needed a brain tumor operation. Not knowing what to say, again I remained silent. Ted went on to tell me that three days later, he finally heard from the mother, who apparently had had the brain tumor removed and was now alive and well and living in Texas. I thought, all this in the span of one week? I was incredulous, hoped it didn't show, bit my lip and wondered how Ted could be taken in by that story. It sounded to me more likely that they had to skip town.

Shortly after that he granted another student's plea for a guitar, "*7/22/04 Because of his love for it, sell Jim D. my X500 Blonde mid '70s Gina.*" I truly was glad that the guitars were going to deserving students and loving homes, but where was the money going? Other than coins, I shuddered to think.

Nonetheless a beam of light was always shining on him. Evidently, Spazio's management was so pleased with the turnout for Ted's playing debut that he was hired again, on Sunday July 25th to play another brunch. Ted charmed and transfixed the room, drenched it in music for three sense-stimulating hours. These were some of his best playing and fantasy improvisations. Although he was glad when it ended, it wasn't as stress-laden the second time. He wrote, *"July 25 Fabulous sounds from my Tele (Esq.) tuned a whole step down, through that Vibrolux Reverb. Best things I played: Fantasy on West Side Story's "America" Fantasy on "On Broadway," Ticket to Ride, Hey Jude (not really a fantasy here), Hard Day's Night."*

● X □ △ ★

Soon beautiful tropical clouds graced the morning, although no chance for a storm, the day became gloomy before noon. Lori held my hand through the appointment with the oncologist. I could have been given worse news, but this was bad enough by my standards: 35 days radiation, 5 days a week, 7 weeks. Given the odds of the cancer returning if I chose to forgo this therapy, I relented. There would be no chemotherapy because of the CREST, way too risky, but the radiation was sort-of like insurance. I silently swore to myself, that this would be all. I had had enough. From the beginning there was never a clear picture of the process, or how many steps, and it seemed to be endless. I was overwhelmed and just wanted it all to be over. Ted understood my frustration, but encouraged me to go through the procedure considering the odds were in both our favor. I suppose I only did it for him. It was the beginning of August 2004 and in retrospect, had I not, we might have both left this planet together, around the same time.

The moon, a tiny smile on its way up. We watched the Angels play while Ted worked on his counterpoint and studied for hours. Then he practiced for his upcoming seminar on Sunday, his playing almost ethereal. Compelled to listen, I lay in bed for hours in a sort of half sleep reverie, thought I'd be tired Sunday and was surprised how energized I felt. The music penetrated my being, awakened my senses. Ted said he felt a similar energy flowing through him as he played and had entered a similar state. Sunday's seminar at Calif. Vintage Guitar was as successful and incredible as all the others had been. Some time ago we both had stopped taking extensive notes, and all Ted jotted in his datebook was, *"Aug. 8 Workshop at Calif. Vintage Guitar, bring Chubbie, Banana Crème and black face Vibrolux, which all sound terrific. Hand out sheets for solo guitar: Over the Rainbow and Our Love is Here to Stay."* Fortunately that seminar was videotaped and transferred to DVD.

Mid August fraught with trepidation, I faced my first radiation treatment. I dreaded the days upon waking. I recoiled from the idea of rising every morning, weekdays, for the next seven weeks. The drive was five times longer than the treatment, and the treatment glared harshly like a single light bulb, intense in an empty room. Ted knew I was very blue and surprised me with three bunches of flowers, blueberries, chocolate eclairs, and drew from me the widest smile when he gave me his old Rogers & Hammerstein Songbook, identical to the one I had as a child. By Saturday I was drained, so I rested and listened to him practice for his upcoming seminar. Afterwards he noted,*"Aug. 22 Seminar at Boulevard Music: Bring Regina (my lovely '65 Blonde Capri) and Banana. Wonderful time, everything flowed. We talk mainly about ways to touch the strings and set amp tones and such."* That seminar was also videotaped and transferred to DVD.

● X □ △ ★

I guess the stress from the breast cancer compounded with discontinuing the use of Estrogen intensified the symptoms of menopause, which were again full-blown and magnified the underlying irritation I felt about Ted's helping the "homeless" women. All that converged when Ted accused me of treating him like a child and said I viewed him as incapable of making sound decisions. It was the same complaint from months ago about his judgment. No matter how I responded he didn't believe me, I only questioned his actions regarding the homeless women, but he still considered this so-called criticism an attack on his entire ability to make accurate assessments of any situation. He truly felt I thought he was incapable of acting like an adult.

I really couldn't say what happened, or if it was even only one thing that caused it, perhaps I had become more critical of him, but when I thought about everything, I ached so much inside, and was also angry. Perhaps he just needed me to sanction his actions, which in all good conscience I could not do. Earlier in the year Ted had come home with a speeding ticket and lied to me for the first time ever, saying he was rushing to post bail for a student's daughter in jail for drunk driving, then recanted and confessed he was posting bail for one of the homeless women, and having confessed, realized how much more fuel it added to my argument against them, which he was trying to avoid doing, by lying. As to why she was in jail, he said she had sassed a policeman. Even if so, regardless of why, should that not have been an omen? He chose to ignore it. Whatever instigated the now circular argument was irrelevant, but somehow it had to be resolved.

For a few more days the tension brewed. Perhaps Ted's stress was heightened and manifested fears about my cancer, as if he were experiencing all of my difficulties and we were both on edge. He accused me of not making any effort to change my view of him. Everything I said he took as criticism and was ultra-defensive and ultra-sensitive. I was at my wits end and without a hint about how to fix things. On the last day of August we separated. (Which turned out to be for six days.) Under these sad and unresolved circumstances, Ted seemed glaringly absent from my life and I missed him terribly.

How many visible and invisible scars would mar our lives? A lifetime's worth, like collected relics. If fortunate, perfection formed one's origin, soft and flawless; then soon a skinned knee, a gash here and there or a hurtful word was inescapable. A heartless remark and the inevitable shin against table leg, or the edge of the kitchen knife slicing into a finger; it all added up as deductions from that perfection we knew was impossible to maintain.

Monday, the 6th was Labor Day and mid-afternoon Ted came back. He told me he couldn't bear to stay away any longer and promised not to press the issues disturbing us. He said he realized I had enough to deal with already. At that moment, a sudden flooding of love swept away all the past pain. That our love above all else sustained us was undeniable, and nothing else mattered. We knew that on a few things we would never see eye to eye but on most things we were in complete agreement. One couldn't ask for a better reconciliation.

That afternoon and evening we connected more strongly than we had in a long time. Then for days we reveled in everything, as if the splendor was lent us for the first time. Bach's Keyboard Concertos, a passel of silver Roosevelt dimes, Ted found me a tiny hand-held fan for my hot flashes, and we swooned over the score from "A Summer Place" more than just a few times.

The Sycamore tree in my front yard had begun to shed its leaves and autumn was but a week away. My coughing had come back at night, which soon escalated into something fierce, and I had trouble breathing. Nothing from herbal teas to honey to Hydrocodone helped. I phoned Dr. P, who prescribed a short regimen using high doses of Prednisone and spent the day in bed reading while on September 19th, Ted played his third brunch at Spazio's. He said the place was packed and even admitted to playing to his satisfaction, which meant he must have been fabulous, *"11 to 2:30 Spazio's my 3rd brunch there. My cousins (Gershon's, Klein's & Kopp's) surprised me! Lulu for 1st 1 1/2 hours then Banana Crème and my beloved Fender Electric Vibrolux Reverb."*

● X □ △ ★

In a small round silver cardboard box tied with purple ribbon were placed 5 old silver coins I selected especially for Ted's 58th birthday. Also, his astrology forecast from the newspaper promising him a very special year ahead (alas, alas). We had a relaxing afternoon, a favorite dinner and watched the Angel's win, just his kind of day, which he graciously accepted, and I was grateful to have provided everything to his liking.

Soon the days became partly cloudy and cool and leaves were strewn about the lawn. The fall always had a sense of sweet melancholy, I didn't know why, and I felt that sentiment inside as I silently gazed at Ted engrossed in a baseball game and sorting through his new coins. Ted's passion for coin collecting had reached a feverish pitch. Several times a week he frequented different coin shops and he began to accumulate a vast array of favorite coins. As he started arranging the coins in sets, it became a treasure hunt to find the missing ones he needed to complete them. There was only slight remorse when he sold two more guitars we weren't playing, then headed straight to Valley View Coins, *"10/4/04 Sell off 2 guitars that deserve more love to Danny at Calif. Vintage: Giavana, light blonde '65 X175 Francesca, '55 Aristocrat M75. To Valley View Coins: many beautiful proof sets, and nine gorgeous Peace & Morgan Silver Dollars. To B"*

By the second week in October I had completed my radiation treatments, but the same night I was having trouble breathing. I sounded like out of tune woodwinds, wheezing high dissonant pitches. Around two in the morning I ended up in the emergency hospital where they plied me with Prednisone, pure oxygen and put me on a nebulizer for a while. I was diagnosed as having a CREST-related asthma-like attack, possibly from too rapid a withdrawal from the high dose of Prednisone I had recently taken and I had developed a severe case of Bronchitis.

We shook off the dust from the winter utilities, our old faithful space heaters. Rinsed out the teapot, searched the shelves for chamomile, ginger and orange spice. Over the coming weeks I wrapped myself in Ted's old warm flannel shirts, analyzed Bach's French Suite in Eb, while Ted marveled over silver dollars and the Yankees battled it out with Boston. L. A. had its first measurable rain in 181 days, and we used the oven to make baked potatoes and had the extra benefit of the warmth. Soon I was feeling better.

Mid October we listened to the newly re-mastered CD of Ted's old solo guitar album and were pleased with the sound and the new order of songs. For two days straight it rained like crazy, rain kept us awake pounding on the roof but astonishingly not one drop seeped through the roof in the kitchen.

On the 23rd the 100th World Series and we watched Boston take Game 1 at home against the St. Louis Cardinals. That night Ted filled in coin boards with quarters and when he finished there was only one missing. Then coincidently, I chanced to look and much to our amazement, there in my wallet happened to be that very 1968 quarter, which filled in the last empty round space.

Ted's 4th Spazio's brunch occurred the same day as the Sherman Oaks Street Fair. Ventura Boulevard blocked off from Van Nuys Boulevard to Kester Avenue, hence not a large crowd due to the inconvenience of getting there. We just about had the whole place to ourselves. Nonetheless his playing was profoundly magical and it was wonderful for me to listen, eat and read. Afterwards we negotiated a roundabout way home and watched Game 2 of the World Series, which gave Boston their 2nd win. Then we watched the first Lakers exhibition game. It was that time of year when the seasons merged and mingled for a short time before diverging, summer into autumn.

October 27th: Rain, thunder, lightening, lunar eclipse, full moon, Boston Red Sox win World Series. Ted was ecstatic, he penned the memory in his datebook, *"Oct. 27 Boston Red Sox Win the World Series! Wow! The Curse Is Over! BoSox stage the great post-season rally (down 0-3 in ALCS) and defeat the powerful Yankees and the powerful Cardinals 8 straight games! and win their 1st World Series in 86 years!"*

Halloween. Cool blustery winds, not a soul at our door, branches scratching the windows. Once we thought we heard voices or laughter, probably the wind rustling something. To discourage little visitors, the porch light wasn't lit, but I bought candy in case anyone was brave enough to venture through the darkness to our door. Not surprising we ate most of those treats. My health had much improved, I did errands for us again, bought Ted some most welcome delicacies, and he bought his first coin hoard, unsought, spectacular timing, dimes, nickels, pennies and quarters. He began filling in the Jefferson nickels coin board, I sorted through hundreds of old pennies while we watched a documentary on Broadway musicals.

● X □ △ ★

I mistook the dimness in the room for a day grown late, but it was just the sun falling behind a blind corner belying another hour of light. In the book I marked my place with a thumbprint smudge, chocolate, unmistakable trace of mine. By the time Ted arrived I was watching the Lakers trounce New Orleans. He surprised me with chocolate eclairs, earlier I had bought his favorite potato wedges, what a dinner! Afterwards we did a jigsaw puzzle, I the bottom half, Ted the top and we finished at the exact same time, give or take a few seconds. As we pieced the puzzle together we listened to Fredrick Delius (twice), second disc of the Sir John Barbarolli little box set he had gotten me. It was rapturous. Ted asked the ether, "Does music ever get any better than this?"

Towards the end of November a box of CDs arrived from Paul Kohler. The 1977 Solo Guitar album was now officially available. Ted took some time to finalize what would be his last published interview, *"Computer: many hours of new & final work on Jim Carlton interview. He has pleaded for me not to change too much (after originally giving me more leeway) He's a great guy so I'm restoring MUCH of what he wrote & clarifying, which he's cool with."*

On Thanksgiving Day, Ted played at Spazio's from 1 to 4 p.m. I went with Lori and her family to my brother's house, where Ted was to meet me after his gig, but never did. Actually I had a feeling he wouldn't show up at my brother's. When I came home, just as I thought, Ted was here, chose to relax, have some quiet time. He said Spazio's went well, some of his student's were there and everyone appeared to enjoy the music. *"Spazio's, play Chubbie for the whole 3 hours, was doing too well to hunger for the Telecaster sound."*

The last month of this difficult year, in between seminars and small gigs, Ted mostly bought and sorted coins or spent the evenings practicing and playing guitar. One night we listened to the soundtrack from "The Sound of Music" and Ted became transfixed, as if hearing it for the first time, the coins became an after thought. Late night hours he used to refine his song list on the computer

On December 12, 2004 Ted played his fifth brunch at Spazio's. When we arrived, all the tables around the stage had been reserved so I sat at a small table in the bar area. While he was warming up I got some breakfast from the buffet. By the time Lori and Andi arrived, Ted was sounding spectacular. He played many songs just for me. I was enraptured, could not hold back tears, it was so poignant, all the songs had special meaning which he expressed so deeply it penetrated my being. That was his beautiful early Christmas gift to me. In his datebook he noted, *"I surprise Barbie (who's with her best friend Lori & her sis*

Andi) & play many tunes for her. She is thrilled. Angela for first two hours, Banana Crème for Christmas medley, spontaneous last half hour. This '54 Esquire & my equally beloved Fender Vibrolux Reverb is now producing the sounds I've wanted all my life. Part of it is sitting to the side of the amp (all tuned down one whole step-no-1/2 step I found out later) Then very last half hour, as fine a sound as I've ever gotten. Spectacular, ringing, throaty, chimey on #4: my beloved '54 Esquire with '60's Vibrolux Reverb: Have Yourself a Merry Little Xmas, O Xmas Tree, Silent Night, White Xmas, The Xmas Song."

The following Sunday Ted played a two-hour early afternoon private party at The Getty Center's Scholar's Lounge. When he came home, he found Lori and I attempting to surprise him by making homemade chocolate chip cookies sans electric mixer, hard work but we succeeded. The three of us, stuffed with warm cookies fresh from the oven, chips melting on our fingers, watched (for the millionth time), and still marveled at the Wizard of Oz. Then he caught another cold.

Christmas Eve Ted came over unknowingly bringing his illness with him. He'd felt better when he left his apartment then the illness manifested again here. We knew he shouldn't stay, as much as we wanted to spend the evening together, especially to share the music of the season but it seemed to be the season itself that caused his illness. I recalled that almost every year, around the same time, Ted would catch a cold. Yet before he left we exchanged our meager but heartfelt gifts. Photographs and silver coins for an electric mixer (so thoughtful), and a wonderful puzzle.

Ted remained very sick throughout the last week of the year, he taught a student or two, transcribed a few Colombo cues, and worked on some guitars, *"Bend 2 contacts for neck pick up and repair (Guild T100D SB) Sadie's toggle switch which wouldn't stay in position, but in order to access her I had to drill out (in 4 stages) one of the stripped, old rusted pick up wiring screws. Success. Readjust. And what a jazz tone, controls full up and neck pick up now very low in its ring in the Peavy Special 130. Even sounding 2 - perfect thick rounded hollowish mid range tone."*

Sad at not having seen Ted for a week it was a surprise to hear him come in on New Year's Eve afternoon, completely recovered from his illness. So glad to see each other and I was relieved that he was again well. Impromptu, we met Lori and Andi for a late lunch at Solly's Deli. Later spent a quiet, enjoyable evening joined by Lori for a while, the three of us watched "De Lovely," not great, but okay. Ted and I stayed up 'til midnight, saw the ball drop and at the very moment when I exclaimed it's 2005, Quincy kissed me! My first kiss of the New Year, then I asked Ted for my second kiss. I was so glad this year was over, and Ted echoed my sentiment, *"B thrilled to be done with 2004 & Quincy's kiss of her right after midnight seals the deal."*

Prelude

How much we leave undone, dictated by the weight of what we think is more important at the moment. Day dreaming, forming thoughts, great ideas put off. The other things first, then one day when the light is just right, maybe at a table placed by a window with a beautiful view, in some sunny quiet place in the future......

Despite his premonition, Ted lived his last seven months as if there were yet many years ahead. Essentially that was his natural attitude, graced with optimism. He was fortunate to be able to live in the moment most of the time, although it was not a conscious choice, it was there from birth. Without realizing it, he was the ultimate risk taker.

Chapter VI
What Fate Had Waiting

Ted and I had become what might be termed as "an old couple" having fallen into a comfortable place, when after many years together, all our idiosyncrasies, habits, had long gone unnoticed and were unquestionably accepted. Our relationship formed the core of our world, a world of two, a dyad. We had long since discovered we preferred not having much company, enjoyed our time most with just the two of us alone. Daily routines, chores, all became part of and embellished that core, and now included long forays to the coin shops. The coin collecting had become fervent and he frequented various coin shops twice a week.

Ted's teaching schedule in the Encino apartment had changed radically over the past five years or so, slowly shortening his teaching hours, and incorporating Tuesdays, and finally Fridays. By 2004 he was teaching five days a week but only 4 or 5 students per day, and thus it would remain. A nearly constant clamor from upstairs neighbors was one factor that caused him to alter his hours. He tailored his days to coincide with the quietest times, began and ended each day earlier. Long gone were all those late night lessons (he used to end at 11:00 p.m.), and on rare occasion when engrossed in a particularly interesting discussion lingered until 2 a.m. His student roster had also begun to decrease and he spent less time teaching, intending to follow up on the many requests for lessons, but rarely getting around to doing so. He had his monthly brunch gig at Spazio's, played some private events and had been giving more seminars, these opportunities were adequate to fill in the blank spots left in his student roster.

January 2005 began just like any other month, Ted was working on the computer by the time I came home from my friend Mary's New Year's Day open house. I joined him in the room and as he worked I practiced piano until midnight. He kept working beyond. Did we even have dinner? Probably not since I'd eaten at Mary's and he could go without food for the longest time, just munching occasionally on carrots or a bell pepper.

Southern California had been experiencing unprecedented and prolonged days of heavy rain. Despite the downpours, Ted came back to my place every afternoon. Once he was soaked to the bone when he arrived, he had walked quite a distance to where he'd parked his car, waded through ankle deep puddles and of course, was dressed totally inappropriately for such doings. During this terribly inclement weather, Ted, ever thoughtful, would always call before leaving his apartment after teaching to see if there was anything I needed him to bring, or if there was a special meal I was craving. Oftentimes he would surprise me anyway, whether with food goodies, DVDs, CDs, puzzles, what ever happened to catch his eye, usually something we could enjoy together.

We continued being loyal to the Lakers, and also became engaged and entertained by another show, which actually became a ritual. Don't laugh, we got hooked on American Idol. We found it fun, interesting and enjoyed comparing our reactions and opinions on the blooming talent of some of these youngsters. Lori was hooked too, and all three of us would gather Tuesday evenings to share this crazy fun fixation.

Another aspect in my life had changed that in a way affected us both. For a long time we had both held out hopes that my fingers would heal, but that had not happened. Tearfully I realized I could not continue to play the guitar with any regularity, which was painful both physically and emotionally. That also saddened Ted, but ever encouraging and optimistic, he helped me learn to accept it, and would write me piano exercises, and offered me useful learning tools. Ted noted a plea from me and wrote a formula I found particularly clever and very helpful. *"Her request: give her 2 to 4 chord progressions that will use all 7 triads in a key. She responds pretty well to the formulas."*

Ted's triads formulas 2005

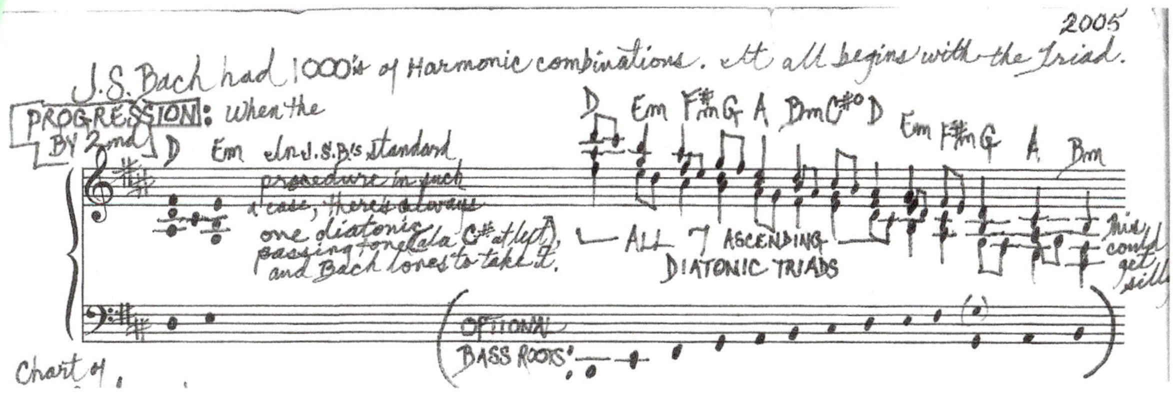

● X □ △ ★

Eventually the rain abated, but Ted continued to bring surprises. One night he bought the Ray Charles movie, the new biography, and we watched it and thought it was so wonderfully well done. We absolutely loved the movie. Ray's unique soulful voice had always surpassed any other male singer for us both. Then airing late in the season, the first Sunday in February Ted and I watched the Superbowl, (Patriots/Eagles). It was a good game but we were rooting for the Eagles (lost by 3). We noted that it was nice to not have company with us, easier to enjoy the game since no one else we knew actually cared enough to really watch. It was just an event blown way out of proportion, but most people thought it warranted a party.

Also in February, much to Ted's chagrin, Lori and I booked our flight to Dublin via London. We would spend a few days in London, then head to our main destination, the National Library in Dublin for a James Joyce exhibition which featured interactive displays enabling visitors to browse through his notebooks, and offering greater insight into his thought process plus so much more. We were to leave on July 20th and return on the 31st. We couldn't possibly let this opportunity pass; it was our last chance, as the exhibit was to close forever to the public at the end of summer.

At Ted's sixth Spazio's brunch gig on February 13th, we were shocked to find everything rearranged and the buffet tables encircled the skirt of the stage. Ted, highly sensitive to smells, sat as far back as possible to fend off nausea from the platters of food. Regardless of the restructured room, Ted played brilliantly his exquisite music with a now customary aplomb. At a back table I sat in the bar, unbeknownst that next to me sat friends of Ted's I would soon meet. When Ted introduced the extraordinary pianist/guitarist Steve Ferguson, *"the most talented and/or accomplished musician and composer I've ever met, and I'm thrilled to have his friendship"* and singer/songwriter Wendy Waldman to me afterwards, there was instant chemistry. We conversed easily about everything, covering a gamut of subjects including literature. The four of us remained at the restaurant long after everyone had gone. We lingered late into the afternoon as each idea formed a discussion that segued easily into another. Finally with the sun slanted low we realized how late it had grown, the restaurant long empty and now preparing for the dinner hour, we had to leave. "*Feb. 13 Spazio's "Bring Chubbie & Banana Crème (down a half step) Beloved vibrolux reverb blows fuse, student Andy M gets more, she blows those too. My back up, trusty Peavey Special 130 stands in."*

When his residual check arrived, "*a surprisingly good amount,"* it was not guitars he sought this time, but coins. *"Feb. 19 Bad rain then sun showers To Gold Coast Coins - spectacular Franklins, Washingtons, Winged Cap Libertys, tons o' coins."* Yet the following day he opted for Tower, *"Feb. 20 To Tower, surprise, Ray Charles 'A Recipe for Soul' for Barbie- reason: Over the Rainbow, You'll Never Walk Alone, Ol' Man River, That Lucky Ol' Sun & much more stunning stuff from 1963."* I was ecstatic, a better gift he could not have found, but he knew that, because he knew me so well. An hour to swoon over this treasure before the NBA All Star Game, but before the game began Ted battled the massive rain again and got us spaghetti from Maria's. Nothing could match the love I felt from him, and I burst with love for him in turn, we were so very blessed.

The rain continued with a vengeance, steady hard heavy, breaking records and wreaking havoc. One morning the rain was so strong and dense I could barely see across the street. Not a deterrent for Ted and within that storm fraught week he visited four more coin stores. Our living room was filled with stacks of coin books, boxes and bags of coins; one would think the weight alone would cause the floor to cave. Ted was euphoric with it all.

● X □ △ ★

Sometime in early March, Ted became suspicious of the homeless women. Even though they had moved to another state, they maintained a bank account here and Ted would periodically deposit money in it for them, but around this time Ted sensed something was amiss. He cleverly set about tripping them up, and discovered they had in fact lied to him. He caught them in the act and that was the end. He was extremely upset, wouldn't tell me any of the details and didn't want to talk about it at all. The deception was distressing and painful for him; how could this be after all he had done for them. He had given them thousands of dollars over the past year. In spite of that particularly disheartening experience, he was not disillusioned by humanity in the least, and still determined to seek out others in need in his never-ending quest for a better world.

Foggy mornings gave way to warm humid afternoons and I was prickly enough with my wacky metabolism, but I was determined to provide a soothing evening to uplift Ted's wounded spirits. After a favorite meal, I dumped out a jigsaw puzzle on the dining table and chose some music. As Ted always said, use music as a healer. It worked like a charm and he noted what I chose, *"Ozawa & the Boston (or S.F.) Orchestra versions of Ravel: Le Trombeau de Couperin, La Valse & Mother Goose Suite, then Max Steiner's 1959 A Summer Place - what great music!"*

On March 13th Ted played his seventh brunch at Spazio's. The one Sunday a month at Spazio's had become somewhat of a salon, a meeting place for friends. It was a comfortable environment to which Ted had now grown more accustomed. Ted's playing continued to be dazzling but he grew braver and braver and this time he culminated with a twenty minute Bachian improvisation that was totally brilliant and stunned everyone.

Many of Ted's friends and students attended regularly now. Afterwards coffee and conversation, and one never knew who would join us. There was always a fabulous array of interesting people. As an indication of how stimulating the entire day was, when leaving Spazio's, Ted, Steve Ferguson, and I, still engrossed in conversation entered the elevator to descend one floor. How much time elapsed before we realized no one had pressed the button? At some point we noticed it was taking an awfully long time to hit ground level. We just weren't moving! Ted also recollected much of that Sunday, *"Spray the military special CAIG De-ox wonder product into pick up selector switches electronics of both*

Chubbie & Esquire. Bring my now almost customary '54 detuned Esquire, Chubbie and the reliable fabulous mid '80s Vibrolux Reverb to Spazio's 11:00 a.m. brunch gig. Remembering some of what I played: blues, Gospel blues, a bunch of forms, I'm In the Mood for Love, Only Have Eyes for You, Unchain My Heart, many more choruses of 2 bar Gospely blues. Can't Buy Me Love, Hard Days Night, Something, A Day in the Life: bridge of 1st replaced by front end of 2nd, near identical. Bluesy/Gospely tho' not too aggressive version of "I'm Into Something Good." "You'll Never Walk Alone" reverential: C/Eb concert to please me and B, surprise : Steve & Wendy loved it. Sort of a personal milestone, drenched in reverb - long final improvisation ala J.S. Bach - 1st time unleashed upon the public. Went very well, as well as the 10's of 1000's of times I've done this in solitude."

Low clouds and fog hung around the valley most of the day; the sun broke through late sending an hour or two of warm rays into the living room to grace our celebration of J.S. Bach's 320th birthday on March 21st. The entire evening was devoted to Bach listening. Although we availed ourselves of this pleasure frequently, we felt particularly inspired to pay special tribute that night.

Soon a new moon ushered in Tom Bocci's 60th birthday. Lori and I took Tom and Wendy for a sumptuous dinner at Petite Jaques. Ted had declined to go due to his *"current heightened sensitivity to killing the animals for their taste and everyone jolly and laughing while partaking, and me partly wanting to revisit that territory."* However, with impeccable timing, Ted arrived as we finished, the dessert dish emptied, four spoons idle, stuffed and giddy, he couldn't have thought of a better surprise for Tom. Afterwards the five of us enjoyed a laughter filled evening.

This thought or that, a moment split by the minds' idle chatter or a tune running through it and a week flies by. Once again back at Spazio's, Ted recounted some memories brought about by this brunch, *"April 17 11:00 My 8th near - monthly Spazio's brunch gig. Guild '58 X350 dear friend Chubbie 1st hour she sounds great, I play old standards in a jazz with romantic tinge (or vice versa) manner for 1st half hour or so - for cousin Howard mainly who along with mom's bro Cy introduced me to jazz when I was 3 or 4 years old. Then Lulu, my beloved stock '52 Tele comes out & dazzles all of us, especially me and my beloved black face Vibrolux Reverb sounded simply spectacular today. This combo soared & sung & was extremely gorgeous. Lee Ving (nee James, nee Caballero) comes up and sings 4 songs beautifully in his new soft style - 'My One and Only Love' in C 'Here's that Rainy Day' medium swing in G, Gb."*

● X □ △ ★

The time moved quietly by, April into May, Ted and I found comfort in each other and in each new mutual joy. Bundles of new book purchases brought us many an evening of reading for hours, sharing passages we thought would interest or amuse the other, laughing a lot, the cats nestled next to us. The living room had become a library in disguise. During one of those contented moments Ted mentioned he had recently met some sweet homeless people and stopped to visit with them for a while, then surprised each with some money. Unquestionably, the pleasure he derived from small acts of kindness was immense, and as much a necessity for his own wellbeing. He had moved forward from the pain of his unrealized dream for the now aptly put con-women and was eager and ready to help turn other people's lives around for the better.

Ted's ninth and final Spazio's brunch came on May 15, 2005 and that day Ted's playing surpassed any performance prior - possibly the best I'd ever heard. He absolutely mesmerized the crowd and me! The bar area where Ted performed was absolutely packed and while he played, reverential silence, no conversation, everyone completely attentive. Ted brought and played our "Gigi" for the first time in public. Later we surmised, with the bar packed and the restaurant almost empty, the management must have felt he wasn't bringing in a large enough brunch crowd. Ted penned some thoughts of that day, *"The most intense one yet: 11:00 Spazio's brunch, our beloved X500 Gigi's 1st gig and boy did she sound great, Lulu my beloved '52 stock Tele. Lee sings "Once in a While" & Here, There & Everywhere."*

The remainder of May included two seminars, one at Musician's Institute that Ted referred to as "open counseling." Then on the 22nd at Boulevard Music, about which he jotted meager and somewhat irrelevant notes, *"May 22 Seminar at Boulevard Music 11-1 Bring Chubbie & Lulu & the Peavey. Buy 10 little books, 9 little paperback 'fake books' (thematic types) & 1 acoustic guitar type book."*

Late spring days with nothing scheduled, no upcoming brunches or seminars, things that would never fluster Ted, who made so much out of each moment and maintained a faith that something would always come up. He was elated by simple joys. He replaced a broken toilet arm and was delighted with the new part, a steal at $1.99. He said it was the best feeling arm ever and found such satisfaction when something worked the way it should. Something that others might consider trivial and insignificant, for Ted was remarkable and warranted a positive response and set the tone for the day. In a humorous mood, he picked up dinner for Lori and me from Panda Express at the mall, but first he took a detour through the bookstore. When he arrived, along with our dinner, he also brought us books, claiming that he had won the books in a contest. We actually believed him for maybe one or two seconds, and loved the surprise. The three of us were gathered together to watch the American Idol 4th season two-hour finale. Ted felt it was well done, and was surprised at Carrie Underwood winning the contest.

Now allowing himself some extra time to catch up on many things he'd put off, Ted followed his intuition on this one, *"June 4 The voice in my head, even when I didn't want to listen: This is the best day - Go to Norm's - 1st time in year and a half. Bring him the 1000 Album Covers book I got for him a few weeks ago. Great to see him again & looking trimmer than ever. He's very happy to see me too. Strum the 3 X500's Norm has. I love the 2 sunbursts but something about the blonde, oh my god! It's got that behind-the-bridge echo louder than any Guild I've ever heard! I'm in trouble again."*

That was the first new guitar purchase in a very long while, and in order to afford such extravagance, a trade was proffered. A week later Ted went back to Norm's with his beautiful cherry red '61 ES 345 and made the trade, and as an extra bonus spent many hours visiting and enjoying friends he hadn't seen for some time. Ted, of course was delighted with his new Guild, he really loved the X500's. Days later with the guitar on his lap, we watched game one of the NBA finals, Detroit at San Antonio.

All too soon I was at the mercy of another birthday and with Ted's penchant for buying presents, I could not escape being the recipient of many gifts. Nonetheless, the best aspect about the things Ted picked out for me was that they were always really for us. On my 53rd he came over with DVDs, CDs and jigsaw puzzles galore. Our preference that night was the music and we listened to Tchaikovsky's 'delicious' serenade for strings, with the fantastic waltz we loved, then we listened to the Tchaikovsky Violin concerto 1st movement - twice. As Ted expressed, *"It's the epitome of romantic harmony and Russian art music."*

The last lingering June evenings were given over to the NBA finals, Spurs claimed the title in game 7, and the Angels who always piqued Ted's interest, were suddenly playing exceedingly well and looked stunning.

● X □ △ ★

July came blazing hot upon us, and our beloved cat Quincy became quite ill resulting from a congenital problem, a defective colon, which was now not functioning properly. We had taken him to the clinic but their remedy had proven ineffective.

Then on the 4th of July, Quincy disappeared. Given the pain in his cry and his behavior the day before, we mostly gave up hope. Our tears flowed as the hours passed late into the night and he was nowhere to be found. I cried, paced the room and periodically went outside to call his name. Ted equally upset had more ability to remain calm and was lying on the floor reading and finally urged me to join him. He held me in his arms; my head buried in his chest, and let me cry it out. Sometime after midnight Quincy appeared in the backyard, but would not come in the house. Comforted considerably by his sudden appearance, and weary from waiting, I got in bed. Ted stayed up to work on his song list, and later noticed Quincy had gotten in bed with me.

Unfortunately Quincy's illness continued, and the next week on top of that we heard the horrible news about the terrorist attacks on the London subways. Despite the attacks and much to Ted's total distress, Lori and I decided not to cancel our upcoming trip. We rationalized that the security would be especially tight and prevalent, even though the mood of the city might be somber. After all it was our only opportunity to see the James Joyce presentation. And Ted, although even more concerned than ever, knew how much this meant to me.

Ted and I were both very blue on our 13th anniversary, Quincy was still not doing well, and my impending departure was a strain for us both. But Ted was not wont to linger in sadness, and did manage to bring some cheeriness when he got us the Sunday New York Times and Haagen Dazs coffee ice cream, which I ravaged. Two days later our veterinarian came and tended to Quincy, who needed to be hospitalized overnight. Dr. E brought him back the next day sedated, disoriented, a bit skittish, and with no appetite to speak of, but the vet was confident that Quincy would be fine. It was the same night as the All Star Baseball Game. For the first time since Ted's father died, Ted again experienced the strange severe pains in his arms. Ted wrote in his datebook, *"Bad Arm attack. B sees it. Sad, I've tried to shield her from this. Treat with hot water, Naproxin Sodium. Her massage of my arms is instantly healing, a Wonderment. Was it the last step or is there some magic to learn from there? We shall see if the situation happens again, we'll reverse the process."*

The departure date for my trip was drawing near and I was at least glad that Quincy had rapidly begun to improve. On July 17th Ted and I watched the first three-fourths of what would turn out to be our last movie together, "Gone With the Wind," elegantly and thematically scored by none other than Max Steiner. Ted told me he abhorred this film when he first saw it thirty-five years ago, but now was able to see it with vastly different eyes as a fantastic piece of movie-making and loved the new perspective he had gained.

● X □ △ ★

Strange that neither of us wrote in our journals what we did on our final two evenings together. I must have packed my luggage. I do remember the coffee table and surrounding area being laden with coins and related material. And there is no doubt that the TV was on, whether we were watching it or not. Of two things I am certain, whatever we did acted as a distraction from my impending departure and that there was no lack of love between us.

Early in the morning, just past the verge of July 20th we said a tearful goodbye, not knowing it was to be our last, but fortunately, we had rarely taken saying good-bye lightly, especially the long ones. Later that day I left with Lori for London.

We arrived at Heathrow on the 21st to the news of another terrorist incident, and all I could think about was how worried Ted must be. As soon as I was able, I called Ted to reassure him I was safe and pleaded with him not to worry. As always, I told him I loved him, he told me he loved me. That was the last time we were ever to speak.

If one's exit could be orchestrated at all, Ted could not have orchestrated his exit any better. The way in which Ted left this earth was so reflective of his nature, to slip away silently, when no one would notice him going.

Afterthoughts:

Is it really far, far easier to realize things in hindsight? Particularly something nebulous or untenable? Such as an incident that gets one's attention, but the underlying intention of the incident is sketchy, or not readily apparent?

Ted took many incidents or coincidences to be a sign, but if he did sense some foreboding in the end, he did not mention anything to me.

Consider:

The timing of Quincy's illness, a cat's hyper-sensitivity, perhaps Quincy sensed Ted was very ill, and also that I was leaving, therefore manifested the illness as a possible way to sideline my trip and prevent the impending tragedy?

OR: Had the terrorist attacks in the exact city I was destined for (coincidence? a sign in itself?), brought on extra stress to cause Ted's severe arm pains? Arm pains that I thought had ceased in 2001 after his father died. Why did it happen now? for me to bear witness to?

Were these subtle warnings? Were they indications I should have stayed home? Why didn't I see or heed them? Was I not supposed to, as per Ted's premonition? Ted believed there was a reason for everything, he was also a fatalist, therefore according to Ted's beliefs, had I stayed, I couldn't have prevented his death.

These and other thoughts I have pondered thousands of times. Not one day has gone by that hasn't brought me to tears. I hold on to the promise Ted made to me a long while back, that no matter what happened we would find each other and be together again. Somehow.

And finally, from Ted's Datebook (written in August 1988),
Somebody asks, "What would you like to be remembered for?"
"As somebody who loved the guitar, loved music, loved passion & enthusiasm, loved ideas & words, loved gentle humor, movies, kindness, and whose big kick was finding somebody else who did…
"Listen to that TONE!!!!!……" "Look at that look on Jean Arthur's face!……."
"What a GORGEOUS color……"
That's who I am (was?), so I might as well be 'remembered' as that, if there's a reason to remember me at all."

I am forever blessed to have been that *"somebody else"* to share Ted's last 13 years on this earth.

● X □ △ ★

May 1947 - Ted at 8 months with parents Irwin and Bertha Greene

Ted and Barbara 1993 - Our first photo together

Ted High School Graduation
Summer 1967

Ted, Barbara and "Gigi" self-portrait 1997

Ted circa 1977

January 1999 - NAMM Show weekend at Papashon. Ted giving a seminar.

1999 - Ted at Papashon (L to R) Barry Zweig, John Pisano and George Van Eps

June 2000 at the Jazz Bakery (L to R) Russell Malone and John Collins Photo:Bob Barry/Jazzography

Group photo from Rocco's 1st anniversary of Guitar night Photo:Bob Barry/Jazzography

2004 - Ted at Spazio's - photo:Nick Stasinos

1994 Display of Ted's guitars - apartment #8 bedroom

Ted's living room in apartment #8 - 2 months after the earthquake

Ted & Quincy

January 2002 Ted cleaning out Betsy (left) and the Bronco.

2002 Living room apartment #8 - looking better.

I think this photo captured all the love I felt for Ted. I don't even remember it being taken.
I found it in the apartment after Ted passed away

2005 - Ted's living room in apartment #8

Part IV

In Ted's Own Words

This is the interview I referred to in Part III of "My Life with the Chord Chemist," in its entirety. Ted never completed it, but these are thoughts Ted intended to share with everyone. Other than "sewing up the seams" as best I could, I left it intact. Towards the end you will find some sentences that were not completed, and also some fragments of thought Ted intended to develop. Ted had his own 'idiomatic' way of writing, using words or making up phrases, which he felt gave a personal touch and really enjoyed "making up scenarios" to convey ideas. I feel it is his best and most insightful "interview" and contains a wealth of information.

Again, this is Ted's self-constructed interview, as he felt no one else could formulate an interview that would meet his own high standards. I know he wanted to put these thoughts out into the world. Some of these ideas and thoughts were most important to him and very close to his heart.

The Interview

Began:12-01-00; continued: Sun. 3-7-04 The new cover-story article.

Ted Greene : the Chord Chemist shares his deeply musical background and unique take on things in a part interview-part conversation. If you don't know, Ted is renowned around the world for his guitar teaching abilities, magnificent playing (although he's a reluctant hero here), and possibly most of all, for some widely acclaimed books on guitar instruction which he authored when he was fairly young, the most famous of which is titled *Chord Chemistry*. We hope you find some illumination and laughter in this somewhat different cover-story, which is actually a chapter in a book being prepared on Ted's life in music.

AA: What are the most vivid memories you've retained of your musical childhood?
TG: Oh there are so many......hiding under the piano when my mom was playing the hauntingly beautiful music from *Porgy and Bess* when I was supposed to be in my room doing homework. Staying home from school (playing sick) so I could listen to music all day coming out of the TV. There was *live* jazz guitar playing in the house bands on some shows! And fantastic classical music scoring of many cartoons where these mice were running around all over the place.

AA: So it was the standard music education.
TG: Nothin' but.
AA: Any other strong memories of music in your early years?
TG: Running home from school at full blast to catch Scotty Moore's ultra-alluring guitar on Elvis Presley's " My Baby Left Me " which they played on this one radio show every day. Walking miles to the keyboard section of dept. stores, where they had electric pianos and beguiling-sounding organs, so I could try to imitate my hero Ray Charles' incredible feel and hipness on cuts like," What'd I Say," "Sticks and Stones " and, "One Mint Julep"--not that I could really, but anything even vaguely close was chartin' high on my body's hit parade; though safe to say not on the store floor peoples'. They'd throw me out as soon as they realized I wasn't there to buy--I had no dough--but I'd get in at least a few notes before such an unfortunate turn of circumstances. Then it was on to another store--for more of the same of course. If you didn't do this *too* often, they wouldn't remember you and couldn't arrest you (people were always threatening to arrest us in those days for almost everything we liked to do). I meant no harm but I just had to hear those sounds up *close*. Some of us seem to be born to experience the excitement of hearing and feeling the music we care about coming out of our *own* fingers.

The most exciting experience of all was unquestionably the whole thing of going to see my favorite groups and artists perform live around the New York City area. That was and still is one of the all-time thrills in my lifetime so far. And it wasn't uncommon for certain performers I loved, to have an even better feel live than they did on records. As we used to say, 'too great.' Or as some might say now, "too 'bad' to believe."
AA: You speak of the feel of music so often with such love and respect in your eyes. What else besides this attracted you to music so much? I think you once told me it was the tone.
TG: Indeed it was. The *sound* of the jukeboxes in the diners, luncheonettes, pizzerias, poolrooms, you name it. So non-hifi but so warm and rich-sounding, especially the voluptuous lower-end instruments. A tonal feast. How 'd I ever go to school? Yeah, this is what did it for me, the tones on those wonderful records coming out of those big-sounding wonderboxes. Also, the radios--at home, in the car, record players too... all these. Short on fi, long on high--this stuff definitely got you that. Kept a lot of kids out of worse trouble.
AA: Were you playing guitar yet, practicing every day?
TG: I was supposed to be, but listening was top priority.
AA: Really? I haven't heard anyone mention this before. Kind of an interesting problem.
TG: I guess it was. I know it was intoxicating, all that music back then. Heck, it still is.
AA: What made it so compelling that you would rather listen than practice?
TG: Well, what a time it was. So many, many terrific songs, artists, styles. And that's the thing. You see, in those 1950's and early `60's days, the popular music umbrella was huge. Tune in a rock'n'roll radio station and you'd hear for instance, such a gorgeous range of rhythm and blues--the original rock 'n' roll (begun way back in the `30's and `40's) which included lots of New York street vocal music ('doo-wop') with all these gifted singers--not to mention a few out of tune ones too sometimes. And once Elvis Presley showed up on

the national record charts, young music lovers all over the United States and beyond got to hear this very up-to-date amalgam of blues, country and more --what the press later called 'rockabilly;' and this fortunately also included other rockabilly cats--great artists who might otherwise never've had a shot at the big airwaves. Carl Perkins, Eddie Cochran, Gene Vincent, others. And yet even with the already large diversity all these sounds were providing, definitely the big wild card was the fact that many of these same radio shows routinely snuck in so many other musical styles as well.

AA: Yeah? Any special things?

TG: Where to begin... Gospel or heavily gospel-influenced things to name just one.

Like so many Ray Charles cuts in the `50's, or Curtis Mayfield's group, the Impressions in the early`60's, or the Isley Bros."Shout." Supremely fine sounds. All this stuff was gospel music really. Right out of the black church, musicwise. With a few other little touches too, it's true. The lyrics--well, they fluctuated between heavenly and earth(l)y. The musicians, dj's, the press eventually called it soul music. I think you knew all this maybe.

AA: I wasn't thinking in those terms. Please continue.

TG: On these same radio stations you also occasionally heard some pretty thrilling jazz and jazz hybrids, a stone city blues tune, even a little skiffle from England (the Beatles early inspiration right before rock bit them on the fanny and changed a few lives). There was also a period of many years where the station programmers played lots of wild novelty and comedy records, tv and movie themes, rich-sounding orchestral music, show tunes, pop songs and a whole bunch of folk music comin' at us for quite a few years. Always some country in there too--country and *western* they called it then. Just western for short. I mean, rock 'n' roll became a marketing vehicle for almost anything in music. Anything. From "here we go with the #39 song this week, Prim & the Properettes singing their new smash, "I Fell In Love At The Bakeoff," to "appearing tonight at your local vomitorium, for one night only, Puke and the Antacids."

So, just about anything might show up at just about any time(!)--all either passed off as rock'n'roll, by association, or thought of as more 'product ' that kids who wanted r'n'r might be coaxed, or maybe fooled, into buying. There was actually a lot more going on here than meets the eye, but we'll leave it for some other time, some other place.

I and many other young people knew what the marketing cats were doing, and even though it could get frustrating at times, like when you were really dying for some jumpin' stuff and instead were fed some sounds just simply beyond hope--overall, I've got to say that frankly I was at least intrigued by the hearing of all these different styles, and ended up loving a lot of it. I guess many other people did too because *all* this music sold. So there were 1000's of great recordings to listen to. And even disallowing nostalgia, many of them still sound...simply incredible.

AA: You were mad about music.

TG: This cannot be denied.

AA: What does your girlfriend say... "encaptivated." Completely "encaptivated."

TG: Yeah mama. Truly. Just couldn't get enough of the sounds then. My friends were the same way. It was deep for us. The deepest actually--we lived for music.

AA: Your waters could be running deep on many things musical, from what I've observed. And it's so clear that listening to music was the dominant theme of your childhood. May I also say that it seems likely to really have paid off for you later, judging by the brilliant, wide array of sounds and depth of feeling you do put out as a player.

TG: You're very kind. My skills are not that far-reaching yet-- though I do keep my hope card turned up--but thank you yes, in a few places, I've stayed in the water a long time, so to speak. The car crowd would tend to say there's been a bit of valve float. The plumbing boys might suggest a 'language reversal' here,[*in strange accent*] "dat float valve's been open for quite some time Pugnacio--you sure dis's good for da brain?" (apparently not).

Shooting straight now--you know, many musicians can find the chord changes and melodies by memory or by ear to hundreds, even thousands of songs and things.

AA: So, out of all the instruments, what made you want to play the guitar?

TG: The same reasons as many people, I guess. The sound of it. The look of it. A kid across the street's dad had a tremendously beautiful electric archtop that he left out on a stand in their den. That thing just glowed when I looked at it. I'd be in my house and I couldn't stand it--I'd have to go across the street and find a way to see it again. I wasn't allowed to play it--I didn't know how anyway--but I do remember touching it and inspecting it, turning it at different angles in the light and being hit like a rocket with waves of ecstasy coursing through my 11 year old body. I'd had a lot of fun in my life already but just standing there looking at that guitar was the most deeply satisfying feeling I'd ever felt. And also, the strongest yearning...wanting so much to be a part of that world where people held gorgeous objects like this and made delicious sounds of their own choosing with them, and other people sometimes gathered around and seemed as happy as the people actually making these nectar-like noises.

AA: Some reaction, T.G. What did you make of all this then?

TG: I was pretty stunned by my feelings and knew enough not to try to describe these experiences to anyone because a) I couldn't anyway, b) I had more questions than I'd ever had before, far more questions than answers--a trait which had not been well-received before by people I cared about, even when it was in a lesser state and c) friends, family and teachers all thought I was 'gone' anyway already due to lots of other stuff I won't bore you with. So I kept it to myself. But that guitar was the prettiest thing I'd ever seen. Not long after this, I used to roam the streets where I knew all the cool pawn shops and music stores were and would stand transfixed, gazing in the windows at all the guitars hanging on the walls, lost in deep pleasure for long periods of time until I'd get chased away or have to go home and eat dinner eventually, and catch hell for being late yet again. Yep, the handwriting was sure on the wall for me, no pun intended. Off the wall too, I guess.

AA: You were a wild child, Theo. And how does it feel to have fulfilled your childhood dream?

TG: Deeply satisfying. Even in periods where I haven't enjoyed my playing very much, I've still thought the guitar is a very beautiful thing and I'm extremely lucky to have been allowed to spend as much time with her as I have. And since I have such a great lot of more stuff to write and publish about this instrument so many of us are gaga over, I'm hoping and praying for many more 1000's of hours of successful engagement in said pursuit.

AA: So how did you get started playing?

TG: My parents eventually got onto me and then figured, "let's get this lad some music lessons, and maybe it'll also keep him from getting into trouble," for which I'd had a more than serious affinity. They always had their feet on the ground, my parents.

AA: You grew up in a city of about 50,000 people outside of New York City followed by a brief stay in Atlanta, then back to Los Angeles where you had lived your first 4 or 5 years. What I'm curious about in order to get a better feel for the period under discussion is, were there a *lot* of kids like you--in each city?

TG: I'd have to say yes, although in certain aspects, not so many. But, 'you find your own.' There were enough.

AA: Did you join bands fairly soon, as did so many other guitarists of that era it seems?

TG: Not soon enough for my hungry nature, but yeah, pretty soon--within a few years.

AA: Were you playing well already?

TG: My playing was just barely passable except that I found ways to set my amp to get some pretty righteous tones, and I had a kind of nice feel--thank God--which, luckily, fit the situation since what we were playing was dance music--for just the coolest-looking dances I'd ever seen by the way. Such a groove back then in 1960,`61,`62.

AA: There *was* alot of cool dancing going on then. And was that something that also affected you in a more personal way somehow--because of all that music? I'm wondering if there's a tie-in because you almost always seem to be moving your feet a little, or swaying your body to some rhythm inside of you.

TG: You're a good people-watcher. Yeah, besides playing in this one dance club, we also *went* to a lot of dances, primarily in old fantastic sounding churches. They were like sound palaces, truly great places to hear live bands or records. I sure wasn't practicing much guitar. But I *was* thrilled from head to toe in that world of sound. A little later though, after I had come back to L.A., it was me playing now again at those same kinds of dances.

AA: What kind of music were you playing?

TG: Mostly all rhythm and blues.

AA: By choice?

TG: Oh yeah. That was my favorite. Certainly my favorite that I could play. I dreamed of playing jazz but other than the feel of it in terms of a little bit of rhythm guitar, I couldn't touch it. Likewise those beautiful songs from shows, movies and things. I simply didn't know enough about music or the guitar to do this. But r 'n' b, wow. That was plenty good enough in a number of ways. I was one of those lucky people who swooned hard from that music and it seemed to just go right into my bones or something. To this day, these are musical flavors I savor with great pleasure when I hear them.

AA: What did your playing sound like by then?

TG: To be fair to myself but not overly so, my playing sounded highly rhythmic, which is what the music called for. They don't call it rhythm 'n' blues for nothin'. Yeah, I was almost all feel and practically zero knowledge in those days.

AA: What a surprise to hear you say that. And what came next?

TG: We discovered cars. Uh-oh. Lost a lot of years of practicing to this one. Talkin' truth, I couldn't practice for beans back then anyway. Very little discipline, lots of emotion. Lazy but excited--hmm, that sounds better than 'excited but lazy' doesn't it.
AA: So how on earth did you ever acquire your fantastic work habits and ability to focus so intensely--qualities somewhat legendary among those close to you when your name comes up. Did some thing or someone play a key role?
TG: Yeah. The doctors. They took out a lot of excess catnip from my blood. But seriously, eventually I went through a lot of changes as a person, probably grew up a bit, and reached a dead end as far as 'feel' getting me through everything--because the music I really wanted to play asked for lots of discipline. There was no way out. I *had* to change--I was a sad guy.
AA: You say 'sad'..... .
TG: Sad about the state of my playing not providing a zing any more, and sad because I didn't want to work, certainly not work hard. Especially not at music, which I started up with to have fun. I fought with the work part of it--I still fight with it. But I dig results an awful lot so I'll stay in there. Most people like me don't have any choice really, you know. Music is too great to say goodbye. Terrible grammar but I know you can dig what I mean. Even when the work knocks a person out of their sleep over and over. 'Wake up, there's work to do, toneman.' 'I don't think so.' 'Alright, just forget the whole thing.' 'Wait a minute, I'm up, I'm up.' 'Now you're talkin. What are we workin' on today?'
AA: Did you set goals?
TG: That's exactly it. Goals, little goals. Step by step. That gets it done. No news to anyone I guess but it's sometimes good to remind oneself. Time out for playing too--groovin'--so I wouldn't get too grouchy about it all. That's still me. My work habits aren't *that* strong.
AA: What did you study?
TG: Everything I could get my hands on that seemed to have any knowledge I was attracted to.
AA: In many fields of music?
TG: Yes, it's true, many fields.
AA: Were you trying to develop your mind?
TG: No, I just wanted to be a righteous player. I did have to develop my mind some in order to help my playing. I don't regret it. I found out it's a good thing to do.
AA: You wrote books.
TG: Yeah. It happened. I couldn't stop it. No kidding, I often do seem to behave like a cat, and this is close to catnip when it happens. No shakin' it. Close the doors and put in 5 to 15 hours a day until it's done. My mom used to say, when she'd see me in this state, " ah, you're pregnant with a new book are you?" Terrific lady my mom was.
AA: What's the story on those great organizational skills you've shown? Were they there as a kid?
TG: Nah, except for a school project once, they were hidin' out. But they just seemed to gush up huge suddenly, God knows from where. I was certainly overjoyed to see them, showing up and all like they did, right when I needed them most. Maybe it's about just

wanting something so much.

AA: I know you believe in this.

TG: I think human beings have pretty deep unsuspected reservoirs of strength that kick in when they really love something and have to work to get it. I know *I* certainly was surprised. Anyway, I'm grateful for the passion I've been given. I need it.

AA: Ted, you've gone into the teaching business more and more through the years. How did all this happen?

TG: Right place, right time. I got hooked on it and it felt like something I was supposed to do. Very much. That's the simple truth.

AA: How about a little more on this, if you would?

TG: The right place thing happened three different times initially--once each in 1963, `64, and `65. Then again at other times over the years. I gradually got the message.

AA: And the job fits your temperament?

TG: More than I would ever have dreamed as a kid but yeah, it sure does.

AA: Also because you don't like performing all that much?

TG: You're doing really well here. Except that's how it *was* not how it is anymore. At least not 100%. I'm out there playing and enjoying it when I can get a party, wedding or something... though I'm still not real keen on concertizing.

AA: Why, Ted?

TG: Aw, it's embarrassing. I've had trouble handling that much love coming at me. It's a bit overwhelming. Everybody showering me with praise when I only occasionally think I deserved it. Crazy. People are crazy. 'Course, I know that includes me. A wise person might say, "take it you chucklebunny, even if you don't think you played well--it makes up for the times when you played so beautifully and nobody cared. Lord knows you've had some gigs like that." This is a not-without-some-sense attitude and I normally embrace it outwardly, but I know inside when I've played up to my potential and my mind wants to know why when I haven't --so I can do my part towards making it right next time. This is more important to me than basking in the praise of others when I haven't earned it by my standards. I do console myself in such a situation with the glow that at least I made other people feel good.

AA: You're really hard to please.

TG: I tend to be this.

AA: Towards others too?

TG: Not towards others. I keep a watchful eye on that thing. Otherwise you squash the majority of your students, just to name one group of people in my life--and that's the thing. They are people and most people wither from the harshness of tough standards. And since many of them are in this thing primarily for the pleasure, it behooves one to keep sight of this so as to add to their joy for the short time that we have on this earth. Every now and then though, I get a student who's not afraid of the work involved in trying to be *really* good on the guitar, someone who wants the praise *and* the gentle or even not so gentle criticism where it's fair, so they know how to be even better--step by step, obstacles dropping away, finding great joy in the work, or especially at least in the results.

I've always seemed to have had at least one student like this right from the beginning of my serious teaching days in 1964. Count me lucky, in spades.

It's also pretty darn satisfying to work with people who just want to play a little better- - they deserve assistance too, if they ask. There's no shame in needing help. Seeing a 1st year guitar player get say, a Bm chord to ring for the 1st time--this is a beautiful thing. Yet if it happens on the 10,000th try, then they are disconsolate in the extreme and I'd be in the wrong business for sure. So it's my job to make sure they're more likely to get it on the 100th try or 10th try. And my patience would run way out anyway, considerably before 10 thou'. I do have my bad days in this area, try as I may. But I'm slowly getting the upper hand here, a little more patient every year.

AA: What other kinds of students come to you for help? I hear there are some world-famous ones amongst the many.

TG: Sometimes.

AA: Care to name one or two?

TG: Nope.

AA: Hmm. It must feel good that they would seek you out.

TG: It does. You work at something for a long time and hope you do a good job. So sure, this can occasionally be a nice extra, but truth be talkin', it doesn't matter alone much that they come to me, what counts is, can I be of assistance? Can I deliver on what they want? That's what really matters.

AA: What do they want from you?

TG: Ah, it's different for every student. All kinds of different things. For instance, I do so much enjoy helping players who are kind of bored with their playing--a specialty of mine since I was bored with my playing for such a horrendously long time. (Don't ask). And it's not about just helping the famous here. Put yourself in my ampseat for a moment: someone who's *not* famous but who's been playing for 20 or 30 years comes to you and is embarrassed, full of bad feelings towards himself because they think they should be so far better a player than they are. Helping them break out of ruts and seeing them smile about their playing again, watching them fall in love with the guitar all over again--how good are you going to feel?

AA: What styles of music do you teach?

TG: Whatever the students ask for--if I can.

AA: I want to go back, please, to you and performing. Many famous guitarists I've talked with about you just lit up when I mentioned your name. And they said things, continue to say the most wonderful things, statements of praise that I think would make even you sit up and feel proud. Can't you find it in your heart to accept this?

TG: It's very flattering, but... I'm afraid not, not all that often. I do feel some pride when I do really well, but since that's not too common for me, most other pride I might start to feel usually feels near-instantly like false pride and I have to say goodbye to it or try to beat that sucker down if it keeps coming back. Sometimes it lingers and gets the best of me for a little while, and sometimes I let it because praise is such a nectar. But ultimately, I have to chase that drug away each time and go forward.

AA: But Ted, you are one of the greatest of guitarists. How can you deny this--and deny others the pleasure of hearing you? Why can't you accept this?
TG: I sure wish I could, I certainly did when I was younger--when my playing at the time was close to everything I dared ever dream it could be. Ah, now *that* was sweet, and it lasted for years, actually *so* many good years of loving my playing, and receiving such heart-warming high compliments from others about it. It was really something. This was from about 1965 to 1977. But life moves on and gradually as I was able to really better hear more of what the very greatest players, arrangers, and composers were doing, my playing paled before me, and wouldn't sound even adequate to me on any consistent basis again for many years. I've been fighting to come up with sounds and ways to play that I could enjoy again for quite some time now and I'm happy to say that it's working some of the time, so I'm excited to be on the right track. All I need is more consistency and then I'll be ready to try to share it more. Given my nature, I do know there'll still be some problems--things I haven't mentioned--but I'll try to deal with them as best I can.
AA: You can mention them. Someone else may draw comfort in knowing that even respected players have to deal with the same problems they do. It might provide hope.
TG: Let me try to put it this way, when things are working well for me I like the way I play very much, am genuinely thrilled and honored to make others so happy, and I know that there are accolades and applause that come with this. But it's a strange feeling to have a lot of love directed at you at once. Maybe it's something one gets used to. I never have. So I'll have to do better there. Another big trouble is, playing in public, I often have to turn up way too much for the sound I like getting so I'm unhappy about that from moment no.1. I'm working to find ways to deal with that. Additionally, the feels that I love can too often for my taste, refuse to show up in anywhere near their full form. Not a good thing. This is a huge part of the consistency thing I had just mentioned. And, last but far from least, if my hands aren't working right--which happens too much--I'm in big trouble. I've limped home from a lot of gigs. But then there's always hope that the next one will be a thrill. I never gave up hope altogether. Well maybe at one point. But that's the past. We were talking about the future. Look--are those some Zen picketers in the back there? What do those signs mean, "the future is now," " the moment is all we have, all we'll ever have? I guess they're not on their way to that Moody Blues *Days of Future Past (Passed)* reunion concert tonight. A pity."
AA: You crazy guy--good crazy though. By the way, what's the deal with the hands?
TG: Not complaining, just explaining--my hands have to be in such great shape in order to play the textures and grooves I love.
AA: Can't you keep them at this level?
TG: Life doesn't always allow it. I do try to get in the tough practicing on days where I can. When I get to that level where things are sounding *really* good, I'm a pretty happy guy. It just doesn't happen all that much.
AA: It seems a shame.
TG: I'll say. But again, no complaints overall. The big picture is I've been very fortunate in this life. And who knows, maybe I'll have some more breakthroughs. One way that has

worked for me is to get into one of those staggering practice sessions of 10 to 15 hours, and then do that again for a few days in a row. This can carry me for weeks afterward even if I can only get in say, 3 hours a day during the follow-up period.

AA: I hope you find a way to do this whenever you need to. And going back now to something you said--why don't the feels you want to play stay with you consistently? Any answers?

TG: A lot of musicians experience this or other comparable challenges, and 1001 plausible reasons and answers have been discussed, suggested, and tried.

AA: And?

TG: Reliability has not proven to be a reliable thing. It's the damnedest thing. I've been in a truly fine state of mind, looking forward to a gig, in great health, hands working an hour earlier, and have sat down at gigtime and then played like a seasick love otter, and gotten the worst tone since Bozo the Clown and Granny Goose honked it up at the local bar after a few drinks. Other times--just a toejam of a day, where I'm sure the human race was one of God's least pleasant experiments, and then I go out on stage and suddenly start playing on some whole other level where near-magic stuff seems to come from the fingers.

AA: It has to be frustrating and I shouldn't laugh at your plight, but you do make it a bit funny to hear about.

TG: That's good. I laugh about it more than I cry. I have to. The truth is I do truly, deeply hate disappointing myself. It's happened way too many times. But my vision and belief is that I'll beat all this some day. Truth be told, I'm banking on it--otherwise I would've just quit years ago in disgust... .I'd still have been an enraptured listener though. That never goes away for long, if at all, for those who've been bitten at birth by the blues bug, to name just one infectione di musica.

AA: And so, is there a certain type of playing job that you do find fulfilling?

TG: Yes, actually a few. Restaurants can be great if the room sounds good and isn't too huge. I've loved playing at the N.A.M.M. shows out on the floor, most recently for Guild and DeArmond in 1999. Weddings are a joy if I get to be the organ. What a groove it is to go after the pipe organ sounds on the Fender Telecaster or other favorite string honeys. Clinics, workshops, seminars--call them whichever pleases you--these can be a fine experience *if* the people who attend really want to be there and, if they don't expect me to be something I couldn't possibly be if my life depended on it. Because most people, since they enjoy having heroes, like it if you're superhuman. And so I walk in and it's, " Ted, could you demonstrate how you would play 4 Beatles songs, one each on 4 different strings, all together of course, and then maybe 2 or 3 of them backwards--or upside down--against the rest ? Maybe not. No."

Anyway, the clinics are great sometimes. I love it if they have questions, lots of questions. I'm bound to have at least a few of the answers and then I feel I'm really earning my money honestly, and at least some of the attendees are getting something they may want. If all else fails, a little humor doesn't hurt. Oh heck, admit it Ted--I like to use it anyway. To lighten the mood, take some of the tension out for them, get rid of any intimidation they may be feeling.

Parties are probably my favorite gigs, quiet parties. Getting a *great* sound at a modest volume usually makes me want to play so much--quiet but fantastic sounds. This is all so ironic because I used to be quite possibly the loudest guitar player in Los Angeles, around 1966 and 1967. Two old 4x10" Bassmans cranked was ridiculous. Great for nasty music. I loved it at the time. But that's so hard on the body. More than a few rock players, from big stars to stay-at-home Sammys, have lost up to 50-70% of their hearing. That says it all. Sad, bad Leroy Brown, the deafest cat in town. Might as well have stood next to planes during takeoff for 4 hours a day. This *is* sad. I don't know how I, for one, escaped the ravages of a culture gone mad on volume. I was a lot lucky, especially, given my own participation and I try not to forget this; and to be thankful for being allowed my hearing.

AA: Even if you are hard to please in regard to your playing, it's easy to see that you know gratitude can feel so good, so it's nice to at least see *that* in you. And switching gears now, what is all this about you and equipment, as one of the world's best guitar 'setup' guys? Your reputation here is literally phenomenal you know, amongst every single guitarist I spoke to who knows you. Maybe you have some words on why you got so involved in this, and possibly some advice in this area for any players who need to hear it ?

TG: Well, this is a treacherous subject if I go way back in my life. And as you know, sometimes there are many incidents that push a person towards something. So we won't be here all night, let me just cite one aspect of this and say that it's something a bit on a down note, but with a moral, a tough but necessary lesson. Now please know that I came to terms with this a long time ago so don't feel bad for me but the thing is, I had three of my all-time favorite guitars butchered and effectively ruined, destroyed, by repairmen who had come highly recommended. You think this had an effect on me? There were a variety of reasons why these hideous things happened and I won't trouble you with the specifics but the biggest cause was that I forgot to heed my mom's sage counsel, ' evaluate the evaluator, son, ' because I was so dazzled with people's words that fit my wishful thinking--dare I say, such a common human failing in so many areas. Ah, if I could only go back. Life definitely will knock us down if we're not paying attention, proper attention to the important things, huh?

I learned and I tell others to please be very careful who you allow to ever work on one of your guitars. See a sample of their current work of a similar type to the work you want done. If you need them to be extremely careful, you must risk offending them by gently letting them know. And most importantly, please make sure that their concept of what you want done is *exactly* the same as yours. Spend a little time discussing all the little areas you might regret later if you didn't--before the guitar is worked on. A typical example: do you like your fingerboard shape to be flat on top, or do you go for an arched board? Are you sure? Why? How do you know? Have you tried your preferred string action on both types? What was each better suited for, in your opinion? Could you tell? And did you care? If not, then it's one less thing to hassle with in a decidedly unhassle-free world.

Anyway, this is just one area and there are many areas in the big area of how a guitar plays and feels and sounds and looks that're of value--different ones for different hands, different ears, different souls. Saying something like 'make it play great,' just doesn't begin to cover the specific areas of personal taste that may well need to be discussed. If I may put it another way: one guy's high fret is another guy's low; one guy's low action is another guy's impossible--impossibly high... or impossibly low. Find out what *you* love. Play 100's of guitars until you start to know for sure. Some people are very flexible and like or at least can adapt to many different setups; others are very particular in their preferences. Find out who *you* are in this area.

Put it in writing too, if it makes you feel better when you leave your guitar with someone to have any work done--with the words as finely-tuned as you need them to be. At least until you know your repairperson really well. Some wonderful, conscientious craftsperson may feel insulted and get upset with you for doing this. You must do it anyway and also, do tell them the truth: you are having all this in writing, on the invoice, to help prevent any problems that could come up later. If they're still mad at you, in my humble opinion, they're making a big mistake in treating their customers like this, and you need to wish them well and take your business elsewhere. You need to be treated right. I mean, if they're just grouchy as burnt heine, but do incredibly good work, do jobs exactly as you asked for, some of us sure can live with this. But if you fear that their being told by you as to the ultra-specifics of what you want has poisoned their incentive to do a fine job for you, get your guitar out of there. Don't let anybody touch your guitar unless it is with love. If that means you'll have to learn to do certain things yourself, this is not a bad thing. In fact, it's a great plus. For things you can't handle, keep looking for that right person.

As for *me* as a setup guy, I have close to 40 years of some very good feelings that I probably should make more time to luxuriate in at least once a year or something, although it's also fair to say that my setup skills only go so far and always have. But I did spend 1000's of hours on it, so naturally, results showed up. I did it for myself initially then a bonus came. I could make other people happy. I get to surprise players who long ago had given up hope that their guitars could ever feel or sound beautiful. Very, very satisfying. Feeds my sense of self-worth, I get to be party to some happiness vibes, and occasionally it helps at least somewhat restore somebody's faith in the human race and our ability to find solutions to things. I don't work on guitars all that much anymore--nothing like the 10-15 hour days I used to put in trying to learn what works. But I still hate to see a student struggling with a guitar that's tough to play, so that'll usually be enough to motivate me to action. One thing hasn't changed--we still try to get it oh-so-smooth and pretty feeling, and sounding like a dream.

AA: Speaking of which, what's goin' on with all those beautiful different tones that come out of just your Telecaster and amp, nothing else. Sometimes it seems like a whole little band is playing. At various other times it's reminiscent of a church organ, a harpsichord, steel guitar, swing vocal group, and even a choir. Besides the Hammond B-3 organ with the walking foot pedal bass. And a big luscious jazz guitar. Sometimes at least two."

TG: Thanks for noticing, for listening.

AA: How'd you learn all this?

TG: Same thing--same answer, meaning, I was able to put in some hours. Except this was the thing I *really* spent some time on. Searching, dreaming.

AA: What do you remember searching for at first; and did it change over time?

TG: Trying for different tones that I loved, still love. Which led me to different styles of music. Every now and then, vice versa. It's all very basic you know. I'm a pretty basic guy. As to your other point, yes it did change later, because I began to work with logic--using reason to find resources beyond my wildest dreams, most of which I still haven't completely absorbed, but the dance goes on.

AA: Many people are drawn to something but don't invest so heavily to the point where they could be said to have chosen a focal point far north of 'highly interested', a level of involvement that many people will never experience with anything. What made you choose to, as you like to say, 'do the time'--that is, give it *so much* of your time? And how did you go about it?

TG: I didn't choose it. It seemed to choose me. I was completely compelled,
virtually no choice. I had to study it for there was nothing in the world that I wanted more than to find out how to make those tones, and then work on learning to do that.
As for how, I was 'gone' for a long, long time. Buying as many guitars as I could and comparing everything that seemed to matter.

AA: Along with being as you say, 'a basic guy', you're also kind of a maniac.

TG: Yeah, ever since I was a baby. You got me right. But I hide it a lot so I can function in many normal situations and not bother or scare other people.

AA: Speaking of scary, and just to stay on this subject of something you spent so much of your life on, someone told me you were improvising a lot of that music we heard for hours. Is it so?

TG: So. I like to let it flow out and hang on. Alot of what shows up I've visited before. They know me. To be more accurate, often really, much of what I tend to play is similar to but not the same as things I've played before. Like a lot of musicians.

AA: It's safe to say then that improvising, in and of itself, is just not your main goal.

TG: That's right. Of course some nights you notice that you want to try and find lots of beautiful things that you've never played before--*true* improvising. I love when I have a night like *that*. But at other times, I'm looking to recreate, virtually note for note, things I've already played, maybe earlier that day, maybe many years ago. Certainly when I play arrangements of tunes, there'll often be favorite chord progressions or combinations of lines that I will go after. Sometimes this is out of necessity--I can't hear anything better--and sometimes it's because I just want to visit an old friend. What's important for me is to be relaxed or excited--I'll take either--and let the beauty pour out of me if I can, and not hassle myself too much about anything. Not as long as it's feeling good. Sounding good. Creating nice flavors, colors, and moods that I love.

AA: And as far as your awareness of every different audience's expectations--how much is this a factor?

TG: Thanks for reminding me: sometimes I play what I want to hear, other times, it's about what others are hoping for. And which way it goes here depends upon more factors than you'd care to hear, I suspect. I do try to make the right decision that I won't have regrets about later.

AA: On the break last night, I think you said the last thing I'd heard and asked about was a

'New Orleans' straight 8ths piano style. Yes?

TG: Yeah, that's it.

AA: It had a great as you say, 'feel', to it. Who should I listen to for more of this? Any special guitar players?

TG: It's not primarily a guitar music, lady of curiosity, but let me think......... you might try some discs by Ry Cooder or Taj Mahal. You may not know that Ry and Taj had a band *together*. In the mid `60's, they were the core of the Rising Sons, a group who caught some very hip feels, one of which was the rolling New Orleans thing if memory serves. Then there's Jerry Reed, the king of the southern piano style of guitar. The cleverest and coolest stuff ever on our beloved string instrument for this style. You'd want to hear him to gain a good window on the thing. And the great Bonnie Raitt gets a righteous straight 8ths slinky groove--although actually I think her fine feel on say, a cut like "Let's Give Them Something To Talk About" gets over more towards the ever-delicious Stax-Volt Memphis sound ala say, "Knock On Wood" by Eddie Floyd. But the feel of the two regions are highly related. And both are *so* funky. Either will do quite nicely thank you, at all hours of the day. My girlfriend has used this music to cure depression in me at times.

AA: And if I want to hear the piano sources of this music?

TG: Ah, then you have to listen to Professor Longhair, Dr. John, Allen Toussaint, Huey 'Piano' Smith, Brother Ray [*Ray Charles*] on non-swing 8th things, people like that. Also try the easily findable music of this type, meaning, the songs which sold very well in the late `50's and early `60's, and actually made it onto the R&B, Rock & Roll, and pop charts, some of the better examples of which might be cuts like "Sea Cruise" by Frankie Ford, "Ooh Poo Pah Doo" by Jessie Hill, "I Know" by Barbara George, "Mother-In-Law " by Ernie K-Doe and "Ya Ya" by Lee Dorsey. I think Allen Toussaint or Huey Smith played on most any one of these--and scads of others like them. All these cuts have a certain flavor and feel that you'll easily identify after awhile as a New Orleans thing. I can't express how much these sounds meant to me when I was a young man in the waiting, and the love affair continues on, possibly deeper now, since I'm finally playing these sounds on the guitar--something I thought I'd only do in my dreams.

AA: Thanks for the info as well as your feelings, and now I'd like to bring our talk back to guitar if you'd like.

TG: Please.

AA: Any advice to other guitar players as far as how to 'get good'? Maybe especially to those even just starting out but already really deeply desiring greatness to be theirs.

TG: Find out what you love and chase it with all your heart.

AA: And if they don't know how to bring those sounds into their hands?

TG: Turn to others for help. Find out all the things it takes to get a beautiful tone, a tone that turns you on (even though it may let you down once in awhile or more, as I was saying earlier). Make your playing have a good feel--always--as much as possible. This is the most crucial area because it is the most delicious area in many styles of music. Don't be blown away by all the failure that usually happens at first. Don't give up, results will come. Accept the work and aches and pains, they're part of it. I still have aches after over

40 yrs. of playing. So what. Just part of the deal. Nobody wants to hear us complain about something that is as beautiful as the guitar and the magic music that can come out of it. Stay with this amazing instrument and near-miracles happen. And for some people, it is simply so important that they look for more and more ways to make their practicing enjoyable, even a real pleasure. One big thing for me has always been to put rhythmic life into everything I'm working on as soon as possible. It's got to groove. If a person can't, please get with someone who will patiently show you how. You'll probably have to learn to count and tap your foot while playing. A certain % of players who love music so deeply but can't get the feel to come out of them, simply have to do this. Don't let embarrassment stand in your way. Life humbles all of us in one area or another. I should probably stop here though there's got to be more to say.

AA: Go ahead, say as much as you feel is right--for any musicians who might take value from your words, especially for those who are having trouble learning...if you'd care to...

TG: Practice slowly, *very* slowly if need be, on anything that is difficult or not sounding right. And listen very carefully to yourself to hear what you are doing well and what you are not. Tape your playing from time to time. But don't always listen back immediately. Give it a day or two. It can be a real eye-opener. The tape doesn't lie. Just us humans do, sometimes to ourselves. Don't do it, it's a trap that will keep a person from ever getting really good on their instrument. I've seen it in almost more cases than my heart can bear. Search your soul to make sure you are being honest with yourself and then peacefully accept the consequences of who you are, or find out how to elicit changes for the better in yourself or your life, changes that will help you live your dreams. Keep the goals in your mind, in your heart, and in your ears. It may take a long time, but good things will happen.

AA: Ted, musical advice is one area where you really shine and it's a very fine answer you've given--all the things you've mentioned.

TG: Thank you. I'm still shocked that I'm a better teacher than a player.

AA: Thank *you* and now possibly to bring this subject to a close--and this may sound a bit negative although I don't mean it to, but I just have to ask it: many people who play guitar, after experiencing so many of the problems the instrument throws their way, have been known to say "maybe I just don't have talent for this." Should they quit? Shouldn't some of them?

TG: No way. Not if they hunger for it. Because a simple truth is that talent often blooms very gradually, and even late for some. I've seen many remarkable transformations.
Nobody loses at guitar if they put in the time. *Some*thing good always shows up. It's all consistent with life's big lessons. Patience. Determination. Love. Goals. Finishing a job. The guitar seems impossibly hard in the early stages for so many who attempt it. But the transformation always starts to happen as the practicing hours begin to accumulate. Suddenly one day you realize you're doing something you couldn't do last month or last week, simply because of the nice effort you've shown.

AA: Such good things I hope for at least some to hear. And do you remember going through such a transforming period, Ted?

TG: There've been more than a few transformation periods that have opened my eyes, my heart, put the electricity of Life in my hands and shaped me as a player. There were a few misery periods in there too, some real nasty ones actually, but mostly it's been a 40+ year good ride. A *great* ride if I look at the big view. There are so many worse things one could do with their time.

AA: And with these words of encouragement ringing in the air, please don't be upset with me for also asking: how about guitarists who work so hard for each leg of their progress while they know other players for whom everything is easy and who make progress at a far faster rate. Do you have anything to say to them since this can be *so* discouraging?

TG: I'll personalize it a little again I guess. I've had lots of students who, in a matter of days, could play things it took me years to get. Shocking isn't it. My job is a humbling one, though not humiliating if I keep my attitude on straight. Periodically, it's good to remind myself that there'll always be very talented people in any field. But that doesn't change the fact that for most of us, pretty regular practice is what it will take to keep progress alive. Or at least a few hours a week for those who can only afford this much time. And even just this small amount will produce terrific things in each pair of hands over time if a person will just stay the course. This is especially true when someone works on something they love or crave results from. Of course, it massively helps if they're practicing *well*, doesn't it. But the gift of music is so large that even those who don't or can't or won't do a good job at practicing well--even they--get quite a lot of the goodies eventually.

AA: I'm very heartened again by your answer. I thought we were basically through with all this earlier but you said more good things than I had hoped for even on this whole rather large general area so I'm well pleased that we kept going. And in that spirit, I'll get greedy and now ask for one more little gem as a closer, if your patience has not been exhausted... .

TG: Maybe many already know this but for those who don't: Visualization--imagining yourself as a very fine player, how you're going to sound, and how incredibly good you're going to feel. This is a very fine thing to do. Every day. It's helped so many musicians immensely. Dreaming good things is good for the soul, especially if it goes hand in hand with working. And practicing in your mind--imagining the fretboard and eventually, hearing the sounds inside--this is one of the greatest aids to real progress I know of. Stuck in line at the market? Fine, visualize the guitar fingerboard and see the music you're working on *there*. Just see the places where your fingers touch down, you don't have to see the fingers themselves. Can't do it? Keep at it. You'll get it. I promise. Works wonders too. Doubles or triples how much information you can absorb--and retain. This guitar thing--it's worth all the hours it takes.

AA: Not to embarrass you but there's something else to what you're saying T.G., that I love.

TG: The part about me selling you my Nuvo D'Angelicorrina ouchtop for $100?

AA: Yes, that's it. No, you jellybean brain. I love that you care so much.

TG: Fooled you, did I? Seriously now, you know, that's birth. You start out with that. Everybody cares about something. And environment counts. You just heard my story of what music did to me as a kid, thrilling me beyond description, and saving me from a life that no doubt, given certain things in my inherent nature and my past, would've ended

up in the slammer like many of the guys I knew. And what did I do to make all those life-changing music moments happen? Nothin'--I was just *there* --lucky to be alive and *exposed* to these sights and sounds. So lucky.
AA: Exposure to great music is such a gift to young people. As I've heard you say, "sad that so many miss out. Lucky that so many don't. "
TG: I'll say--on both counts. Of course, fortunately, it's close to never-too-late on this front. Whether one hears Bach's E Major Violin Concerto at age 1 or 81, it still has a beautiful effect on most people. Debussy's *Afternoon of a Faun*... forget it--ridiculous ecstasy for just about anybody--a baby doing their first day on the planet or an elderly person in their last, at age 184--whoa. This is *some* piece of music.
AA: And if somebody was exposed to this music or any widely loved music and responded unfavorably--what do you make of that? Also, earlier you mentioned Scotty Moore and I was wondering about other guitar players *you* were exposed to when you were younger, and your reactions please?
TG: Oh it's fairly involved stuff as to your first point, that is, what all could be going on here. Having to do with images inside that the music conjures up for anyone. Music triggers stuff. Images of people they admire, others they don't, people who've treated them well and those who haven't, old memories, dreams of tomorrows, hopes and fears, praise and ridicule, triumph and shame, and most especially, how any of this makes them *feel*--feel about themselves--all churning around inside often because of music they are hearing. Also, it might shock you--or maybe not--how often it relates back to how and what and where and when and why the situation was what it was when they first heard anything even moderately similar, and how *that* made them feel. Again, about themselves, others, life itself. Man, don't think two ways about it, this is powerful stuff. But, at least half the time, just forget all this junk--there's the not uncommon possibility that if they hear something and don't like it, they simply just don't like it! You know, birth taste and all, everybody born with their own taste. But again, exposure counts. Many of us like things, even love things now that we didn't really like when we first heard them. Same with people, places, foods, you name it. Familiarity doesn't always breed contempt (tho' too much for my taste).

I was in my teens when I was first exposed to most of the guitar players who would affect me the most. So as to your second point, the first time I heard Albert King, I basically drove off the road. I could think of little else for days. How was I going to get that tone and those phrases I had heard him do? Who *was* this guy? Back then, in early 1966, I had to go deep into the bowels of the black section of L. A. to get that record. It was called "Laundromat Blues " and it meant the world to me. The other side,"Overall Junction," a shuffle groove for the ages, and talk about a band... ! So that was my first exposure to Albert King. When I saw him live at the old Ash Grove club, his backup band 'warmed up' the room for... ever it seemed. The crowd was going crazy, virtually none of them had ever seen him before, and then suddenly there he was, coming down the aisle from the back of the club with his guitar strapped on, ready to go. And he jumped up on that stage, with the band wailing and hit just 2 notes, his signature riff. And that crowd exploded with such a roaring approval, which in itself was such a wonderful sound, all of us just screaming and shouting. An ecstasy feast, that's what it was, that's what music can be when it connects to our emotions and more. Just think, there was no sound on earth that virtually every person in that room would have rather heard at that moment than that soulful, preachin', moanin' guitar of Albert King. He played and sang so well for so many years...made so many people happy or occasionally, left them dumfounded as his thumb sounded those particular note groupings which were only his

AA: You really do love this man still. I had no idea you were so involved in the whole blues revival of the `60's.

TG: What can I tell you, I was madly in love with this music many years ago and the residual effect has never really gone away, even when I think it has.

I simply couldn't believe a person could play that much guitar when I first heard Chet Atkins in 1962. By the time I heard the rest of the album, I was speechless and just sat around thinking for a long time. How could he have made all those sounds? How had he learned all this great music that had poured out, song after song? How could I ever learn to hear and understand all that was going on at once on so many of the cuts? Why didn't my guitar get any of those great tones I had just heard him get? Why did every song sound like it was in a different style? How would I ever be able to go to school the next day and concentrate? This man and Les Paul probably rang more musical bells for more people than any other guitar players in history. Other than that, nothing much. Well actually wait, yes, Les did invent multitrack overdubbing and did a lot in the pioneering of successful solidbody guitar design, but these don't count for much I'm sure. Ooh.

You know, the truth is, I could go on literally for weeks about so many guitar players. But, it's probably time to cool it.

AA: This talk reveals one thing for sure Ted: you could be accused of loving music. Just a little.

TG: We're born to love music it appears--I mean, certainly some of us are...as well as at the least, a few people along the way, not to mention a few other creatures, things, places--you name it. Leave it to a slightly 'out there' musician to put it in this order..just kidding (maybe not).

AA: And there's another thing, Mr. tone rascal. You're kind of a philosophical guy even when you're not trying to be.

TG: So is Woody Woodpecker. Sorry. I'll just say 'thank you'. That's what I should have said. c. Ted Greene 2001

***/////////* Extra stuff--optionally, include in some other article :**

Do the best you can here... Doing a *good* job...Put that music on and watch people try to sit still. 'Love it' instead of 'o.k.' in response to a request...Those tones. The low-end, especially the interaction of the drums and bass on those records really spoke to me.

Take "The Hucklebuck." It was just a silly dance tune c.1960, (tho' based on an earlier more sophisticated jazz thing) but the low-end, the interaction of the drums and bass, was something else. That cut sounded like an express train *and* a band when played on a jukebox. "Let Me In" by the Sensations, the Ist ska hit in this country, way back in `62. I've never heard that sound and feel again since. "Dance With Me" by the Drifters. It was pure magic. The jukeboxes had real power over my life in such a great way. Hi-fi they surely weren't. Throbbing, thick, irresistible tone, they had in spades. (or: ---they had it in spades). My whole generation likes to get funky. This is an early form of a swampy version of it. Love tryin' to get it. It's lean, spare but groovin' hard. A form of rhythm and blues. Made its way onto the rock 'n' roll charts too eventually--in the early `60's, pre-Beatle days. The period most of the rock critics and historians call a waste-land--what a box of toilet cleaner.

AA: How could so many writers get it so wrong, if this is true?

TG: Lack of experience. Non-experiential writing. Not listening with their hearts open instead of being overly swayed in judgment by the images of things, and media frenzy--rather than the substance of the music itself. I'll tell you, a lot of these guys weren't there, playing at those dances, watching the ladies move, hearing some pretty terrific-sounding things. For every terrible song, there was a really fine sounding one around at the same time. You just had to keep your ears open. The truth is, there never was a bad year in rock 'n' roll in the `50's or `60's.

AA: So it's the old human problem of ignorance--writing about something they don't really know enough about. Using 2nd and 3rd-hand sources rather than knowledge picked up by 'living' a subject. Being fooled by the look of things. Things that are new to them, which compounds the issue further. Unfortunate.

TG: You're on the case.

AA: Thank you. Do you think this type of thing will ever end?

TG: Maybe if the human race evolves a bit. So far, image has ruled an awful lot of things. If girls weren't screaming for some music like they did for Elvis and The Beatles, the critics often figured it must be less worthy. Yet, even in the rowdy world of rock, there has always been music that's a little more subtle, but equally valuable; and certainly equally appealing to many ears. The marketing people have always kept the rock umbrella open wide. They love to call some pretty ballad with strings, rock and roll.

AA: This is kind of stimulating to think of all this mild craziness but I'd like to bring our talk back to guitar.

...Izdatun Island? I've found many different answers to this one, but if I had to distill it all down into one thing, it would be that. I've found many seemingly different answers to this one, but believe it or not, it all distilled down into one thing, near exclusively. it would be that 'Desire is the engine of life, at least the main engine. To put it in a simpler way... It's easy to forget that, amazingly, it's an experience shared by literally millions of young people since the end of World War II--we've been so extremely lucky. And the *look* of it all often counts too when you're young--especially if it looks a little dangerous. You know this, it's a story as old as time--a sizeable amount of young people are going to go for something that even suggests the pushing of the envelope a little beyond what society says is right. Even though I, like many other people, adopted the outer trappings of some performers I admired, it was still mostly about the music for me--and the shared experience of it with my friends and a whole generation of kids. I'm sure that we loved having our own music and feeling part of something great--a common thing for quite a few generations of kids in the 20th century, right? And later, in the Beatle era, lots of people believed that this music could and would help straighten out the world.

AA: Your take on why the old records sound so incredible?

TG: Sure, thanks for asking. The music biz, with a few gargantuan exceptions, was an industry mostly geared to *talent* back then. Many of the musicians on the records had been professionals or at least playing at this level on their instruments for a long time, and it really shows. Likewise, the singers--the vocals are often the most wondrous, awe-inspiring part of the old records--along with the feel of course. Other than the hideous racial issue, image was way back in the pack. And a performer's dancing ability was just a welcome bonus--if it was there at all--not the ultra-huge selling point it would often become later.

AA: I have a feeling you could tell me more about these old records' appeal if you wanted to... .

TG: Certainly. Since you asked--guitar players used big fat strings which often gave a deep, rich tone. Bass players primarily used the huge standup basses, and with warm studio mics--no built in pickups, this produced an amazing though often subtle feel and tone--they weren't mixed up front very often. When they used electric basses--primarily the legendary Fender P basses in various incarnations, they tried to imitate the standup's tone in most cases (for lots of reasons). Recording gear had luscious, warm tone--seldom equaled or bettered since. 'Room sound' was a given on almost every recording. Equipment didn't change and update overnight so engineers really knew their boards and how to get the best sounds out of them. People have certainly done wonderful things with recording in the last 30 years as well, but there's no denying that there's magic in so many recordings of the first few decades of the post-ww II era, the era that I was lucky enough to be born to.

AA: Any recommended listening cuts come to mind?

TG: Oh do they ever. But maybe we'll come back to this later because I may not want to talk about anything else once we start on that. Some of the best memories of my life are here.

AA: I like when I've heard you talk about this aspect before. You've had some interesting ideas.

TG: Thanks, sometimes you have a question that you keep coming back to. One of those for me is 'why people do what they do'--I guess I've phrased it here as a non-question for ease of discussion.

AA: Would you explain what this is really about for you? And do I recall correctly that it's something you've heeded because it paid dividends in your teaching?

TG: Yes it's true. You see, since I'm in a business where human motivation plays a key role in whether the people I work with (meaning my students) get what they came to me for, it's proper for me to observe many things if I am to do a good job in helping them--helping them learn to get all the particular pleasures they yearn for with the guitar and music in general sometimes too.

So if somebody asked me, "in regards to human behavior, what do you think 'runs the planet' --what's the one most powerful thing?, expressed in one or two words if possible, and leaving God and nature out of it, I'd have to say 'desire'. Desire is it, as best I can tell. Desire runs the show for the human race. Also not uncommonly, intense desire, if you prefer two words. A way I'm fond of speaking about all this is to simply say, "Desire is the Engine of Life." At least the main engine. It's the one lens through which you can include most actions of the human race. And more. I like it. I would have preferred it to have been Love but it isn't--though it's running a close second and oftentimes, is just about the same thing. 'Instinct' and 'Intuition' are in there too, battling for 'best supporting actor.'

AA: Why do you think 'desire' is number one, Ted?

TG: Well, when you look at why people do what they do, and look for one constant reason or root cause, this is just what shows up over and over, at least to my sense of things. You know, I'm just one guy, one opinion. Somebody else may see it differently.

AA: I haven't given it enough thought. I'll throw it around with some friends and get back to you with some feedback, okay?

TG: Love it. Now, don't expect it to be more than it is. The desire concept is a surface concept at times. Meaning, it doesn't get down to the 'ultra-base' of why we all have these desires in the first place. No matter. It's still powerful stuff and has been a great help to me in many areas of my own life and like I said, in figuring out what to give people to get them where they long to go with their music.

Musically speaking, I'm interested to get just a bit more of the flavor of the period you're alluding to; 'tho when I can't stand not to have something anymore, I'll go after it pretty strong and endure the work. One thing after another. A lot of grief for my parents. This seemed a good way out. And it eventually proved to be true... outtasight people, both of them, 'tho you couldn't have convinced my wretchedly ungrateful self of this during my teenage years. My love of music got me through a lot of rough times when I was young Actually, and so I had to begin a whole the price of growth is often pain of one sort or another--that's clear to see. but I can't change my inner standards, because they're directly linked to how I hear.

AA: One last reason you could give to do music?

TG: Yeah, well you know, ever since Mick Jagger sang "I'm a queen bee, baby..." in tribute to his beloved black brethren, he's never been stung again (except in court).

don't you think, especially if when people hear music they might like or even be moved by, they're in a good situation so that the experience is felt mainly as high pleasure.

AA: You mean if say, a person says " but I don't *like* 'country,' it could well be because they were exposed to it under unfavorable circumstances.

TG: That's exactly right although it also has to do with *images* -- the images a person gets inside when they hear each type, any type--every type of music, not to mention any individual artist in any style. If it reminds someone of something they feel bad about, then that particular music doesn't stand much of a chance. Read about Babe Ruth and you know for sure, this guy was superhuman. Likewise, Charlie Parker--scientists once put him through an extensive series of tests and he scored superior to super-human on all of them. The Bird was undoubtedly operating a few penthouses above what even most talented musicians could do with a horn in their hands and a thirst for life in great huge amounts. Even tanked up, Bird sounded better than most of us will ever be. Staggers the imagination.

AA: Care to name some?

TG: I wouldn't know where to begin.

AA: Whatever comes to mind. A few favorites perhaps? How about only some where both the performances and sound merit high honors?

TG: You win. I like your proposal. Maybe we'll just go with 45's that lit up my youth.

"I Only Have Eyes For You" by the Flamingos (and their follow up, "Mi Amore" which never got the airplay). Still unmatched for dreamy, floating in paradise vibe. A recording to hear a million times and never tire of.

"Money Honey" by the Drifters (also the Elvis version). The height of vocal 16 bar medium shuffle blues, with wild lyrics and super-rich singing. As you may know, almost all early rock 'n' roll records were shuffles or triplets, with a few 2 beat bounces as a third main type. So when you talk about "Be-Bop-A-Lula" by Gene Vincent and his Blue Caps, I mean, I just don't know of a better med.-slow shuffle record than this. Nothing else of its type has the magic elixir of the super-potent 1/4 notes of this recording combined with the simply astonishing overall gorgeous tone. Nothing that grooved this hard ever *sounded* this good. It was shocking, but in the greatest way. It was like you were in the room right next to the players and yet they were also far away. In its field, there's simply nothing else to equal it. It stands alone. You can define one whole huge chunk of r'n'r with this record.

"There Goes My Baby" by the new-era Drifters in 1959. A new sound at the time, with fantastic 'far-away' vocal against a never-heard-before backdrop of tympani and strings. Especially fine in the moments where the background vocals come in with the counterpoint. Again, an overall recorded sound that seduced whenever you heard it.

"He Will Break Your Heart" by Jerry Butler. The incomparable Curtis Mayfield and the Impressions laying down a wonderful story in super-appealing lyrics over a unique and extraordinarily influential groove coupled to the seeds of a brand new guitar style, which would emerge fully-formed in the years to come (early `60's), culminating in 1965's "People Get Ready," possibly Curtis's greatest overall triumph, and in all the best of Jimi Hendrix's soul music-chord stuff, he being the supreme 'Curtis player' of his generation, and even more directly influential in this than Curtis himself. All this is widely known by afficianados of this genre, so my apologies to any who may be reading this.

"Whole Lotta Woman" by the Radiants. Chicago soul at its harmonic richest. The 2nd chord of each 'A' section has to be heard to be believed.

"This Can't Be True" by Eddie Holman. I remember sitting with some guys and playing this record all night long when we first discovered it. No one wanted to hear anything else. All night long until the sun came up. We talked about this event for years after. One of the most exquisite and hypnotic records one will likely ever hear. Especially if your taste includes a love of beautiful R&B/soul ballads with incredible writing, production, stunningly perfect guitar tone and playing, and highly stylized but super-effective singing-

-both lead and background--and masterful building in the arrangement. "Don't Stop Now" by the same artist is almost as good and in the exact same vein.

"Red Beans and Rice" by Booker T. and the M.G.'s. Still the funkiest, most soulful instrumental I've ever heard. There are moments in there where time stands still and where they've captured part of the essence of how I feel inside.

"Peter Gunn," Duane Eddy's 1960 version. The break in the middle where it all falls out and then gradually comes back, layer upon layer, fusing into this kind of musical paddlewheel.....wow. This is a study in the art of ebb and flow, pacing, building, dropping back down, coming back. Sly Stone did it so well in "Dance To The Music" almost a decade later. But I'm still kind of shocked at how little this technique's been used on record. It is *so* effective. I used to see live bands do it and I was part of some bands that did it, and what a blast... The simple pleasures of life--sometimes that's all we need.

"Money" by Barrett Strong. The original. Impossible major bass line under dorian minor key triads. Should've been a musical trainwreck and maybe it even was but no young person who grew up hearing this record didn't at least smile when it came on, if not flat out love it. What a wild bunch of maniacs played and recorded this. As if the foregoing weren't enough, compared to almost everything else that had ever been a popular record, this one had this noticeable, wild (if mild by today's gonzo standard) distortion in all the low-end instruments. And to add to the embarrassment of riches, what a time feel--the almost floating feeling is because of the every-other time habanera rhythm under the driving straight 8th's with that huge hesitation in every-other line. Talk about rhythmic counterpoint. And a cake that already was frosted really high received one final cherry on top--just a riot of sarcastic lyrics. Talk about a singular moment in recording history. This has to be one.

"Hey, Bo Diddley" by who else, Bo Diddley. Well, here we are in unique artist land again. And on this track, he outdoes himself for excitement. I remember being at more than one party where this song just tore the house down. His guitar sounds like you're flying around in the sky and he just got this floating, yet throbbing sound that no one else that I know of ever did on record--before or since-- and without any flanging, chorusing, digital delaying. I mean, it's a guitar but it's not a guitar. And the drummer.

Certainly a graduate of Rimshot U., but what did *he* have for breakfast? Try to duplicate the whole sound of this recording. Good luck.

"Theme From A Summer Place" by Max Steiner, Percy Faith's recording. This one is so beautiful that many people were swept away with emotion when they heard it. Used to win the most requested song award, even on otherwise rock'n' roll stations. I've known more than one person who's told me that this is their all-time favorite song or record. And I can see why. A gorgeous and memorable romantic-sounding melody over an irresistible orchestration of high piano, french horns, and one of the finest-recorded string sounds in the history of the industry, coupled to a modulating, building arrangement with the best lines appearing late in the game. Even the fadeout is absolutely nectarlike. I wonder how many people fell in love to this only-one-of-its-kind recording. I could barely stand up sometimes when I'd hear it while walking down the street with my little radio. My friend

Vivian Sanchez used to tease me about this but I didn't care--I just wanted to hear that song. Others to come: Wiggle Wobble Thank you Mr. Poobah Overall Junction The Jam, Pt. 1," Been So Long" by the Pastels.

AA: Was it all centered on Albert King?

TG: It wasn't just Albert King. I have many similar feelings and stories about B.B. too. And Freddy. 3 Kings.

AA: Who else?

TG: Michael Bloomfield and Eric Clapton in 1966 &7. These two shattered all notions for my generation as to what an electric guitar should be doing in the field of electric blues and more. Of course Jeff Beck and Jimi Hendrix were showing what an electric guitar *could* do--such innovators! And Jeff's still at it all these years later. Absurdly brilliant talent. With brain and hands to match. Jimmy Page, he may have been outplaying them all back then. Roy Buchanan...for those who were lucky enough to hear him at his peak, you may have heard the very best--of Telecaster magic. Although when I think of Danny Gatton at the top of *his* game, I just can't imagine anyone playing the guitar much better. Then there's Albert Collins--a volcano...white heat. Jimmie Vaughn seems to have absorbed alot of this flame and is keeping it alive so well. And we've heard rumors that his brother could play a little. What a stunning loss it still is even 10 years later. I think Stevie gave so many people such a thrill, the type they'll remember for the rest of their lives, and his command by the end of *his* life, was fantastic. And in this context I'd be wretchedly ungrateful not to mention T-Bone Walker, the father of all of this, and I believe, the most influential guitarist. In history. No joke.

AA: Why Ted?

TG: Well for starters, out of T-Bone you get Chuck Berry, and you get B.B. King--and you know what these two guys spawned. That's a humungous amount of rock 'n' roll guitarists and not much less in the blues. Check the numbers game, the number of guitarists that come from these two guys and it boggles the mind. Not to belabor the point but I think we're talkin' millions.

Anyway, with musicians, some people have a little more heart than others, some have more beautiful knowledge, others more skill. But all *these* guys I just mentioned, set a standard, showed the way for hundreds of thousands of other guitar players, maybe millions.

And it's beautiful that there's an artistic line here--if you listen to the early work of B.B., Albert, and Freddy King, you can joyfully spot so much of who for instance, Bloomfield and Clapton were to become, and yet, each of the younger pups brought their own voice to the instrument, and in turn, influenced the next guy, and so on. By the way, I didn't mean to focus so much on blues when I started to answer that gentle-man's question from the audience. Sorry 'bout that.

AA: Then you'd like to say a few words about some guitarists in other fields who had a major impact on you?

TG: This is where I would have gone naturally if I had continued talking. Because it was also love at first sound with Wes Montgomery and me in 1964 or 5 when I heard

"Caravan" from that breathtaking *Movin' Wes* album. He remains my favorite guitar player to this day. His best stuff is near unbearably perfect to me. It's practically pulverizing to listen to him at the top of his game. One could mention the powerhouse first album he did with Jimmy Smith, *The Dynamic Duo* . Or the ultra-fine 1963 album, *Boss Guitar*. Likewise the live, classic, *Smokin' At The Half-Note* . The lush beauty of the *Bumpin'* album. All of these albums--real stunners. The *Body And Soul* live album from his SRO dates in England at Ronnie Scott's, the famous jazz club. *Live At Jorgie's*, in St. Louis in the early `60's, with his brothers playing *and* reacting to Wes playing his heart out on "Summertime." Incandescent, would be a starting word to describe Wes at his best. Don't put those recordings near any booze or anything.

Guitarists such as the afore-mentioned Scotty Moore; the initially young and soon to be super-influential James Burton and Cliff Gallup; older legend Joe Maphis and whiz kid Larry Collins; Johhny Meeks, Hank Garland. Plenty more. Very special players all. Not that the public knew who these guitarguys were. But at least their fascinating playing made its way to alot of ears, even if they were often paid little. They certainly had the respect of all those whose business it was to know who the great players were, and this could be a mighty nice porridge for those hungry bank accounts, tho' as the song says, 'your love don't pay no bills.'

AA: But your point is a bit shocking. And I don't think I like the sound of it.

TG: I don't blame you, and I was just about to say...you know, what I said is real, but it's also fallacious as can be from a fairness standpoint, so unfair, even though I didn't mean it to be, didn't mean it in that sense at all.

AA: Maybe the fairness thing is what bothered me too but please explain a bit anyway.

TG: Musicians are drawn to what they love and if they're lucky, get to focus on it, work on this music they love so much. And for many players, it may be just one field, and it may keep them busy for their whole life, just becoming hugely accomplished in there.

Now, nobody lives long enough yet to even hear, let alone learn, all the fine music in maybe *any* of so many different fields in music. There's so much. It boggles the mind if you really think about it. That's why I said we're musical poopers. But it seems so misleading to then think we must therefore be very poor musicians just because compared to the whole, we're the weensiest little noteheads on the cosmic staff that is Music--with the big M.

So a fair picture of the thing is that none of us is all that accomplished when we consider how large music is. But if you were at a Segovia concert in the`60's, or saw Clarence White in his prime--which was what, from about the age of four on?, or heard Michael Bloomfield in person with the Paul Butterfield Blues Band or saw the impossible things that Wes Montgomery did with great ease and laughter, the type of thing I was mentioning may have been the last thing on your mind. So it's a paradox, a thing which some of us can at least look at a little from time to time, use for whatever good we can gather from it. And *I* gather that I may have talked too long already of something that's possibly too self-evident to too many.

AA: No, no. The imagery you stirred up was stimulating. And I have many questions for you.

TG: Shooting straight now--you know, many musicians of my generation are able to play the melody and chord changes to hundreds, even thousands of songs and things, but did you know that this isn't even one *ten-thousandth* of all the great music that's been written? So most of us are still babies here, musical diapers all around.

AA: Kind of shocking. How do you deal with this since you're fond of so *much* music?

TG: Well, first let me say that musicians are drawn to what they love, especially to what they love the most and for many, this may well be just one field or style; and they'll work on this their whole life, becoming hugely accomplished in there if they're lucky enough to find a way to be a good worker, and if they're also fortunate enough to have the time, energy and circumstance to do it. Now, nobody lives long enough to even hear, let alone learn, all the fine music in any of so many fields--that is, even in any one field of music. But...and I don't mean this in a punk way but...... "so what ." People have to do what they have to do, especially when it doesn't hurt others.

In my case, and it too isn't all that rare, there's no way I can stay away from at least dipping my toe in the water of at least a little bunch of different musical pools. For the same reason--usually love--as the player who spends his or her whole life on one style. I already gave up drugs, I'm not giving up R&B, Bachian counterpoint--how could I say goodbye to that? Head over heels in love with it I am and have been for over 30 years. So many styles of jazz. A banquet here alone.

Anyway, I don't need to, nor am I qualified to gig in all the areas I love, but as long as I get to play in them a little... And if the specialist becomes a master of their chosen style while guys like me maybe end up staying down on some lesser rungs, who cares if you're playing the music you love? I can live with this if I remind myself that it's the least objectionable alternative. I'm not looking for trouble with the universe. No contest.
Things are the way they are and it's hip to deal with that, deal with what is. My only regrets here happen when I see a phenomenally accomplished player in some style I love where I'm just a babe, and then I find myself thinking, "ah, if I only could." But again, one has to deal with what is, change it, or change oneself. I doubt that I'll ever change my roving nature in music and I've stopped bothering trying. There's too much else to beat oneself up about, too many other areas of personal growth to work on. And too many beautiful sounds to get down with to sit around and worry about what one'll never do.

AA: I like your style Ted which is part of why I wanted to do this interview, and do this in front of an audience, in case it never got to print. But as you know, I still don't agree with some of your assessments as to your own accomplishments.

TG: Free country. And thanks.

AA: Speaking of country, what was that thing you started to tell me the other day, about a country player learning classical music?

TG: Oh yeah, it was on something not dissimilar from what we just were mentioning before... let's say a truly fine country guitarist also plays 20 superb classical pieces, and plays them very well; this is terrific, quite a decent achievement. But it's just the romper room at Julliard. Still in the musical pooping stage there.

AA: Pretty funny, T. G.

TG: You could of course also reverse it--a bunch of Julliard graduates go to Nashville for the summer and take a country gig through a great misunderstanding, and end up sounding like The Vienna Stringbean Orchestra on Nyquil. A lot of chuckles or a lot of sourpusses at the end of that one.

AA: You are a wild spirit, Ted. Which some of us love, but we do have to do this thing seriously too you know.

TG: You're certainly right. Yes. I'll behave.

AA: And I think you were serious about the fellow at Julliard.

TG: Sure. How could it be otherwise, since the output in the classical music world is easily over 100,000 pieces. If you only like one out of 10 of these, you're either still in a veritable sea of ecstasy, or in really big trouble, depending on how you look at it, how you feel about it. And that's why most all of us *are* musical poopers in this, or most other musical areas--but at least we're all in it together.

AA: You've retained your sense of wonder, which is hard for many adults to do although it does seem like a worthwhile thing, at least to this set of eyes. And now, if you would, let's go back to your story for a while please.

Regrets? Oh sure--would I ever like to have even half that time back... .But the world of fast-travel, gorgeous-looking machines is particularly alluring to some of us who inhabit this planet, and it took quite awhile to get myself to say goodbye to that scene, which takes *so* much of your time if you fall in love with it. No lie.

I can live with some bad notes--I take a million more chances now than I used to--but not with everything 'off' in the feel dept. and a non-satisfying tone. As many in the older generations would say, "so, you can't have everything you want in life--what else is new?" Next day, Gonzo the clueless dogface boy again.

Notes

The lists in the Appendix

The following lists were compiled after the first stages of my organization of Ted's lesson material. To say it was a massive task is an understatement. As I labored through that project I constructed these lists for my own use at that time. There are a few minor inaccuracies. I had not planned to publish this list.

After the writing of this book I decided to include the lists (as they were) to give a visual example of just how much work Ted produced. I thought it was a precise way for the reader to gain a proper perspective of the scope of Ted's writings.

Yes, at some point in the future the lists will be revised. For now, I just wanted to share with you an idea of the immensity of Ted's productivity throughout his lifetime.

Ted Greene - Music Studies Listed Chronologically

1967/1968 March and Roman Type Themes (experiment)

1968-1970
Chord Formulas and Families
Poly Chords
Essential Chords
Chord Substitution
Voice Leading
Triads
Dominant 7ths
Scale Harmonies

1971
01/26/71 Renaissance
10/19/71 Modulation
11/22/71 Dominant 7th Sounds - Step 1 Pg. 5
Ideas - Gospel, Neapolitan etc.

1972
03/24/72 Chorales
08/28/72 Bach Chord Progressions

1973
03/27/73 Standard Resolution of the Dominant 7th Chords
06/05/73 The Related Triads and Maj. 7 Chords
09/14/73 Triads in Root Position (with upper 3 voices in close pos.)
09/15/73 Sequences Using Root Position, Close Position Triads
09/15/73 Triads in 1st Inversion
09/15/73 Triads in 2nd Inv. and Figured Bass
10/02/73 Some Resolutions of Modern Dominants to Tonics
10/12/73 Modern Chords Viewed from Melody 2 Pgs.
10/12/73 mi7 family (+ relative major) Viewed From Melody
10/27/73 Modulations
10/30/73 Harmonic Patterns
11/16/73 Chord Construction (Formulas) & Substitution 10 Pgs.
11/16/73 Essential Chords (Standard Inversions) 3 Pgs.
12/17/73 Modern Chord Progressions
12/18/73 Systematic Inversion Families
1973 Closed Voicing Triads

1974

02/19/74 Major Triad Fingerings
02/19/74 Melodic Patterns (key of C)
04/21/74 Chords for Chord Melody Playing 5 Pgs.
04/27/74 Vocabulary Reference Page
04/27/74 "Sentimental Journey" Analysis
05/26/74 Chord Construction Formulas
08/01/74 I bVI7 ii7 I
08/08/74 Good Ways to Establish Tonality
08/16/74 Modern Chords Grouped According to Bass
09/02/74 Intervals 4 Pgs.
09/09/74 Dominant 7th Sounds
09/15/74 Tonality
09/16/74 Melodic Patterns (key of C)
09/23/74 Tonality Pg.2
10/19/74 Bach Type Pedal Points
10/21/74 Variations on I vi ii V 2pgs.
10/12/74 Construction of Chords by Location & String Grouping 2 Pgs.
11/02/74 Chords for Stretching the Hand
11/26/74 Whole Tone Modulations
11/26/74 Whole Tone Modulations inc. permutations of whole tone scale
12/18/74 Single Note Scales for miMaj7, mi6, mi7b5, 7b9+ (& diminished) Families
12/18/74 Melodic Minor Scales for: mi6, miMaj7, mi7b5, 7#9#5(b9b5), and 13+11 Families
12/29/74 Common Chord Progressions & Principles
12/29/74 Common Chord Progressions & Principles
12/29/74 Most Common Chord Progs & Harmonic Principles Used in 20th Century Popular Music 4 Pgs.
12/31/74 Modern Chords - Condensed List
12/31/74 Chord Construction Formulas

1975

01/11/75 Modern Chords
01/11/75 Examples of Common (Maj. Key) Chord Progressions
01/19/75 Common Progressions & Principles - Dim7 Chords
01/26/75 Other "Major Type" Tonalities
02/---/75 Dim.7 Family Voicings (all listed on C)
02/09/75 Triad Spelling
02/22/75 20th Century Harmonic Vocabulary
03/11/75 Tonal Centers of Different Types of Tonalities
03/25/75 Tonality Types (Dealing more with Norms than Exceptions)
04/21/75 Modern Tonality and Rhythm Types/Classical Tonality & Rhythm Types
05/03/75 Tonality and Rhythm Types (Organization for Improvisational Thinking)
05/13/75 Basic Chord Forms
05/18/75 Ear Training Exercises Pt.2 - Chord Progressions
05/19/75 Basic Chord Progs. (for Ear Training)
06/19/75 Blues Progressions (Bb)
06/26/75 Styles (Tonality Types) and Harmonic Resources
07/08/75 Condensed Tonality Sheet
07/15/75 Major Scale Sounds for Single Note Playing
07/15/75 7th Chord Scales (mixolydian) Pg.1
07/15/75 7th Chord Scales Pg.3

07/25/75 mi7b5 Sounds & more Pg.2
07/31/75 More Variations on iii vi ii V
08/22/75 I (or iii) VI ii V - Variations Stemming from Different Types of VI's Pgs. 2&3
09/14/75 iii VI ii V Variations Consonant Style
09/19/75 List of Favorable Matings of Qualities & Degrees
09/20/75 iii biii ii V (bii) Contrary Motion 2 Pgs.
09/27/75 Melodic Chord Streams ala George Van Eps
09/27/75 Melodic Chord Streams
09/27/75 Melodic Chord Streams (change of position w/connecting melodies
09/30/75 7th Chord Melodic Chord Streams
10/12/75 Tonality Types (Modulation & Tonality Transitions are Very Important) 2 Pgs.
10/17/75 III VI II V with Contrary Motion 2 Pgs.
1975 Modes, Scales, Tonal Resources

1976
02/27/76 Single Note Playing (Explanation) Pg. 1&2
02/28/76 Common Diatonic Chord Progs. Examples (Maj.)
02/28/76 Single Note Playing -Building 7th Chords Pg.3
02/28/76 Single Note Playing - Arpeggios Pg. 4
02/28/76 Diatonic Major Scale Arpegios Pg.5
03/25/76 Single Note Playing in Minor Keys Pg.1
03/25/76 S.N.P. Harmonic Minor Pg.2
03/27/76 S.N.P. Dorian Minor Pg.4
03/28/76 S.N.P. Melodic Minor Pg.3
03/28/76 Diatonic Harmonic Minor Arpeggios
03/30/76 Diatonic Melodic Minor Arpeggios
04/20/76 Altered Dominant Scales Pg. 2
04/30/76 Illustrations of Dom.7ths on All 12 Degrees in a Maj. Key 2 Pgs.
04/29/76 Illustrations of Dom.7th's on all 12 Degrees in Maj. Keys
04/29/76 Harmonic Patterns Diatonic Major Key
05/05/76 Systematic Inversions
05/10/76 Tonalities
05/16/76 Modern Chords in Common Progressions
05/25/76 Musical Priorities
05/26/76 Chord Const. (Formulas)
05/28/76 Chord Reference Charts and the Nucleus Concept 5 Pgs.
05/29/76 Modern Chord Progressions
05/30/76 Tonality 6 Pgs.
05/31/76 Musical Goals and Necessary Areas of Study
05/31/76 Learning the Names of Notes on the Fingerboard 2 Pgs.
06/07/76 Blues Progressions
06/08/76 Longer Progs. Using Modern Chords
06/30/76 Tonalities Pg.2
07/09/76 Phrases in Chord Melody Style
10/07/76 mi7b5 Scales and more
10/19/76 Melodic Patterns (apply to all scales & keys)
10/28/76 General Harmonic Tendencies - Tonality Oriented
10/21/76 Non Diatonic V7 I Progressions 10-21-76
10/21/76 20th Century Harmonic Vocabulary & Progressions
11/09/76 vi7 (or I) II7 ii7 V7 (I) 3 Pgs.

1977

01/03/77 Tonality Types
01/24/77 Whole Tone Derived Chords
02/01/77 Small Chords for Group Playing 3 Pgs.
02/03/77 Tonality Types
02/14/77 The Elements of Chord Progressions
02/18/77 Modern Chords in Basic Chord Progressions
02/22/77 Chord Voicings on the Top 4 Strings (level 1)
02/26/77 Chord Voicings on the Middle 4 Strings (level 1)
02/26/77 Chord Voicings on the Top 4 Strings (level 1)
03/09/77 Chords for Group (or Solo) Playing (on top 4 stgs.) 2 Pgs.
03/19/77 Harmonic Patterns - Type 1 "held note sound"
04/08/77 Examples of I Chord Vamps
04/---/77 Blues Progressions
05/04/77 Chord Voicings on the Middle 4 Strings (level 1)
05/06/77 Progressions to Illustrate Different Types of II7 Chords
06/16/77 Summary of Most Common Chord Movements in Modern Jazz Harmony
06/24/77 Tonality Types
07/19/77 The Blues
07/20/77 Blues Chord Forms for Chord Melody Playing
07/20/77 Melodic Blues Progressions
08/08/77 Root in the Bass iii7 VI7 ii7 V7 Progressions
08/08/77 Modern Jazz-Blues Progressions
08/10/77 Modern iii7 VI7 ii7 V7 Progs. 2 Pgs.
08/10/77 Voicing Reference Page (showing General Areas Only)
08/15/77 Some Basic Chord Forms for "Walking" Bass Style
08/17/77 Fundamentals
08/19/77 Chord Forms for Chord Melody Playing (Level 1) 3 Pgs.
08/25/77 The 5 Main Areas of the Fingerboard
09/17/77 Walking Bass Style "Satin Doll"
10/02/77 III7 (or I) VI7 II7 V7
10/02/77 bVII7 VI7 bVI7 V7
10/12/77 Solo Based on the Chords to "Cute"
10/15/77 Reference Page
10/16/77 Dominant Family Tones Chart
10/22/77 Learning Aaltered Dominant Sounds - Type 1 Pg.5 Arpeggios
10/24/77 Playing in One Position (as a tool for learning Maj. scales & transitions)
11/02/77 Playing Through Chord Changes in Position
11/05/77 Learning the Dominant 7th Scale: I bVii7
11/08/77 Learning mi7 Sounds in Context: I biii7 ii7 V7 I
11/12/77 Diatonic Major Scale Runs 7 Pgs.
11/15/77 Overtone Dominant Scale: playing "in position" 2 Pgs.
11/18/77 Learning Altered Dominant Sounds Type 1
11/19/77 Learning Altered Dominant Sounds Type 2
11/20/77 Learning Altered Dominant Sounds Type 3
11/24/77 Dominant 7th Sounds - Step 1 7 Pgs.
12/06/77 Visualizing and Fingering
12/07/77 The Dim7th Chord
12/14/77 Diminished 7th Sounds 4 Pgs.
12/28/77 Major Chord Runs Using Only Chord Tones 7 Pgs.

12/30/77 The Dominant 7th Scale

1978

01/07/78 More Major Chord Runs 4 Pgs.
01/15/78 Overtone Dominant 7th Runs 4 Pgs.
01/18/78 Playing Through Changes 4 Pgs.
01/18/77 Group 4 Dominant Type Chord Forms "Altered Dominants"
01/28/78 Extra Arpeggios for High Register
01/28/78 Dominant 7th Runs 8 Pgs.
02/09/78 Imitation and Melodic Patterns
03/24/78 More on Playing Through Changes (Basing Solo on Arpeggio Fragments)
03/28/78 The Melodic Minor Scale 2 Pgs.
04/01/78 Melodic Minor Sounds (runs) 8 Pgs.
04/07/78 Basing Your Solo on Condensed Arpeggios 10 Pgs.
04/15/78 mi7b5 Arpeggios, Scales & Chord Forms 2 Pgs.
05/01/78 The Blues: Harmonic Vocabulary and Progressions
05/22/78 Melodic Patterns (various) 11 Pgs.
05/25/78 Arpeggios
05/29/78 Melodic Patterns Repeated at the 4th
07/04/78 Blues Progressions
07/08/78 Melodic Patterns (specific intervals)
07/17/78 Chord Forms for Visualizing Scales, Arpeggios & Runs 3 Pgs.
08/18/78 Modern Chord Reference Page
08/30/78 Whole Tone Sounds - Using one structure at a time
09/03/78 Melodic Chord Streams ala George Van Eps 3 Pgs.
09/04/78 Harmonic Patterns Based on 6th Intervals
09/05/78 Harmonic Patterns Diatonic 4th or 5th Type
09/16/78 Melodic Chord Streams ala GVE
10/18/78 "Right-Hand" Chords
10/10/78 V7 I Progs. (org. by Melodic Considerations) Resolving from V7 which has a 13th on top Pg.1
11/19/78 V7 I Progs. (organized by Melodic Considerations)Resolving from V7 with #5 on top Pg .2-3
11/19/78 *Important Dom.7th Family Chord Voicings *(Rejected)
11/26/78 Locating the Tones in the Main Chord Forms 2 Pgs.
11/28/78 String Transference Chart (modern dom. Family nucleus voicings)
12/02/78 I IV II VI II V I Variations (organized Melodically)
12/08/78 Blues in F - Upper Register Modern Voicings
12/18/78 Modern Dom.7th Chord Forms Catalogue
12/27/78 Preliminary V7 I Resolutions (organized by Melodic Considerations) 3 Pgs.

1979

01/09/79 Progressions to Learn Dominant 7th Type Pg.3
01/09/79 Progressions to Learn Minor 7th Type
01/09/79 Learning the Basic m7 Chord Forms: iii7 vi7 ii7 V7 Imaj.7
01/09/79 Learning the Basic Dom7 Chord Forms: Imaj.7 VI7 II7 V7
01/09/79 Learning the Basic Chord Forms thru Various Progressions
01/15/79 Progressions to Learn Major Type Chord Forms Pg. 1&2
02/02/79 Outlining Modern Dominant Progs. Using 3 Note Voicings 2 Pgs.
02/02/79 More Progressions Using Modern Dominant Voicings
02/20/79 Pentatonic Melodic Patterns (asc. & desc.)
03/01/79 Learning Basic Chords for Comping, Chord Soloing or? 4 Pgs.

04/03/79 Progressions for Learning #11 Dominants (Overtone Dominants)
04/07/79 Chords for Chord Soloing & Comping - mi7th Type
04/08/79 Chords for Chord Soloing & Comping Dom. 7th Type & Dom. & Companion mi7th Exercises
04/27/79 Gospel Blues -Key of A
05/15/79 Turnarounds to Get from I7 to ii7
06/08/79 Turnarounds to Get from I7 to ii7 or II7
06/15/79 Visual Shapes for Learning Octave Style
07/28/79 Minor7 Family Runs
10/13/79 Minor Chords and Astronomy 10-13-79
10/14/79 Learning the Basic Chord Forms: Root in the Bass Voicings
12/10/79 Jazz Progressions Descending Bass - Small Texture

1980
01/24/80 Jazz Tags
02/28/80 Foundation Chords - Major 3 Pgs.
03/04/80 Minor 7th Type Chords for Comping & Chord Soloing
03/04/80 Dominant 7th Type (and companion minors)
03/04/80 Major 7th Type Chords
06/09/80 Chart of "Bass" Harmonization for Baroque Period
06/09/80 Beginning Counterpoint
07/07/80 Baroque Chord Progressions Contrapuntal Style 3 Pgs.
07/25/80 Pentatonic Practice Program
08/09/80 Romantic Harmony: vi6 (and friends) I Examples
08/30/80 Be-bop Lines
08/31/80 4 Note Melodic Fragments for Be-Bop Single Line Study
09/09/80 Ear Training & Progression Catalogue
09/15/80 Condensed List of Ear Training Progs/ (geared for jazz & pop)
09/16/80 20th Century Harmonic Vocabulary & Progressions - Diatonic Sounds
10/31/80 Baroque Progressions Using 1st Inversions
10/31/80 Successive 1st Inversion Triads: Progressions by Step
11/01/80 Harp Harmonic Forms on the Top 5 Strings: More Consonant Forms 3 Pgs.
11/01/80 Harp Harmonic Forms on the Top 5 Strings: More Dissonant Forms 2 Pgs.
11/09/80 Close Harmony Derived Voicings (organized by string group-bass up)
12/03/80 Position Playing on ii half dim.7 V7 alt. & i6
12/18/80 Baroque Melodic Tendencies - Organized Over Basses

1981
02/11/81 iii7 VI7 ii7 V7
02/20/81 BeBop Solos & Progressions
02/25/81 Melodizing Chord Progressions Primary Diatonic Treatment
06/04/81 "Meditation" #1 & #2
06/04/81 "All the Things You Are" /"Cherokee" #1 Chord Tone Outline
06/05/81 "Cherokee" #2 Chord Outtline
11/04/81 Foundation Chords - Dominant (unaltered)
11/05/81 Foundation Chords - Minor 7th

1982
03/08/82 ii7 V7 I Examples
03/25/82 Major Type Chord Forms - Melodically Grouped- Root in Bass Only
03/31/82 Minor 7th Type Chord Forms: Melodically Grouped - Root in Bass Only

07/01/82 Voicing Centers Applied to Common Progressions
07/11/82 Walking Bass & Walking Chords Guitar Style
07/21/82 Application of Harmonic Improvement Concepts
11/28/82 Progressions Derived From Triad Chord Streams and Harmonized Melodies
11/30/82 Harmonization - Studies in the Main 4 Ingredients: Color, Texture, Harmonic Rhythm, Register

1983
02/15/83 Cumulative Chord Learning: Forms from the 5th String Root
02/15/83 Cumulative Chord Learning: Forms from the 5th String Root - 4 Note Forms
03/14/83 Cumulative Chord Forms From the 6th String Root
03/22/83 Cumulative Chords - 4th String Root
03/28/83 Cumulative Chords Grouped by Color and Visuals
03/30/83 Diatonic Cycle of 4ths
05/10/83 Diatonic Harmonization through Counter Lines
05/21/83 Learning to Hear Dorian and Aeolian Melodies
06/07/83 Moving Lines for Added Beauty and Interest
06/26/83 Cumulative Chords 3rd in the Bass - from the 5th String
06/26/83 Cumulative Chords (Color and Visual Groupings) 1st Inversion from 5th String
06/29/83 Chord Forms by Soprano (and Bass) - One Top String at a time (3rd str. Soprano)
06/14/83 Harmonized Triads in 5 Tonalities (from light to dark)
07/31/83 Minor 7th Colors - Single String
08/03/83 Chord Forms: Cumulative Melody from the Bass up (minor 7th types)
08/03/83 Chord Forms by Soprano (and Bass) - One String at a time (2nd str, Soprano)
09/23/83 Chord Soloing with Chord Hearts (supplement to Pg.2)
09/28/83 Inner Hearing-The Visual Fingerboard
12/28/83 Ear Training Progressions 3 Pgs.

1984
02/22/84 I VI7 ii7 V7 & Friends on the Top 4 Strings
02/23/84 There are 12 Major Triads in Every Major Key
02/26/84 Cumulative Chords 3 Note Major Types -2nd String Anchor
02/28/84 Harmonic Vocabulary: Progression Study I ii Pg.1
02/29/84 Harmonic Vocabulary: Progression Study I ii and I iii ii Pg.2
03/01/84 Chord Progressions for Intro Pge of 6 String Root)Major Chord Forms)
03/04/84 Cumulative Chords - 6th String Root- Major Types - Memorize Layout 2 Pgs.
03/04/84 Cumulative Chords - 6th String Root - Sus. Types - Memorize Layout
03/06/84 Cumulative Chords - Dominant 7ths Group 1 Colors - 1st Inversions - 4th String
03/06/84 Cumulative Chords 3 Note Major & Minor Close Triads and Friends
03/11/84 Interval Layout and their Combinations - Middle Strings 5th String Root
03/11/84 Cumulative Chords - 5th Str. Root - Middle Stgs. Only- 4 Note - Bottom Notes Constant
03/12/84 Chord Progressions Using Middle 4 Strings - Root in the Bass Types
03/16/84 Interval Layout & Some Common Combinations - 6th String Root - No 1st String
04/01/84 3 Note Voicings - 5th String Root in the Bass 2 Pgs.
04/01/84 3 Note Voicings - 6th String Root in the Bass
04/29/84 Harmonic Vocabulary - Major Key Pg.1
05/01/84 Harmonic Vocabulary - Maj. Key Pg.3
05/01/84 3 Voice Major Triads - Soprano Organization
05/01/84 3 Voice Major Triad - Soprano Organization #2
05/01/84 3 Note Triad Inversion Rows (Chord Streams)
05/02/84 Harmonic Vocabulary - Major Key Pg.2

05/02/84 Implied Triad Inversion Rows Through Intervals
05/02/84 3 Note Triad Inversion Rows - One String Set at a Time - Sop. Org.
05/03/84 Intervals Used in Implied Triads - Soprano Organization
05/03/84 Intervals Used in Implied Maj. Triads - Bass Organization
05/06/84 3 Note Triad Inversion Rows - Minor
05/08/84 Low End Mi. 7th Syst. Inv. & Friends 4
05/09/84 Low-End Dim.7th Syst. Inv. & Friends
05/09/84 Low-End Dom. 7th Syst. Invs. & Friends
05/11/84 Low-End Mi.7b5 Voicings : Syst. Inv. & Friends
05/12/84 2nd Set of Low-End Maj.6 Voicings Syst. Inv. & Friends
05/12/84 2nd Set of Low End Dom.7th Syst. Inv. & Friends
05/12/84 2nd Set of Low-End Dom. 7th Syst. Inv. & Friends
05/20/84 Low-End Mi.6th Voicings Syst. Invs. & Friends
05/29/84 III7 VI7 II7 V7 - Top 4 Strings
06/12/84 2nd Set of Low-End Mi.6th Syst. Invs. & Friends
06/12/84 2nd Set of Low End Mi7b5 Syst. Inv. & Friends
06/12/84 2nd Set of Low End Dim.7th Syst. Inv. & Friends
07/14/84 Major Triad Voice Leading: IIV V
07/14/84 Harmonic Vocabulary - Major Key Pg.4
07/18/84 Harmonic Vocabulary - Major Key Pg.5
09/01/84 Introductory Page for Root in the Bass Chord Forms from the 6th String
09/08/84 Harmonic Vocabulary Pgs. 6-8
09/08/84 3 Note Minor Triad Inversion Rows - One String at a Time - Sop. Org.
09/12/84 I IV & V Connecting 3 Voices - Ascending Stepwise 1 to 1 Melodies
09/15/84 Mixolydian Chord Progressions for taping
09/15/84 Diatonic Major Scale Chord Progs. for taping
09/15/84 Diatonic 4ths I vi7 ii7 (I7) V7 Ascending Diat. Melody Stepwise 2 Pgs.
09/15/84 Beginning Progressions to Apply to Cumulative Chords
09/16/84 Stepwise Diat. Bass Harmonization (via diat. Flavors)
09/28/84 Introductory Page for 3rd in the Bass Chord Forms
09/29/84 Introductory Page for 5th in the Bass Chord Forms
10/17/84 String Crossing with Diat. Chord Scales - Maj. Key 4 Note 7th Chords
10/17/84 V-4 String Crossing with Diat. Chord Scales - Maj. Key 4 Note 7th Chords Pg.3
10/20/84 Applying minor 9 Chords in Desc. (from root) Line Progressions
10/28/84 Harmonization: 1st Phrase of "There Will Never Be Another You" 2 Pgs.
10/31/84 IV I in Open Triads - Ascending Chain
10/31/84 IV I in Open Triads - Descending Chains

1985

01/23/85 Maj. Pentatonic: 2 Voices Sounding Like 3 - 2 Positions at a Time 2 Pgs.
01/23/85 2 Note Pentatonic w/Dots and Ties in the Soprano
01/24/85 Maj. Pentatonic: 2 to 1 Soprano Line in 2 Non-Adjacent Positions for Full Range Tone & Vision
01/25/85 2 Note Pentatonic w/Dots and Ties in the Lower Voice
01/27/85 2 Voice - 2 to 1 Soprano Weaving Through Adjacent Positions 4 Pgs.
02/21/85 Light Colors: Diat. Major Key - Upper Register Opening & Expanding Thickness Gradually
02/23/85 Harmonizing Melodic 3rd Intervals: Using IV or V7sus4 Types to Begin
02/26/85 Harmonizing 3rd Interval-Oriented Melodies w/"Triads & Basses" (consonant Maj. Polychords)
03/02/85 V-2 Syst. Inv. Learning mi7b5 via Chord Transformation 4 Pgs.
03/02/85 V-2 mi7b5 Chords on the Bottom & Middle Strings
03/02/85 V-2 mi7b5 Chord Streams on All 3 Sets

03/02/85 V-2 Mi.7b5 Chords Middle & Top Strings
03/13/85 Diat. Major Harmony: Asc. Bass Starting from Various I's (2 to 1 melody) Pg.1
03/14/85 Diat. Major Harmony: Asc. Bass Starting from Various :ii's (2 to 1 melody) Pg.2
03/26/85 Neo Baroque Descending Bass Progs. Diat. Bass & Chord Colors 2 Pgs.
04/04/85 4 Note Pentatonic Chord Scales - Top 4 Strings 2 Pgs.
04/04/85 4 Note Pentatonic - Top Strs. 2 to 1 Textures via Neighbor Tones
04/20/85 Walking Chord Blues
04/21/85 Varying Harmonic Rhythm Under a Melodic Pattern
04/27/85 Harmonized blues melodies (1 to 1)
05/03/85 2 to 1 Diat. Asc. Stepwise Bass Motion w/Delayed Ent. as the Generator of the Harmony 2 Pgs.
05/05/85 Ear Training, Chord Progs. & Broken Chord Texture (right hand) 2 Pgs.
05/07/85 'Night Wes
05/08/85 V-2 dim.7 Forms - Introduction & Progression Application
05/26/85 Diat. Harmonization of a 3 Note Theme: Frozen Notes Underneath
05/27/85 Learning the 8 Note Dominant Scale in ii7 V7 I Runs (area 3)
05/28/85 Ascending Melodic Fragments (area 1)
05/28/85 Ascending - area 2
05/28/85 Ascending - area 3
05/29/85 Descending Melodic Fragments (area 1)
05/29/85 Descending - area 2
05/29/85 Descending - area 3
05/29/85 Ascending - area 4
05/31/85 Descending - area 4
06/14/85 Establishing a Major Tonality: Diatonic Colors I IV
06/16/85 Basic Minor 7th Type Chords (& their Intervals) from the 5th & 6th Str. Root
07/05/85 R35 Triads & 7R3 7th Chords (in Short Melodic Phrases): Diat. Maj. Key - Top 3 Strs.
07/05/85 5R3 Triads & 7 R 3 7th Chords: Diat. Maj. Key - Top 3 Strs. (in short phrases)
07/05/85 Phrases Using Diat. Maj. Key 1 5 7 3 Voicings
07/05/85 1 5 7 3 Diat. Maj. Key Voicings: String Crossing in Chord Scales
07/06/85 Diat. Maj. Key R35 and 7R3 Chord Scales
07/06/85 Diat. Maj. Key 5R3 and 7 R 3 Chord Scales
08/15/85 Approach Chord Blues (key of F)
08/15/85 Approach Chord Blues (Variation 1 - key of E)
08/15/85 Approach Chord Blues Variation 3 - key of F)
08/16/85 Dominant Approach Chord Catalogue for Blues &
08/16/85 Approach Chord Blues (Variation 2 - key of E)
08/17/85 Dominant Approach Chord Catalogue for Reference & Gradual Learning 6 Pgs. (Pg.4-6 Similar Outer Voice Motion)
08/20/85 Polyrhythmic Diatonic Triads in the Major Scale
08/21/85 Diatonic Triad Chord Scales 4 Pgs.
08/21/85 A Foggy Day - A Study in Color Choosing and Placement
08/23/85 Ear Training & Analysis List of (initial or semi initial) Intervals of Songs
08/25/85 Approach Chord Blues (key of C)
08/25/85 Blues Prog. Skeletons
08/25/85 Blues Progs. Skeletons (2nd set of strs.)
08/27/85 Approach Chord Blues (key of F)
08/28/85 Using Altered Dom. Chords from the 5th Str. Root
08/29/85 Triad Exercises in Minor Broken Chords (Right Hand Delays)
08/30/85 Using 3 Note Triads and 7th Chords in Short Phrases-Major Key
08/31/85 Diatonic Maj. Key: R 3 5 Triads and Pedals in Short Melodic Phrases

08/31/85 Diatonic Maj. Key Triads: R35 Triads (top 3 strs.) and Pedals in Short Melodic Phrases
08/31/85 Mixing Functions of Close Harmony 3 Note Maj. Extensions
08/31/85 Diat. Maj. Key: 1st Inv. Triads (3R5) and Pedals in Short Song-like Passages
09/01/85 Warm Harmonization of Diat. Maj. Scale Melodies or Approach Chords Studies
09/04/85 Chromatic & Semi-Chromatic Harmonization and Approach Chords Studies 6 Pgs.
09/09/85 Ear Training Progressions Organized by Soprano 6 Pgs.
09/15/85 Using R 3 7 3 Voicings (5th Str. Root) in Short Primarily Diat. Phrases
09/15/85 Pg.1 Mixing Chords with 6th String and 5th String Roots in the Diat. Cycle of 4ths
09/15/85 Pg.2 Mixing Chords with 6th & 5th Str. Roots: Linear Texture Through Rt. Hand Delays
09/15/85 Pg.3 Mixing 5th & 6th Str. Root Chords: Diat. Cycle Starting on IV
09/15/85 Pg.4 Mixing 6th & 5th Str. Root Chords: Diat. Cycle of 4ths from IV: Linear Texture thru Rt. Hand Delays
09/15/85 Combining 6th & 5th Str. Root in Short Progs
09/16/85 Basic Major & Dominant Type Chords (& their Intervals) from the 5th Str. Root
09/16/85 Combining 6th & 5th Str. Root Chords in Short Progs
09/17/85 Open Triads: Low-End Maj. & Mi. 1st Inv. 2 Pgs.
09/17/85 Open Triads: Low-End Maj. & Mi. 2nd Inv.
09/18/85 Using All 3 Open Triad Major Forms
09/18/85 Combining Low-End Open Triads in I IV Progressions
09/20/85 Low-End Open Triads: Using iii and vi
09/20/85 Low-End Open Triads: I IV iii I and I IV bIII I Chains
09/20/85 I ii Low-End Open Triads (w/some IV too)
09/20/85 Low-End Open Triads Using I IV w/Voice Leading
09/29/85 Using Low-End 1st Inversions in Diat. Chord Scale Derived Passages
09/29/85 Using 4 Note 1st Inv. Middle Strs
09/29/85 1st Inv. Maj. Triads with the Bass on the 5th String
09/30/85 R 5 3 Voicings from the Bottom String
10/02/85 1 5 7 3 Voicings on the Top 4 Strings
10/04/85 1 5 7 3 Voicings on the Middle Strings
10/04/85 1 5 7 3 Voicings on the Top & Middle Strings
10/11/85 1 5 7 3 Voicings on the Bottom 4 Strs.
10/27/85 Approach Chord Blues (key of Bb)
10/27/85 Approach Chord Blues Pg.2 (Variation - key of F)
10/29/85 Time Zone Blues (key of F)
10/29/85 Time Zone Blues (key of D)
11/07/85 Slow Blues Lines in Triplet Speed
11/28/85 Diat. Chord Progs. Pg.2
12/03/85 Minor Key: 2 to 1 Stepwise Asc. Bass Motion as the Main Generator of the Harmony
12/22/85 Getting Acquainted with Triads: Diat. Maj. Key Close Triads I through IV- 5 Pgs. Pg 1&2
12/23/85 Lazy Blues Chordal Style

1986
01/07/86 Diat. 6th and Inner Pedals Leading into 6th & Soprano Pedals (& other sounds for taste's sake)
01/08/86 Longer Phrases Using Diat. 6ths and Inner Pedals (& other sounds at end for variety)
01/10/86 More of Wes Blues
01/11/86 Using R 3 7 3 Diat. Maj. Scale Voicings in Short Phrases
01/11/86 I IV in Low-End Open Triads (w/some ii also)
01/11/86 Complete String Crossing w/Decorated Triads (Diat. Scale-wise Close /3 w/ 2 to 1 Soprano)
01/12/86 Decorated Triads: Diat. Maj. Key Close 1st Inv. w/ 2 to 1 Melody 3 Pgs.
01/15/86 Tonality Establishment and Modulation using Close 1st Inv.'s w/2to1 Soprano

01/19/86 Diatonic 4th Chords (Maj. Scale) as a Harmonic Device and a Means of Learning 4 Pgs.
01/20/86 Mixolydian Harmony and Melody
01/24/86 Approach Chord Concept - Overview via Constant Lower Voices
01/29/86 Major Scale Harmony & Melody: 1 to 1 1-29-86 01/25/86 V7 I in Diatonic 4th Chords: Melodic Moves From 1st Chord
01/25/86 Non-Diatonic Spicy Approach Chords "Constant Soprano Groupings" 5 Pgs.
02/08/86 Modern Dominant Flavored Blues
02/28/86 Advanced Approach Chord Based Material: "East Side Blues"
03/14/86 Jazz Single Texture - 2 Beats per Chord Pg. 1&2
03/30/86 I7 bVII7 bVI7 V7 Turnarounds (contrary motion) 2 Pgs.
04/02/86 Broken Chord Practice
04/09/86 Harmonization Studies for Intros, Endings, Interludes & Fills 2 Pgs
04/19/86 Uptown Blues
04/20/86 IV iii7 ii7 w/Contrary Motion Melody 4 Pgs. 4-20-86
04/20/86 Harmonic Improvement - VI iii7 ii7 w/Contrary Motion Melody 4 Pgs.
04/20/86 Harmonic Improvement - VI iii7 ii7 V7 I w/Contrary Motion Melody
04/24/86 Harmonic Tendencies & Common Progressions Pgs 1-2 4-24-86
05/29/86 Learning to Use Altered Dominants on One Degree At A Time 4 Pgs.
06/02/86 The Pentatonic Blues Scale 3 Pgs.
06/10/86 Jazz Single Texture - 2 Beats per Chord Pg. 3
07/25/86 High Register Dom.7th Type Chords - Root on Top - Group1 Colors Pg.1
07/26/86 High Register Dom.7the Type Chords- 5th on Top - Group 1 Colors Pg.2
07/26/86 High Register Group 1 Doms. In 12 Bar "I7 IV7 V7" Blues Pg.3
07/27/86 High Register Group 2 (sus4 or 11's) Type Dom. Colors - Root on Top Pg.4
07/27/86 High Register Group 2 to 1 Dom. Resolutions - Root on Top Pg.5
08/03/86 Dorian Tonality
08/03/86 Aeolian Tonality
08/06/86 Combining Diat. & "Extra-Diat." Colors (Heading in a subdominant direction) "Extra-Diat." Progressions
08/09/86 W/Beautiful Majors
09/19/86 Harmonic Tendencies & Common Progressions Pgs.3-4 9-19-86
09/20/86 Developing Fingerboard Sense in a Harmonic-Melodic Style
09/21/86 Intense Focus on Diatonic Maj. Key V7/R I/R 4 Pgs.
09/22/86 2 to 1 Soprano in Diat. Maj. Key V7/R I/R 2 Pgs.
09/30/86 Harm. Studies: Using V and iii to Catch the 5th Degree of the Key
10/01/86 Harmonization of Scale Step 1 via the IV Chord
10/01/86 Using V for the 2nd Degree
10/06/86 More Diatonic Major Key Voicings (and Progs. w/same)
10/07/86 Descending Progs. From 5/3/9 : Mainly Diat. Harmony - Diat. Melody
10/07/86 More Desc. Progs. Conceived From: The Bass, The Melody or Soprano, The Harmonic Tendencies
10/10/86 Getting Acquainted with Triads: Diat. Maj. Key Close Triads I through IV- 5 Pgs. (Pg.1a)
10/10/86 Getting Acquainted with Triads: Diat. Maj. Key Close Triads I through IV- 5 Pgs. (pg.4)
10/11/68 R 3 7 Voicings on the Top 3 Strs.
10/11/86 R 3 7 Voicings w/String Crossing
10/11/86 R 3 7 Voicings on the "High" Middle Strs.
10/11/86 R 3 7 Voicings on the "Low" Middle Strs.
10/12/86 R 5 3 7 Voicings on Both Normal Sets
10/12/86 R 5 3 7 Voicings from the 5th String
10/12/86 R 5 3 6 Voicings from the Bottom String

10/12/86 R 5 3 7 Voicings from the Bottom String
10/12/86 Long Open Triad String Crossing Passages
10/13/86 Diat. Maj. Key Triads and Soprano Pedal
10/13/86 R 5 3 7 with R 5 3 6 on Both Normal Sets
10/13/86 More R 5 3 6 and R 3 5 7 Studies
10/15/86 R 3 7 3 Voicings on the Top Strings
10/16/86 R 3 7 3 Voicings with String Crossing
10/16/86 R 5 3 Diat. Chord Scale Studies - Lower Set
10/16/86 R 5 3 Middle Strings: Chord Scale Studies
10/16/86 R 3 7 3 Voicings on the Middle Strings
10/16/86 R 5 3 on the Top Strings: Chord Scale Studies
11/15/86 Close 1st Inv. Triads w/Inner Voice Motion 2 to 1 - 5 Pgs.
12/23/86 Getting Acquainted with Triads: Diat. Maj. Key Close Triads I through IV- 5 Pgs. (pg.3)
12/16/86 Triad "Relocations" As Means of Learning the Fingerboard 3 Pgs.
12/30/86 Walking Chord Style Blues
12/31/86 Walking Chord "Gospel Style" Blues

1987
01/01/87 Expanded Diatonicism Using Maj. Add9 and mi. add9
01/04/87 Using Patterns for Intros, Interludes & Endings
01/07/87 Diatonic Scale Derived Passages I ii IV ii I in Close Triads 3 Pgs.
01/07/87 Open Triads: I ii IV ii I
01/21/87 A Taste of Tonality Types: Triads Over Bass Pedals Mainly
01/24/87 A Taste of Tonality Types: Triads Over Bass Pedals Mainly
02/04/87 Cumulative Chord Phrases Starting From IV 7/3/R Types
02/05/87 Chord Passages Starting From I 7/3/R Types
02/09/87 i7 bVI in Large Voicings
02/24/87 Overview of Some Friendly Low End Major Voicings (Geared to the Given Key) 4 Pgs.
03/14/87 Harp-like Right Hand Studies 8 Pgs.
03/15/87 16 Bar Blues w/Walking Bass: "Glued to the Blues"
03/17/87 Walking Bass Blues w/out IV in Bar 2 (key of D)
03/21/87 Harmonization of the 1st Phrase of "How High the Moon" Pg.1
03/29/87 (with)Darker Colors Pg.2
03/30/87 (with) Desc. Diat. Stepwise Bass w.2 to 1 Soprano Pg.3
03/30/87 (with) Diat. 4ths w/ 2 to 1 "Texture" or Harmonic Rhythm Pg.4
04/19/87 Learning R 4 7 5 ("3 Notes and a Skip") Diat. 4th Chords - Maj. Key
04/21/87 Diat. 4th Chords: R 4 7 9 Types - Middle Strs.
05/03/87 Blues with a Walking Bass: Approach Chords used to Harmonize a Riff
05/03/87 Top 4 Strs. Dom.7th Types: Root on Top - V7 to I as Learning Device
05/06/87 Walking Bass Blues w/out IV in Bar 2 (key of Bb)
05/08/87 3 Note Low End Chord Streams Type 1 mi7b5 (adj.str.) 2 Pgs.
05/08/87 Type 2 mi7b5 (adj. str.) 1 Pg.
05/08/87 Type 1 mi6 (adj. str.)
05/08/87 Type 2 mi6 (adj. str.)
05/10/87 Walking Bass Blues: inadvertently, a study in contrasts & right hand selectivity
05/12/87 R 4 7 9 Type 4th Chords on the Top Strs.
05/12/87 R 4 7 9 with String Crossing
05/13/87 4 Note Diat. 4th Chord Studies on the Top 4 Strs.
05/13/87 4 Note Diat. 4th Chord Studies on the Middle 4 Strs.
05/23/87 Variation on Key of E Page: Blues with a Walking Bass

05/24/87 Slow Blues w/Walking Bass and Melodically & Rhythmically Derived Theme
05/28/87 Soprano View of Low End Dominant Chords (3rd Str. on Top) 2 Pgs.
06/10/87 Developing Jazz Lines from Arpeggios" ii 1/2dim7 V7alt. .i6 2 Pgs.
06/13/87 Dorian and Aeolian 6ths w/Inner Pedals
06/18/87 Top 4 Strs. Doms. w/b9's Root on Top
06/21/87 I IV V with Consonant Polychords (or "slash chords") and friends
06/21/97 Developing Inner Harmonization Hearing: Targeting Each Note of the Scale 2 Pgs.
06/21/97 Developing Inner Harmonization Hearing: Targeting Each Note of the Scale 2 Pgs.
07/04/87 Developing Inner Harmonization Hearing: Targeting a root of the Maj. Scale as Soprano 2 Pgs.
08/12/87 Consonant Maj. Slash Chords: I IV V
08/31/87 Progressions Using Only R 3 5 9 & R 3 5 9 w/Others
09/28/87 Using 3 Note Chord Fragments & Chord Hearts in Common Progs.
09/29/87 Using 3 Note Voicings in Phrases w/Larger Chords
09/30/87 Small Voiced Mi7th Types in Semi-Chord Streams 2 Pgs.
09/30/87 String Crossing with 3 Note mi7 Types small voiced
09/30/87 String Crossing with 3 Note mi7 Types small voiced 3rd set
09/30/87 Small 3 Note mi7th Type Chord Voicings in Cumulative Chord Stream Phrases
09/30/87 Variations
10/12/87 Hearing Chord Progressions and their Basses 2 Pgs.
11/22/87 The Aeolian flavor

1988

01/13/88 Voicing Twins: Studies by Shape Affinity
04/22/88 Exercises for the Right Hand
04/24/88 Triad in I IV and V I Sequences within a Key 2 Pgs.
05/31/88 Top End Open Triad Diat. Cycle of 4ths
06/15/88 I IV's with Melodizing & Bell-like Rings
07/22/88 Advanced String Transference Studies - All 3 Sets of V-2
08/03/88 String Transference Studies: Bottom 4 Strings to Top 4 Strings
08/03/88 String Transference Studies: Top 4 to Bottom 4
08/08/88 Systematic Inversions "Staple Chords" Top 4 to Middle 4
08/10/88 Systematic Inversions "Staple Chords" Middle 4 to Lower 4
08/29/88 Cycles - (Overview)
09/03/88 Systematic Inversions "Staple Chords" - Bottom 4 to Top 4
09/30/88 Double Pick-Up Chord Walking Bass Blues 9-30-88
10/02/88 Diat. 4/3/4/4 4th Chords with Alternating Delay in Top 2 Voices 2 Pgs.
10/03/88 Integrating 4/3/4/4 Diat. 4th Chords into Other Settings
10/13/88 Hearing the Different Tonalities by Direct 'No Modes' Comparisons
10/25/88 The Blues Scale(s)
12/25/88 Guitar Solfege (The Inner Fingerboard) Pg.1
12/31/88 10th and Inner Pedal: 3 Note Baroque Harmony 2 Pgs.

1989

01/01/89 10ths and Contrary Motion or Stationary (Pedals or Sustained) Voices
01/02/89 Alternate Voice Leading - Cycle of 4ths Prog. Starting on the 2nd 1/2 of the Beat Pg.1
01/16/89 10ths and Inner Pedal: 3 Note Baroque Harmony
02/10/89 New Choice Voicings Course Top 4 Strs. Doms. w/Root on Top "Sus" Doms. W/b9
02/10/89 New Choice Voicings Course Middle 4 Strs. Dom. w/b9's Root on Top
02/10/89 New Choice Voicings Course Middle Strs. Dom. w/Root on Top - "Sus" Doms. W/b9's
02/11/89 Guitar Solfege Pg. 2

02/20/89 3 Note Close Harmony Major Extensions Used in Little Melodic Phrases
02/22/89 3 Note Chord Hearts: Major
03/01/89 Jazz Style Walking Chord Blues (Ab)
03/11/89 Major Chord Hearts Type 2
03/11/89 Major Chord Hearts Type 3
03/11/89 Learning the Fingerboard: Major Scale
03/12/89 3 Note Close Harmony Major Extensions 2 Pgs.
03/12/89 3 Note Close Harmony mi7 Extentions & Friends
03/14/89 New Choice Voicings Course ii7 V7 I: Using Doms. w/b9's Root on Top - Top 4 Strs.
03/20/89 Learning the Fingerboard: Mixolydian Scale
03/25/89 Baroque Counterpoint Top 2 Strs.(mainly) Pg.1 1-9-89 Pg. 2
03/25/89 Walking Bass Blues #2 Key of C
04/29/89 Chord Color - Adds, 2 Note Comping 2 Pgs.
05/04/89 New Choice Voicings Course Top 4 Strs. Dom.7 Types- Root on Top V7 to I Application
05/23/89 Learning 3 Note Open 1st Inv. Diat. Maj. Key Middle String Voicings
06/06/89 One Four
07/08/89 Cycle of 4ths Progression - 2 Bass Notes per Chord
07/11/89 Walking Chord Blues (key of E)
07/16/89 Neo-Baroque Counterpoint Colors
07/17/89 Introduction to Expanded Diatonicism: Extensions on bIII & bVII
07/20/89 3 Note Close Harmony Dominant Extensions
07/20/89 3 Note Close Harmony Dominant Extensions Top Set 2 Pgs.
07/20/89 3 Note Close Harmony Dominant Extensions 1st Series 2nd Set of Strings
07/20/89 "Old" Counterpoint Converted into Baroque Counterpoint
07/23/89 2 Voices Yielding 3 (or 4) via Ties
07/29/89 High Register Piano Voicings in ii7 V7 I Progressions
07/20/89 Jazz Walking Chords
08/08/89 Adding a Part to an Ascending Minor Scalewise Bass
08/16/89 Using "Slash Chords" in V7 I Type Applications
08/18/89 Minor Blues
08/20/89 Trills in Blues Triplet Runs
08/20/89 Freddie King Triplet Shuffle Run
08/30/89 Focusing on 3rds with 3,4, & 5 of the Key in the Soprano
09/03/89 Aeolian Colors with Pedal Tones
09/06/89 Mixing Minor & Major Triads in Minor Key Progressions
09/06/89 Tri-Level Chords and their Progressions: A Beginning
09/21/89 Power Bass Triads: List 1
09/24/89 Chord Hearts in ii7 V7 I (series 1 pg.2)
09/24/89 Chord Hearts & Blocks: ii7 V7 I Comping or Chord Soloing Series 1 pg.1
10/03/89 Bass Energized Triads in Harmonization of Ascending Maj. Scale: {5 6 7 & 8 degrees}
10/09/89 Walking Bass Jumpback Blues w/50s Ray Charlesish Theme
10/14/89 Power Bass Triads: Harmonizing 4 5 6 & 7 Soprano Tones of a Maj. Scale (Key)
10/24/89 Chord Prog. Vocab. (Key of E) Pg.1
10/28/89 Deep Into Mixolydian by Writing Melody, Creative Structure
10/29/89 Chord Prog. Vocab.(Key of A) Pg.1a
11/11/89 High Register Opening for ii7 V7 ii7 vi7 ii7 V7 I or III or VI
11/12/89 Triads and Bass Enhancement: Harmonizing A Long Scale Line- Beginning on the 4th Degree
11/12/89 Triads and Bass Enhancement: Harmonizing A Long Scale Line- Beginning on the 3rd Degree
11/12/89 Jazz Turnarounds: one-six-two-five 10 Pgs.
11/19/89 "V-4 Blues" 11-19-89

12/01/89 More Harmonization of 5 6 7 & 8 via Bass Enhanced Triads
12/14/89 Mixed Major Tonality bIII bVII IV I
12/17/89 Multi Tonal Major "Diat. Mixed Major" 2 Chords per Change
12/22/89 The Guitar Fingerboard: Learning the Layout through Scale Fragments
12/31/89 The Guitar Layout - Chord Twins

1990

01/90 Neo-Baroque Ascending Diatonic Bass Progressions
01/01/90 Secondary Dominants Pgs. 2&3
01/10/90 Long Diatonic Cycle of 4th Progression
01/15/90 Short Intros: Using Chord Scales (Diatonic Maj. Key)
01/16/90 Short Intros Using Modest Decoration
01/17/90 Short Intros Using Right Hand 'Delays'
01/20/90 Secondary Dominants in Common Progressions
02/06/90 Blues Scale (inc. 6 and b5) Run w/Slides (actually grace note slides)
02/23/90 Open Triad 2nd Inv. 2 Pgs.
03/19/90 Minor Key Progressions Generated by Chromatic Inner Voices
03/22/90 Using mi7b5 Types in iidim.7 V7 I Progressions: some favorites 2 Pgs.
03/22/90 Open Triad 1st Inversions
04/03/90 Alt. Voice Leading w/Open Triads in Diatonic Maj. Key Cycle of 4ths Prog. Pg.3 (4/4/90 Pg. 2)
04/25/90 Expanded Diatonic Colors: bIII & Friends as "Extra Diatonic Color" & Momentary New Keys
05/08/90 The Guitar Fingerboard: Learning the Layout thru Scale Fragments 3 Pgs.
05/08/90 Dorian Progs. For Taping
05/09/90 Aeolian Progressions for Taping
05/09/90 Harmonic Minor Progs. For Taping
07/31/90 The Guitar Fingerboard: Learning the Layout thru Song Fragments 3 Pgs.
08/17/90 Chicago Blues ala Jimmy Reed
08/30/90 Learning Baroque Minor Key Vocabulary Through Cycle of 4ths Prog.
09/02/90 Contemporary Bass Enhanced Triads in Expanded Diatonic Chord Prog : I IV bvii V (I)
09/08/90 Developing Facility with Low-End 3 Note 7th Chords
09/14/90 Neo-Baroque Contrapuntal Harmony: Mixing 7ths & Triads
10/10/90 Jazz Blues Runs in G - 7th Position
10/10/90 Gospel-Influenced Blues
10/16/90 Ear Training Studies: 7th Type Chords w/ their 3rd on Top
09/23/90 (& 12/25/90) One- Flat7-Five (or Four Dominant for an occasional spice)
11/15/90 Color Shifts (also to be called Changing Tonalities) In One Key at a Time
11/16/90 Ear Training Studies: 7th Type Chords w/5th on Top

1991

01/13/91 Wes-Type Chord Phrases
04/06/91 Ear Training & Harmonization: The Primary Colors Maj. Key or Dom.7th Key: for Dom. 7 type chords
04/17/91 Learning to Use 8 Note Dominant Scale Chords (1/2 - Whole)
05/02/91 Common Progs. For Taping, Ear Training & More: More use of bVII (& bVII Dom. now too)
05/05/91 Common Progs. For Taping, Ear Training & More: Using bIII as friend of iii
04/30/91 Common Chord Progs. For Taping & More: Using bVII to Expand the Sense of
03/05/91 Learning to Hear Major going to Minor (w/sus 4's thrown in to spice things us)
03/03/91 Learning to Hear V7b9
03/03/91 Learning to Hear dim.i dim6 (7), dim.iMaj7
07/14/91 Blues Runs Key of E - Lower Positions

08/28/91 Learning Harmony through Harmonization of Scale Lines: More Parallel Intervals w/Pedal Tones
08/28/91 Learning Harmony through Harmonizing Scale Lines: Mostly 6th Intervals & Pedal Tones
08/30/91 The II Maj. Chord in the Major Key

1992
01/05/92 Introduction to Diatonic 6th & Inner Pedals 2 Pgs.
01/05/92 Diatonic 6th and Inner Pedals: A Form of 'Sustained Scale' Technique
01/16/92 Jazz Turnarounds Based on Rhythmic Figures Mated to Common Progressions
04/17/92 Voice Leading as Helpful Tool & More
04/25/92 Harmonized Scales & More Using Open Triads (Low End)
05/09/92 New Diatonic Maj. Contrary Motion Progresions: 1 to 1 Motion in the Outer Voices
05/10/92 Ear Training Progressions: The Condensed List 2 Pgs.
05/10/92 Bass Ear Training Course
06/02/92 Bass Ear Training (Pg.2)
07/01/92 Application of Contemporary Harmonized Scales 2 Pgs.
07/11/92 Comping Vocabulary 3 Notes, Major Family General Overview
07/18/92 Understanding Voice Leading and Voice Splitting
08/09/92 Learning to Hear V 11th's & its Extensions 2pgs.
08/11/92 Progressions Through Voice Leading
08/17/92 The Major Scale: Learning to See & Hear the Harmonized Scale
11/08/92 Descending 5ths, Ascending 5ths and their Combination
12/31/92 String Transference - To the next Lower String Set

1993 - 2001
11/27/93 Turnarounds (a beginning) Key of G
04/13/95 Open Triads: Smoothest Voice Leading
05/08/98 Gapped 3rd Stacks: mi9 & its extensions with Favorable String Crossing (2-17-79)
12/30/01 Secondary V7 Chords Pg. 1

Ted Greene - Music Studies by Category

Fundamentals
Chord Construction Formulas (last dated 5-26-74)
Intervals 4 Pgs. 9-1,2-74
Musical Priorities 5-25-76
Triad Spelling 2-9-75
Tonality 6 Pgs. 5-28-76 thru 5-30-76
Musical Goals and Necessary Areas of Study 5-31-76
Learning the Names of Notes on the Fingerboard 2 Pgs. 5-30, 31-76
Fundamentals 8-17-77

Learning the Guitar Fingerboard
And The Related Triads and Maj. 7 Chords 6-5-73
The 5 Main Areas of the Fingerboard 8-25-77
Developing Fingerboard Sense in a Harmonic-Melodic Style 9-20-86
The Guitar Layout - The Fingerboard as Friend 1-5-88
Voicing Twins: Studies by Shape Affinity 1-13-88
Major Scale 3-11-89
Mixolydian Scale 3-20-89
The Guitar Layout - Chord Twins 12-31-89
Learning the Layout thru Scale Fragments 3 Pgs. 12-22-89, 4/29 & 5/8-90
Learning the Layout thru Song Fragments 3 Pgs. 7-16,20,31-90

Guitar Mechanics
Chords for Stretching the Hand 11-2-74
Exercises for the Right Hand (and the left a little) 4-22-88
Developing Facility with Low-End 3 Note 7th Chords 9-8-90

Triad Diagonals
Learning the Fingerboard through the 3 Triad Diagnols 2 Pgs. 8-31-89
Mixing Minor & Major Triads in Minor Key Chord Progressions 9-6-89
Triad Conversion: Close to open

Harp-Like Right Hand Studies
"Right-Hand" Chords (6-30-76) 10-18-78
Harp-Like Rt. Hand Study w/ Symmetrical Root Progs. In V-2 Dom. 7ths Top 4 Strs. Pg.2 3-6-89
Harp-Like Rt. Hand w/Symmetrical Dom. Progs. : V-2 Top Strs. Pg.1 3-14-87
Harp-Like Rt. Hand Study w/ Symmetrical Root Progs. In V-2 Dom. 7ths Middle 4 Strs. Pg.2 3-13-87
Middle Strs. V-2 Symmetric Dom. Progs.: Mi3rd Stuff Pg.3 3-13-87
Middle Strs. V-2 Symmetric Dom. Progs. Mi3rd & b5 Intervals 3-14-87
Top Strs. V-2 Symmetric Dominant Progs. Mi3rd Material Pg. 3 3-14-87
Top Strs. V-2 Symmetric Progs. Mi3rd & b5 Material Pg.4 3-14-87

Harp-Like Rt. Hand Study w/Symmetrical Dom. Progs. V-2 Middle Strs. Pg.1 3-14-87

Ear Training
Basic Chord Forms 5-13-75
Ear Training Exercises Pt.2 - Chord Progressions 5-18- 75
Basic Chord Progs. (for Ear Training) 5-19-75
Examples of I Chord Vamps 4-8-77
Ear Training & Progression Catalogue 9-9-80
Condensed List of Ear Tr. Progs. (Geared for Jazz & Pop) 9-15-80
Progressions Derived from: Triad Chord Streams & Harmonized Melodies 11-28-82
Inner Hearing - The Visual Fingerboard 9-28-83
Ear Training Progresions - Triads I V 12-28-83
I IV: Triads and Maj.7th Only 12-29-83
I and V Triad Progs. (inc. Sus 4's) 12-31-83
There are 12 Maj. Triads in Every Maj. Key (4-17-76) 2-23-84
Ear Training, Chord Progs. & Broken-Chord Texture (Rt. Hand) 2 Pgs. 5-5-85
Ear Training & Analysis List of (initial or semi-initial) Intervals of Songs 8-23-85
Triad Exercises in Minor Broken Chords (Rt. Hand Delays) 8-29-85
Using 3 Note Triads and 7th Chords in Short Phrases (Maj. Key) 8-30-85
Ear Training Progressions Organized by the Soprano Pg.1 9-7-85
Ear Training Progressions Organized by the Soprano w/Expanded Diatonicism (stage one) Pg.2 9-8-85
Ear Training Progressions Organized by the Soprano -Expanded Diatonicism (stage two) Pg. 3
Ear Tr. Sop. Org. Special Expanded Diat.: Lydian (&contrasting review) Pg. 4 9-8-85
Ear Tr. Prog. Sop. Org. Special Expanded Diat.: Lydian (&contrasting colors) 9-9-85
Ear Tr. Progs. Sop. Org. Special Expanded Diat. : Diminished 9-9-85
Developing Inner Harmonization Hearing: Targeting the Root of a Maj. Scale as the Sopr. 2 Pgs. 7-4-87
Developing Inner Harmonization Hearing: Targeting Each Note of the Scale 2 Pgs. 6-21-87
Hearing Chord Progs. And their Basses 2 Pgs. 10-12-87
Guitar Solfegge (the Inner Fingerboard) Pg.1 12-25-88 Pg.2 2-11-89
Ear Training Studies: 7th Type Chords w/ their 3rd on Top 10-16-90
Ear Training Studies: 7th Type Chords w/5th on Top 11-16-90
Learning to Hear dim.i, dim.6 (7), dim.iMaj7 3-3-91
Learning to Hear V7 3-3-91
Learning to Hear V7b9 3-3-91
Learning to Hear Major going to Minor (w/sus 4's thrown in to spice things us) 3-5-91
Ear Training Progressions: The Condensed List 2 Pgs. 5-10-92
Bass Ear Training Course 5-10-92
Bass Ear Training (Pg.2) 6-2-92
Ear Training Progs. Three-six-two-five 7-11-92
Learning to Hear V 11th's & its Extensions 2pgs. 8-9-92
Learning to Hear Minor 3-3-01

Tonality Types
Learning to Hear Dorian and Aeolian Melodies 5-31-83
Harmonized Triads in 5 Tonalities (from Light to Dark) 6-14-83
Establishing a Major Tonality : Diatonic Colors I IV 6-14-85
Diatonic Triad Chord Scales 4 Pgs. 8-20,21-85
Mixolydian Harmony & Melody 1-20-86
Dorian Tonality 8-3-86
Aeolian Tonality 8-3-86

A Taste of Tonality Types: Triads Over Bass Pedals Mainly 1-24-87
The Aeolian Flavor(s) 11-22-87
Hearing the Different Tonalities: by Direct 'No Modes' Comparisons 10-13-88
Aeolian Colors w/Pedal Tones 9-3-89
Mixed Major Tonality: bIII bVII IV I 12-14-89
Multi Tonal Major "Diatonically Mixed Major" 2 Chords per Change 12-17-89
Open Triad 2nd Inv. 2 Pgs. 2-23-90
Open Triad 1st Inversions 3-22-90
Aeolian Colors w/Pedal Tones 9-3-89
Dorian Progs. For Taping 5-8-90
Aeolian Progressions for Taping 5-9-90
Harmonic Minor Progs. For Taping 5-9-90

Tonality (sub-category)
Diatonic Maj. Scale Chords Progs. (for taping) 9-15-84
Mixolydian Chord Progs. (for taping) 9-15-84
Common Chord Progs. For Taping & More: Using bVII to Expand the Sense of Key 4-30-91
Common Chord Progs. For Taping & Ear Training: More use of bVII (& bVII Dom. Now too) 5-2-91
Common Chord Progs. For Taping & Ear Training: Using bIII as friend of iii 5-5-91

Tonality Types - Reference Sheets
Modes, Scales, Tonal Resources 1975
Other "Major Type" Tonalities 1-26-75
Tonality Types (Dealing more with Norms than Exceptions) 3-25-75
Tonal Centers of Different Types of Tonalities 3-11-75
Modern Tonality and Rhythm Types/Classical Tonality & Rhythm Types 4-21-75
Tonality and Rhythm Types (Organization for Improvisational Thinking) 5-3-75
Condensed Tonality Sheet 7-8-75
Tonality Types (Modulation & Tonality Transitions are Very Important) 2 Pgs. 10-10,12-75
General Harmonic Tendencies -Tonality Oriented 10-28-76

Chord Studies
Gapped 3rd Stacks: mi9 & it's extensions with Favorable String Crossing (2-17-79) 5-8-98

Diminished Family Voicings:
Common Chord Progressions & Principles 12-29-74
Common Progressions & Principles - Dim7 Chords (12-29-74) 1-19-75
Dim.7 Family Voicings (all listed on C) 1,2 -75
Using mi7b5 Types in iidim.7 V7 I Progressions: some favorites 2 Pgs. 3-22-90

Chord Function Color by Color:
The II Maj. Chord in the Major Key 8-30-91
Color Shifts (also to be called Changing Tonalities) In One Key at a Time 11-15-90
Chord Color -Adds, 2 Note Comping 2 Pgs. 4-28,29-89
A Foggy Day- A Study in Color Choosing and Placement 8-21-85
Ear Training & Harmonization: The Primary Colors - Maj. Key (One,Four & Five) 4-6-91

Favorable Matings:
Favorable Matings of Quality (Chord Ext. & such) & Degree (of the key) Maj. Or Dom. 7th Key:

For Dom.7 Type Chords - 6-18-90
Progressions for Learning #11 Dominants (Overtone Dominants) 4-3-79
Learning to Use Altered Dominants on One Degree At A Time 4 Pgs. 5-27,28,29-86

Descending Progressions:
Descending Progs. From 5/3/9 : Mainly Diat. Harmony - Diat. Melody 10-7-8
More Desc. Progs. Conceived From: The Bass, Melody or Soprano, The Harmonic Tendencies 10-7-86
Desc. 5ths, Ascending 5ths and their Combination 11-8-92
Applying mi/9 Chords in Desc. (from Root) Line Progressions 10-20-8?

High Register Voicings and Progressions:
High Register Piano Voicings in ii7 V7 I Progressions 7-29-89
High Register Opening for ii7 V7 ii7 vi7 ii7 V7 I or III or VI 11-11-89

New Secondary Dominants:
Secondary V7 Chords (also called Secondary Dominants) Pg.1 12-30-01
(The Principle: Many Chords can be Preceeded with their OWN V)
Secondary Dominants Pgs.2 & 3 1-1-90
Secondary Dominants in Common Progressions 1-20-90

Individual Chord Studies:
Variations on I vi ii V 2 pgs. 10/20-21/74
Non Diatonic V7 I Progressions 10/21/76
Successive 1st Inversion Triads: Progressions by Step (6/24/80) 10/31/80
iii7 VI7 ii7 V7 2-11-81
Progressions in 3 or 4 Voices 5/18/83
Dissonant Turnarounds: III7 VI7 II7 V7 - Top 4 Strings 5/29/84
Applying m9 Chords in Descending (from root) Line Progressions 10/20/84
IV I in Open Triads- Ascending Chain 10/31/84
i7 bVI in Large Voicings 2 Pgs. 2/8,9/87
Using 3 Note Voicings in Phrases with Larger Chords 9/29/87
Triads in "I IV" and "V I" Sequences Within a Key 2 Pgs. 4-24-88
One Four 6/6/89
Minor Key Progressions Generated by Chromatic Inner Voices 3/19/00

Aggregate Chord Exposure Program
Modern Chords - Condensed List 12/31/74
Chord Reference Charts and the Nucleus Concept 5 Pgs. 10/11/74 thru 5/28/76
Modern Chord Reference Page (1/11/75) 8/18/78

Approach Chord Concept and Catalogue
Diatonic 4ths I vi7 ii7 (I7) V7 Ascending Diatonic Melody (Stepwise) 2Pgs. 9/1,15/84
Dominant Approach Chord Catalogue for Blues & 8-16-85
Dominant Approach Chord Catalogue for Reference & Gradual Learning 6 Pgs. 8/17/85
Dom Approach Chord Catalogue for Reference & Gradual Learning Pg.4-6 Similar Outer Voice Motion
Diatonic 4th Chords (Maj. Scale) as a Harmonic Device and a Means of Learning 4 Pgs. 1/19/86
Non-Diatonic Spicy Approach Chords "Constant Soprano Groupings" 5 Pgs. 1/24,25/86
Approach Chord Concept - Overview via Constant Lower Voices 1/24/86
V7 I in Diatonic 4th Chords: Melodic Moves From 1st Chord 12/7/86

Bass Enhanced Triads
I IV V with Consonant Polychords (or "slash chords") and friends 6/21/87
Consonant Maj. Slash Chords: I IV V 8/12/87
Using "Slash Chords" in V7 I Type Applications 8/16/89
Tri-Level Chords and their Progressions: A Beginning 9/6/89
Power Bass Triads: List 1 9/21/89
Bass Energized Triads in Harmonization of Ascending Maj. Scale: {5 6 7 & 8 degrees} 10/3/89
Power Bass Triads: Harmonizing 4 5 6 & 7 Soprano Tones of a Maj. Scale (Key) 10/14/89
Triads and Bass Enhancement: Harmonizing A Long Scale Line- Beginning on the 4th Degree 11/12/89
Triads and Bass Enhancement: Harmonizing A Long Scale Line- Beginning on the 3rd Degree 11/12/89
More Harmonization of 5 6 7 & 8 via Bass Enhanced Triads 12/1/89
Contemporary Bass Enhanced Triads in Expanded Diatonic Chord Prog.: I IV Bvii V (I) 9/2/90

Choice Voicings Course (old course)
High Register Dom.7th Type Chords - Root on Top - Group1 Colors Pg.1 7/25/86
High Register Dom.7the Type Chords- 5th on Top - Group 1 Colors Pg.2 7/26/86
High Register Group 1 Dominants In 12 Bar "I7 IV7 V7" Blues Pg.3 7/26/86
High Register Group 2 (sus4 or 11's) Type Dom. Colors - Root on Top Pg.4 7/27/86
High Register Group 2 to 1 Dom. Resolutions - Root on Top Pg.5 7/27/86

New Course
Top 4 Strings Dominant7th Types: Root on Top - V7 to I as Learning Device 5/3/87
Top 4 Strings Dominants w/b9's Root on Top 6/16/87
Top 4 Strings Dominants w/Root on Top "Sus" Doms. W/b9 2/10/89
Middle 4 Strings Dom. w/b9's Root on Top 2/10/89
Middle Strings Dom. w/Root on Top - "Sus" Doms. W/b9's 2/10/89
ii7 V7 I: Using Dominants w/b9's Root on Top - Top 4 Strs. 3/14/89
Top 4 Strings Dom.7 Types- Root on Top V7 to I Application 5/4/89

Chord Basics: Progressions to Learn Chord Forms
Major Type Forms Pg. 1 & 2 1/5/79
Dominant 7th Type Pg.3 1/9/79
Minor 7th Type 1/9/79

Foundation Chords
Foundation Chords - Major Pg. 1-3 2/7,12,28/80
Foundation Chords - Dominant (unaltered) 11/4/81
Foundation Chords - Minor 7th 11/5/81
Essential Chords (Standard Inversions) 3 pgs. 11/15, 16/73
Modern Chords Grouped According to Bass Note 8/16/74
Learning the Basic m7 (and other) Chord Forms 1/7/79
Learning the Basic m7 Chord Forms: iii7 vi7 ii7 V7 Imaj.7
Learning the Basic Dom7 Chord Forms: Imaj.7 VI7 II7 V7
Learning the Basic Chord Forms thru Various Progressions

Chord Construction Formulas & Substitutions 10 Pgs. 11/16/73

Chord Construction Formulas (& Symbols)
Chord Construction Formulas (11-16-73) 1/31/74
Construction of Chords by Location & String Grouping 2 Pgs. 10/11,12/74

20th Century Harmonic Vocabulary 1/6/75 & 2/22/75
Chord Construction (Formulas) Last dated 5/26/76
Reference Page - Last dated 10/15/77
Dominant Family Tones Chart 10/16/77
Minor Chords and Astronomy 10/13/79
Chord Formulas 2/4/95

3 Note Chord Hearts and Chord Fragments
Using 3 Note Chord Fragments & Chord Hearts in Common Progressions 9/28/87
Small Voiced Mi7th Types in Semi-Chord Streams 2 Pgs. 9-30-87
String Crossing with 3 Note mi7 Types "small voiced" 9-30-87
String Crossing with 3 Note mi7 Types "small voiced" 3rd set 9-30/87
Variations 9-30-87
Small 3 Note mi7th Type Chord Voicings in Cumulative Chord Stream Phrases 9/30/87
3 Note Chord Hearts: Major 2/22/89
Major Chord Hearts Type 2 3/11/89
Major Chord Hearts Type 3 3/11/89
Chord Soloing with Chord Hearts (supplement to pg.2) 9-23-83
Chord Hearts in ii7 V7 I (series 1 pg.2) 9-24-89(?)
Chord Hearts & Blocks: ii7 V7 I Comping or Chord Soloing Series 1 pg.1 (last dated 9-24-89)

Chord Progressions
20th Century Harmonic Vocabulary & Progressions 10/21/76
vi7 (or I) II7 ii7 V7 (I) 3 Pgs 11/9/76
The Elements of Chord Progressions 2/14/77
I IV II VI II V I Variations (organized Melodically) 12/2/78
Turnarounds to Get from I7 to ii7 5/15/79
Turnarounds to Get from I7 to ii7 or II7 6/8/79

Voicing Centers
Voicing Reference Page (showing General Areas Only) 8/10/77
Applied to Common Progressions (8/10/77) 7/1/82

Chord Progressions Vocabulary
Harmonic Vocabulary: Progression Study I ii Pg.1 2/28/84
Harmonic Vocabulary: Progression Study I ii and I iii ii Pg.2 2/29/84
Using I/TR I/3 ii/3 Imaj.7 ii7 and Various I IV or Sus Dom V's in Short Phrases 8/31/85
Mixing Maj. Scale Ext. Primary Colors 8/31/85
Chord Progression Vocabulary (Key of E) Pg. 1 10/24/89
Chord Progression Vocabulary (Key of A) Pg.1a 10/29/89

Vocabulary Reference Page 4/27/74
Harmonic Vocabulary of Standard Tunes 5 pgs. 8/4,31/84

Melodic Chord Streams
Melodic Chord Streams (change of position w/connecting melodies) 9/27/75
7th Chord Melodic Chord Streams 9/30/75
Melodic Chord Streams ala George Van Eps 3 Pgs. 9/3/78
Melodizing Chord Progs. - Primarily Diatonic Treatment 2/25/81
Moving Lines for Added Beauty & Interest 6/7/83

3-Note Low End Chord Streams
Type1 m7b5's (adjacent strs.) 2pgs. 5/8/87
Type2 m7b5's (adjacent strs,) 1pg. 5/8/87
Type2 m6's (adjacent strs.) Pg.1 5/10/87
Type1 m6's (adjacent strs.) Pg.2

Chord Voicings Overview
Overview of Some Friendly Low End Major Voicings (Geared to any given key) 4 pgs. 2/22,24/87
Soprano View of Low End Dominant Chords (3rd String on top) 2 pgs. 5/28/87

Chord Voicings
Chord Voicings on the Top 4 Strings (level 1) 2/22/77
Chord Voicings on the Top 4 Strings (level 1) 2/26/77
Chord Voicings on the Middle 4 Strings (level 1) 2/26/77
Chord Voicings on the Middle 4 Strings (level 1) 5/4/77

Chords by Melody Note
Chord Forms for Chord Melody Playing (Level 1) 3 Pgs. 8-19-77
Major Type Chord Forms - Melodically Grouped - Root in the Bass Only 3-25-82
Minor 7th Type Chord Forms: Melodically Grouped - Root in the Bass Only 3-31-82
Chord Forms By Soprano (&Bass) - One Top String at a Time (3rd str. Soprano) 6-29-83
Chord Forms: Cumulative Melody From the Bass Up (maj. Types) 7-1-83
Chord Forms: Cumulative Melody From the Bass Up (minor 7th types) 8-3-83
Chord Forms by Soprano (&Bass) - One Top Str. At a Time (2nd str.Soprano) 8-3-83
Modern Chords Viewed from Melody 2 Pgs. 10-11,12-73
mi7 family (+ relative major) Viewed From Melody 10-12-73
Chords for Chord Melody Playing 5 Pgs. 4-20,21-74
Phrases in Chord Melody Style 7-9-76
I VI7 ii7 V7 & Friends on the top 4 Strs. 2-22-84
I IV's with Melodizing & Bell-like Rings 6-15-88
Melodic Chord Studies: One Flat7-Flat6-Five (or Four Dom/occasional spice) 2 pgs. 9-23-90 & 12-25-90

Comping
Small Chords for Group Playing 3 pgs. 2/1/77
Chords for Group (or Solo) Playing (on top 4 strings) 2 pgs. 2/2/77 & 3/9/77
Basic Chords for Low End Accompaniment 5/2/79
Comping Vocabulary - 3 Note-Major Family General Overview 7/11/92

Cumulative Chord Program #1
Locating the Tones in the Main Chord Forms 2 Pgs. 11-26-78
Cumulative Chords - 5th Str. Root- Middle Strs. Only - 4 Notes - Bottom Notes Constant 3-11-84
Interval Layout and their Combinations - Middle Strs. 5th Str. Root 3-11-84
Chord Progs. Using Middle 4 Strs. - Root in the Bass Types 3-12-84
Interval Layout & Some Common Combinations - 6th Str. Root - no 1st Str, 3-16-84
Beginning Prog. To Apply Cumulative Chords (2-2-84) 9-15-84
Basic Minor 7th Type Chords (& their Intervals) from the 5th & 6th Str. Root 6-16-85
Using Altered Dom. Chords from the 5th Str. Root 8-28-85
Combining 6th & 5th Str. Root in Short Progs. 9-15-85
Basic Major & Dominant Type Chords (& their Intervals) from the 5th Str. Root 9-16-85
Combining 6th & 5th Str. Root Chords in Short Progs. 9-16-85

Intense Focus on Diatonic Maj. Key V7/R I/R 4 Pgs. 9-21-86
2 to 1 Soprano in Diat. Maj. Key V7/R I/R 2 Pgs. 9-21,22-86
More Diatonic Major Key Voicings (and Progs. w/same) 10-6-86
Mixing in Upper Voices with the Basic Ones 1-1-88

Cumulative Chord Program #2
Learning the Basic Chord Forms: Root in the Bass Voicings 10-14-79
Cumulative Chord Learning: Forms from the 5th Str. Root (last dated 2-15-83)
Cumulative Chord Learning: Forms from the 5th Str. Root - 4 Note Forms (last dated 2-15-83)
Cumulative Chords: Forms from the 6th Str. Root 2 Pgs. (last dated 3-13,14-83)
Cumulative Chords - 4th Str. Root 3-22-83
Cumulative Chords: Grouped by Color & Visuals 3-28-83
Cumulative Chords: 3rd in the Bass - from the 5th Str. 6-26-83
Cumulative Chords (Color & Visual Grouping): 1st Inv. from the 5th Str. 6-26-83
Cumulative Chords 3 Note Major Types (2nd Str. Anchor) 2-26-84
Introductory Page for 3rd in the Bass Chord Forms (9-28-83) 2-29-84
Introductory Page for 5th in the Bass Chord Forms 2-29-84
Chord Progressions for Intro. Page of 6 Str. Root (Maj. Chord Forms) 3-1-84
Cumulative Chords - 6th Str.Root - Sus Types - Memorize Layout 3-4-84
Cumulative Chords - 6th Str. Root - Maj. Types - Memorize Layout 2 Pgs. 3-3,4-84
Cumulative Chords-Dom.7ths Group 1 Colors - 1st Inv. 4th Str. 3-6-84
Cumulative Chords 3 Note Major & Minor Close Triads & Friends 3-6-84
3 Note Voicings - 5th Str. Root in the Bass 2 Pgs. 4-1-84
3 Note Voicings - 6th Str. Root in the Bass 4-1-84
Introductory Page for Root in the Bass Chord Forms from the 6th Str. 9-1-84

Modern Chord Progressions
Modern Chord Progressions 12-17-73
Examples of Common (Maj. Key) Chord Progs. 1-11-75
More Variations on iii vi ii V 7-31-75
I (or iii)VI ii V - Variations Stemming from Different Types of VI's Pgs. 2&3 8-11,22--75
iii biii ii V (bii) Contrary Motion 2 Pgs. 8-6-75 & 9-20-75
III VI II V with Contrary Motion 2 Pgs. 10-17-75
Illustrations of Dom.7ths on All 12 Degrees in a Maj. Key 2 Ogs. 4-29,30-76
Progressions to Illustrate Different Types of II7 Chords 5-6-77
Root in the Bass iii7 VI7 ii7 V7 Progs. 8-8-77
Modern iii7 VI7 ii7 V7 Progs. 2 Pgs. 8-8,10-77
III7 (or I) VI7 II7 V7 10-2-77
bVII7 VI7 bVI7 V7 10-2-77
I (or iii Modern Voicings on iii7 VI7 ii7 V7 (8-8-77) 3-2-79
I bVI7 ii7 I 8-1-74
Most Common Chord Progs. & Harm. Principles Used in 20th Century Popular Music 4 Pgs. 12-28,29-74
Modern Chords 1-11-75
iii VI ii V Variations Consonant Style 9-14-75
Modern Chords in Common Progs. 5-16-76
Modern Chord Progressions 5-29-76
Longer Progs. Using Modern Chords 6-8-76
Modern Chords in Basic Chord Progs. 2-18-77
Modern Chord Reference Page (1-11-75) 8-18-78

Modern Chord Voicings (Dominant 7th)
Modern Chords in Common Progs. 5 Pgs. 5-16-76 thru 7-11-76
V7 I Prgogs. Resolving from V7 which has a 13th on top Pg.1 11-10-78
V7 I Progs. Resolving from V7 with #5 on top Pg.2-3 11-12,19-78
V7 I Progs. (organized by Melodic Considerations)
String Transference Chart (modern dom. Family nucleus voicings) 11-28-78
Preliminary V7 I Resolutions (organized by Melodic Considerations) 3 Pgs. 12-17,18,27-78
Modern Dom.7th Chord Forms Catalogue 12-18-78
*Important Dom.7th Family Chord Voicings Pg.1 11-9-78 Pg.2 11-19-78 *(Rejected)

Dominant 7th Studies
Standard Resolution of the Dominant 7th Chords 3-27-73
Some Resolutions of Modern Dominants to Tonics 10-2-73
Dominant 7th Sounds 9-9-74
Illustrations of Dom.7th's on all 12 Degrees in Maj. Keys 4-29-76

String Transference Studies
Advanced String Transference Studies - All 3 Sets of V-2 7-22-88
String Transference Studies: Bottom 4 Strings to Top 4 Strings 8-3-88
String Transference Studies: Top 4 to Bottom 4 8-3-88
Systematic Inversions "Staple Chords" Top 4 to Middle 4 8-8-88
Systematic Inversions "Staple Chords" Middle 4 to Lower 4 8-10-88
Systematic Inversions "Staple Chords" - Bottom 4 to Top 4 9-3-88
String Transference To the Next Lower String Set 12-31-92

Systematic Inversion Families 12/18/73
Systematic Inversions 5/5/76
Low End Mi. 7th Syst. Inv. & Friends 5-8-84
Low-End Dom. 7th Syst. Invs. & Friends 5-9-84
Low-End Maj.6th Voicings - Syst. Inv. & Friends 5-9-84
Low-End Dim.7th Syst. Inv. & Friends 5-9-84
Low-End Mi.7b5 Voicings: Syst. Inv. & Friends 5-11-84
2nd Set of Low-End Dom. 7th Syst. Inv. & Friends 5-12-84
2nd Set of Low-End Maj.6 Voicings Syst. Inv. & Friends 5-12-84
Low-End Mi.6th Voicings Syst. Invs. & Friends 5-20-84
2nd Set of Low End Mi7b5 Syst. Inv. & Friends 6-12-84
2nd Set of Low End Dim.7th Syst. Inv. & Friends 6-12-84
2nd Set of Low-End Mi.6th Syst. Invs. & Friends 6-12-84
Dim.7ths - Outside Strings Hook Up 6-12-84
V-2 Syst. Inv. Learning mi7b5 via Chord Transformation 4 Pgs. 3-1,2-85
V-2 Mi.7b5 Chords Middle & Top Strings 3-2-85
V-2 mi7b5 Chords on the Bottom & Middle Strings 3-2-85
V-2 mi7b5 Chord Streams on All 3 Sets 3-2-85
V-2 dim.7 Forms - Introduction & Progression Application 5-8-85

Triad Studies
Closed Voicing Triads 1973
Major Triad Fingerings 2-19-74
Triads in Root Position (with upper 3 voices in close pos.) 9-14-73
Sequences Using Root Pos., Close Pos. Triads 9-15-73

Triads in 1st Inversion 9-15-73
Triads in 2nd Inv. and Figured Bass 9-15-73

Harmony

Application of Harmonic Concepts
"Misty" Analysis 5-15-74
Phrases in Chord Melody Style (2-72) 7-9-76
The Technique of Diat. Harmonization (as derived from bass lines) 7-17-77
Different Chord MelodyTreatments of the 1st Phrase of "I'll Remember April" 12-2-77
Chord Melody - Various Treatments - Bridge of: "You Are the Sunshine of My Life" 3-16-78
Ear Training and Harmonizing Melodies (using "There Will Never Be Another You"1st Phrase) 2-26-79
"Here's That Rainy Day" - 1st Phrase w/Various Harmonizations 7-16-79
Warm Harmonization of Melodies with b7 / Approach Chord Studies 10-1-80
Reharmonization, Substitutions, & Counterlines 10-24-81
Application of Harmonic Improvement Concepts 7-21-82
Harmonization - Studies in the 4 Main Ingredients: Color, Texture, Harm. Rhythm, Register 11-30-82
Stepwise Diat. Bass Harmonization (via diat. Flavors) 9-16-84
Harmonization: 1st Phrase of "There Will Never Be Another You" 2 Pgs. 10-28-84
Harmonizing Melodic 3rd Intervals: Using IV or V7sus4 Types to Begin 2-23-85
Harmonizing 3rd Interval-Oriented Melodies w/"Triads & Basses" (consonant Maj. Polychords) 2-26-85
Diat. Major Harmony: Asc. Bass Starting from Various I's (2 to 1 melody) Pg. 1 3-13-85
Diat. Major Harmony: Asc. Bass Starting from Various :ii's Pg. 2 3-14-85
Varying Harmonic Rhythm Under a Melodic Pattern 4-21-85
2 to 1 Diat. Asc. Stepwise Bass Motion w/Delayed Entr. as the Generator of the Harmony 2 Pgs. 5-2,3-85
Diat. Harmonization of a 3 Note Theme: Frozen Notes Underneath 5-26-85
Warm Harmonization of Diat. Maj. Scale Melodies or Approach Chords Studies 9-1-85
Chromatic & Semi-Chromatic Harmonization and Approach Chords Studies 6 Pgs. 9-2,3,4-85
Minor Key: 2 to 1 Stepwise Asc. Bass Motion as the Main Generator of the Harmony 12-3-85
Major Scale Harmony & Meldoy: 1 to 1 1-29-86
Harmonization Studies for Intros, Endings, Interludes & Fills 2 Pgs. 4-9-86
Harmonization of the 1st Phrase of "How High the Moon" Pg.1 3-21-87
Darker Colors Pg.2 3-29-87
Desc. Diat. Stepwise Bass w.2 to 1 Soprano Pg.3 3-30-87
Diat. 4ths w/ 2 to 1 "Texture" or Harmonic Rhythm Pg. 4 3-30-87
Application of Contemporary Harmonized Scales 2 Pgs. 7-1-92

Harmonic Vocabulary Pt. 1
Harmonic Vocabulary - Major Key Pg. 1 4-29-84
3 Voice Major Triads - Soprano Organization 5-1-84
3 Note Triad Inversion Rows (Chord Streams) 5-1-84
3 Voice Major Triad - Soprano Organization #2 5-1-84
Harmonic Vocabulary - Major Key Pg. 2 5-2-84
3 Note Triad Inversion Rows -One String Set at a Time - Sop. Org. 5-2-84
3 Note Triad Inversion Rows - Minor 5-6-84
Harmonic Vocabulary - Maj. Key Pg. 3 7-6-84
Major Triad Voice Leading: IIV V 7-14-84
Harmonic Vocabulary - Major Key Pg. 4 7-14-84
Harmonic Vocabulary - Major Key Pgs. 5 7-18-84

3 Note Minor Triad Inversion Rows - One String at a Time - Sop. Org. 9-8-84
Harmonic Vocabulary Pgs.6-8 9-8-84
I IV & V Connecting 3 Voices - Ascending Stepwise 1 to 1 Melodies 9-12-84
IV I in Open Triads - Ascending Chains 10-31-84
IV I in Open Triads - Descending Chains 10-31-84
Close Harmony Derived Voicings (organized by str. group - bass up) 11-9-80

20th Century Harmonic Vocabulary and Progressions
Minor Key Vocab. Reference Page 6-11-74
Complete Normal Vocab. for 20th Cent. (Max Steiner) Sounds 11-26-74
Normal 18th & 19th Cent. Harmonic Vocab. (listed in keys of C and Ami) 2-22-75
20th Cent. Harm. Vocab. (1-6-75) 2-22-75
20th Cent. Harm. Vocab. & Progs. -Diatonic Sounds (10-21-76) 9-16-80

Harmonic Improvement
The Cross Cycle or b5 Substitution Principle (Harm. Impr. Pg.3) 2-20-75
Harmonic Improvement 7 Pgs. 6-2,5,6-76
Common Harmonic Improvement Concepts 10-14-79
Application of Harmonic Improvement Concepts 7-21-82
IV iii7 ii7 w/Contrary Motion Melody 4 Pgs. 4-20-86

Harmonic Tendencies and Common Progressions Pg. 1&2 4/24/86 Pg. 3&4 9/19/86

Early 20th Century Romantic Progressions - Chromatic Bass Line Voice Leading 9/19/77
20th Century Chord Progs. 1-18-75
20th Century Minor Key Chord Progs. 2-22-75
Classical & Romantic Progs. (11-8-75) 5-9-76
Romantic Chord Progressions 7-15-78
Romantic Harmony: vi6 (& friends) I Examples - Last Dated 8-9-80

Harmonization of Scale Lines
Learning Harm. Through Harmonization of Scale Lines: More Parallel Intervals w/Pedal Tones 8-28-91
Learning Harmony Through Harmonizing Scale Lines: Mostly 6th Intervals & Pedal Tones 8-28-91
Harmonized Scales & More using Open Triads (low-end) 4-25-92
The Maj. Scale: Learning to See & Hear the Harmonized Scale 8-17-92
IV and V in the Major Scale (undated)

Using Degrees of the Key
Harm. Studies: Using V and iii to Catch the 5th Degree of the Key 9-30-86
Harmonization of Scale Step 1 via the IV Chord 10-1-86
Using V for the 2nd Degree 10-1-86

Voice Leading
Voice Leading as Helpful Tool & more 4-17-92
Understanding Voice Leading and Voice Splitting 7-18-92
Progressions Through Voice Leading 8-11-92
Open Triads: Smoothest Voice Leading 4-13-95
Approach Chords into /R ii on top (contrary motion Soprano (splitting voice) 10-30-85
Using m7/R ii on top & m7b5/R as ii Chords (undated)

11 V7 I Harmonization Studies 3 Pgs. (4/30/87) 5/1,2/87

3 Note Close Harmony Extensions
3 Note Close Harmony Major Extensions Used in Little Melodic Phrases 2-20-89
3 Note Close Harmony Major Extensions 2 Pgs. 3-12-89
3 Note Close Harmony Dominant Extensions 7-20-89
3 Note Close Harmony Dominant Extensions Top Set 7-20-89
1st Series 2nd Set of Strings 7-24-89

Harmony Fundamentals
The Maj. Scale and the Foundations of Harmony 6-5-73
Non-Harmonic Tones 2 pgs. 9-16-73
Structures 10-22-73
Common Chord Progressions & Harmonic Principles 10-22-73
Understanding Chord Progressions 11-11-73
Modern Chords & Extensions 1-23-74
Theory of Chord Progression 2-17-74
Maj. Scales (cont.) 2-19-74
Maj. Scales (cont.) "rewritten" 2-19-74
Minor Scales 2-26-74
Drill Sheet 4-7-74
Why Study Chord Progressions in Minor Keys 8-3-74
Harmony or Theory? 9-7-74
Main Harmonic Resources 10-5-75
Fundamentals 2-17-77
Harmony: Basic Chord Types & their Uses 2 pgs. 10-30-77
Harmonic Minor Scale 2-12-78

Neo Baroque Counterpoint
Sampler of Some Uses of Harmonic Resources in Different Styles 11-13-75
Light Colors: Diat. Major Key - Upper Register Opening & Expanding Thickness Gradually 2-21-85
Neo Baroque Descending Bass Progs. Diat. Bass & Chord Colors 2 Pgs. 3-15,26-85
Neo-Baroque Counterpt. Colors 7-16-89
Neo Baroque Ascending Diat. Bass Progs. 0-1-90
Neo Baroque Contrapuntal Harmony: Mixing 7ths & Triads 9-14-90
String Crossing With 7ths and Triads (undated)

'Classical' Harmony for Guitar I IV V7 I Pg. 1&2 10/18/83
'Classical' Harmony for Guitar I IV V7 I - Pg. 3 Upper Close Triads w/added Bass Root 10/15/88

Baroque Counterpoint
Counterpoint Exercises -Imitation 7/21/78
Counterpoint Based on Harmonic Intervals from Bass (2/10/78) 8/16/78
Counterpoint Exercises Focusing on Bass in Motion (8/14/77) 8/25/78
Modern Counterpoint Studies 11/24/78
Counterpoint Exercises - Lower Voice Movement 2/23/79
Counterpoint Exercises - Motion in Alternative Voices (6/5/78) 12/31/79
Implied Triad Inversion Rows Through Intervals 5/2/84
Intervals Used in Implied Triads - Soprano Organization 5/3/84
Intervals Used in Implied Major Triads- Bass Organization 5/3/84

Application of 1 to 1 Counterpoint and Introduction to 2 to 1 5/22/85
Baroque Counterpoint and the Guitar Fingerboard 12/26/88
Baroque Counterpoint Top 2 Strings (mainly) Pg. 1 1/1/89 Pg. 2 3/25/89
Cycle of 4th Progressions - 2 Bass Notes per Chord 7/8/89
"Old" Counterpoint Converted into Baroque "Counterpoint" 7/20/89
2 Voices Yielding 3 (or 4) via Ties 7/23/89
Adding a Part to an Ascending Minor Scalewise Bass 8/8/89
Focusing on 3rds with with 3, 4, & 5 of the key in Soprano 8/30/89

Baroque Harmony
Understanding Chord Progs. (Pt.1 - Baroque) 2 Pgs. 11-11-73
Standard Resolutions of V7 to I (or i) 11-16-73
Bach Key Changes & Progs. 1-20-74
Voice Leading Reference Chart - 3 Note Triads 2-8,24-74
Some of the Most Common Chord Progs. In Baroque Major Harmony 6-12-74
Some of the Most Common Resolutions of V7 I 6-13-74
Some Ways to Make Music with Triad Chord Scales 9-26-74
ii7 V(7) I 2 Pgs. 11-28,29-74
Baroque Major Key Vocabulary 12-3-74
Baroque Minor Key Vocabulary 12-3-74
Exercises 12-4-74
Triads in 1st Inversion 12-7-74
Embellishing Tones, Broken Chords & Decoration 12-14-74
The Chromatic Scale 12-18-74
Progressions. Using 1st Inversions, Figured Bass 12-27-74
Catalogue of Common Baroque Harmonies and their Progressions 4-6-75
Voice Leading 2 Pgs. 1-8-75
Triads in 2nd Inversion 1-11-75
Baroque Modulation 1-13-75
Triad Spelling 2-9-75
Voice Leading Reference Charts (Triads Only) 3 Pgs 2-5-75 thru 4-27-75
Some Ways to Learn a Scale Fingering 2-8-75
Maj. Triad Voicings 2-9-75
Progs. Using 2nd Invs. 2-21-75
Phrases with Root Position Triads (Chorale Style) 3-8-75
Voice Leading and Parallelism on Guitar 2 Pgs. 3-9-75
Phrases with Inversions & Embellishing Tones (Chorale Style) 3-14-75
Short Phrases to Illustrate Diat. Chord Progs. 3-16-75
Seventh Chords 3-16,30-75
Summary of Diat. Chord Progs. In Baroque Harmony 3-24-75
Baroque Modulation Schemes 3-27-75
Cadences 3-29-75
Common Diat. Chord Progs. In Baroque Harmony 3-29-75
Baroque Practice Program 4-1-75
Exercises to Learn Triad Fingerings in Inversion Rows 4-17-75
Maj. And Mi. Scales, Chords, & Arpeggios 4-28-75
Secondary Dominants, Tonicization 5 Pgs. 5-15-75 thru 5-18-75 (7-1-75)
Secondary Dominants 7-1-75
Catalogue of Common Cycle of 4ths Patterns (inc. Secondary Doms.) 7-4,10-75
Bass View of Baroque Harmonic Vocabulary (12-3-74) 7-8-78

Examples of Progs. Using 1st Invs. (2-9-75) 8-8-75
Diatonic Cycles of 4ths 3 Pgs. 5-31-75 thru 8-9-75
Modulation 6 Pgs. 10-1,2,3,4,5-75
Cadential Bass Formulas 11-8-75
Open Triad Inversions 2-26-76
Progs. Using Open & Incomplete Triads (4 Notes - Root in Bass) 2-26-76
Study Areas (6-30-75) 3-4-76
Examples of Melody & Harmony Relationships in Minor Keys 3-5-76
Melody and Harmony Relationships in Minor Keys 3-5,12-76
Unusual Diat. Chords in Baroque Minor 3-6-76
Resolutions of V7b9 - i 3-19-76
Incomplete V7b9 - i (diminished triads to i) 3-20-76
Voice Switches 2 Pgs. 3-20-76
Common Baroque Harmonic Tendencies 7-8-78
Counterpoint Exercises (Maj. Key) 2 Pgs. 2-10-78 thru 8-16-78
Harmonic Patterns Using Root Pos. Close Triads (last dated - 5-3-79)
String Crosses Using Open Triads 2 Pgs. 12-19-79
Beginning Counterpoint 6-9-80
Chart of "Bass" Harmonization for Baroque Period 6-9-80
Baroque Chord Progs. Contrapuntal Style 3 Pgs.7-4,5,6,7-80
Baroque Progs. Using 1st Inversions (6-24-80) 10-31-80
Sample Solutions to "Fill-In" Page 11-30-80
Baroque Melodic Tendencies - Organized Over Basses 12-18-80
10ths and Contrary Motion or Stationary ("Pedals" or Sustained) Voices 1/1/89
10ths and Inner Pedal: 3 Note Baroque Harmony Pg. 1 12/31/88 Pg. 2 1/16/89

Cycles
Diat. Cycle of 4ths 3-30-83
Diat. Cycle of 4ths Pg. 2 (5-31-75) 8-9-75 Pg.3 8-9-75
Top End Open Triad Diat. Cycle of 4ths 5-31-88
Cycles - (Overview) 8-28-88
Alternate Voice Leading Cycle of 4ths Prog. Starting on the 2nd 1/2 of the Beat Pg.1 1-2-89
Long Diat. Cycle of 4ths Progs. 1-10-90
Alt. Voice Leading w/Open Triads in Diat. Maj. Key Cycle of 4ths Prog. Pg.2 4-4-90 Pg.3 4-3-90
Learning Baroque Minor Key Vocabulary Through Cycle of 4ths Prog. 8-30-90
Baroque Minor Key Cycle of 4ths Prog. : Triads, Prepared 7ths 9-23-90

Diatonic 4th Chords
Learning R 4 7 5 ("3 Notes and a Skip") Diat. 4th Chords - Maj. Key 4-19-87
Diat. 4th Chords: R 4 7 9 Types - Middle Strs. 4-21-87
R 4 7 9 Type 4th Chords on the Top Strs. 5-12-87
R 4 7 9 with String Crossing 5-12-87
4 Note Diat. 4th Chord Studies on the Top 4 Strs. 5-13-87
4 Note Diat. 4th Chord Studies on the Middle 4 Strs. 5-13-87
4 Note Diat. 4th Chord Studies on the Middle Strs. 5-15-87
Diat. 4/3/4/4 4th Chords with Alternating Delay in Top 2 Voices 2 Pgs. 10-2-88
Integrating 4/3/4/4 Diat. 4th Chords into Other Settings 10-3-88

Diatonic 6th and Inner Pedals
Diat. 6th and Inner Pedals Leading into 6th & Soprano Pedals (& other sounds for taste's sake) 1-7-86
Longer Phrases Using Diat. 6ths and Inner Pedals (& other sounds at end for variety) 1-8-86
Dorian and Aeolian 6ths w/Inner Pedals 6-13-87
Introduction to Diat. 6th & Inner Pedals 2 Pgs. 1-5-92
Diat. 6th and Inner Pedals: A Form of 'Sustained Scale' Technique 1-5-92

Diatonic Chord Scales and More
Phrases Using Diat. Maj. Key 1 5 7 3 Voicings 7-5-85
5 R 3 Triads & 7 R 3 7th Chords: Diat. Maj. Key - Top 3 Strs. (in short phrases) 7-5-85
1 5 7 3 Diat. Maj. Key Voicings: String Crossing in Chord Scales 7-5-85
Diat. Maj. Key 5 R 3 and 7 R 3 Chord Scales 7-6-85
Diatonic Maj. Key: R 3 5 Triads and Pedals in Short Melodic Phrases 8-31-85
Using R 3 7 3 Voicings (5th Str. Root) in Short Primarily Diat. Phrases 9-15-85
Pg. 1 Mixing Chords with 6th String and 5th String Roots in the Diat. Cycle of 4ths 9/15/85
Pg. 2 Mixing Chords with 6th & 5th Str. Roots: Linear Texture Through Rt. Hand Delays
Pg. 3 Mixing 5th & 6th Str. Root Chords: Diat. Cycle Starting on IV
Pg. 4 Mixing 6th & 5th Str. R Chords: Diat. Cycle of 4ths from IV: Linear Texture thru Rt. Hand Delays
R 5 3 Voicings from the Bottom String 9-30-85
1 5 7 3 Voicings on the Top 4 Strings 10-2-85
1 5 7 3 Voicings on the Middle Strings 10-4-85
1 5 7 3 Voicings on the Top & Middle Strings 10-4-85
15 7 3 Voicings on the Bottom 4 Strs. 10-11-85
Using R 3 7 3 Diat. Maj. Scale Voicings in Short Phrases 1-11-86
Using R 3 7 Diat. Maj. Scale Voicings in Medium Length Passages w/String Crosses for fluidity
Broken Chord Practice 4-2-86
R 3 7 Voicings on the Top 3 Strs. 10-11-86
R 3 7 Voicings w/String Crossing 10-11-86
R 3 7 Voicings on the "High" Middle Strs. 10-11-86
R 3 7 Voicings on the "Low" Middle Strs. 10-11-86
R 5 3 7 Voicings on Both Normal Sets 10-12-86
R 5 3 7 Voicings from the 5th String 10-12-86
R 5 3 6 Voicings from the Bottom String 10-12-86
R 5 3 7 Voicings from the Bottom String 10-12-86
R 5 3 7 with R 5 3 6 on Both Normal Sets 10-13-86
More R 5 3 6 and R 3 5 7 Studies
R 3 7 3 Voicings on the Top Strings 10-15-86
R 3 7 3 Voicings with String Crossing 10-16-86
R 5 3 Diat. Chord Scale Studies - Lower Set 10-16-86
R 5 3 Middle Strings: Chord Scale Studies 10-16-86
R 3 7 3 Voicings on the Middle Strings 10-16-86
R 5 3 on the Top Strings: Chord Scale Studies
Cumulative Chord Phrases Starting From IV 7/3/R Types 2-4-87
Chord Passages Starting From I 7/3/R Types 2-5-87

Diatonic Contrary Motion Studies
Contrary Motion Studies 7-13-77
Contrary Motion with Lots of 4th Chords 7-22-77
Diat. Contrary Lines with 2 to 1 Melody 9-11-77
Diat. Maj. Key Contrary Motion Sounds with a diversion at end 7-4-78

Stationary Voices & Moving Voices 5-22-79
Diatonic Harmonization Through Counter Lines 5-10-83
Contrary Motion into Modern Chords 5-10-83
(Harmonic Improvement) VI iii7 ii7 w/Contrary Motion Melody 4 Pgs. 4-20-86
Pg. 2 - VI iii7 ii7 V7 I
(New) Diat. (Maj.) Contrary Motion Progressions: 1 to 1 Motion in the Outer Voices 5-9-92

Old Diatonic Course
Harmonic Patterns - Diat. Maj. Key 4-29-76
Examples of Diat. Chord Scales in Maj. Keys 4-3-77
Forms for Building Diat. Chord Scales in Maj. Keys (5-5-76) 8-18-78
Diat. Chord Scales - Maj. Key 9-18-79
String Crossing with Diat. Chord Scales - Maj. Key 4 Note 7th Chords Pg.1 9-15-84 Pg.2 10-17-84
V-4 String Crossing with Diat. Chord Scales - Maj. Key 4 Note 7th Chords Pg.3 10-17-84
R35 Triads & 7R3 7th Chords (in Short Melodic Phrases): Diat. Maj. Key - Top 3 Strs. 7-5-85
Diat. Maj. Key R35 and 7R3 Chord Scales 7-6-85
Diatonic Maj. Key Triads: R35 Triads (top 3 strs.) and Pedals in Short Melodic Phrases 8-31-85
Mixing Functions of Close Harmony 3 Note Maj. Extensions 8-31-85
Diat. Maj. Key: 1st Inv. Triads (3R5) and Pedals in Short Song-like Passages 8-31-85
Combining Diat. & "Extra-Diat." Colors (Heading in a subdominant direction) 8-6-86
"Extra-Diat." Progrs. W/Beautiful Majors 8-9-86
Expanded Diatonic Colors: bIII & friends as "Extra-Diat. Color" & Momentary New Keys 4-25-90

Diatonic Major Key Harmony
Some iii vi ii V (I) Patterns 9-29-74
Diat. Chord Progs. Pg. 3 11-28-75
Diat. Triads and Pedals (Maj. Key) Pg.1 4-15-76
Diat. Sounds & Pedals (Maj. Key) Pg. 2 - 4 4-18,28-76
Chord Progs. (Diat. Maj. Scale Type) Cycle of 4ths I IV vii iii vi ii V I etc. Pg.1 10-1-77
Diat. Sequential & cycle Progression Catalogue (6-21-74) 12-4-83
Diat. Chord Progs. Pg. 2 11-28-85

Diatonic Scale Derived Passages
I and IV Small Triads with 2 to 1 Decoration 4-11-85
Open Triads: Low-End Maj. & Mi. 1st Inv. 2 pgs. 9-17-85
Open Triads: Low-End Maj. & Mi. 2nd Inv. 9-17-85
Using All 3 Open Triad Major Forms 9-18-85
Combining Low-End Open Triads in I IV Progressions 9-18-85
Low-End Open Triads: Using iii and vi 9-20-85
Low-End Open Triads: I IV iii I and I IV bIII I Chains 9-20-85
I ii Low-End Open Triads (w/some IV too) 9-20-85
Low-End Open Triads Using I IV w/Voice Leading 9-20-85
Using Low-End 1st Inversions in Diat. Chord Scale Derived Passages 9-29-85
Using 4 Note 1st Inv. Middle Strs. 9-29-85
1st Inv. Maj. Triads with the Bass on the 5th String 9-29-85
I IV in Low-End Open Triads (w/some ii also) 1-11-86
Decorated Triads: Diat. Maj. Key Close 1st Inv. w/ 2 to 1 Melody 3 Pgs. 1-11,12-86
Complete String Crossing w/Decorated Triads (Diat. Scale-wise Close /3 w/ 2 to 1 Soprano) 1-11-86
Tonality Establishment and Modulation using Close 1st Inv.'s w/2to1 Soprano 1-15-86
Getting Acquainted with Triads: Diat. Maj. Key Close Triads I through IV- 5 Pgs.(12/22/85) 10/10/86

Long Open Triad String Crossing Passages 10-12-86
Diat. Maj. Key Triads and Soprano Pedal 10-13-86
Close 1st Inv. Triads w/Inner Voice Motion 2 to 1 - 5 Pgs. 11-15-86
Triad "Relocations" As Means of Learning the Fingerboard 3 Pgs. -12-16-86
Open Triads: I ii IV ii I 1-7-87
I ii IV ii I in Close Triads 3 Pgs. 1-7-87
Learning 3 Note Open 1st Inv. Diat. Maj. Key Middle String Voicings 5-23-89

Expanded Diatonicism
Examples Using Add9th Chords in I bVI IV II V 7-17-77
Using Maj. Add9 and mi. add9 1-1-87
Progressions Using Only R 3 5 9 & R 3 5 9 w/Others 8-31-87
Introduction to Expanded Diatonicism: Extensions on bIII & bVII 7-17-89
Multi-Tonal Maj. Key Colors: "Diatonic Mixtures" or "Mixed Majors" (7-19-78) 12-17-89
Common Progs. For Taping, Ear Training & More: Using bIII as friend of iii 5-5-91
Common Progs. For Taping, Ear Training & More: More use of bVII (&bVII Dominant now too) 5-2-91

Modulation
Diatonic Modulation 5-1-73
Other Modulations 5-1-73
Modulations & Temporary Modulations 9-17-73
Tonicization (Secondary Dominants) 10-22-73
Modulation & Tonicization 10-23-73
Modulation (using bvii, bIII7, mi6) as Pivot 2-14-74
Modulation Types 11-5-74
Impressionistic Harmonic Tendencies (& Modulation) 2-25, 3-23- 75
Examples of Modulation (from Mozart to Beethoven to Max Steiner Types) 4-8-75
20th Century Modulation 4-29-75
Choice Impressionistic Harmonic Tendencies 5-23-75
Modulation Practice Patterns 12-8-75
Good (Modulating) Progressions in Classical or Romantic Style 3-10,19-76
Modulation (to new I's or other chords in key) 4-8-76
Melodic Continuity as Applied to Modulations up a Maj. 3rd 9-2-76

Mainly Through ii7 V7
Practice Patterns to Learn Chord Forms 3-20-77
Application of Basic Chord Forms in Progressions 3-14-83

Harp Harmonics
Harp-Harmonic Technique 2-3-77
Harp-Harmonic Technique (Sustained Scales) Series-1 3 Pgs. 8-27-79
Harp Harmonic Technique Bottom 5 Strs. (Pg.2) 6-28-78
Harp-Harmonic Technique ala Lenny & Chet 10-14-78
Harp-Harmonic Forms on the Top 5 Strs. More Consonant Forms 3 Pgs.11-1,24-80 & 12-7-80
Harp-Harmonic Forms on the Top 5 Strs. More Dissonant Forms 2 Pgs. 11-1,24-80

Harp-Like Chords/Chimes
Harp-Like Chords Mi.6's 9-21-75
Chord Progressions For Using Chimes 2-17,18-79
Chord Voicings for Chimes 10-28-78

Pentatonic Studies
Pentatonic Chords Pg.2 9-8-74
Pentatonic Practice Program 7-25-80
2 Note Pentatonic w/Dots and Ties in the Soprano 1-23-85
Maj. Pentatonic: 2 Voices Sounding Like 3 - 2 Positions at a Time 2 Pgs. 1-23-85
Maj. Pentatonic: 2 to 1 Soprano Line in 2 Non-Adjacent Positions for Full Range Tone & Vision 1-24-85
2 Note Pentatonic w/Dots and Ties in the Lower Voice 1-25-85
2 Voice - 2 to 1 Soprano Weaving Through Adjacent Positions 4 Pgs. 1-26,27-85
4 Note Pentatonic Chord Scales - Top 4 Strings Pg.1- 3-30-85 Pg.2 - 4-4-85
4 Note Pentatonic - Top Strs. 2 to 1 Textures via Neighbor Tones 4-4-85

Whole Tone Studies
Whole Tone Modulations 11-26-74
Whole Tone (pg.2) includes permutations of whole tone scale 11-27-74
Whole Tone Derived Chords 1-24-77
Whole Tone Sounds - using one structure at a time 8-30-78

Blues

Beginning Blues Runs & Scales
The Pentatonic Blues Scale 3 Pgs. 5-30-86, 6-2-86
The Blues Scale(s) 10-25-88
Blues Scale (inc. 6 and b5) Run w/Slides (actually grace note slides) 2-6-90
Jazz Blues Runs in G - 7th Pos. 10-10-90
Blues Runs Key of E - Lower Positions 7-14-91
Approach Chords
Approach Chord Blues (key of F) 8-15-85
Approach Chord Blues (Variation 1 - key of E) 8-15-85
Approach Chord Blues Variation 3 - key of F) 8-15-85
Approach Chord Blues (Variation 2 - key of E) 8-16-85
Approach Chord Blues (key of C) 8-25-85
Approach Chord Blues (key of Bb) 10-27-85
Approach Chord Blues Pg.2 (Variation - key of F) 10-27-85
Advanced Approach Chord Based Material: "East Side Blues" 2-28-86
Approach Chord Blues (key of F) 10/27/87
Jumpback Blues 4-19-88
Minor Blues 8-18-89

Blues Progression Skeletons
The Blues 7-19-77
Blues Chord Forms for Chord Melody Playing 7-20-77
Melodic Blues Progs. 7-20-77
Modern Jazz-Blues Progs. 8-8-77
Outlining Modern Dom. Progs. Using 3 Note Voicings 2 Pgs. 2-2-79
More Progs. Using Modern Dom. Voicings 2-2-79
Blues Prog. Skeletons 8-25-85
Blues Progs. Skeletons (2nd set of strs.) 8-25-85

Jazz Blues Comping (Key of Bb) 4/2/93

Jazz Blues Ideas for 2nd half of 12 bar Blues (Ab) 11/30/87

Blues Progressions

Blues Progressions (key of Bb) (8-24-74) 6-19-75
Blues Progressions (page1) 6-7-76
Blues Progressions 4-77
The Blues: Harmonic Vocabulary and Progressions 5-1-78
Blues Progressions 7-4-78
Blues in F (upper register-modern voicings) 12-8-78
'Night Wes 5-7-85
Time Zone Blues (key of F) 10-29-85
Time Zone Blues (key of D) 10-29-85
Lazy Blues Chordal Style 12-23-85
More of Wes Blues 1-10-86
Modern Dominant Flavored Blues 2-8-86
Uptown Blues 4-19-86
Walking Chord Blues (key of Bb) 4-20-86
Jazz Style Walking Chord Blues 3-1-87
"V-4 Blues" 11-19-89
Walking Chord Blues (key of E) 7-11-89

Misc. Blues Studies

"Gospel" Blues (key of A) (12/1/78) 4/27/79
Walking Chord Blues 4/20/85
Harmonized Blues Melodies (1 to1) (9/26/73) 4/27/85
Polyrhythmic Diatonic Triads in the Major Scale 8/20/85
Slow Blues Lines in Triplet Speed 11/7/85
Walking Chord Style Blues 12/30/86
Walking Chord "Gospel Style" Blues 12/31/86
Trills in Blues Triplet Runs 8/20/89
Freddie King Triplet Shuffle Run 8/20/89
Chicago Blues ala Jimmy Reed 8/17/90
Gospel Influenced Blues 10/10/90
Multi-Position Blues Run 4/3/91
The 7#9 Scale: Very Bluesy 1/13/93
Jazz Blues (Key of Bb) 7/13/00

Walking Bass Blues

Walking Bass Blues 2 Pgs. 4-27-85
16 Bar Blues w/Walking Bass: "Glued to the Blues" 3-15-87
Walking Bass Blues w/out IV in Bar 2 (key of D) 3-17-87
Blues with a Walking Bass: Approach Chords used to Harmonize a Riff 5-3-87
Walking Bass Blues w/out IV in Bar 2 (key of Bb) 5-6-87
Walking Bass Blues: inadvertently, a study in contrasts & right hand selectivity 5-10-87
Variation on Key of E Page: Blues with a Walking Bass 5-23-87
Slow Blues w/Walking Bass and Melodically & Rhythmically Derived Theme 5-24-87
Double Pick-Up Chord Walking Bass Blues 9-30-88
Jazz Style Walking Chord Blues (Ab) 3-1-89
Walking Bass Blues #2 Key of C 3-25-89
Walking Bass Jumpback Blues w/50s Ray Charlesish Theme 10-9-89

Walking Bass Blues: Mixing Blue & Warm Colors 7-15-91
Walking Bass Blues (key of G) 2-29-92

Jazz

Outlines to Soloing
Jazz Tags 1-24-80

BeBop Lines 8-30-80
4 Note Melodic Fragments for BeBop Single Line Study 8-31-80
BeBop Solos & Progressions 2-20-81
"Meditation" #1 & #2 6-4-81
"All the Things You Are"/ "Cherokee" #1 - Chord Tone Outline 6-4-81
"Cherokee" #2/ "Cute" (chord outline) 6-5-81

Jazz Turnarounds
I7 bVII7 bVI7 V7 Turnarounds (contrary motion) 2 Pgs. 3-28,30-86
Jazz Turnarounds: one-six-two-five 10 Pgs. 11-23-86 thru 11-12-89
Jazz Turnarounds Based on Rhythmic Figures Mated to Common Progs. 1-16-92
Turnarounds (a beginning) Key of G 11-27-93

Misc. Jazz Studies
Summary of Most Common Chord Movements in Modern Jazz Harmony 6/16/77
Most Common Harmonic Tendencies in Jazz and Related Music (10/27/77) 9/14/79
Jazz Progressions Descending Bass Small Texture 12/10/79
Jazz Single Line Texture: 2 Beats per Chord Pg. 1&2 3/14/86 Pg.3 6/10/86
Developing Jazz Lines from Arpeggios ii 1/2dim7 V7alt i6 2 pgs. (5/9/87) 6/10/87
Jazz Walking Chords 7/20/89

Playing Through Changes
Playing Through Chord Changes in Position 11-2-77
Learning the Dom.7th Scale: I bVII7 11-5-77
Playing Through Changes 4 Pgs. 11-5-77 thru 1-18-78
Learning mi7 Sounds in Context: I biii7 ii7 V7 I 11-8-77
The Overtone Dom. Scale: playing "in position" 2 Pgs. 10-25-77, 11-15-77
Basing Your Solo on Condensed Arpeggios 10 Pgs. 3-22-78 thru 4-7-78
Arpeggios (11-8-77) 5-25-78

Single Line Studies

Single Note Playing
Single Note Scales for miMaj.7, mi6, mi7b5, 7b9+, (& dim.) Families 12-18-74
Melodic Minor Scales for: mi6,miMaj.7,mi7b5,7#9#5(b9b5), and 13 + 11 Families 12-18-74
7th Chord Scales Pg.3 7-15-75
Major Scale Sounds for Single Note Playing 7-15-75
7th Chord Scales (mixolydian) Pg.1 7-15-75
mi7b5 Sounds & more Pg.2 7-25-75
Single Note Playing (explanation) Pg.1-2 2-27-76

Common Diatonic Chord Progs. Examples (Maj. Key) 2-28-76
Single Note Playing (building 7th chords) Pg. 3 2-28-76
Single Note Playing (arpeggios) Pg.4 2-28-76
Diatonic Major Scale Arpeggios Pg.5 2-28-76
Single Note Playing in Minor Keys Pg.1 3-25-76
Harmonic Minor Pg.2 3-25-76
Dorian Minor Pg.4 3-27-76
Melodic Minor Pg.3 3-28-76
Diatonic Harmonic Minor Arpeggios 3-28-76
Diatonic Melodic Minor Arpeggios (i chords) 3-30-76
mi7b5 Scales & more Pg.3 (7-25-75) 10-7-76
Single Note Playing- Dominant 7th Scales Pg.1 4-18-86
Altered Dom. Scales Pg.2 4-20-7

Chord Scale Runs
Playing in one Position (as a tool for learning Maj. Scales & transitions) 10-24-77
Major Chord Runs using only Chord Tones 7 Pgs. 12-27,28-77
More Major Chord Runs 4 Pgs. 12-30-77 thru 1-7-78
Chord Forms for Visualizing Scales, Arpeggios & Runs 3 Pgs. (4-27-78) 7-17-78
Lydian Tonality

8 Note Dominant Scale
Learning the 8 Note Dominant Scale in ii7 V7 I Runs (area 3) 5-27-85
Ascending Melodic Fragments (area 1) 5-28-85
Descending Melodic Fragments (area 1) 5-29-85
Ascending - area 2 - 5-28-85
Descending - area 2 - 5-29-85
Ascending - area 3 - 5-28-85
Descending - area 3 - 5-29-85
Ascending - area 4 - 5-29-85
Descending - area 4 - 5-31-85
Learning to Use 8 Note Dominant Scale Chords ("1/2- Whole") 4-17-91

Altered Dominant Sounds
Learning Altered Dominant Sounds Type1 7 pgs. 10-22-77, 11-18-77
Learning Altered Dominant Sounds Type2 7 Pgs. (+ pg.4a) 10-23-77 thru 11-19-77
Learning Altered Dominant Sounds Type3 7 Pgs. (+pg.7a) 10-23-77 thru 11-20-77
Group 4 Dominant Type Chord Forms "Altered Doms." 1-18-78
Extra Arpeggios for High Register 1-28-78

Dominant 7ths
Dominant 7th Sounds - Step 1- 7 Pgs. 11-6-77 thru 11-24-77
The Dominant 7th Scale 12-30-77
Dominant 7th Runs 8 Pgs. 12-30-77 thru 1-28-78
Overtone Dominant 7th Runs 4 Pgs. 1-13 thru 15-78
Group 1 Dominants: Cumulative Single Line Resources 12-18-83

Melodic Patterns
Melodic Patterns (key of C) 9-16-74
Melodic Patterns (apply to all scales & keys) 10-19-76

Imitation and Melodic Patterns 2-9-78
Melodic Patterns (various) 11 Pgs. 5-22-24-78
Melodic Patterns Repeated at the 4th "imitation at the 4th" 5-27,29-78
Melodic Patterns (specific intervals) 7-8-78
Pentatonic Melodic Patterns (asc. & desc.) 2-20-79

Harmonic Patterns
Harmonic Patterns 10-30-73
Melodic Patterns (key of C) 2-19-74
Harmonic Patterns - Diat. Maj. Key 4-29-76
Harmonic Patterns - Type 1 "held note sound" (3-14-76) 3-19-77
Harmonic Patterns - Diat. 4th or 5th Type 9-5-78
Harmonic Patterns Based on 6th Intervals 9-4-78

Minor 7th Single Note
Diatonic Major Scale Runs 7 Pgs. 11-2-77 thru 11-12-77
Minor 7th Family Runs 7-28-79
ii7 V7 I (examples) 3-8-82
Learning to Hear Dorian and Aeolian Melodies 5-31-83
Minor7th Colors 7-31-83

Visualizing & Fingering mi7b5 Runs
mi7b5 Scales 10-7-76
Visualizing & Fingering 12-6-77
The Dim.7th Chord 12-7-77
Diminished 7th Sounds 4 Pgs. 12-8-77 thru 12-14-77
The Melodic Minor Scale 2 Pgs. 3-28-78
Melodic Minor Sounds (runs) 8 Pgs. 3-29-78 thru 4-1-78
mi7b5 Arpeggios, Scales & Chord Forms 2 Pgs. (12-5-77) 4-15-78
Position Playing on ii half dim7, V7alt & i6 12-3-80

Using Patterns for Intros, Interludes and Endings
Dominant 7th Sounds - Step1 Pg.5 Arpeggios 11-22-71
"Sentimental Journey" Analysis 4-27-74
List of Favorable Matings of Qualities and Degrees 9-19-75
Solo Based on the Chords to "Cute" 10-12-77
Learning Altered Dom. Sounds - Type1 Pg.5 Arpeggios 10-22-77
Using Patterns for Intros, Interludes & Endings 1-4-87
More on Playing Through Changes (Basing Solo on Arpeggio Fragments) 2Pgs. 3-22,24-78
Short Intros: Using Chord Scales (Diat. Maj. Key) 1-15-90
Short Intros Using Modest Decoration 1-16-90
Short Intros Using Right Hand 'Delays' 1-17-90

Walking Style Bass (General)
Some Basic Chords Forms for "Walking" Bass Style 8-15-77
Walking Bass Style - "Satin Doll" 9-15-77
Walking Bass & "Walking Chords" Guitar Styles 7-11-82

Wes Approach to Chord Soloing

Learning Basic Chords for Comping, Chord Soloing or? 4 Pgs. 2-3-79 thru 3-1-79
Chords for Chord soloing & Comping - mi7th Type 4-7-79
Dom.7th Type & Dom. & Companion mi7th Exercises 4-8-79
mi7th Type Chords for Comping & Chord soloing 3-4-80
Dom.7th Type (& companion minors) 3-4-80
Maj. Type Chords 3-4-80
Walkin' With Wes 2/26/82
Visual Shapes for Learning Octave Style (5/30/79) 6/15/97)
Wes Type Chord Phrases 1/13/91

Voicing Systems Chronology

Voicing System 1

ii7 V7 I on the Top 4 Strs. (Close Harm. Voicings) 6-23-79
Multi Possibilities of Voice Leading via ii7 V7 I - Top 4 Strs. 11-80
Exercise Progam ii7 V7 I Top & Middle Strs.: Close Harmony Voicings (6-23-79) 11-5-80
Melodizing ii7 V7 I in Close Harmony (Purposes: 1.Music 2.Stretching) (6-23-79) 11-10-80
4 Note Upper Partial Chord Rows - Close Harmony - 1-6-81
Learning Chord Forms Thru Chord Rows: Upper Partial mi7&Sus. Dom.(11th)Types (3-4-80) 7-10-81
3 Note ii7 Voicings in ii7 V7 I Progressions 1-1-84
Maj. Type Chords on the Top 4 Strs. Reg. & Normal Ext. w/out 11 or #11 2 Pgs. 2-3-85
Dominants: 13th on Top - Top 4 Strs. - 8-8-85
Dominants: #5 on Top - Top 4 Strs. 8-9-85
Minor 7th Streams as ii7 or vi7 - Top 4 Strs. Desc. Motion 4-19-85
Maj. Types with String Crossing on Higher Sets (mainly) 8-18-86
Maj. Pentatonic - Both Sets 8-22-86
Long String Cross Chains - Maj. Types Pg.1- 8-18-86 Pg.2 - 8-23-86
Introduction to Maj. Colors on the Middle (and low) Strs. 3 pgs. 8-19,20-86
Maj. Types w/ String Crossing on Higher Sets (mainly) 8-18-86
Maj. Type Colors - Middle Strs. 2 Pgs. 8-19-86
Maj. Colors on the Middle Strs. 5pgs. 8-19,20-86
Introduction to V1 Symmetrical String Crosses w/Maj. Sounds 8-26-86
Dom. 7th Chords- Top 4 Strs. 11-5-86
More Exercises to Learn mi7 "3rd Stack" Types (w/phrase extensions at end of each for fun) 8-5-87
Minor 7th Type Chord Studies Pg.1 - 8-5-87 Pg.2 - 8-10-87
ii7 V7 (I) Studies Mixing V-1 and V-2 2 Pgs. 8-29-87
Chord Voicings: ii7 V7 I w/Connecting Chords (undated)
Close Harmony Derived Voicings mi7 Types 11-9-89

Voicing System 2

1977-1983

06/09/77 Melodic Use of Small Maj. Type Chords (6ths) Key of E
02/01/79 Progressions to Learn Modern Dominant Voicings: Top Strs. (key of Bb)
02/02/79 Progs. To Learn Modern Dominant Voicings: Middle Strs.
12/12/83 Chord Evolution: G7 & Dm7 Types in Voicing Group 2 (& some 1)

1984

03/09 Dominant 7ths - Top & Middle String
Dominant 7ths for Study - String Transference
03/13 Dominant 7ths - Outside Strings Hook-Up

03/16 Minor 7ths - Outside Strings Hook-Up
Major 6ths - Outside String Hook-up
03/17 Dominant 7ths - All 3 String Sets w/Locational Crossing
03/28 Visually Troublesome 7b9's V7 i, V7 I
03/29 Learning to Visualize (& play) 7b9's "all 3 sets"
03/31 Dominant 7ths One Set At A Time - Systematic Inversions
Dominant 7ths One String At A Time - Challenge Exercise
Dominant 7ths - Top 4 & Middle 4 Combined
04/18 3 Note Major 6th Chord Stream Exercises - 2pgs.
06/15 I vi ii V - Organizing Factors: 1 to 1 Soprano Moves - 5 Pgs.
06/18 Root Anchor Points for Chord Visualization "all 3 string sets"
06/19 Dominant 7ths - Low & Middle Strings
Larger Visual Segments of Dominant Inversion Chain
07/19 Practical String Crossing for Minor 7ths in Long Lines (Chord Streams)
Minor 7ths - Top 4 & Middle 4 Strs.
07/20 Minor 7ths - Bottom 4 & Middle 4 Strings
Minor 7ths: Exercises Using All 3 String Sets (5/5/76)
Major 6ths - Bottom 4 & Middle 4 Strings
Major 6ths Exercises Using All 3 String Sets (5-5-76)
Major 6ths Systematic Inv. Studies - Top & Middle 4 Str. (4-18-84)
07/29 Chord Streams w/ Maj. 6ths (& some exts.)
09/04 7b9's all 3 sets Diagonal & Derivatives
7b9 Chords - Outside String Sets Hook-Up
7b9 Chords - Outside String Sets Hook-Up Plus Middle in Same Location
7b9's - More Outside String Hook-Ups Plus Middle in same Location
7b9's Compact Pattern
09/07 7b9's Compact Pattern with Leaps
09/16 Diagonal String Crossing with V-2 Maj. Extensions
Diagonal String Crossing with V-2 Maj. 6ths
10/21 Major Type Chords - List 1 and 1a - Top Set
Major Type Chords - Intermediate List - Top Set - (6-17-84)
10/22 Major Type Chords - List 1 and 1a - Middle Set
10/23 Major Type Chords - List l and 1a - Bottom Set
10/26 Major Type Chords - Intermediate List - Middle Set
11/04 Minor 7th Type Chords - List 1 and 1a - Top Set
11/06 Dominant 7th Type Chords - Top Set - Group 1 Colors
Dominant 7th Type Forms - Middle Strings - Group 1 Colors
Dominant 7th Type Chords - Bottom Strings - Group 1 Colors
Minor 7th Type Chords - List 1 and 1a - Middle Strings
Minor 7th Type Chords - List 1 and 1a - Bottom Strings
11/10 7b9's Longer Chord Connection 11-10-84
11/13 String Transference Quiz
11/14 Major 7th & Maj. 6th Chords on the Top 4 Strings
Dominant 7th & 9th Chords on the Top 4 Strings
Minor 7th and Minor 9th Chords on the Top 4 Strings
Minor 7th & 9th Chords on the Top 4 Strings
11/16 Learning the 7b9 Forms Through V7 - I Progressions
11/23 7b9 Chords on the Middle & Top Strings
Chords in V7 I Progressions - Top 4 Strings
11/24 Drills - 7b9 Chords on all 3 String Sets Pg.1 thru 3

Cycle of 4th Challenge Exercises - 7b9 Chords on all 3 string sets - 4 pgs.
11/25 7b9 Chords on the Middle & Top in V7 I Progressions
11/28 Major 6/9 - Maj.9 and Add9 Chords on the Top 4 Strings
11/30 Minor 9ths on the Middle String
12/02 V7 I Progressions On Top 4 Strings
12/21 Minor 6 & Mi6/9th Chords on Top 4 Strings
Minor 7b5 & minor7/11b5 Chords of the Top 4 Strings
12/22 Dominant 7/6, 13 & 9th (w/root) Chords on Top 4 Strings
Large Leap Drills with 7b9 Chords - Top 4 Strings - 2 pgs.
12/23 Large Leap Drills - 7b9 Extensions (soprano) Top 4 Strings
Large Leap Drills - diminished7 Chords on the Top 4 Strings
Large Leap Drills with diminished Extensions (Soprano) on the Top 4 St.
Large Leap Drills with 7b9 Alto Extensions - Top 4 Strings
Reinforcing Melodic Pattern with dim.7 Chords on the Top 4 Strings
Reinforcing Melodic Patterns with dim7 Soprano Extensions on the Top 4 Strings
2nd Reinforcing Melodic Pattern with dim.7 Chords on the Top 4 Strings
Reinforcing Melodic Pattern with 7b9 Chords on Top 4 Strings - 2 pgs.
Reinforcing Melodic Patterns with 7b9 Soprano Extensions - Top 4 Strings
12/25 Large Leaps with dim7 Alto Extensions on the Top 4 Strings
12/28 7b9+ and 7#9+ on the Top 4 Strs.

1985

01/26 Chord Transformation Exercises - Top 4 Str.
02/01 V1 & V2 Dom. 7th Type Chords - Root on Top - V7 Function - Top 4 Strs.
03/02 Mi7b5 Chords - Middle & Top 4 Strs.
02/03 Maj. Type Chords on the Top 4 Strs. Reg. & Normal Ext. w/out 11 or #11 Pg.1 2-3-85 Pg.2 3-3-85
03/18 String Crossing from Bottom Set to Top - to ease melodic leaps
03/19 Systematic Inversions: Maj.7 Chord Streams
Inversions - Learning Add9 Chords via Short Phrases w/crossovers
03/22 Major 9 Chord Streams
03/23 Major 6/9 Chord Streams
04/15 Linear ii7 V7 I - 2 to 1 Moving Soprano - 2 Forms per Change - Top 4 Str.
04/18 Middle Strs. Descending Dom.-Sub.Dom. Chains Use for "2-5" or co-minor, co-dom. application
04/23 Top 4 Strs. - iii7 VI7 ii7 V7 Chains (5-26-76)
Middle Strs. iii7 VI7 V7 Chains
Middle Strs. Two-Five (Asc.) Chains with Leaps
04/24 Descending Dominant - Sub-Dominant Chains Top 4 Strings
04/27 7b9 in I V7 Chains - 3 pgs.
05/15 Mi9ths Middle Strs. Ii V7 I
05/17 Mi9's Top 4 Strs. ii7 V7 I
Maj.7th & Maj.6th Chords on the Top 4 Strs.
Dim7 and Ext. (Maj.7,9,11 and b13) - Top 4 Str.
05/21 Dominants: Constant b7 and 3 (top 4) 5-21-85
Chord Transformation: 9ths to 7b9's - Top 4 Str.
05/22 Intro Page to Constant b7 and 3 in V7 I Prog. (Middle Str.)
05/24 Review (intro) Page for Constant b7 and 3 (in V7 I prog.)
05/18 Big Band Blues: I IV V and "3 Statement Form" 1. Key of C
06/20 Big Band Blues: I IV V and "3 Statement Form" Key of Bb
06/22 Big Band Blues: 3 Statement Form -Middle 4 Strs.- Key of Bb
Major7ths Syst. Inv. Studies - Middle & Top 4 Strs.

Major 7ths Systematic Inversion Studies - Middle & Top 4 Strs.
Dominant 9ths Syst. Inv. Studies - Top & Middle 4 Strs.
Dominant 9th Chords - Syst, Inv. Studies - Middle & Top 4 Strs.
06/23 Maj. 6/9 and Maj.9 & add9 Chords - Middle Strs.
Chord Transformation Exercises - Middle 4 Strs.
Chord Transformation Exercises - Middle 4 Strs.
06/27 Big Band Blues #2- 3 Statement Form - Key of G - Middle Strs.
06/29 Big Band Blues #2 - 3 Statement Form - Middle & Top Strs. Key of Ab
07/23 9th Chord Streams - All 3 Sets
07/24 9th Chord Streams in a Short Progression: one-four-two-five
Dominant 9th Chords in Melodic Pattern
Minor 9th Chords in Melodic Pattern
12/19 Color Overview of 3rd Inv. Dom. On the Top 4 Str.

1986

01/10 Ear-Eye-Hand Connection Exercises: Dom. 7th Chords - Top 4 & Middle Str.
Ear-Eye-Hand Connection Exercises: Dom. 9th Chords - Top 4 & Middle Str.
Ear-Eye-Hand Connection Exercises: Maj. 6th Chords - Top 4 & Middle Str,
Ear-Eye-Hand Connection Exercises: Minor 7th Chords -Top 4 & Middle Str.
02/05 ii V7 I Starting from R573 Voicing on the Top 4 Strs.
ii V7 I Starting from R5b711 on the Top 4 Strs.
02/08 Top Str. ii7 (R5b7b3) to Altered (& regular) V7 then I
Top Str. b7b35R in ii7 V7 I
Top Str. b7b359 in ii7 V7 I
Middle Str. R5b7b3 in ii7 V7 I - 3pgs. (2-5,7,8-86)
02/15 Organizing Middle Str. 1st Inv. Doms. For Mental & Physical Practice
Organizing Middle Str. 3rd Inv. Doms. For Mental & Physical Practice
Ear Training through Quality-Degree Focus: VI7#9
Ear Training through Quality-Degree Focus: VI#9 (& add 9 as "fragmented 9th") Key of E, F
Ear Training Through Specific Quality-Degree Focus:VI9(& add9 as fragmented 9th)Key of E, Eb
Ear Training Through Specific Quality Degree Focus: VI#9
02/16 Middle & Top ii7 V7 I with String Crossing - 4 Pgs.
Middle Str. ii7V 7 I - 2 Pgs.
Introduction to ii7 V7 I - Top 4 Strings - 2 pgs.
02/18 Focusing on "Regular Dom's" - Top 4 Strings, 1st Inv.
Focusing on V7's w/b9's - Top 4 Strings - 1st Inv.
02/19 Overview of 1st Inv. Dom's. - Top 4 Strings
02/20 Focusing on "Regular" Doms. - Middle Strs.
Overview of 1st Inv. Dom. On the Middle Strs.
Focusing on "Regular" Dom. - Middle Strs.
02/22 Focusing on V7's w/b9's - 1st Inv. Middle 4 Str.
Focusing on V7's w/b9's 1st Inv. - Middle 4 Strs.
02/23 Locking in the 2nd String Visual Root for mi7 Types
Locking in the 2nd Str. Visual Root for mi7 Types
Using Minor 7th Type with the 11th on Top
Minor 7th Exts. : b7 thru b3 in the Soprano - Top 4 Strings
Minor 7th Ext.: b7 thru b3 in the Soprano - Middle Strs.
Minor 7th Ext. b3 thru b7 in the Soprano: Str. Crossing - Middle & Top Forms
02/24 Minor 7th Exts. : 11 thru 13 in the Soprano - Top 4 Strings
02/25 Mi. 7th Ext. : 11 thru 13 in the Soprano - Middle Set

Mi. 7th Ext. 11 thru 13 in the Soprano: Str. Crossing - Middle & Top Forms
Mi7 Ext. 11 thru 13 in the Soprano - Middle Set
Mi7 Ext. 11 thru 13 in the Soprano - String Crossing - Middle & Top Forms
12/19 Color Overview of 3rd Inv. Doms. On the Middle Strs.
Color Overview of 3rd Inversion Dominants on the Middle 4 Strings
12/20 One-Six-Two-Five-One Progs. (1 to 1 Texture) 2 Pgs.
12/21 Learning to Hear & Use 1st Inv. Dom's. (w/b9's & some #9's) on the Top 4 Strings

1987

01/15 Dominant "Sus"Colors on the Middle and Top Str.
Dom. "Sus" Colors on the Middle & Top Strs.
01/16 Dom. 11th Chords (no root) on Top 4 Str. - 4 pgs.
01/18 Resolution of Dom. Type Exts. Top 4 Str.
01/20 Resolutions of SPECIAL Diatonic V Chords - Gp. 2
01/21 Using Mi.7 Types with the 11th on Top
01/23 Dom. 11ths (no roots) on the Middle Strs.
Dom. 11ths (no roots) on the Middle & Top Strs.
Dom. 11ths (w/out Roots) on the Middle & Top Strs. - 2pgs.
Dom. 11ths (w/out Roots) on the Middle Strs.
01/25 Syst. Inv. Middle Str. 7+ Chords - 4 Pgs.
02/22 Maj. Pentatonic: Type 1 - Top 4 Str.
02/23 Maj. Pentatonic Type 1 - Middle and Top Str.
Maj. Pentatonic: Type 2 - Top 4 Str.
Maj. Pentatonic Type 1: Middle and Top Strs.
Maj. Pentatonic Type 3: Middle & Top Strs.
Maj. Pentatonic Type 3 - Top 4 Stg.
03/15 Using 3rd Inversion Dominant Colors: Group 1's Middle 4 Strs.
Using 3rd Inv. Dom. Colors: Group 1 - Top 4 Str.
Using 3rd Inv. Dom. Colors - Group 1- Middle 4 Strs.
Color Overview of Suspended 3rd Inv. Dom. : Top 4 Str. Gp. 2 (unaltered)
04/29 Color Overview of Suspended 3rd Inv. Doms. - Middle Strs. Group 2 (unaltered)
10/18 Introduction to Maj. Pentatonic Type 3's
Melodic Motion in Maj. Pentatonic - Type 3 via Right Hand Delays

1988

01/13 Learning to work with 7b9's in Musical Passages - Top 4 Str.
01/18 Using "Regular" Dom. Exts. In Little Bluesy Phrases
01/30 Using : "Regular" Dom. Ext. in Little Bluesy Phrases
Using : "Regular" Dominant Exts. in Little Bluesy Phrases - Middle & Top Strs.
09/24 Mastering Inner String dominant Chords - Key of E
11/23 Mi7b5's Middle & Top Strs. Tougher Transitions (at the end of each series of 4)
11/24 Mi7b5's Middle & Top Strs. Key Shifting Drills
12/04 Mi7b5's Middle & Top Strs. Tougher Transitions
Mi7b5's - Middle & Top Strs.
(Mi)7/11b5 Middle & Top Strs.

1989

4/3/89 Learning the Companion Minor7 & Dom. 7's
4/3/89 Learning the Co-Mi7 & Dom.7's

1990's
11/13/92Add 9's on All 3 Sets
02/12/94 Voicing Groups Unified: By the Soprano Tone --
Color Overview of Suspended 3 Inv. Doms. : Middle Strs. , Group 2 (unaltered) NO DATE

Voicing System 3
Some Choice Dom. Voicings: 3rd in Soprano 1-25-86
Passages Using 1st Inv. Diat. 7th Chords 7-12-87
The Seven Fundamental Chord Qualities 4-30-89
V3 with V2 (Chord Tone Swap) 7-29-89

Voicing System 4
Both Sets - Dominant 7th Chords: Introduction to Higher Sets - 5 Pgs. 2-9-86
Larger Sounding Leaps with Dom. 7ths - 2 Pgs. 2-9-86
Major 6th Chords - Lower Set 2-9-86
Both Sets of Maj. 6th Chords: Introduction to Higher Set - 2 Pgs. 2-10-86
Dominant 7ths - Lower Set - 12-8-86
Diatonic Chord Scale-Type Passages to Add a Little Life to the Dry Harmonized Scale 6-1-88
Musical Passages Using Chord Scales w/String Crossovers 6-21-88
The Seven Basic Qualities & their Syst. Invs, - Top Set - 9-30-89
The Seven Basic Qualities & their Syst. Invs. - Bottom Set 10-3-89
Common Tone Soprano in Dom. 7ths 10-4-89
Diatonic Maj. Key Cycle of 4th Progs. w/Difficult Ties in the Bass 2-21-89
Using Chord Scales to Get Ideas Started (undated)
Descending Bass Prog. From ii7/5 (undated)
"V-4 Blues" (undated)

Voicing System 5
Sub-Dominant Mixing : IV to ii 3-7-88
Challenging Exercises (Mentally) to Really Sink the Chords In 7-29-89
Learning the Mi7b5's on the Higher, Sparklier String Set 8-5-89
Learning the Mi7b5's on the Lower, Richer String Set 8-5-89
Maj.6th Chords: String Crossing - Units of 4 1-1-90
Dom.7ths: String Crossing - Units of 4 1-2-90
The Seven Basic Qualities - Lower Set 1-3-90
Mi7b5's Leaps w/Backtracking Mostly Top Set 1-3-90
Cumulative String Crossing - Low to High 1-3-90
Intense Drilling using Patterns w/Leaps - Bottom Set - 7 Pgs. 1-3,5,6-90
Intense Drilling w/Leaps - Top Set 7 Pgs. - 1-6-90

Voicing System 6
Basic Colors: 7 Chord Types - the backbone of the V-6 Voicing Group - 11-26-87
Progressions for Learning to Hear V-6 Size Chords & Colors 7-2-91
Gradual Program for Absorption of V-6 Chord Colors 8-31-91
Learning Chord Colors: Baroqueish Harmony V7 I & friends 9-8-91
Progressions Using V-6 Shadings '91

VOICING SYSTEMS 7-8-9-10

The Seven Basic Qualities & their Systematic Inversions
V-7 - 7- 27-89
V-8 - 10-08-89
V-9 - 10-14-89
V-10 - 10-15-89

MISC. VOICING SYSTEM STUDIES

I to 1 SOPRANO MOVES
I vi ii V - ORGANIZING FACTORS: 1 to 1 Soprano, V-2 Voicings, 1st Chord Constant Pg.1 6-15-84
I vi ii V 1 to 1 Starting with High Strings Pg.2 6-16-84
I vi ii V 1 to 1 Soprano Moves on Middle Strs. Pg.2a 6-16-84
I vi ii V 1 to 1 Soprano Moves Starting with High Strs. Pg.3 6-16-84
I vi ii V 1 to 1 Soprano Moves Starting From V2 /9 Pg. 3a 9-1-85
V-2 TOP 4 ONE-SIX-TWO-FIVE-ONE PROGS. (1 to 1 Texture) 12-20-86
V-2 MIDDLE STRINGS ONE-SIX TWO-FIVE ONE PROGS. (1 to 1 Texture) 12-20-86

V-2 SIZE 7+ CHORDS
V-2 CHORDS in V7 I PROGRESSIONS Top 4 Strs. 1-2-84
V-2 CHORDS in V7 I PROGRESSIONS Top 4 Strs (mainly) 11-23- 84
V-1 & V-2 DOM.7th TYPE CHORDS - V7 FUNCTION - Top 4 Strs. Root on Top 2-1-85
V-2 - 7+ Chords Syst. Inv. Top 4 Strs. Pg.2 1-25-87
V-2 -7+ Chords Syst. Inv. Middle Strs. 2 Pgs. 1-25-87
V-2 7+ Chords: Introduction & Resolutions Top 4 Strs. 1-25-87
VOICING GROUPS UNIFIED: By the SOPRANO TONE (V-1,V-4 & V-5) 2-12-94
V-2 ADD 9's on all 3 SETS (undated)

List of Guitars by "Personal Name"

Alphabetically by Make

Fenders

Banana Crème	1954 Esquire
Egg	1976 Tele
Lala	1953 Tele
Lucky	1951 Tele
Lulu	1952 Tele
Mambo	1964/65 Jazzmaster

Gibsons

Bernice	1961 SB ES330 TD
Cherima	1960s Cherryburst ES125 TCD
Goldie	1952 Gold Top Les Paul
The Lady	1960 SB ES5 Switchmaster
Lucia	1970 Blond ES175 D
Stella	1966 Red ES330 TCD

Guilds

Amber	1985 Blond X170
Aphrodite	1977 Blond Artist Award
Bettina	1954 Blond Spruce X375
Brandy	1960/61 SB CE100 DP Special
Camille	1963 Red Starfire II
Carmine	1969 Burgundy Cherry Duane Eddy 400
Chubby	1958 SB X350
Daisy	1960s SB M65 3/4
Danette	1958 SB X175
Deedee	1968 SB M75 Bluesbird
Desiree	1958 SB X350
Duena	1966 SB Duane Eddy 400
Francesca	1955 SB M75 Aristocrat
Gigi	1961 SB X500
Gina	1976 Blond X500
Granny	1959 SB X50 Granada
Lucia	1965 Blond X175
Mona	1961 Ebony Starfire II
Luscious	1956 Blond X550
Ruby	1960s Cinnamon Red Starfire II

Sandy	1972 Blond T100 D
Sadie	1970s SB T100 D
Savannah	1957 SB X150 Savoy
Smokey	1970 SB X175
Toby	1962 SB T100 D

Misc.

Carmelita	1960s D'Angelico copy
Donna	1960s Blond Ibanez L5 copy
Hazel	1963 SB Gretsch Tennessian
Venus	1990s SB Samick L5 copy

Information About References in the Book

Information on DVDs, CDs and other people/things mentioned in the book that may be of interest to some of you.

<u>Ted Greene Seminars on DVD</u>
Musician's Institute June 1993
Calif. Vintage Guitars May 2003
Calif. Vintage Guitars December 2003
Calif. Vintage Guitars August 2004
Boulevard Music August 2004
Musician's Institute May 2005

For information about any of Ted's seminars on DVD contact us at **www.tedgreene.com**

● X □ △ ★

A very special thank you to all the students who videotaped the seminars and somehow made sure these seminars found their way to me.

● X □ △ ★

Solo Guitar CD - Art of Life Records	www.artofliferecords.com
Chris Maybach's Art City DVD Soundtracks	www.artcity123.com
The American Metaphysical Circus	www.amazon.com
Lori Markman	www.markmanart.com

Ted Greene Remembered: www.eldoradorecords.net
A special tribute CD that was produced by Tom Bocci with performances by many of the greatest guitar players around today including Dan Sawyer and Steve Ferguson.

Steve Ferguson www.cdbaby.com/steveferguson
"I have been waiting for Steve Ferguson's THE WELL-TEMPERED PIANO ever since he told he in 1972 that he was writing rags, ballads, impressionistic songs and other pieces in all the 12 major and minor keys. This solo piano recording is so beautiful and encompasses so many moods, inspirations and influences, and yet is deeply one long continuous work from beginning to end; it nurtures me to listen to it every day."
- George Winston

Dan Sawyer www.amazon.com/Uke-Ages-Dan-Soybean-Sawyer
From the first track it becomes quickly apparent that Dan Sawyer is a truly talented professional musician, and as the CD progresses he cleverly uses his skills to provide the listener with not only a tremendously varied selection of tracks of the highest quality, but also musicianship of the highest order. He takes ukulele playing to another level with apparent ease, both to himself by his beautifully smooth but technically advanced playing, and to the listener - who is left thirsting for more!

Russell Malone LIVE AT JAZZ STANDARD VOLUME ONE - www.amazon.com/Russell-Malone
Dedication: Russell dedicated this record to the memories of John Hicks and Ted Greene.
Of Special Note: This is Russell Malone's first "Live" recording as a leader; This recording includes five Russell Malone original compositions; Three different Russell Malone versions of Milt Jackson's "Heartstrings" have been recorded, including this live version in September 2005. "Music, to me, is not math or science. It is a language." -- Russell Malone.

Dan Sindel "Marching In: A Tribute to the March King John Philip Sousa" - www.dansindel.us
"A lot of guitarists claim to be "orchestral" players, and the result is often dreadful to my ears, but Sindel is cagey enough to be both hilarious and enjoyable. His reading of this John Sousa march - perhaps best known as the Monty Python theme - is well arranged and goofy. It's whacked out genius!" Guitar Player Magazine (April 2008)

Dan also makes online guitar instruction available at www.ezgtr.com

KPFK Radio Show recording can be listened to in its entirety at www.tedgreene.com

Ted's Books:
Chord Chemistry
Modern Chord Progressions Volume I
Single Note Soloing Volume I
Single Note Soloing Volume II

Ted's books are available through Amazon or other music book websites. Old copies, with the wonderful cover photos, do appear from time to time on Ebay. The contents are the same as the new copies but there is really something special about having one with one of the old original covers.

All the proceeds from the sale of this book go to TedGreene.com

Made in the USA
Middletown, DE
27 November 2022

16133912R00157